FOR DUMMIES™

BUSINESS AND GENERAL REFERENCE BOOK SERIES FROM IDG

Mutual Fund$ For Dummies™

Quick Reference Card

by Eric Tyson, MBA

Mandates for Mastering Mutual Fund Investing

$ **Use 'em!** Mutual funds offer a low cost way of investing in bonds and stocks. And you get a professional, full-time fund manager on your team!

$ **Look inside and don't be intimidated.** Mutual funds are nothing more than portfolios of individual securities. Understand and learn about what a fund holds before investing.

$ **Pay attention to fees.** Avoid funds that charge sales commissions (loads) and have high ongoing operating expenses. There are more than enough commission-free (no-load), low-expense funds with great managers and track records as alternatives.

$ **Beware the dangers of buying past performance.** Investing in mutual funds solely based on past performance is like buying insurance after an accident. Good historic performance is but one of many factors to consider when selecting funds. Extraordinary prior returns could indicate a fund that happened to be in the right place at the right time or a fund that's taking high risk.

$ **Consider the source.** Always consider the reputation and experience of the parent company offering a mutual fund, as much as the manager and track record of the fund itself. You'll increase your chances for success by sticking with fund companies that have a history of producing winners with the type of fund you're considering.

$ **Fund selection is not a science.** You can be logical, analytic, and sensible and end up with some mediocre funds. Remember, you're trying to increase your chances of success by avoiding funds with high costs and poor performance that are sold by companies with poor reputations. There are no guarantees.

$ **Compare your fund selections to Vanguard's.** If you've found a mutual fund you like, compare it to similar fund(s) offered at Vanguard. You're probably decreasing your chances of successful fund investing if you choose higher cost funds elsewhere that are performing the same or worse than a comparable Vanguard fund.

$ **First things first.** Before you invest in mutual funds, be sure to look at your overall financial situation and take advantage of other good "investments," such as paying off high-cost consumer debt and using your employer's tax-deductible retirement savings plan.

$ **Taxes matter.** Always consider the tax impact of your fund investing decisions. When investing money outside of a tax-sheltered retirement account, understand the taxability of distributions, such as dividends and capital gains, that a fund makes.

IDG BOOKS WORLDWIDE

...For Dummies™: The Best-Selling Book Series

FOR DUMMIES

BUSINESS AND
GENERAL
REFERENCE
BOOK SERIES
FROM IDG

Mutual Fund$ For Dummie$
by Eric Tyson, MBA

Quick Reference Card

Mandates for Mastering Mutual Fund Investing
(continued)

$ **Diversify.** Holding additional mutual funds doesn't have to cost you more. At a minimum, invest some of your longer-term money in stock funds, both U.S. and international, as well as bond funds. If your assets allow, use at least two funds within each category.

$ **Buy when the financial markets are on sale.** Don't dump your mutual funds when they're down. Buy more (or at least keep buying)! If there's a thunderstorm, tornado, or snowstorm this week, you know the weather won't stay that way — be patient — it'll get better!

$ **Don't try to time the markets.** Shifting money around — into and out of mutual funds based on the latest news or predictions — is almost certain to reduce your investment returns. Make fund investment decisions that fit with your goals. If your situation significantly changes or your fund's performance is much worse than its peers, then consider making some changes.

$ **Give up the guru search.** No one, and certainly not a newsletter writer, can predict the future and which mutual funds will rise and fall the most. If they have figured out a new sure-win system, they're sure not going to share it with you and me.

$ **Don't overestimate the value of finding tomorrow's stars.** Over 10+ years, the best fund managers, if they're lucky, beat the market averages by only a couple percent per year.

$ **Don't underestimate the power of saving and regular investing.** These are far more important and valuable habits than your ability to choose tomorrow's top performers.

$ **Remember the power of index funds.** Index mutual funds, which match and track the performance of a broad bond or stock market index, handily beat the vast majority of competing funds. Index funds' low cost and avoidance of major mistakes, which ensure that they won't underperform the markets, are enormous advantages.

$ **Maintain a long-term perspective.** Try to avoid following your mutual funds too closely. Once a month or even a couple times per year is the most you need to check in and see how your investments are doing.

$ **Be fair when comparing your funds.** When comparing the performance and cost of your mutual funds, be certain that you are using funds that are truly comparable in terms of the types of securities they hold. Be mindful that many mutual funds, brokers, and financial advisors use benchmarks that make their funds look better than they really are.

$ **Work with conflict-free advisors.** If you need assistance with investing in mutual funds or overall financial decisions, hire advisors who sell their time and nothing else. Don't assume a person works on this basis simply by looking at their title — titles are often and intentionally misleading.

$ **Priorities.** Remember that the size of your fund portfolio should have nothing to do with your happiness. Don't forget to "invest" in your health, family, and friends.

...For Dummies™: The Best-Selling Book Series

Praise, praise, praise!

Some nice things that people have said about Eric Tyson, this book, and his previous writing:

"You don't have to be a novice to like *Mutual Funds For Dummies*. . . . Author Eric Tyson clearly has a mastery of his subject. He knows mutual funds and he knows how to explain them in simple English. . . . It's hard to imagine a more accessible sourcebook."

— Steven T. Goldberg, *Kiplinger's Personal Finance Magazine*

"Superb! Could have saved me 5 years on research! This is my 4th book — I loan it to family & friends and never get it back!"

— Bruce Mickelson, Campbell, CA

"Eric Tyson . . . seems the perfect writer for a '. . .For Dummies' book. He doesn't tell you what to do or consider doing without explaining the why's and how's — and the booby traps to avoid — in plain English . . . it will lead you through the thickets of your own finances as painlessly as I can imagine."

— Clarence Petersen, *Chicago Tribune*

"I own many finance and investment books — this is <u>by far</u> the best!"

— Mike Dodge, Baltimore, MD

"This book is a primer for those who flinch when contemplating the 7,000 funds you can now buy."

— Brian Banmiller, Fox Television (KTVU), San Francisco, CA

"It is sooo comprehensive. If I would have found this book first, I could have saved (invested) the money I spent on all the other mutual fund books."

— Jean Hawkins, Anaheim, CA

"Eric Tyson is far and away the best writer, most readable author, and most honest and intelligent voice in America today in the areas of personal finance and mutual fund investing."

— David Diaman, enrolled agent, San Rafael, CA

"I thought I'd never understand mutual funds — finance magazines make them look like rocket science! This book made it easy!"

— John B. Sibley, Fairfield, CT

"Best new personal finance book."

— Michael Pellecchia, Syndicated Columnist

"A book that should help investors be smarter. . . . readable, comprehensive. . . Tyson's encyclo-pedic book is chockful of useful examples and advice for both new and experienced investors. . . ."

— Kim Campbell, *Christian Science Monitor*

"Mutual Funds For Dummies *is a terrific introduction to the principles of investing. I was entertained and educated.*"

— Edward Peck, York Beach, ME

"This book provides easy-to-understand personal financial information and advice for those without great wealth or knowledge in this area. Practitioners like Eric Tyson, who care about the well-being of middle-income people, are rare in today's society."

— Joel Hyatt, founder, Hyatt Legal Services, one of the nation's largest general-practice law firms providing personal legal services to families and individuals

"I liked his holistic view. He placed money management in perspective to life's important considerations. Invaluable! I'd like to give a copy to each of my sons just starting their 1st jobs."

— Robin Ketchum, Norfolk, CT

"Finally, a book about finance that I can understand!"

— Michael K. Owens, Knoxville, TN

*"*Personal Finance For Dummies *is, by far, the best book I have read on financial planning. It is a simplified volume of information that provides tremendous insight and guidance into the world of investing and other money issues."*

— Althea Thompson, Producer, PBS Nightly Business Report

"I should never have brought this book into work — everyone wants to borrow it!"

— Maria Zografos, San Francisco, CA

"Confused by finances and taxes? Eric Tyson has written Personal Finance For Dummies, *a friendly, easy-to-follow guide to smart money strategies."*

— Deb Lawler, anchor, WBZ radio, Boston, MA

" This book answered so many questions. Truly, I was completely illiterate financially — now I am becoming the family guru."

— Jean M., Holt, Missouri

". . . straightforward, readable. . .Tyson is an authoritative writer. . ."

— *Orange County CA Register*

"This book cuts through all the jargon so that a novice like myself can understand how to manage money."

— Ronnell Mitchell, New York, NY

"Smart advice for dummies . . . skip the tomes . . . and buy Personal Finance For Dummies, *which rewards your candor with advice and comfort."*

— Temma Ehrenfeld, *Newsweek*

"I purchased copies for each of my children."

— M.G. Sher, Marblehead, MA

"Fun to read, informative. I wish all financial magazines and prospectuses were as fun to read."

— Mike Mendiola, Whittier, CA

"The best book I've ever bought!"

— David Clarke, Chicago, IL

Personal Finance For Dummies is a great book. It addresses everything and helps me feel secure about my finances."

— Phyllis Haber, Kansas City, MO

"An invaluable, easy-to-read financial help book that should be in every family's library."

— Stan Schaffer, reporter, *The Morning Call*, Allentown, PA

" Simplified and demystified personal finance. This book actually made me excited about future investments and taking control of my finances."

— Kathy West, Chicago, IL

Personal Finance For Dummies offers a valuable guide for common misconceptions and major pitfalls. It's a no-nonsense, straightforward, easy-to-read personal finance book… With this book, you can easily learn enough about finances to start thinking for yourself."

— Charles R. Schwab, Chairman and CEO, The Charles Schwab Corporation

"Down-to-earth, straightforward information. It was as if Mr. Tyson was a close friend of mine who really cared about me."

— Arnold L., Monterey Park, CA

". . . smart ideas about mutual funds. The beauty of this book is that you don't have to read it from cover to cover. If you want a simple overview, focus on the highlights; if you want more depth, read the chapters that interest you."

— *The Times-Picayune*, New Orleans, LA

"This book was written for real people."

— Lisa Timco, Westland, MI

"Nothing but accolades for Mr. Tyson."

— R.C. Watkins, Houston, TX

"For those named in the title, such as myself, Personal Finance For Dummies *is a godsend. It's bright, funny, and it can save you money, too."*

— Jerome Crowe, reporter, *L. A. Times*

"The organization of this book is superb! I could go right to the topics of immediate interest and find clearly written and informative material. The author answered questions that I didn't even know."

— Lorraine Verboort, Beaverton, OR

"This is a great book. It's understandable. Other financial books are too technical and this one really is different."

— Shad Johnson, Producer, Business Radio Network

"Well-written, good format. I gave a copy to my 25-year-old, newly married daughter. Her reaction: 'The book is a real eye opener.'"

— Reece Little, Louisville, KY

"Fantastic. I wish I had it 20 years ago. I'll make sure my children get one."

— C.H. Day, Richmond, VA

"Mr. Tyson's unique style of presenting an intimidating topic to beginners in a humorous and interesting fashion should be a lesson to other financial advice writers."

— Gary T. Rzepka, APO, AP, Japan

"Personal Finance For Dummies is a sane and useful guide that will be of benefit to anyone seeking a careful and prudent method of managing their financial world.

— John Robbins, founder of EarthSave and author of *May All Be Fed*

"Easy to understand and hard to put down once you start reading."

— Absolam Deshong, Washington, D.C.

"Mutual Fund$ For Dummie$ by Eric Tyson is an excellent source for not only the novice investor but also for someone looking to enhance their understanding of one of the fastest growing investment tools."

— Tarun Reddy, *Northwest Arkansas Times*

"My life stopped — could not put the book down!"

— Richard Bolton, San Diego, CA

". . . injects common sense into the dizzying world of mutual funds. . ."

— Cliff Pletschet, *Oakland Tribune,* CA

"The minute I read the table of contents, I knew this was a book I should have had 30 years ago. I strongly believe that all young people just starting out in their first job should have this book."

— Ellinor Juarez, Alameda, CA

"Worth getting. Scores of all-purpose money-management books reach bookstores every year, but only once every couple of years does a standout personal finance primer come along. *Personal Finance For Dummies,* by financial counselor and columnist Eric Tyson, provides detailed, action-oriented advice on everyday financial questions . . . Tyson's style is readable and unintimidating."

— Kristin Davis, *Kiplinger's Personal Finance Magazine*

 ™

BUSINESS AND GENERAL REFERENCE BOOK SERIES FROM IDG

References for the Rest of Us!™

Do you find that traditional reference books are overloaded with technical details and advice you'll never use? Do you postpone important life decisions because you just don't want to deal with them? Then our *...For Dummies*™ business and general reference book series is for you.

...For Dummies business and general reference books are written for those frustrated and hard-working souls who know they aren't dumb, but find that the myriad of personal and business issues and the accompanying horror stories make them feel helpless. *...For Dummies* books use a lighthearted approach, a down-to-earth style, and even cartoons and humorous icons to diffuse fears and build confidence. Lighthearted but not lightweight, these books are perfect survival guides to solve your everyday personal and business problems.

> *"More than a publishing phenomenon, 'Dummies' is a sign of the times."*
> — The New York Times

> *". . . you won't go wrong buying them."*
> — Walter Mossberg, Wall Street Journal, on IDG's ...For Dummies™ books

> *"A world of detailed and authoritative information is packed into them..."*
> — U.S. News and World Report

Already, hundreds of thousands of satisfied readers agree. They have made *...For Dummies* the #1 introductory level computer book series and a best-selling business book series. They have written asking for more. So, if you're looking for the best and easiest way to learn about business and other general reference topics, look to *...For Dummies* to give you a helping hand.

by Eric Tyson, MBA

Financial Counselor and Author of the National Bestsellers
Personal Finance For Dummies™
and
Investing For Dummies™
and co-author of
Taxes For Dummies™

IDG Books Worldwide, Inc.
An International Data Group Company

Foster City, CA ◆ Chicago, IL ◆ Indianapolis, IN ◆ Southlake, TX

Mutual Funds For Dummies™

Published by
IDG Books Worldwide, Inc.
An International Data Group Company
919 E. Hillsdale Blvd.
Suite 400
Foster City, CA 94404
www.idgbooks.com (IDG Books Worldwide Web Site)
http://www.dummies.com (Dummies Press Web Site)

Library of Congress Catalog Card No.: 94-73684

ISBN: 1-56884-226-0

Printed in the United States of America

10 9 8 7 6 5

1A/RY/QZ/ZW/IN

Distributed in the United States by IDG Books Worldwide, Inc.

Distributed by Macmillan Canada for Canada; by Contemporanea de Ediciones for Venezuela; by Distribuidora Cuspide for Argentina; by CITEC for Brazil; by Ediciones ZETA S.C.R. Ltda. for Peru; by Editorial Limusa SA for Mexico; by Transworld Publishers Limited in the United Kingdom and Europe; by Academic Bookshop for Egypt; by Levant Distributors S.A.R.L. for Lebanon; by Al Jassim for Saudi Arabia; by Simron Pty. Ltd. for South Africa; by Pustak Mahal for India; by The Computer Bookshop for India; by Toppan Company Ltd. for Japan; by Addison Wesley Publishing Company for Korea; by Longman Singapore Publishers Ltd. for Singapore, Malaysia, Thailand, and Indonesia; by Unalis Corporation for Taiwan; by WS Computer Publishing Company, Inc. for the Philippines; by WoodsLane Pty. Ltd. for Australia; by WoodsLane Enterprises Ltd. for New Zealand. Authorized Sales Agent: Anthony Rudkin Associates for the Middle East and North Africa.

For general information on IDG Books Worldwide's books in the U.S., please call our Consumer Customer Service department at 800-762-2974. For reseller information, including discounts and premium sales, please call our Reseller Customer Service department at 800-434-3422.

For information on where to purchase IDG Books Worldwide's books outside the U.S., please contact our International Sales department at 415-655-3172 or fax 415-655-3295.

For information on foreign language translations, please contact our Foreign & Subsidiary Rights department at 415-655-3021 or fax 415-655-3281.

For sales inquiries and special prices for bulk quantities, please contact our Sales department at 415-655-3200 or write to the address above.

For information on using IDG Books Worldwide's books in the classroom or for ordering examination copies, please contact our Educational Sales department at 800-434-2086 or fax 817-251-8174.

For authorization to photocopy items for corporate, personal, or educational use, please contact Copyright Clearance Center, 222 Rosewood Drive, Danvers, MA 01923, or fax 508-750-4470.

 is a trademark under exclusive
license to IDG Books Worldwide, Inc.,
from International Data Group, Inc.

About the Author

Eric Tyson, MBA

Eric Tyson is a nationally recognized personal financial writer, lecturer, and counselor based in San Francisco, California. Through his counseling, writing, and teaching, he teaches people to manage their personal finances better and successfully direct their own investments.

He has been involved in the investing markets in many capacities for the past two decades. Eric first invested in mutual funds back in the mid-1970s, when he opened a mutual fund account account at Fidelity. With the assistance of Dr. Martin Zweig, a now-famous investment market analyst and frequent guest on PBS's *Wall Street Week*, Eric won his high school's science fair in 1976 for a project on what influences the stock market!

Since that time, Eric has (among other things) worked as a management consultant to Fortune 500 financial service firms, and earned his Bachelor's degree in economics at Yale and an MBA at the Stanford Graduate School of Business. Despite these handicaps to clear thinking, he had the good sense to start his own company, which took an innovative approach to teaching people of all economic means about investing and money.

An accomplished freelance personal finance writer, Eric is the author of the national bestsellers *Personal Finance For Dummies, Investing For Dummies,* co-author of *Taxes For Dummies,* and *Home Buying For Dummies,* and a columnist for the *San Francisco Examiner.* His work has been featured and quoted in dozens of national and local publications, including *Newsweek, Forbes, Kiplinger's Personal Finance Magazine*, the *Wall Street Journal, L.A. Times, Chicago Tribune,* and *Bottom Line/Personal;* and on NBC's *Today Show,* ABC, CNBC, PBS's *Nightly Business Report,* CNN, CBS national radio, Bloomberg Business Radio, and Business Radio Network. He's also been a featured speaker at a White House conference on retirement planning.

To stay in tune with what real people care about and struggle with, Eric still maintains a financial counseling practice and is a lecturer of the Bay Area's (and perhaps the country's) most highly attended money management course at the University of California, Berkeley.

Despite his "wealth" of financial knowledge, Eric is one of the rest of us. He maintains a large inventory of bumble-bee yellow-and-black-covered computer books on his desk for those frequent times when his computer makes the (decreasing amount of) hair on his head fall out.

ABOUT IDG BOOKS WORLDWIDE

WINNER
Eighth Annual
Computer Press
Awards ≥ 1992

WINNER
Ninth Annual
Computer Press
Awards ≥ 1993

IDG BOOKS
WORLDWIDE

Welcome to the world of IDG Books Worldwide.

IDG Books Worldwide, Inc., is a subsidiary of International Data Group, the world's largest publisher of computer-related information and the leading global provider of information services on information technology. IDG was founded more than 25 years ago and now employs more than 8,500 people worldwide. IDG publishes more than 270 computer publications in over 75 countries (see listing below). More than 90 million people read one or more IDG publications each month.

Launched in 1990, IDG Books Worldwide is today the #1 publisher of best-selling computer books in the United States. We are proud to have received eight awards from the Computer Press Association in recognition of editorial excellence and three from *Computer Currents'* First Annual Readers' Choice Awards. Our best-selling ...*For Dummies®* series has more than 25 million copies in print with translations in 30 languages. IDG Books Worldwide, through a joint venture with IDG's Hi-Tech Beijing, became the first U.S. publisher to publish a computer book in the People's Republic of China. In record time, IDG Books Worldwide has become the first choice for millions of readers around the world who want to learn how to better manage their businesses.

Our mission is simple: Every one of our books is designed to bring extra value and skill-building instructions to the reader. Our books are written by experts who understand and care about our readers. The knowledge base of our editorial staff comes from years of experience in publishing, education, and journalism — experience which we use to produce books for the '90s. In short, we care about books, so we attract the best people. We devote special attention to details such as audience, interior design, use of icons, and illustrations. And because we use an efficient process of authoring, editing, and desktop publishing our books electronically, we can spend more time ensuring superior content and spend less time on the technicalities of making books.

You can count on our commitment to deliver high-quality books at competitive prices on topics you want to read about. At IDG Books Worldwide, we continue in the IDG tradition of delivering quality for more than 25 years. You'll find no better book on a subject than one from IDG Books Worldwide.

John J. Kilcullen

John Kilcullen
President and CEO
IDG Books Worldwide, Inc.

IDG Books Worldwide, Inc., is a subsidiary of International Data Group, the world's largest publisher of computer-related information and the leading global provider of information services on information technology. International Data Group publishes over 276 computer publications in over 75 countries. Ninety million people read one or more International Data Group publications each month. International Data Group's publications include: **ARGENTINA:** Annuario de Informatica, Computerworld Argentina, PC World Argentina; **AUSTRALIA:** Australian Macworld, Client/Server Journal, Computer Living, Computerworld, Computerworld 100, Digital News, IT Casebook, Network World, On-line World Australia, PC World, Publishing Essentials, Reseller, WebMaster; **AUSTRIA:** Computerwelt Osterreich, Networks Austria, PC Tip; **BELARUS:** Data News; **BRAZIL:** Annuário de Informática, Computerworld Brazil, Connections, Super Game Power, Macworld, PC Player, PC World Brazil, Publish Brazil, Reseller News; **BULGARIA:** Computerworld Bulgaria, Networkworld/Bulgaria, PC & MacWorld Bulgaria; **CANADA:** CIO Canada, Client/Server World, ComputerWorld Canada, InfoCanada, Network World Canada; **CHILE:** Computerworld Chile, PC World Chile; **COLOMBIA:** Computerworld Colombia, PC World Colombia; **COSTA RICA:** PC World Centro America; **THE CZECH AND SLOVAK REPUBLICS:** Computerworld Czechoslovakia, Elektronika Czechoslovakia, Macworld Czech Republic, PC World Czechoslovakia; **DENMARK:** Communications World, Computerworld Danmark, Macworld Danmark, PC Privat Danmark, PC World Danmark, PC World Danmark Supplements, TECH World; **DOMINICAN REPUBLIC:** PC World Republica Dominicana; **ECUADOR:** PC World Ecuador; **EGYPT:** Computerworld Middle East, PC World Middle East; **EL SALVADOR:** PC World Centro America; **FINLAND:** MikroPC, Tietoverkko, Tietoviikko; **FRANCE:** Distributique, Golden, Hebdo-Distributique, Info PC, Le Guide du Monde Informatique, Le Monde Informatique, Reseaux & Telecoms; **GERMANY:** Computer Partner, Computerwoche, Computerwoche Extra, Computerwoche Focus, I/M Information Management, Macwelt, PC Welt; **GREECE:** GamePro, Multimedia World; **GUATEMALA:** PC World Centro America; **HONDURAS:** PC World Centro America; **HONG KONG:** Computerworld Hong Kong, PCWorld Hong Kong, Publish in Asia; **HUNGARY:** ABCD CD-ROM, Computerworld Szamitastechnika, PC & Mac World Hungary, PC-X Magazine; **ICELAND:** Tolvuheimur/PC World Island; **INDIA:** Information Systems Computerworld, PC World India, Publish in Asia; **INDONESIA:** InfoKomputer PC World, Komputerworld, Publish in Asia; **IRELAND:** ComputerScope, PC Live!; **ISRAEL:** People & Computers; **ITALY:** Computerworld Italia, Computerworld Italia Special Editions, Macworld Italia, Networking Italia, PC Shopping, PC World Italia, PC World/Walt Disney; **JAPAN:** DTP World, HP Open World Japan, Macworld Japan, Nikkei Personal Computing, Open World Japan, OS/2 World Japan, SunWorld Japan, Windows World Japan; **KENYA:** East African Computer News; **KOREA:** Hi-Tech Information/Computerworld, Macworld Korea, PC World Korea; **MACEDONIA:** PC World Macedonia; **MALAYSIA:** Computerworld Malaysia, PC World Malaysia, Publish in Asia; **MEXICO:** Computerworld Mexico, Macworld, PC World Mexico; **MYANMAR:** PC World Myanmar; **NETHERLANDS:** Computer! Totaal, LAN Magazine, LanWorld Buyers Guide, Macworld, Net Magazine, Totaal! Beurskrant; **NEW ZEALAND:** Absolute Beginner's Guide, Computer Buyer, Computer Industry Directory, Computerworld New Zealand, MTB, Network World, PC World New Zealand; **NICARAGUA:** PC World Centro America; **NIGERIA:** PC World Nigeria; **NORWAY:** Computerworld Norge, Computerworld Privat (Datamagasinet), CW Rapport Norge, IDG's KURSGUIDE, Macworld Norge, Multimediaworld, PC World Ekspress, PC World Nettverk, PC World Norge, PC World's Produktguide, Windows World Spesial; **PAKISTAN:** Computerworld Pakistan, PC World Pakistan; **PANAMA:** PC World Panama; **P. R. OF CHINA:** China Computer Users, China Computerworld, China Infoworld, China Telecom World Weekly, Computer & Communication, Electronic Design China, Electronics Today, Electronics Weekly, Game Camp, Game Soft, Network World China, PC World China, Popular Computer Weekly, Software Weekly, Software World, Telecom World; **PERU:** Computerworld Peru, PC World Profesional Peru, PC World Peru; **PHILIPPINES:** Computerworld Philippines, PC World Philippines, Publish in Asia; **POLAND:** Computerworld Poland, Computerworld Special Report, Macworld, Networld, PC World Komputer; **PORTUGAL:** Cerebro/PC World, Computerworld/Correio Informático, Dealer World Portugal, MacIn/PCIn, Multimedia World Portugal; **PUERTO RICO:** PC World Puerto Rico; **ROMANIA:** Computerworld Romania, PC World Romania, Telecom Romania; **RUSSIA:** Computerworld Russia, Mir PK, Sety; **SINGAPORE:** Computerworld Singapore, PC World Singapore, Publish in Asia; **SLOVENIA:** MONITOR; **SOUTH AFRICA:** Computing S.A., InfoWorld S.A., Network World S.A., Software World; **SPAIN:** Computerworld España, COMUNICACIONES World, Dealer World, Macworld España, PC World España; **SWEDEN:** CAP&Design, Computer Sweden, Corporate Computing, MacWorld, Maxi Data, MikroDatorn, Nätverk & Kommunikation, PC/Aktiv, PC World, Windows World; **SWITZERLAND:** Computerworld Schweiz, Macworld Schweiz, PCtip; **TAIWAN:** Computerworld Taiwan, Macworld Taiwan, PC World Taiwan, Publish Taiwan, Windows World; **THAILAND:** Thai Computerworld, Publish in Asia; **TURKEY:** Computerworld Turkiye, MACWORLD Turkiye, PC WORLD Turkiye; **UKRAINE:** Computerworld Kiev, Computers & Software, Multimedia World Ukraine, PC World Ukraine; **UNITED KINGDOM:** Acorn User, Amiga Action, Amiga Computing, Appletalk, Computing, GamePro, Macworld, Network News, Parents and Computers, PC Advisor, PC Home, PSX Pro UK, The WEB; **UNITED STATES:** Cable in the Classroom, CD Review, CIO Magazine, Computerworld, Computerworld Client/Server Journal, Digital Video Magazine, DOS World, Federal Computer Week, GamePro, InfoWorld, I-Way, JavaWorld, Macworld, Multimedia World, Netscape World Online, Network World, PC Entertainment, PC World, Publish, SunWorld Online, SWATPro Magazine, Video Event, WebMaster; **URUGUAY:** PC World Uruguay; **VENEZUELA:** Computerworld Venezuela, PC World Venezuela; and **VIETNAM:** PC World Vietnam. 7/16/96

Dedication

To my wife, Judy; my family, especially my parents Charles and Paulina; and friends; and to my counseling clients and students of my courses for teaching me how to teach them about managing their finances.

Acknowledgments

Many people contribute to the birth of a book, and this book is no exception. First, I owe a deep debt of gratitude to James Collins who inspired me when I was a young and impressionable business school student. Jim encouraged me to try to improve some small part of the business world by being an entrepreneur and focusing solely on what customers needed rather than on what made the quickest buck.

The technical reviewers for this book helped to improve each and every chapter and I am thankful for that. It was a privilege to be able to have the wise input of Kenneth L. Fisher, who knows more about investing and the history of the field than is fair for one person to know. My heartfelt thanks also to the American Association of Individual Investors and John Bajkowski for many helpful and insightful comments and to Dennis Ito, Robert Taylor, and the other tax savvy professionals at KPMG Peat Marwick.

Special thanks also to Frederic Lowrie, Chris Doyle, Brian Mattes, John Woerth and Mariann Lindsey for helping provide forms, documents, and answers to my many questions.

Thanks to all the good people in the media and other fields who have taken the time to critique and praise my previous writing so that others may know that it exists and is worth reading. And to those too lazy to open the book just because of its bright yellow color and title I say, "Don't judge a book by its cover!"

And a final and heartfelt thanks to all the people on the front lines and behind the scenes at IDG Books who helped to make this book and my others a success. A big round of applause, please, for Kathy Cox as project editor and Jeff Waggoner as copy editor. Special thanks to Kathy Welton, publisher, for her many timely and thoughtful ideas, and to John Kilcullen for cajoling me into writing these books in the first place. Thanks also to Andy Cummings, Diane Giangrossi, Pam Mourouzis, Michael Simsic, Tammy Castleman, Beth Jenkins, Cindy Phipps, Sherry Gomoll, Mary Breidenbach, Linda Boyer, Theresa Sanchez-Baker, Gina Scott, Carla Radzikinas, Sherry Massey, and Jenny Kaufeld for their great efforts in producing this book.

P.S. Thanks to you, dear reader, for buying my books.

Publisher's Acknowledgments

We're proud of this book; please send us your comments about it by using the Reader Response Card at the back of the book or by e-mailing us at feedback/dummies@idgbooks.com. Some of the people who helped bring this book to market include the following:

Acquisitions, Development, and Editorial

Project Editor: Kathleen M. Cox

Copy Editors: Andy Cummings, Diane Giangrossi, Pam Mourouzis, Michael Simsic, Jeffrey Waggoner

Technical Editors: John Bajkowski, Kenneth L. Fisher, Dennis Ito, Robert Taylor

Editorial Manager: Kristin A. Cocks

Editorial Assistants: Constance Carlisle, Chris Collins, Ann Miller, Kevin Spencer

Production

Project Coordinator: Sherry Gomoll

Layout and Graphics: Cameron Booker, Linda Boyer, Mary Breidenbach, Elizabeth Cárdenas-Nelson, J. Tyler Connor, Maridee Ennis, Angela F. Hunckler, Carla Radzikinas, Gina Scott

Proofreaders: Jennifer Kaufeld, Dwight Ramsey

Indexer: Sherry Massey

Special Help

Executive Assistant: Michelle Vukas

General & Administrative

IDG Books Worldwide, Inc.: John Kilcullen, President and CEO; Steven Berkowitz, COO and Publisher

Dummies, Inc.: Milissa Koloski, Executive Vice President and Publisher

Dummies Technology Press and Dummies Editorial: Diane Graves Steele, Associate Publisher; Judith A. Taylor, Brand Manager

Dummies Trade Press: Kathleen A. Welton, Vice President and Publisher; Stacy S. Collins, Brand Manager

IDG Books Production for Dummies Press: Beth Jenkins, Production Director; Cindy L. Phipps, Supervisor of Project Coordination; Kathie S. Schutte, Supervisor of Page Layout; Shelley Lea, Supervisor of Graphics and Design; Debbie J. Gates, Production Systems Specialist

Dummies Packaging and Book Design: Patti Sandez, Packaging Assistant; Kavish+Kavish, Cover Design

◆

The publisher would like to give special thanks to Patrick J. McGovern, without whom this book would not have been possible.

◆

Contents at a Glance

Cartoons at a Glance

Reprinted with permission

By Wiley

page 129

page 7

page 309

page 241

page 319

More Cartoons at a Glance

Reprinted with permission

By Wiley

page 349

page 373

page 315

page 11

Table of Contents

· ·

Foreword

I admit it. I am a "Dummy" — at least when it comes to personal finances. But like a smart dummy, I know where to turn for trusted information and advice. Fortunately, Eric Tyson wrote *Personal Finance for Dummies*. I knew Eric so I've had a copy to serve as a valuable and trusted quick reference guide whenever I have a money question.

Like you (if you've picked up this book), I know that I should be wiser about investing my savings. Magazine articles about mutual funds clutter my desk and mutual fund literature piles up in a corner of the living room — mountains of reading that, "I'll get to later, when I have a few minutes." Friends tell me over dinner that they've invested in this fund or that fund. They spout off sage advice about "load" and "no-load" and "growth funds" and "income funds" and risk and — well, I usually just go back to the menu and try to figure out what to order for dinner.

"You know, we really should invest some of our money in a few of those funds," I might comment to my wife on the drive home. But, like most of us, I put it off or — worse — make bad decisions. Like the novice mountain climber, I know just enough to get myself into trouble.

However, unlike exotic activities such as mountain climbing, the task of managing our personal finances is one we all face. It's as if we are all stuck in the mountains, but few of us really know how to climb. Wealthy people hire personal guides to help them out. But most of us can't afford or don't feel comfortable doing that. And as Eric points out, and my own experience suggests, financial advisors may have their own agendas that conflict with yours.

I first met Eric when he was a graduate business student of mine at Stanford; I was impressed by the strength and clarity of his personal purpose: to help people at all income levels to take control of their financial futures. He nurtured his vision while he worked to pay off all his student loan obligations. Then he boldly quit his high-paying and prestigious management consulting career to devote full time to making his vision a reality. Like Henry Ford, Eric wants to make that which is available only to the wealthy widely accessible to middle-income Americans. Ford did it with automobiles; Tyson aims to do it with thoughtful financial planning. This book is yet another important step toward that goal.

We live in a knowledge age. Those who "know" will be better-off in the long run than those who "have." I do not see the widening cleavage in our society to be between the "haves" and the "have-nots," but between the "knows" and the "know-nots." Those who know will have; those who know-not...

Eric knows a lot about mutual funds and making intelligent investing decisions in funds within the context of one's overall personal financial situation. And he makes that knowledge accessible to all of us "Dummies" here in this book. I hope you learn and apply his lessons. I intend to.

James C. Collins
Palo Alto, CA

Co-author of the national bestseller *Built to Last: Successful Habits of Visionary Companies* and *Beyond Entrepreneurship: Turning Your Business into an Enduring Great Company,* and Lecturer in Business, Stanford Graduate School of Business

Introduction

*T*hanks for choosing *Mutual Funds For Dummies.* Whether you're a regular reader of investing books or this is your first, *Mutual Funds For Dummies* will teach you practical techniques of mutual fund investing that you can put to work now and for many years to come.

Mutual funds are smart investments for people at all income and educational levels. They offer low-cost access to professional money managers so that you can spend your time doing the things in life that you enjoy. Mutual funds should improve your investment returns as well as your social life!

How This Book Is Different

Many investment books confuse folks. They present you with some newfangled system that you never figure out how to use without the help of a mainframe computer, several mathematicians, and a Nobel Laureate as your personal consultants. Books that bewilder more than teach may be intentional because the author may have another agenda: to get you to turn your money over to him to manage or to sell you his newsletter(s). These authors may generally lack a financial planning perspective and an "in the trenches" understanding of the challenges real investors face. And these writers with an agenda may imply and sometimes say that you really can't invest well on your own.

Going another route, too many investment books glorify rather than advise. They place on a pedestal the very, very few who, during decidedly brief periods in the history of the world and financial markets, managed to beat the market averages by a few percentage points or so per year. Many of these books and their publishers suggest that reading them will teach you the strategies that led Superstar Money Manager to the superlative performance that the book glorifies. "He did it his way; now you can, too," trumpets the marketing material. Not so. Reading a book about what made Michael Jordan a phenomenal basketball player, Shakespeare a great playwright, or Henry Kissinger a successful Secretary of State won't teach you to shoot a basket, versify, or negotiate stately alliances like these famous folks. By the same token, you can't learn from a book how to become the next Wall Street investment wizard. These types of books make their publishers wealthy, not you.

Almost as bad, most mutual fund books are too technical; they overwhelm you with tons of data on lots of different funds. Those that do a good job explaining the fundamental concepts typically don't delve into the nuts-and-bolts issues that frustrate some financial novices. None deal well with the critical subject of how and when to buy funds from the perspective of holistic financial planning.

When you want to buy or sell a mutual fund, your decision needs to fit your overall financial objectives and individual situation. Fund investors make many mistakes in this regard. For example, they invest in funds instead of in their employer's tax-deductible retirement savings plan or instead of paying off debt. It's also common for investors to choose funds that don't fit their tax situation. *Mutual Funds For Dummies* helps you avoid those common fund-investing pitfalls.

Mutual Funds For Dummies also covers pesky issues completely ignored by other mutual fund books. For novice fund investors, just obtaining and finding the correct application and other forms in the mountain of literature that fund companies send you can be a challenge. And if you invest in mutual funds outside of tax-sheltered retirement accounts, you're greeted by the inevitable headache about how to report distributions at tax time. This book puts you on the path you need to be on in order to avoid these problems.

Truth is, investing is not all that difficult — and mutual funds are the great equalizer. There's absolutely no reason, except perhaps a lack of time and effort on your part, why you can't successfully invest in mutual funds on your own. In fact, if you learn some basic concepts and how to avoid major mistakes that occur for some fairly obvious reasons, you can be even more successful than most so-called investment professionals.

In my practice as a financial counselor, I help investors make successful investing decisions with mutual funds as part of comprehensive personal financial management. So I know the questions and challenges that you face when you invest in funds. I wrote this book to answer, in plain English, your fund investing questions.

Eliminating Mutual Fund Confusion

You have good reason to be here because mutual funds are a huge and confusing business. Although mutual funds began in the U.S. in 1924, as recently as 1978 they held only $57 billion in assets. Today, thousands of mutual funds account for about three *trillion* dollars (*$3,000,000,000,000!* — count all those zeros!) under management — a 50-fold increase in just the last 18 years. In the near future, the total money invested in mutual funds will, for the first time in history, surpass the total invested through traditional bank accounts.

Mutual funds are investment companies that pool your money with that of thousands of other people and invest the money in stocks, bonds, and other securities. The basic principle sounds simple enough, but you have to understand the different types of investments, such as stocks and bonds, and how they work, because funds are a package deal.

The second thing you have to understand is that there are so *many* individual funds — more than 8,000. Hundreds of companies in many different kinds of businesses (mutual fund companies, brokerage firms, insurers, banks, and so on) are trying to sell funds. Even experienced investors suffer from information overload. Lucky for you, you'll be presented in this book with short lists of great funds that work for you and your situation.

And because no investment, not even one of the better mutual funds, is free of flaws and shortcomings, I show you sound alternatives to mutual funds — and help you tell when investing in funds probably isn't appropriate for you.

Using This Book Effectively

You don't need to read this book cover to cover. But if you're a beginner or you want to fully immerse yourself in the world of fund investing (or if you're just a glutton), there's no reason why you can't.

On the other hand, you may have a specific question or two that you want to focus on today, but you'll want something else tomorrow. No problem there, either. *Mutual Funds For Dummies* is lighter on its feet and on your brain than most reference books. Use the table of contents or index to speed your way to what you need to know and get on with your life.

Getting There from Here

Part I: Appetizers: Prerequisites and Background

Before you start to eat in a foreign country, you need to know what all the appropriate utensils are, what comes with each course, and how not to look like a pig! By the time you catch a whiff and finally a bona fide taste of the big meal, you're primed to dine with pleasure and maybe even enjoy the view.

Your mutual fund investing will work the same way — so Part I of this book whets your appetite for fund investing itself by helping you learn general investing basics. If you don't understand the different types of investments, such as stocks and bonds, you won't fully understand funds. Part I defines and demystifies what mutual funds are and discusses what funds are good for and when you should consider alternatives.

You also learn how to pick great funds, how to avoid losers, where and how to purchase funds, and how to read all those pesky reports such as prospectuses and annual reports that fund companies stuff in your mailbox. You'll also learn the critical but often misunderstood ways to fit funds into your future financial plans and how to get advice if you need or want it.

Part II: The Main Course: Nothing but the Best

Dig into the main course and learn all you need to know to enjoy money market, bond, and stock mutual funds. Our smorgasbord includes fare from around the world and options that you may not even know about. For all the major fund types, you get specific recommendations. You learn how to select funds to lower your income tax bill and funds to make your money grow. Best of all, you get recipes to whip up the best meals to meet the special needs of your own discriminating and unique palate.

Part III: Nuts and Bolts: Indigestion

Here you learn all the aggravating but necessary things you need to do to get started with investing in funds and managing your portfolio in the years ahead. Think of these chapters as your antacids in the medicine cabinet. Part III answers your questions about how to complete fund application and account transfer forms and how to fix glitches that cause unnecessary hassles for fund investors. You also learn how to track the performance of your funds, whether you should feel devastated or elated with your returns, and how to decide whether and when to dump your holdings. Come tax time, you'll also have the information you need to decipher those confusing tax documents fund companies send you.

Part IV: For the Glutton: More Information and Advice

If you're still not full, you can learn some critical information about the scores of companies and individuals who rate, rank, and predict financial market gyrations. You learn the dangers of blindly following gurus and which, if any, of them really are gurus. You also learn how to use the best mutual fund information sources, the differences between good and bad newsletters, and where to turn for more information. You may want to know how to use your computer to track and even invest in mutual funds using on-line services and software — so Part IV tells you that, too.

Part V: The Part of Tens: Desserts, for the Mind

Broaden your thinking even further with these chapters of ten-somethings that cover other important fund issues and concepts. Here you get answers to your fund investing concerns and learn about concerns you may not have but perhaps should. You also get guidance on how to use funds for other goals — such as saving for college costs — and the ten questions you should ask before you hire a mutual fund advisor.

Part VI: Appendix: Other Useful Stuff about the Best Mutual Funds

So as to not clutter up the book unnecessarily, I stuck some useful things at the end of book. Here you find the telephone numbers, addresses, and other vital statistics of all the top-notch funds recommended in this book.

Icons Used in This Book

Throughout this book, you will find friendly and useful icons to enhance your reading pleasure and to flag and demarcate special types of information. So, when you meet one of these margin-hugging doo dads, imagine this conversation with yourself:

Hey, I'll bet Eric just pointed out something that can save me time, headaches, money, or all of the above!

Uh, bombs normally ain't real popular in polite company, so maybe Eric's trying to steer me away from mistakes and boo-boos others have made investing in mutual funds.

Sharklike life-forms dead ahead. *Some*thing around here could really cost me big bucks (maybe even an arm and a leg!) if I don't devote my raptest attention to Eric here.

Yowza! Finally, a book that tells me what to do, where to do it, and whom to do it with. What a neat idea — a Dummies seal of approval that flags specifically recommended funds and other trustworthy stuff on the market!

Eminently skippable stuff here (especially if something important like a call from Mother Nature is pressing upon me), but I may not seem as astute at the next cocktail party when mutual fund Trivial Pursuit begins. Neat but nonessential stuff — read at leisure.

An invite from His Tysonship to get out my trenchcoat, sagging pipe, and Sherlock Holmes hat and look into something on my own. Eric's told me as much as he can, but he thinks I may need or want to check it out more on my own before I make a move.

I'll bet what Eric's telling me is *so* important that I should *make sure* I don't forget it when I'm at large in the real world making my own fund investing decisions!

Part I
Appetizers: Prerequisites and Background

Reprinted with permission

In this part...

If you don't know the difference between a stock and a bond or between a growth mutual fund and an expense ratio, this part gives you those key definitions — and others — to tease and whet your investing appetite. In five rollicking, action-packed chapters, you'll get everything under your belt and into your cerebral cortex that you need to know to understand and converse about mutual funds. You'll also get an inside look at where, how, and when to invest in the best mutual funds and how to make sure your mutual fund decisions fit nicely and neatly with the rest of your finances.

Chapter 1

Smart People, Dumb Investments

· ·

In This Chapter

▶ Determining your needs and goals

▶ Understanding investments

▶ Investment risk and returns

▶ Benefits of diversification

· ·

I was learning about Chris's financial history and personality, as is often the case in my first meeting with someone new. "I've made every investing mistake there is to make," she said with a sigh. "If you have done the opposite of what I have always done, that would have been a good strategy."

Chris's investing career began in the late 1970s when she bought stock (shares of ownership in a company) in her employer's company. Unfortunately, the employer was a manufacturing company whose days were numbered. In 1980, Chris's company filed for bankruptcy, and she got a pink slip from her boss. In this way, Chris found herself sitting on a pile of stock that no longer had a price per share — the stock was essentially worthless. Few things could have been more depressing than sitting at home, unemployed, and seeing company stock account statements show a balance of $0.00.

Being a little bit gun shy, Chris did not foray into another major investment until 1983. While vacationing in Florida, she went to a presentation that extolled the virtues of purchasing a share in luxury condominiums being built near Disney World. "How could you lose," the presenter asked, "with the never-ending attraction of Disney?" Chris concurred: Kids would always be dragging their money-toting parents to Disney.

Chris found out what far too many time share owners know: Time shares are grossly overpriced ways to purchase a week's ownership in a place you wish you hadn't bought. Ten years later, Chris unloaded her investment for 20 percent of what she paid for it. And her 80 percent loss was *after* she'd paid annual maintenance and other unanticipated fees — all of which had been conveniently left out of the initial sales pitch (er, I mean, presentation).

Chris's next investment decision came as the result of an unfortunate family occurrence. In 1984, her father passed away and left her $200,000. Since Chris had learned from experience that putting too many investment eggs in one basket causes problems for investors, she was all ears when Louis, a financial consultant, recommended "a diversified, professionally managed investment." After all, she thought, the advice made sense to her, and the attorney who handled her father's estate highly recommended Louis. Louis's investment firm advertised everywhere and had, it seemed, nearly a hundred employees.

These limited partnerships (LPs), as Louis called them, would end her string of bad luck in investments. "Each partnership holds dozens of individual investments, so if one of them does poorly or even becomes worthless, it's just a small portion of the whole. Besides, you'll get all these great tax write-offs to boot," Louis assured her.

Louis wore an expensive business suit and had an office with a nice view of the financial district. "I've invested in limited partnerships myself and so have my parents," he said. Well, Chris reasoned, if limited partnerships were good enough for Louis's company, an obviously successful brokerage firm, and for Louis and his family, then limited partnerships were good enough for her, too. She put three-quarters of her inheritance money into a couple of them.

More than a decade later, here's the news on Chris's limited partnerships:

Total invested = $150,000. Current value = $8,000.

In addition to high sales commissions and high ongoing management fees, the LPs made poor investments. Oh, and Chris still has to have her accountant fill out those nasty special income tax return schedules for LPs every year.

Luckily, Chris kept $50,000 of the inheritance reserved for a home down payment. By 1987, however, real estate prices in northern California seemed to be heading into the stratosphere, so when Louis called again with his stock recommendations, Chris was receptive to his advice. If she could just make her money grow, Chris thought, she could afford to buy a good home she'd be really happy with.

She bought a half dozen stocks — which promptly nose-dived 40 percent when the stock market crashed in October. Monday never was Chris's favorite day, but when she heard on the news that the market had dropped more than 500 points on Monday, October 19, she knew that that day was indeed Black Monday.

She had a hard time getting through to Louis, whose secretary said, "He's very busy today helping clients make changes with their investments." When she finally got through to him, Louis helped Chris make changes to her investments, too. "A money market fund will provide a safe haven from the turbulent financial markets," he reasoned.

Chris didn't want to jeopardize the future home purchase, so she took Louis's seasoned advice to sell and put the proceeds into a money market fund. The $50,000 was now worth about $28,000. Her money stayed in the money market fund until I found Chris sitting at my doorstep, her portfolio and ego both deflated.

Although Chris was being hard on herself when she said that she had made every investing mistake there is to make — actually, there are many more — she had made other financial mistakes that she wasn't even aware of. Sadly, during her two decades of investing horrors, she had missed out on the opportunity to contribute to tax-deductible investment accounts through employers she had worked for. She also had racked up more than $10,000 in high-interest consumer debt, mostly on credit cards. At the risk of having you think I enjoy finding fault, I also must tell you that Chris had no long-term disability insurance or life insurance when she called me, even though she had started a family following her marriage in 1992.

Mutual Funds: An Investment

If you don't have a portfolio of limited partnerships, stock options, and vacation home time shares, fear not. And don't feel stupid! Many people don't have these kinds of investments or even understand how they work. And many people who do have fancy-sounding investments — including people who have lost millions of dollars — don't have the slightest notion of how their fancy-sounding investments work. No wonder they got socked with horrendous losses!

Chris made her investing mistakes for one simple reason: she didn't understand investments. She didn't know what her investing options were and why particular options were inferior or superior to others.

Reprinted with permission

This book is about mutual funds and, if it had been available to Chris two decades ago, she could have saved herself from much financial and accompanying emotional hardship. You're no dummy (the publisher made me use this book title), and by selecting and reading this book, you'll prevent yourself from making big mistakes. You'll learn how to invest in one of the best investment vehicles ever created: mutual funds — which offer you instant diversification and low-cost access to outstanding money managers. And you'll learn how to do this in the context of your overall financial plans and goals.

Now, I'm not going to try to fool you by saying that you can't make mistakes with mutual funds, because you can. But, because the best mutual funds are superior in many respects to other investments, they help you minimize your risk while maximizing your chances of success. People from many walks of life and many income levels use funds because of this.

But first things first. Mutual funds are an investment.

"Tell me something I don't know; I'm not that dumb," you say.

Fair enough. But we have to agree on this point because mutual fund writers almost always assume that you already know and understand the different types of investments available. The author starts talking about "small cap value stock funds" and "asset allocation" and before you know it, you're lost in the weeds and frustrated. You have every right to be.

Sadly, sometimes writers — and financial advisors, for that matter — intend to confuse you and make things seem complicated, or they don't want to give you answers for how to buy investments on your own. Some "writers" write as a marketing tool — to sell their investment newsletter or investment products. This is how Charles Givens got himself in trouble selling limited partnerships and other yucky commission-based investments. (He wrote these books telling you how to get wealthy without taking risks — a most difficult proposition unless you're blessed with an inheritance or an extraordinarily high paying job. Turned out, his books referred you to his investment salespeople.) You learn all about the dangers of gurus and their advice in Chapter 14.

A mutual fund is just a big pile of money that the mutual fund manager uses to buy a bunch of stocks, bonds, and/or other assets that meet the fund's investment criteria. Each fund has investment criteria so that you, the trusting investor, know what you're getting. It's like buying a car: You want to make sure that if you want a silver four-door sedan you don't get a red sports car.

The description of a mutual fund tells you whether you're getting a sedan or a sports car. That's easy because we all know what "sedan" and "sports car" mean. But what if the car salesman asked you, Do you want a Pegasus or a Stegasaurus? How can you decide if you don't know what those names mean? In this chapter and the next, I tell you what most of those irritating investment words mean.

If you already understand what stocks and bonds are, their risks and potential returns, terrific. You can skip this chapter. Most people don't really understand the basics of investments. That's one of the major reasons people make investing mistakes in the first place, by overlooking mutual funds as an option.

Once you understand the specific types of securities that funds can invest in, you've mastered one of the important building blocks to understanding mutual funds. But before we dive into the different types of things a fund can own, we need to talk about why you're investing money (besides trying to give yourself a headache choosing among the morass of available investments).

Determining Your Needs and Goals

Before you pick funds to invest in, you have to know your investment goals and how much risk you want to take. A good fund for your next-door neighbor is not necessarily a good fund for you. You're different. You're unique. Know thyself.

Before you go shopping, you have to think — just for a minute — about what goal you're trying to meet. Why are you investing this pile of money? What are you going to use it for? You can't earmark *every* dollar, but you should set some major objectives.

You need to set goals because time is one of the most important variables in the investment world. There's a big difference between the investments you want for retirement 20 years down the road and the ones you want for a new car six months from now. Your future use of the money helps determine how long you can stick with an investment and which investment you choose.

For example, if you're trying to accumulate money toward buying a house in a few years, you can't afford much risk. You'll need that money sooner rather than later. Putting that money into the stock market, then, is not a smart move. As you'll see later, the stock market can drop a great deal in a year or over several consecutive years. So stocks are probably too risky an investment for down-payment money that you plan to use soon.

But if you're saving toward a longer-term goal, such as retirement that's 20 or 30 years away, you can risk more value fluctuations because you have time to bounce back from temporary losses or setbacks. Here's where you should consider investing in stocks, which offer greater growth potential. You can tolerate year-to-year volatility in the market because you've got time on your side.

The thought of putting retirement money into the stock market horrifies some people. You want to make sure that your retirement nest egg is intact, and you know what a roller coaster the stock market can be. These concerns are valid, and you have to weigh these fears against the potential benefits. The risk level of your investments has to meet your ability to sleep peacefully with your investing decisions as well as meet your time frame.

One of the nice things about mutual funds is that they have equivalent liquidity. *Liquidity* just means how easy it is to convert your investment into green cash. Think about the difference between selling your house and withdrawing money from your local bank account. The bank account will get you to the travel agent to pay for a trip to your friend much faster than the house will. Similar to that bank account, all mutual funds can be sold any business day for cash. They can differ greatly, however, in how volatile they are. A volatile investment is okay if you're planning to hold it a long time, but if you plan to sell it soon, you might find yourself forced to sell just after one of its big nose dives.

Putting the puzzle together

Many people plunge into mutual funds without first coming up with an overall financial plan. Would you start out on a long trip without picking a destination? Before you ask for directions, you have to know where you're trying to go. And you have to know what you want to do along the way. Some investors leap into the task of picking a fund before they know what they want their mutual funds to do. They might pick a fine fund, but they also might make a big financial planning mistake that leads them to pay far more in taxes than they need to. If you haven't planned, you're not alone. You work hard and want to have a life; developing a financial plan is probably the last thing on your mind when the weekend rolls around.

In recent years, too many people have found out the hard way that recessions and natural disasters aren't just bad things that happen to other people. You need a safety net in case you lose your job or are hit with unexpected expenses. This safety net needs to be invested in something you can sell quickly, something whose value you can count on *not* to drop at inconvenient moments (see Chapter 6).

A great deal of what's written and published on mutual funds completely ignores the financial planning implications of mutual fund decisions. In some cases, the writer doesn't have enough space to go into these important details. In other cases, writers don't know what they're overlooking.

If you've determined your financial needs and goals already, terrific! Understanding yourself is a good part of the battle. But don't shortchange yourself by diving in before you put your mask and flippers on. Dress for success! And be sure to read Chapter 5.

Making Sense of Investments

There are tens of thousands of investment options for you to choose from. That's one of the reasons that investments seem so confusing, and why you're likely to make some poor choices.

For a moment, though, imagine a simple and more pleasant world to be living in. Suppose that you have only two investment choices. The investment world can be just that simple. If you have money that you don't plan to spend right away on your daily necessities, you have just two choices for how to use it: lending investments and ownership investments.

Lending (money market and bond) investments

You're a *lender* when you invest your money in a bank certificate of deposit, a U. S. Treasury bill, or a bond issued by, say, Nike. In each case, you are lending your money to an organization — the bank, the federal government, or Nike. You are paid an agreed-upon rate of interest for lending your money. You are also promised to have your original investment (the *principal*) returned to you on a specific date.

(You're also a lender when your buddy Bob asks for $7 to cover his lunch because he left his wallet at home. In this case, you'll get no interest — and you may not even get your $7 back!)

The best that can happen with a lending investment that you hold until it matures is that you are paid all of the interest in addition to your original investment as promised. (In Chapter 7, you see how lending investments can also appreciate if interest rates fall.) This result isn't so bad, given that the investment landscape is littered with the carcasses of failed investments (such as lunch money loans to friends).

The worst that can happen is that you don't get everything you were promised. Under extenuating circumstances, promises get broken. When a company goes bankrupt, for example, you can lose all or part of your original investment.

Another risk is that you get what you were promised, but, because of the ravages of inflation, your money is simply worth less than you expected it to be worth; it has less purchasing power than you thought. Back in the 1960s, for example, high-quality companies were issuing long-term bonds that paid approximately 4 percent interest. At the time such bonds seemed like a good investment because the cost of living was increasing only 2 percent a year. But when inflation rocketed to 6, 8, 10 percent and higher, those 4 percent bonds didn't look quite so attractive. The interest and principal didn't buy nearly the amount it did years earlier when inflation was lower.

Here's a simple example to illustrate. Suppose you had put $5,000 into an 18-year lending type investment yielding 4 percent. You planned to use it in 18 years to pay for one year of college. Although a year of college cost $5,000 when you invested the money, college costs since then had risen 8 percent a year; so in 18 years when you needed the money, one year of college cost nearly $20,000. But your investment would only be worth around $10,100, nearly 50 percent short of the cost of college.

A final drawback to lending investments is that you do not share in the success of the organization that you lend your money to. If the company doubles or triples in size and profits, the growth is good for the company and its owners, and it ensures that you'll get your interest and principal back. But you don't reap any of the upside. If Steven Jobs had approached you many years ago for money to help build some easy-to-use computer that he wanted to sell to people to use in their homes, would you rather you had loaned him the money or done what Forrest Gump did and *owned* a piece of "that fruit company," Apple?

Ownership (stock and real estate) investments

You're an *owner* when you invest your money in an asset, such as a company or real estate, that has the ability to generate earnings or profits. Suppose that you own 100 shares of IBM stock. With hundreds of millions of shares of stock outstanding, IBM is a mighty big company; your 100 shares represent only a tiny piece of IBM.

What do you get for your small piece of IBM? As a stockholder, you share in the company's profits in the form of annual dividends as well as an increase (you hope) in the stock price if the company grows and becomes more profitable. That's what happens when things are going well. The downside is that, if IBM's business declines, your stock can plummet or even go to $0 per share.

Real estate is another type of ownership investment. It can yield profits by being rented out for income (profits come when rental income exceeds the expense of owning the property) or by being sold at a higher price than you paid to buy it.

As with other ownership investments, the value of real estate depends on the health and performance of the economy as well as on the specifics of the property you own. If the local economy grows and more jobs are being produced at higher wages, then real estate should do well. If companies in the community are laying people off left and right and excess housing is sitting vacant because of previous overbuilding, then rents and property values are likely to fall.

Speculation

There's a big difference between investing and gambling. The two may seem similar, but that's only because people hope to make a lot of money in both arenas, whether by skill or by chance.

But unlike investing, gambling is putting your money into schemes that are sure long-term losers. That's not to say that everyone loses, or that you lose every time you gamble. However, the deck is stacked against you. The house wins most of the time, and the longer you play, the more likely you are to lose.

There are gambling equivalents in the investment world — putting your money into futures, options, and commodities. Financial instruments whose values are derived from another security (such as a stock or bond) are called *derivatives*.

You may have heard the radio ad by the investment firm of Fleecem, Cheatem, and Leavem, advocating that you buy heating oil futures because the cold-weather months lead to the use of more heating oil. You call and are impressed by the smooth-talking "vice president" who spends so much time with little ol' you. His logic makes sense, and he's spent a lot of time with you, so you send him a check for $10,000.

Such an investment isn't much different from blowing $10,000 shooting craps in Las Vegas. Futures prices depend on short-term price movements. Commodities and futures are quite volatile in price. As with gambling, you occasionally win, as Hillary Rodham Clinton did, when the market moves the right way at the right time. But, in the long run, you're gonna lose. In fact, you can lose it all. (Hillary was smart or lucky enough to quit while she was ahead.)

Options are the same as commodities and futures: you're betting on short-term movements of a specific security. If you have inside information, as Ivan Boesky did, so that you know in advance when a major corporate development is going to occur, you can get rich. But don't forget one minor detail: insider trading is illegal. You too may end up in the slammer, like Boesky did.

Beware of greed and "advisors" who encourage it

Greed has a long history of exacting harsh punishment on those who fall prey to it in the world of investing. Dating back three centuries from the tulip bulb mania in Holland, the south sea bubble in England, and the extraordinary margin and leverage investors took in the U.S. stock market in the 1920s to the Japanese real estate market speculative bubble that finally burst in the 1980s, for investors willing to learn from others' mistakes there are lessons aplenty.

The 1994 Orange County investment fund debacle (not a mutual fund but a pool of money privately managed by the county treasurer in Orange County, CA) is chock full of mistakes that easily could have been avoided. The fund engaged in insanely complicated and risky investment practices — including borrowing up to 200 percent of the value of the fund to buy more risky derivative investments.

Robert Citron, Orange County Treasurer, made critical investing decisions based almost exclusively on advice from commission-based brokers like Michael Stamenson of Merrill Lynch. According to the *Wall Street Journal*, Stamenson is one of Merrill Lynch's top salesmen, reported to have earned in excess of $5 million in commissions yearly during 1993 and 1994, a period during which Merrill Lynch earned an astounding $80 million in its dealings with Orange County.

Lured by the success of higher-than-average returns while interest rates were falling, Citron's fund took on greater risk and more investors. The legend of his success surely attracted many to blindly jump on board as a number of smaller city and county governments (nearly 200 in total) handed their money over to Citron and his legions of brokers to invest.

Orange County and the other governments could have avoided making the same mistake that officials of San Jose, CA, did a decade earlier when they made aggressive interest-rate risky investments that plunged when rates turned tail. Stamenson was heavily involved in this investment disaster as well, which led to Merrill Lynch and a number of other brokerage firms coughing up a legal settlement of $26 million.

Some municipalities are getting the same investing education in the school of hard knocks that individual investors got who were sold limited partnerships by the same brokerage firms involved in the Orange County fiasco.

Honest brokers who help their clients invest in stocks, bonds, and mutual funds tell you the truth about commodities, futures, and options. A former broker I know who used to work for Merrill Lynch and Shearson told me, "I had one client who made money in options, futures, or commodities for 12 years, but the only reason he came out ahead was that he had to pull money out to close on a home purchase just when he happened to be ahead. The commissions were great for me, but there's no way a customer will make money in them."

Wealth without risk

If only Charles Givens had focused on these items in his book, he might have been right after all. There are just a few ways to almost guarantee yourself high returns without taking much risk. They are:

- ✔ **Your health.** Eat healthy, exercise, relax.
- ✔ **Friends and family.** Improve your relationships with loved ones. Invest the time and effort it takes to make relationships better.
- ✔ **Personal and career development.** Learn a new hobby, improve your communication skills, read widely. Take an adult education course or go back to school for a degree. Your investment will surely pay off in higher paychecks and greater happiness.

The Major Investment Options

In the investment world, you can put your money into many types of investments. Decent investment vehicles work their way methodically around the track, rarely deterred but never speedy. The best ones make their way through the course at a faster clip, only occasionally slowed by a bump or detour. The worst ones sputter in fits and starts and sometimes crash and burn in a flaming heap.

Which vehicle you choose for your trip depends on where you're going, how fast you want to get there, and what risks you're willing to take along the way. Here's a list of vehicles to choose from and some of my thoughts on what vehicle would be a good choice for your situation. Caution signs label the ones you should avoid.

Bank and money market accounts

Checking accounts are best used for depositing your monthly income and paying out your expenditures. If you need to have unlimited privileges to write checks for all amounts and to access your money with your ATM (Automated Teller Machine) card, checking accounts at local banks are your best bet. Make sure that you shop around for accounts that don't ding you $1 here for use of an ATM machine and $10 there for a low balance.

Savings accounts can be found at banks; money market funds are available through mutual fund companies. They are nearly identical in that they generally pay a better rate of interest than checking accounts. The interest rate paid, also known as the *yield,* fluctuates over time as the level of interest rates changes.

Bank savings accounts are backed by the federal government through Federal Deposit Insurance Corporation (FDIC) insurance. If the bank goes broke, you still get your money back (up to $100,000). Money market funds are not insured. Should you prefer a bank account because your investment (principal) is insured? No. Savings accounts and money market funds have almost equivalent safety. The next chapter provides more background on money market funds.

Bonds

Bonds are the most common lending investment traded on securities markets. Bond funds also account for about 26 percent of all mutual fund assets invested.

When a bond is issued, it includes a specified maturity date at which you will be repaid your principal. Bonds are also issued at an interest rate, which is typically fixed.

Bonds fluctuate in value based mainly on changes in interest rates. If, for example, you're holding a bond issued at 8 percent, and rates increase to 10 percent, your bond decreases in value. (Why would anyone want to buy your bond at the price you paid if it yields just 8 percent and she can get a bond yielding 10 percent somewhere else?)

Bonds differ from each other in the following ways:

- **The type of institution to which you are lending your money.** Institutions include state governments (municipal bonds), the federal government (treasuries), mortgage holders (Government National Mortgage Association — GNMA), and corporations (corporate bonds).

- **The credit quality of the borrower to whom you lend your money.** The probability that a borrower will pay you the interest and return your principal varies from institution to institution.

- **The length of maturity of the bond.** Bonds generally mature within 30 years. Short-term bonds mature in a few years, intermediate bonds in around 10 years, and long-term bonds within 30 years. Longer-term bonds generally pay higher yields but fluctuate more widely in value with changes in interest rates.

You learn more than you ever wanted to know about bonds in Chapter 7.

Stocks

Stocks are the most common ownership investment traded on securities markets. They represent shares of ownership in a company. Companies that sell stock to the general public (called *publicly held* companies) include automobile manufacturers, computer software producers, fast food restaurants, hotels, magazine and newspaper publishers, supermarkets, wineries, zipper manufacturers, and everything in between!

Besides occupying different industries, companies also vary in size. In the financial press, you often hear companies referred to by their *market capitalization,* which is the total value of their outstanding stock. This is what the stock market and the investors who participate in it think a company is worth.

You can choose from two very different ways to invest in bonds and stocks. You can purchase individual securities, or you can invest in a portfolio of securities through a mutual fund. You learn all about stock mutual funds in Chapter 8.

Overseas investments

Not only can you invest in stocks and bonds in companies that trade on the U.S. stock exchanges, but you also can invest in securities internationally. Aside from folks with business connections abroad, why would the average citizen want to invest overseas?

There are several good reasons to invest overseas. First, the majority of investment opportunities are overseas. If you look at the total value of all stocks and bonds outstanding worldwide, the value of U.S. securities is now in the minority. We are not the world!

Another reason for investing in international securities is this: when you confine your investing to U.S. securities, you're missing a world of opportunities, not only because of business growth available in other countries, but also because you get the opportunity to further diversify your portfolio. International securities markets don't move in tandem with U.S. markets. During the 1987 U.S. stock market crash, for example, most international stock markets dropped far less than ours. Some actually rose in value.

Some people hesitate to invest in overseas securities because they feel that it hurts the U.S. economy and contributes to a loss of American jobs. Fair enough. But I have two counterarguments. One is that if you don't profit from the growth of economies overseas, someone else will. If there is money to be made, Americans may as well be there to make some of it.

Also, you should recognize that we already have a global economy — making a distinction between U.S. companies and foreign companies is no longer appropriate. Many companies headquartered in the U.S. also have overseas operations. Some U.S. firms derive a large portion of their revenue from their international divisions. Conversely, many firms that are based overseas also have operations here. Increasing numbers of companies are worldwide operations.

It is not unpatriotic to buy from a company that is based overseas or that has a foreign name. In fact, that product you thought was foreign-made may be made right here at home. Profits from a foreign company are distributed to all stockholders, no matter where they live. Dividends and stock price appreciation know no national boundaries.

Real estate

Real estate has made many people wealthy. Not only does it produce consistently good rates of return (averaging around 10 percent per year) over long investment periods, but it can be bought with gobs of borrowed money. This leverage can help you to generate an even higher rate of return on your investment.

For investors who have time, patience, and capital, real estate can make sense as part of an investment portfolio. If you don't want the headaches that come with purchasing and maintaining a property, you can buy mutual funds that invest in real estate properties (see Chapter 8).

Precious metals

Gold and silver have been used by many civilizations as currency or as a medium of exchange. One advantage of precious metals as a currency is that the government can't debase them. With a paper-based currency, such as U.S. dollars, the government can always just print more currency to pay off its debts. (To date, gold is much harder than paper money to make. Just ask Rumpelstiltskin.) This process of casually printing more and more currency can lead to a currency's devaluation — and to our old friend, inflation.

Holdings of gold and silver can provide a so-called *hedge* against inflation. In the U.S. in the late 1970s and early 1980s, inflation rose dramatically. This rise depressed stocks and bonds. Gold and silver, however, soared in value, rising more than 500 percent (even after adjusting for inflation) from 1972 to 1981.

But don't purchase precious metals futures contracts. They are not investments; they are short-term gambles on which way gold or silver prices might head over a short period of time. You also should stay away from firms and shops that sell coins and *bullion* (not the soup, but bars of gold or silver). Even if you can find a legitimate firm (which is not an easy task), storing and insuring gold and silver is costly. You don't get good value for your money. I hate to break the news to you, but the Gold Rush is over.

Gold and silver can profit long-term investors, but if you want to invest in precious metals, you'd be wise to do so through mutual funds. For more information about determining how these types of funds may fit with the rest of your investments and how to buy them, be sure to read Chapters 3 and 8.

Annuities

Annuities are an investment product with some tax and insurance twists. They behave like a savings account, except that they give you slightly higher yields and they're backed by insurance companies.

As in other types of retirement accounts, the money you put into an annuity compounds without taxation until withdrawal. However, unlike most other types of retirement accounts — 401Ks, SEP-IRAs, and Keoghs — an annuity gives you no tax deductions. It also carries extra expenses. That's why it makes sense to consider contributing to an annuity only after you fully fund the tax-deductible retirement accounts that are available to you.

The best annuities available today are distributed by no-load (commission-free) mutual fund companies. For more information about situations where annuities may be appropriate and which ones are best, be sure to read Chapter 9.

Limited partnerships (LPs)

Always avoid limited partnerships sold directly through brokers and financial planners. They are inferior investment vehicles. That's not to say that no one has ever made money on them, but limited partnerships are so burdened with high sales commissions and investment-depleting management fees that you can do better in other vehicles.

Limited partnerships invest in real estate and a variety of businesses, such as cable television, cellular phone companies, and research and development. They pitch that you can get in on the ground floor of a new investment opportunity and make big money. And they also usually tell you that while your investment is growing at 20 percent or more per year, you'll get handsome dividends of 8 percent or so per year. Sound too good to be true? It is.

Many of the yields on LPs have turned out to be bogus. In some cases, partnerships propped up their yields by paying back investors' principal (without telling them, of course). The other hook with LPs is tax benefits. What few loopholes did exist in the tax code for LPs have largely been closed. Amazingly, some investment salespeople hoodwink investors to put their retirement account money — which is already tax-sheltered, just the way you want it — into LPs! The other problems with LPs overwhelm any small tax advantage, anyway. If you want tax-friendly investments, check out Chapters 6 through 8.

The investment salesperson who sells you such an investment stands to earn a commission of up to 10 percent or more. That means that only 90 cents (or less) per dollar that you put into an LP actually gets invested. Each year, LPs typically siphon off several more percentage points for management and other expenses. Most partnerships have little or no incentive to control costs. In fact, they may have a conflict to charge more to enrich the managing partners. Efficient, no-load mutual funds, in contrast, put 100 percent of your capital to work and charge 1 percent per year or less in management fees.

Unlike a mutual fund, in a limited partnership you can't vote with your feet on where your dollars go. If the partnership is poorly run and expensive, you're stuck. That's why LPs are called *illiquid* — you can't get your own money back until the partnership is liquidated, typically seven to ten years after you buy in. If you want to sell out to a third party in the interim, you'll have to sell at a huge discount. Don't bother unless you're totally desperate for cash. You're better off sticking it out.

The only thing limited about a limited partnership is its ability to make you money. If you want to buy investments that earn profits, stick with stocks (using mutual funds), real estate, or your own business.

Life insurance?

Life insurance should not be used as an investment, especially if you haven't exhausted contributing money to retirement accounts. Agents love to sell it for the high commission. Life insurance that combines life insurance protection with an account that has a cash value is usually known as *universal, whole,* or *variable life.*

The only reason to consider cash-value life insurance is that the proceeds paid to your beneficiaries can be free of inheritance taxes. You need to have a fairly substantial estate at your death to benefit from this feature.

Cash-value life insurance is not a good investment for many reasons. First, you should be saving and investing as much as possible through tax-deductible retirement savings plans such as 401Ks, IRAs, and Keoghs. Contributions to a cash-value life insurance plan provide you no up-front tax benefit. Second, you likely can earn better investment returns through mutual funds. If you've exhausted contributing to retirement accounts, you can either choose tax-friendly mutual funds and/or invest in variable annuities that use mutual funds as an investment option (see Chapters 6 through 9).

Term life insurance is best for the vast majority of people. Because this is not a book on insurance (thankfully), I advise you to consult my first book, *Personal Finance For Dummies,* which has all sorts of good stuff on life and other types of insurance.

Many Happy (Investment) Returns

Now you know the differences among the major types of investments.

"That's all well and good," you say. "But how do I choose which type of investments to put my money into? How much can I make and what are the risks?"

Good questions. I'll start with the returns you *might* make. I say "might" because I'm looking at history, and history is a record of the past. Using history to predict the future, especially the near future, is dangerous. History may repeat itself, but not always in exactly the same fashion and not necessarily when you expect it to.

Over time, ownership investments like stocks and real estate have returned around 10 percent per year, handily beating lending investments such as bonds (around 5 percent) and savings accounts (roughly 4 percent) in the investment performance race. Inflation has averaged around 3 percent per year, so savings accounts and bonds barely would have kept you up with increases in the cost of living. Factoring in the taxes you pay on your investment earnings, bonds and savings account returns would even be losing ground relative to the cost of living.

Wouldn't it be interesting to see where those who have some discretionary funds to toss around invest their money? They must know some secret. Many millionaires are financially savvy; that's how some of them make their millions. But others are financial dummies. The difference between poorly informed millionaires and poorly informed average investors is that poorly informed millionaires are (or feel) wealthy enough to hire advisors — or else they have so much money that it doesn't matter if they lose a few thousand every year on bad investments.

As a group, millionaires invest most of their wealth — almost three-quarters of it — in ownership investments such as corporate stock, real estate, and businesses. The remaining quarter they invest mainly in lending-type investments.

Investment Risks

Obviously, you should put all of your money in stocks and real estate, right? The returns sure look great. So what's the catch?

Investments with a potential for higher returns carry greater risks.

The main drawback to ownership investments is volatility. For example, during this century, stocks have declined by more than 10 percent in a year approximately once every five years. Drops in stock prices of more than 20 percent have occurred about once every ten years (see Figure 1-1). In order to earn those generous long-term returns of 10 percent per year, you must be willing to tolerate volatility. That's why you absolutely should *not* put all your money in the stock or real estate market.

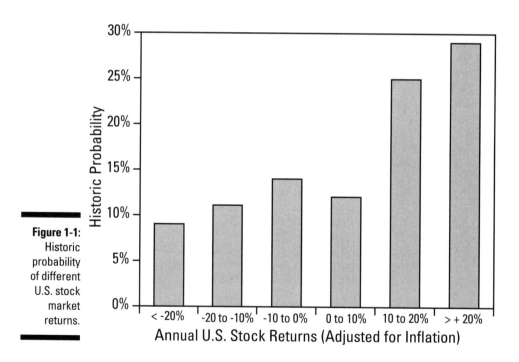

Figure 1-1:
Historic probability of different U.S. stock market returns.

As you can see from Figure 1-2, bonds have had fewer years where they have provided rates of return that were as tremendously negative or positive as stocks have. Bonds are less volatile but, as I discussed in the preceding section, on average you'll earn a lower rate of return in bonds.

Some types of bonds have higher yields than others — but nothing is free here, either. A bond generally pays you a higher rate of interest as compared with other bonds when it has:

- ✔ **Lower credit quality** to compensate for the higher risk of default and the higher likelihood that you will lose your investment;

- ✔ **Longer-term maturity** to compensate for the risk that you'll be unhappy with the bond's interest rate if interest rates move up; and

- ✔ **Callability** to retain the right to pay back (buy back) the bonds issued before payback is required. (Companies like to be able to pay back early if they have found a cheaper way to borrow the money. Early payback is a risk to bond holders because they might get their investment money returned to them when interest rates have dropped.)

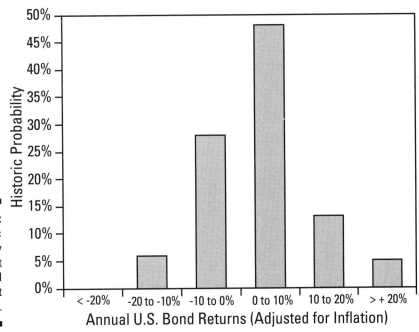

Figure 1-2:
Historic probability of different U.S. bond market returns.

Diversification: Eggs in Different Baskets

Diversification is one of the most powerful investment concepts. All diversification really means is that you carry and save your eggs (your investments) in different baskets.

Diversification requires you to place your money in different investments with returns that are not completely correlated. Now for the plain-English translation: With your money in different places, when one of your investments is down in value, the odds are good that others are up.

To decrease the odds that all of your investments will get clobbered at the same time, put your money in different types or classes of investments. The different kinds of investments include money market funds, bonds, stocks, real estate, and precious metals. You can further diversify your investments by investing in international as well as domestic markets.

Within a given class of investments, such as stocks, you should diversify by investing in different types of stocks that perform well under various economic conditions. For this reason, mutual funds, which are diversified portfolios of securities, are a highly useful investment vehicle. You buy into the mutual fund, which in turn pools your money with that of many others to invest in a vast array of stocks or bonds.

You can look at the benefits of diversification in two ways. First, diversification reduces the volatility in the value of your whole portfolio. In other words, when you diversify, you can achieve the same rate of return that a single investment can provide, but with reduced fluctuations in value. Another way to look at it: diversification allows you to obtain a higher rate of return for a given level of risk.

Chapter 2

Mutual Funds: Awesome Money Management for All of Us

. . . .

In This Chapter

▶ Mutual funds versus individual securities

▶ Ten reasons to choose mutual funds

▶ Funds defined

▶ Drawbacks to mutual funds

▶ Money-managed alternatives to mutual funds

. . . .

Consider this: a young man with his first paycheck, a child with some gift money from loving grandparents, our good friend Chris, and bigwigs like Steve Jobs, Hillary and Bill Clinton, Charles Schwab, Michael Jackson, Danielle Steel, and Michael Jordan all can hire the same professional money managers — for the same price — by investing in mutual funds.

It's true that some wealthy people prefer to invest their money in things that you and I can't — such as private jets, yachts, savings and loans, cattle futures, or beach-front vacation homes. But most well-heeled investors choose to invest in mutual funds for the same reasons that make sense for you and me:

✔ Easy diversification

✔ Access to professional money managers

✔ Low investment management costs

Some of the big-time investors who haven't invested in mutual funds probably wish they had — instead of in now-vacant office buildings, barren oil fields, lame racehorses, and other "promising" investments.

What's a Mutual Fund?

A mutual fund is a large pool of investment money from lots and lots of people. When you invest in a fund, you buy shares and become a *shareholder* of the fund. A fund manager and his or her team of assistants figure out which specific securities (for example, stocks, bonds, money market securities) they should invest the shareholders' money in to accomplish the objectives of the fund and keep you as a happy customer.

Because good mutual funds take most of the hassle and cost out of figuring out which companies to invest in, they are one of the best investment vehicles, if not the best, ever created. They allow you to diversify your investments — that is, invest in many different industries and companies instead of in just one or two. Funds enable you to give your money to the best money managers in the country — some of the same folks who manage money for the already rich and famous. And they are the ultimate couch potato investment! But, unlike when you're watching *Hard Copy* or playing Nintendo, you'll be doing yourself a big favor by investing in mutual funds.

While I don't know the origins of usage of the term "mutual" funds, perhaps it's used because these funds allow a large group of people to mutually invest their money. And by spreading the risk among a number of complementary companies and industries, you lessen your chances of loss, while the companies have the funds they need to stay profitable and expand.

Financial intermediaries

A mutual fund is a type of financial intermediary (now that's a mouthful). Why should you care? Because, if you understand what a financial intermediary is and how mutual funds stack up to their competition, you'll better understand when funds are appropriate for your investments and when they probably are not.

A financial intermediary is nothing more than an organization that takes money in from people who want to invest and then gets the money to those who need capital. Suppose that you want to borrow money to invest in your own business.

You go to your friendly neighborhood banker, who examines your financial records and agrees to loan you $20,000 at 10 percent interest for three years. The money that the banker is lending you

has to come from somewhere, right? Well, the banker got that money from a bunch of people who deposited money with the banker for three years at, say, 5 percent. Thus, the banker acts as a financial intermediary or middle-man, one who receives money from depositors and lends it to borrowers who can use it productively.

Insurance companies do similar things with money. They may sell you investments such as annuities (see Chapter 1), and then turn around and lend your money — in the form of a bond, for example — to businesses that need to borrow. (Remember, a bond is nothing more than a company's promise to repay borrowed money over a specified period of time at a specified interest rate.)

What's really cool about mutual funds is that — once you understand them — you realize that they can help you meet a bunch of different financial goals. Maybe you have an emergency savings stash of three to six months' living expenses (a prudent idea, by the way). Perhaps you're starting to think about saving for a home purchase, retirement, or future educational costs. You may know what you need the money for, but you may not know how to protect the money you have and make it grow.

Don't feel bad if you haven't figured out a long-term financial plan. And don't feel bad if you don't have a goal in mind for the money you're saving. Many people don't have their finances organized. That's why there are books like this one!

Ten Reasons to Choose Mutual Funds

Funds are super investment vehicles for many people. To understand why funds are so sensible is to understand how and why funds can work for you. Read on to discover their many benefits.

Professionals, professionals, professionals

Mutual funds are investment companies that pool your money with the money of hundreds, thousands, or even millions of other investors. The investment company hires a portfolio manager and researchers whose full-time job is to research and purchase suitable investments for the fund. These people screen the universe of investments for those that best meet the fund's stated objectives.

Typically, fund managers are graduates of the top business and finance schools in the country, where they learn the principles of portfolio management and securities valuation and selection. (Despite the handicap of their formal education, most of them still do a good job of investing money.) In addition to their educational training, the best fund managers typically have five or more years of experience in analyzing and selecting investments.

A (brief) history of mutual funds

Mutual funds date back to the 1800s, when English and Scottish investment trusts sold shares to investors. Funds hit the U.S. in 1924. They were chugging along and growing in assets until the late 1920s, when the Great Depression derailed the financial markets and the economy. Stock prices plunged, and so did mutual funds that held stocks.

As was common in the stock market at that time, mutual funds were *leveraging* their investments — which is a fancy way of saying that they put up only, for example, 25 cents on the dollar on investments they actually owned. The other 75 percent was borrowed. That's why, when the stock market plunged in value in 1929, some investors and fund shareholders got clobbered. They were losing money on their investments *and* on all the borrowed money, too. But, like the rest of the country, mutual funds, although a little bruised, pulled through this economic calamity.

In 1940, the Investment Company Act established the ground rules and oversight by the Securities and Exchange Commission (SEC) over the fund industry. Among other benefits, this landmark federal legislation required funds to gain approval from the SEC *before* issuing or selling any fund shares to the public. Over time, this legislation has been strengthened by requiring funds to disclose cost, risk, and other information in a uniform format through a legal document called a *prospectus* (see Chapter 3).

During the 1940s, 1950s, and 1960s, funds grew at a fairly high and constant rate. From less than $1 billion in assets in 1940, fund assets grew to more than $50 billion by the late 1960s — more than a 50-fold increase. (At this point in our brief history of funds, it's interesting to note that they are on track to grow at a similar rate over the subsequent three decades — the 1970s, 1980s and 1990s.)

Before the early 1970s, funds focused largely on investing in stocks. Since then, however, money market mutual funds and bond mutual funds have mushroomed and now account for about two-thirds of all mutual fund assets.

Today, thousands of mutual funds manage more than $3 trillion. That's a mighty big number — but still less than *half* the amount of the U.S. government's debt outstanding and just about five percent (one out of every $20) of the total financial assets in our economy.

For most fund managers and researchers, finding the best investments is more than a full-time job. Consider the following activities (all of them unpleasant) that an investor should do before investing in stocks and bonds:

✔ **Analyze company financial statements.** Companies whose securities trade in the financial markets are required to issue reports every three months detailing their revenue, expenses, profits and losses, and assets and liabilities. Unless you're a numbers geek, own an HP-12C financial calculator, and enjoy dissecting these tedious statements, this first task alone is reason enough to invest through a mutual fund and leave the driving to them.

✔ **Talk with the muckety-mucks.** Fund managers log thousands of frequent flier miles and incur massive long distance phone bills talking to the folks running the companies to get a sense of the companies' business strategies and vision. Because of the huge amount of money they manage, large fund companies like Fidelity even get visits from company executives, who fly in to grovel at Fidelity's feet (er, I mean, to talk to them).

Now, do you have the correct type of china and all the place settings that etiquette demands of people who host such high-level folks? If not, avoiding this activity will be another savings for you when you invest through mutual funds.

✔ **Analyze company and competitor strategies.** Corporate managers have an irritating tendency to talk up what a great job they're doing. It's not that they fib; they just want rich investors to feel warm and fuzzy about forking over their loot. Some companies may look as if they have their act together — but what if they're really light-years behind the competition? Fund managers and their researchers take a skeptical view of what a company's execs say. Fund reps read the fine print and check under the rugs. They also keep on top of what competitors are doing. Sometimes they discover better investment ideas this way.

✔ **Talk with company customers, suppliers, and industry consultants.** Another way the mutual fund managers find out if a company's public relations story is full of holes is to talk to the company's customers, suppliers, and other industry experts. These people often have more balanced viewpoints and can be a great deal more open about the negatives. These folks are harder to find but can provide valuable information.

✔ **Attend trade shows and review industry literature.** It's truly amazing how specialized the world is becoming. Do you really want to subscribe to business magazines that track the latest happenings with ball-bearing or catalytic-converter technology? They'll put you to sleep in a couple of pages. Unlike *People*, *Newsweek*, and *TV Guide*, they'll cost you an arm and a leg, too.

Are you, as the investor, going to do all these tasks and do them well? Nothing personal, but I doubt that you will. A mutual fund management team, though, will happily do all these yucky things for you, do them well, and do them for a fraction of what it would cost you to do them haphazardly on your own.

In short, a mutual fund management team does more research and more number-crunching and applies more due diligence than most of you could ever possibly have the energy or expertise to do in what little free time you have. Investing in mutual funds will help your friendships and maybe even your sex life. Don't miss this time-saving opportunity!

They're a great value

The concept of mutual funds sounds great, you say, but what's it going to cost to hire such high-powered talent to do all of this dreadful research and analysis? A mere pittance. In fact, when you invest your money in a good, efficiently managed mutual fund, it will likely cost you less than it would to trade individual securities on your own.

Years ago, most investors handed their money to a broker from big-name firms like Prudential, Shearson, and E.F. Hutton, all of whom recommended and traded individual securities. Because a broker could work with only so many people in a workday — especially before voice-mail, fax machines, and car phones! — and because he or she had to share a big chunk of his commissions with the firm, each trade cost an investor about 3 percent of the investment.

When fund managers buy and sell securities, they can do it for a fraction of the cost that you would pay. Because mutual funds typically buy or sell tens of thousands of shares of a stock at a time, their transaction fees generally run 80 to 90 percent less per share than what you would pay to buy or sell a few hundred shares on your own.

Mutual funds are a cheaper, more communal way of getting the investing job done. How do they do it? They spread out the cost of their extensive — and expensive — research over thousands of investors. The most efficiently managed mutual funds cost less than one percent per year in fees (bonds and money market funds will cost much less — good ones charge just 0.5 percent per year or less). Some of the larger and more established funds can charge annual fees as low as 0.2 percent per year.

And today, many funds do not charge a fee to purchase or redeem shares (such funds are called no-load funds). Such opportunities used to be rare. Fidelity and Vanguard, the two largest distributors of no-load funds today, exacted sales charges as high as 8.5 percent during the early 1970s. Even today some mutual funds, known as load-funds, charge you for buying or selling shares in their funds.

If you decide that you want to withdraw money from a fund, most funds — particularly no-loads — do not charge you a redemption fee. (Think about that — some investments require that you pay to get your own money back!)

Mutual funds are also able to manage money more efficiently through effective use of technology. Innovations in information management tools enable funds to monitor and manage billions of dollars from millions of investors at a very low cost. In general, it doesn't cost them much more to move around $5 billion in securities than $500 million. Larger investments just mean a few more zeros in the spreadsheet columns.

Diversification

Diversification is a big attraction for many investors who choose mutual funds. Here's an example of why.

Say you heard that Nirvana Pharmaceuticals has developed a drug that stops cancer cells in their tracks. You run to the phone, call your broker, and invest all of your savings in a few hundred shares of Nirvana stock. Five years later, the Food and Drug Administration denies Nirvana approval for the drug, and Nirvana goes belly up, taking your $10,000 with it.

Your $10,000 would have been safer in a mutual fund. A mutual fund can buy a few shares of a promising, but risky, company like Nirvana without exposing investors like you to financial ruin. The fund owns stocks or bonds from dozens of companies, diversifying against the risk of bad news from any single company or sector.

It would be difficult — and expensive — to diversify like that on your own, unless you have a few hundred thousand dollars and a great deal of time to invest. You would need to invest money in at least 8 to 12 different companies in different industries to ensure that your portfolio could withstand a downturn in one or more of the investments.

Mutual funds typically invest in 25 to 100 securities, or more. Proper diversification ensures that the fund receives the highest possible return at the lowest possible risk, given the objectives of the fund.

I'm not suggesting that mutual funds escape without share-price declines during major market downturns. For example, mutual funds that invested in U.S. stocks certainly declined during the October 1987 U.S. stock market crash. However, the most unhappy investors that month were individuals who had all of their money riding on only one or a handful of stocks. Some shares plunged in price by as much as 80 to 90 percent.

While most mutual funds are "diversified," some aren't. For example, some stock funds invest exclusively in stocks of a single industry (for instance, health care) or country (such as India). I'm not a fan of such funds because of this lack of diversification and because such funds typically charge higher operating fees.

I had a dream — an investment for all us

With mutual funds, all investors are treated equally.

If you have $500 or more to invest, you should consider mutual funds. Most funds have low minimum investment requirements. Nearly a quarter have minimums of $500 or less, and nearly two-thirds have minimums of $1,000 or less. Retirement account investors often can invest with even less. Some have monthly investment plans — so you can start with as little as $50. Best of all: when you invest in a mutual fund, you get the same attention given to the rich and famous.

Even if you have a whole pile of money to invest, you also should consider mutual funds. Join the increasing number of companies and institutions with big bucks (millions) to invest who are turning to the low-cost, high-quality money management services that you can get from a mutual fund.

Regulatory oversight — the SEC's checking on 'em

Before a fund can take money in from investors, it must go through a tedious scrutinizing process with the Securities and Exchange Commission. Once it offers shares, every mutual fund is required to publish in its prospectus historical data on the fund's earnings, its operating expenses and other fees, and its rate of trading (turnover) in the fund's investments.

It should go without saying that government regulators are far from perfect. Remember the Savings & Loan fiasco of the 1980s. Conceivably, a fund operator could slip through some bogus numbers. I wouldn't lose sleep worrying about this, though — especially when investing through the larger, reputable fund companies.

Flexibility in risk level

Choosing from a huge variety of mutual funds, you can select the funds that take on the kinds of risks that you're comfortable with and that meet your financial goals.

- **Stock funds.** If you want your money to grow over a long period of time (and you can put up with some bad years thrown in with the good), you want to select funds that invest more heavily in stocks.

- **Bond funds.** If you need current income and don't want investments that fluctuate as widely in value as stocks do, you may choose bond funds.

Are mutual funds too risky?

One of the major misconceptions about mutual funds is that they all invest entirely in stocks and therefore are risky. They don't, and they're not. Mutual funds allow you to invest in a whole array of securities, ranging from money market funds, bonds, stocks, precious metals, and even real estate.

It might surprise you to learn that, of the more than $3 trillion currently invested in mutual funds, only about 48 percent is invested in stocks. The rest (more than half of it) is *not* invested in stocks: It's in money market securities and funds and bonds.

When you hear folks talk about the "riskiness" of mutual funds, even in the media, you'll know that they're overlooking this fact: All mutual funds are not created equal. Some funds, such as money market funds, carry virtually *no* risk that your investment will decline in value. Bond funds that invest in shorter-term bonds don't budge by more than several percentage points per year. And you may be surprised to learn in Chapter 8 that some funds that invest in stocks aren't all that risky if you can plan on holding them over time periods of a decade or more.

▸ **Money market funds.** If you want to be sure that your invested principal does not drop in value because you may need to use your money in the short term, you may choose a money market fund.

Most investors choose a combination of these three types of funds to diversify and help meet different financial goals. I get into all that in the chapters to come.

Virtually zero risk of bankruptcy

Hundreds of banks and dozens of insurance companies have failed in the past decade alone. Banks and insurers can fail because their liabilities (the money customers have given them to invest) can exceed their assets (the money they have invested or lent). When a big chunk of a bank's loans go sour at the same time that its depositors want their money back, the bank fails. That happens because banks have less than 20 cents on deposit for every dollar that you and I place with them. Likewise, if an insurance company makes several poor investments or underestimates the number of claims that will be made by insurance policy holders, it too can fail.

Such failures can't happen with a mutual fund. The situation in which the investors' demand for their investment back (the fund's liabilities) exceeds the value of a fund's investments (its assets) simply cannot occur. Why not? Because the mutual fund's investors have purchased shares in the fund — and the value of the fund's shares fluctuates. So the value of a fund fluctuates as the securities it is invested in fluctuate in value. For every dollar of securities they hold for their customers, mutual funds have a dollar's worth of securities.

The worst that can happen is that a fund investor who wants his or her money back may get less cash than originally put into the fund — but he or she won't lose all of the investment. In fact, since the Investment Company Act of 1940 was passed to regulate the mutual fund industry, no fund has ever gone under. (A money market fund run by and invested in by banks did disband after losing a small portion of principal — see Chapter 6.)

You may be interested to know that the specific stocks, bonds, or both that a mutual fund has bought are held at a custodian — a separate organization independent of the mutual fund company. The employment of a custodian ensures that the fund management company can't embezzle your funds and use assets from a better-performing fund to subsidize a poor performer.

Freedom from those sharks

Stock brokers (a.k.a. financial consultants) and commission-based financial planners make more money by encouraging trading activity and by selling you investments that provide them with high commissions — limited partnerships and mutual funds with high load fees, for example. Brokers and planners also get an occasional message from the top brass asking them to sell some new-fangled investment product. All of this creates inherent conflicts of interest that can prevent them from providing objective investment and financial advice and recommendations.

No-load (commission-free) mutual fund companies do not push products. Their toll-free telephone lines are staffed with knowledgeable people who earn a salary. Their recommendations don't carry inherent conflicts of interest. Of course, they want your money.

EZ access to your dough

What's really terrific about dealing with mutual funds is that they are set up for people who don't like to waste time going to a local branch office and standing in line waiting for "the next available representative."

With mutual funds, you can make your initial investment from the comfort of your living room by filling out and mailing a simple form and writing a check.

Later, you can add to your investment by mailing in a check or by authorizing money transfers by phone from one mutual fund account to another.

Selling shares of your mutual fund for cash is just as easy. Generally, all you need to do is call the fund company's toll-free 800 number. Some companies have representatives available by phone 24 hours a day, 365 days a year.

Still not easy enough for you? Well, here's another path to your loot. Most money market funds offer check-writing privileges. These accounts often carry a restriction that your bank checking account doesn't have: money market checks must be greater than a specified minimum amount — typically $250. Many mutual fund companies also allow you to wire money back and forth from your local bank account; you can access your money almost as quickly through a money market fund as you can through your local bank. (As I discuss in Chapter 6, you'll probably need to keep a local bank checking account to write smaller checks and for immediate ATM access to cash.)

But if you do want to do some transactions in person, some of the larger fund companies, such as Fidelity, and some discount brokers, such as Charles Schwab, have branch offices in convenient locations so you can give money to or get it from another living, breathing human being. But they won't give you cash on the spot the way a bank would. Schwab, for example, will issue you a check only if you give them a day's notice.

Don't worry about the crooks

Don't worry about others having easy access to your money. If someone were able to convince a fund company through the toll-free phone line that he were you (say, by knowing your account number and Social Security number), the worst that could happen is that the impostor could request a transaction — but one could do that only among accounts registered in your name. You'd find out about the shenanigans when the confirmation arrived in the mail, at which time you could call the mutual fund company and undo the whole mess. (Just by listening to a tape of the phone call, which the fund company records, the company could confirm that you did not place the trade.)

No one can actually take money out of your account, either. Suppose that someone does know your personal and account information and calls a fund company to ask that a check be sent from a redemption on the account. Even in such a scenario, the check would be sent to the address on the account and made payable to you.

The only way that someone can actually take money out of your account is with your authorization. And there's only one way to do that: by completing a full trading authorization or power-of-attorney form. I generally recommend that you do not grant this authority to anyone. If you do, make sure the investment firm makes the check payable only to you, not to the person disbursing the money from the account.

Because you're not a dummy and you have a life!

You work hard; you have family and friends. Chances are, the last thing you want to do with your free time is research where to invest your savings. If you're like many other busy people, you've kept your money in a bank just to avoid the hassles. Or maybe you turned your money over to some smooth-talking broker who sold you a high-commission investment you still don't understand.

Mutual funds — which you can purchase by writing a check or calling an 800 number — can pay you a much better rate of return over the long haul than a dreary, boring bank account or an insurance company account. Just don't forget that mutual funds, like all investments, carry their own unique risks, which you need to know before you take the plunge.

Talking the Talk — Are There Open-Ended Families?

In addition to understanding fund prospectuses and performance numbers (which are discussed in Chapters 3 and 11, respectively), I need to clarify some important terms right now to avoid confusion.

Of families and funds

Throughout this book, I discuss mutual fund companies as well as individual funds. To better illustrate the difference between the two, I'll compare a mutual fund family to a real family — one with parents and children. Mutual fund companies, such as Vanguard and Fidelity, can be thought of as parent organizations that act as the distributors for a group of funds. The parent doesn't actually take your money. Instead, it is responsible for distributing and managing the individual mutual funds — the kids, if you will, in the family.

You actually invest your money in an individual mutual fund — one wayfaring child of the whole family — such as Vanguard's Wellesley Income fund or the Fidelity Balanced Fund. Vanguard and Fidelity are the parent organizations. (Don't worry: children don't actually manage the funds, although some portfolio managers are on the young side — in their 30s!)

As with real families, good parent organizations tend to produce better off-spring. That's why you should understand the parent organization that's responsible for overseeing the fund before you ever invest in it. What is the parent's track record with similar funds? How long has the parent been managing the types of funds you're interested in? Has the parent had any disasters with similar funds? The funds I recommend later in the book will satisfy these concerns.

Open-end or closed-end

I'm not talking about whether you remembered to place the cap back on the tube of toothpaste! Open-end and closed-end are general terms that refer to whether a fund issues an unlimited or set amount of shares in a particular mutual fund.

The vast majority of funds in the marketplace are open-end funds, and they're the funds that this book focuses on. Open-end simply means that the fund issues as many (or as few) shares as investors demand. In open-end funds, there's no limit to the number of investors or the amount of money in the fund.

Closed-end funds decide up front, when they issue their original shares, exactly how many shares they will issue. Thus, once a closed-end fund is issued, the only way you can purchase shares (or more shares) is to buy them from an existing investor.

Sorry to complicate things, but there's an important exception to what I just said. Open-end funds can and sometimes do decide at a later date to close their fund to new investors. This does not make it a closed-end fund, because investors with existing shares can still buy more shares from the fund company.

Generally speaking, the better open-end funds are preferable to closed-end funds for the following reasons:

- ✔ **Bigger and better.** The best open-end fund managers can attract more investors over time. Thus, they can afford to pay the necessary money to hire better managers. That's not to say that closed-end funds don't have some good managers, too, but as a general rule, open-end funds attract better talent.

- ✔ **Lower cost.** Because they can attract more investors, and therefore more money to manage, the better open-end funds charge lower annual operating expenses. Closed-end funds tend to be much smaller and therefore more costly to operate. Remember, operating expenses are always deducted before a fund pays its investors their returns. Just because of the principles of basic accounting, then, the returns for closed-end funds are depressed by higher annual fees.

When closed-end funds are originally sold, such sales generally occur through brokers who receive a healthy (for them, not for you) commission. Brokers' commissions usually suck anywhere from 5 to 10 percent out of your investment dollars. Even if you're smart and wait to buy shares in a closed-end fund on the stock exchange after the initial offering, you'll still pay a brokerage commission. You can avoid these unhealthy commissions by purchasing a no-load (commission-free), open-end mutual fund (say that ten times real fast!).

✔ **No haircuts when you sell.** With an open-end fund, the value of a share always equals 100 percent of what the fund's investments are currently worth. And you don't have the cost and trouble of selling your shares to another investor as you must with a closed-end fund. Because closed-end funds trade like securities on the stock exchange, and because you must sell your shares to someone who wants to buy, closed-end funds sometimes sell at a discount. Even though the securities in a closed-end fund may be worth $20 per share, you may be able to get only $19 per share if sellers outnumber buyers.

There can be a good side to a closed-end fund selling at a discount. You could buy shares in a closed-end fund at discount and hold onto them in hopes that the discount disappears or — even better — turns into a premium (which means that the share price of the fund exceeds the value of the investments it holds).

Unless I specify otherwise, funds discussed and recommended in this book are open-end funds. For the information gluttons among you, investing in closed-end funds is covered in Chapter 14.

Mutual Funds versus Individual Securities

Some folks just don't, won't, or can't enjoy having all of their money tied up in mutual funds. Some people say that funds are, well, kind of boring. It's true that following the trials, tribulations, successes, and failures of a favorite company can provide you plenty of excitement (often much more than you want). A fund, on the other hand, is a little like a black box. You pour money into it and don't have specific company events to follow.

While I've never been one to enjoy stereotypes, I've noticed some common characteristics among investors who prefer to have at least some of their portfolios in individual securities. No offense, but see if you recognize yourself:

✔ **The Boaster.** You only go to parties when you've just made a sweet deal in the stock market. You give unsolicited advice to everyone you talk to, including the personal financial planner you met on the airplane.

If you couldn't tell others of your latest killing in the market and shrewd stock picks, there'd be little point to owning securities. While the thought has hopefully never crossed your mind of sending copies of a brokerage statement out to friends and relatives, you've been known on more than a few occasions to offer unsolicited tips and investment advice.

✔ **The Controller.** You hate delegating jobs to others, especially important ones, because no one will do as good a job as you. Investing much or all of your money in mutual funds and leaving all of the investment decisions to the fund manager won't make you a happy camper.

✔ **The Free Spirit.** You're the type who says, "I don't care if there's $3 trillion invested in mutual funds. I don't care if everyone's using word processors instead of typewriters." You like to be just a little bit different and independent.

Although investing a small portion of your money in individual securities may be a compromise, be realistic as to why you're investing in them. And before you plunk down too much money in them, remember the sage words of Jack Bogle, the mutual fund investor's best friend:

> "Attempting to build an investment program around the selection of a handful of individual securities is, for all but the most exceptional investors, a fool's errand. . . . Specific stock bets should be made, if at all, in small portions, and more for the excitement of the game than for the profit."

Yes, Bogle is the founder and CEO of a large mutual fund company, Vanguard. No, his comments aren't self-serving: Vanguard also operates a discount brokerage company that handles individual securities trades for Vanguard customers who wish to do them.

In the long haul, you're not going to beat full-time professional managers who are investing in the securities of the same type and risk level that you are. As with hiring a contractor, you need to do your homework to find a good money manager. Even if you think that you can do as well as the best, remember that even superstar money managers like Peter Lynch have beaten the market averages by only a few percentage points per year.

My experience is that more than a few otherwise smart, fun-loving people choose to invest in individual securities because they think that they're smarter or luckier than the rest of us. If you're like most people, it's safe to say that, in the long run, your investment choices will not outperform those of a full-time investment professional.

I've noticed a distinct difference between the sexes on this issue. Perhaps because of differences in how people are raised, testosterone levels, or whatever, men tend to have more of a problem swallowing their egos and admitting that they're better off not going with individual securities. Maybe it's genetically linked to not wanting to ask for directions.

The dangers of individual securities

Generally, you should avoid investing in individual stocks and bonds unless you have a lot of time and money to invest. There are many drawbacks to selecting and trading individual securities, including the following:

✔ **Significant research time and related expenses.** Before buying an individual security, you should know a great deal about the company you're investing in. Relevant questions that you need to answer include these: What products does the company sell? What are the company's prospects for future growth and profitability? How does the company's performance compare to its competitors' performances — both recently and over the long haul? Are technological changes in the works that might harm or improve their business? How much debt does the company have?

You need to do your homework on these questions, not only before you make your initial investment, but also on a continuing basis as long as you hold the investment. And you have to expend this legwork for every company you invest in and every company you consider investing in.

Be honest with yourself. If you're really going to research and monitor your individual securities, the extra work ultimately will take time away from other pursuits. In worst-case situations, I've seen busy people spend almost as many hours on the weekend and in the evenings with their portfolios as they do with family and friends. If you can really afford the time for this type of hobby, more power to you. But remember, no one I know of has ever said on her deathbed, "I wish I had spent more time watching my investments."

✔ **High transaction costs.** Even when you use a discount broker (described in Chapter 4), the commissions you pay to buy or sell securities are not cheap. It may cost you about $40 to buy 100 shares of a $20 security through a discounter, which amounts to 40 cents per share, or 2 percent of the amount invested. A large institution, such as a mutual fund, that buys securities in blocks of 10,000 shares or more pays a penny or two per share when trading. If you invest in securities on your own, you're effectively paying 20 to 40 times more per share in commissions than mutual fund companies do.

Note two exceptions to the rule of individual security purchases costing too much: (1) government bonds can be purchased directly from the Federal Reserve without charge, and (2) deep discount brokers (see Chapter 4) can be quite cheap for investors making large purchases.

✔ **Less likelihood of diversification.** Unless you have several hundred thousand dollars or more to invest in dozens of different securities, you probably can't afford to develop a diversified portfolio. For example, when you're investing in stocks, you should hold companies in different industries, different companies within an industry, and so on. And not diversifying adds to the risk of losing your shirt.

✔ **More accounting and bookkeeping chores.** When you invest in individual securities outside retirement accounts, every time you sell a specific security, you must report that transaction on your tax return.

Even if you pay someone else to complete your return, you still have the hassle of keeping track of statements and receipts. (On the other hand, you control selling decisions with individual securities, whereas with funds, managers who trade can lead to capital gains distributions.)

Dividend reinvestment plans for individual stocks

There's an interesting spin on investing that may sound attractive, but it's often more bother than it's worth. Increasing numbers of corporations allow existing holders of shares of stock to reinvest their dividends (known as DRIPs) in more shares of stock without paying brokerage commissions. In some cases, companies allow you to make additional cash purchases of more shares of stock, also commission-free.

In order to qualify, you must first buy some shares of stock in a company that seems attractive. Ideally, you should purchase these initial shares through a discount broker to keep your commission burden as low as possible. The National Association Investor Corporation (NAIC) also has a plan that allows you to buy one or a few shares to get started.

While DRIPs reduce your stock commissions on future purchases, DRIPs have their shortcomings. Here's why you're probably better off in the long run using professional money managers such as those available through no-load mutual funds:

✔ Investing in DRIPs is only available and cost-effective for investments held outside retirement accounts. You should be doing as much investing as possible through the retirement accounts that are available to you.

✔ You need to complete a lot of paperwork to invest in a number of different companies' stock. Life is too short to bother with these plans for this reason alone.

✔ Some companies that offer these plans are hungry — for whatever reason. They need to drum up support for their stock. These investments may not be the best ones for the future.

Should I join an investment club?

Investment clubs are a little bit like having your own hands-on mutual fund. You get a group together for periodic meetings where you discuss investment ideas.

Each group member chips in a bit of money. The group then selects individual investments and invests in and monitors them over time.

These groups can be valuable as an educational forum so long as you utilize good information sources. If the group members are somewhat clueless and the meetings are rambling, these groups can end up degenerating into the blind leading the blind.

They may have social or hobby value (which are most clubs' major benefit), but investment clubs aren't likely to help your finances much. In fact, they can hurt your checkbook more than they help. First of all, let's face it — you're a bunch of part-time amateurs. You could end up making some real bone-headed decisions and losing money (or not making nearly as much as if you had been in some good mutual funds). Secondly, it's highly unlikely that everyone in the group is in the same tax situation. Thus, the club's investments may work for some members' tax situations but not for others.

Beware of stock brokers who have been known to participate in investment clubs and volunteer as leaders as a so-called business development tool. Although their participation may be harmless, more often than not, they have a hidden agenda to reel in new clients to whom they've been able to demonstrate their vast investment knowledge.

Consider forming a financial reading club instead of an investment club. You can get together and discuss financial periodicals, books, and investment strategies. This way, you can advance your level of financial knowledge, learn about new resources from others, and have the fun, camaraderie, and other benefits that come from doing things in a group.

Better yet, join a bowling league or a softball team and leave the investing to fund managers!

Mutual Fund Drawbacks

The mutual fund industry is a success story. Never before have investors been able to take more responsibility and have access to some of the best money managers in the world for such a low cost.

The growth of mutual funds has received some bad press. Some of it is deserved; some of it isn't. Investors who still don't understand what funds are and how they work harbor some prejudices. Herewith is my take on some of these concerns and criticisms.

Don't worry about these . . .

The investment Goliath

One of the concerns I still hear about is the one that, because funds are becoming large, if fund investors head for the exits at the same time, they may get stuck or trampled at the door.

Here's a fear you can just chuck. Mutual funds hold just 12 percent of outstanding U.S. stocks. They're growing in importance simply because they're a superior alternative for a whole lot of people.

Where's the building?

Some people, particularly older folks who grew up doing all of their saving through a local bank, feel quite uncomfortable doing business with an organization that they can reach only via an 800 number or through the mail. I understand where they are coming from. I hate putting things in the mail, too, given the reliability of the U.S. Postal Service! Seriously, though, there are some enormous benefits to mutual funds' not having branch offices all over the country. Branches cost a lot of money to operate. That's one of the reasons why the interest rates on bank accounts are so cruddy.

If you feel better dropping your money off in person to an organization that has local branch offices, invest in mutual funds through one of the firms recommended later that maintain branch offices, such as Charles Schwab or Fidelity. Or do business with a fund company headquartered near your abode.

Worry about these . . .

Mutual funds, like any other investment, are not without warts and scars. Here are some things you should be aware of:

Volatility of your investment balance

When you invest in mutual funds that hold stocks and/or bonds, the value of your funds fluctuates with the general fluctuations in those securities markets. This doesn't happen if you invest in a bank certificate of deposit or a fixed insurance annuity that pays a set rate of interest yearly. With these investments, you get a statement every so often that shows steady — but slow — growth in your account value. There's never any great news, but there's never any bad news (unless your insurer or bank fails, which could happen).

Over the long haul, if you invest in decent mutual funds — ones that are efficiently and competently managed — you should earn a better rate of return than you would with bank and insurance accounts. And if you invest in growth-oriented funds (such as stock funds), you'll be more likely to keep well ahead of the double bite of inflation and taxes.

But if you freak out and sell when the market value of your mutual fund shares drops (instead of taking advantage of the buying opportunity), then maybe you're not cut out for funds. Take the time to read and internalize the investment lessons in this book and you'll soon graduate from Mutual Fund University!

The borders between banks, insurers, and mutual fund companies have come a-tumblin' down. Insurers and banks have piled into the mutual fund business in recent years. As you see in Chapter 4, most of their offerings have been high-cost (commissions and ongoing operating expenses) and poor-performance funds. They are new to the mutual fund scene, so they are still playing catch-up.

Mystery (risky) investments

In recent years, some mutual funds have betrayed their investors' trust by taking unnecessary and, in some cases, undisclosed risks by investing in volatile financial instruments such as futures and options (a.k.a. derivatives). Since these are basically short-term bets on the direction of specific security prices (see Chapter 1), they are very risky when not properly used by a mutual fund.

An arm and a leg

Not all mutual funds are created equal. Why else would there be thousands of them? Some charge extremely high annual operating expenses that put a real drag on returns. Expense ratios, for example, in excess of $3/4$ percent for bond funds and $1^1/4$ percent for U.S. stock funds take away a good deal of your expected returns.

Taxes. Taxes. Taxes.

The taxable distributions that funds produce can also be a negative. When fund managers sell a security at a profit, the fund must distribute that profit, minus the losses from any securities sold for less than they were purchased for, to fund shareholders. These taxable distributions can be a negative. This is an often overlooked problem for investors purchasing mutual funds outside of tax-sheltered retirement accounts. I fill you in on taxes and mutual funds in Chapter 5.

Some — especially brokers who advocate investing in individual securities — have argued that taxes on mutual fund distributions are a big problem, especially for higher tax-bracket investors.

They don't have to be. If you are concerned about the money you're investing outside of tax-sheltered retirement accounts, don't worry — there's a solution: Flip to Chapters 6 through 8 to see the recommended tax-friendly funds.

Managed Investment Alternatives to Mutual Funds

The unbelievably wide variety of mutual funds enables you to invest in everything from short-term money market securities to corporate bonds, U.S. and international stocks, precious metals, and even real estate.

Mutual funds can fill many needs, but as I discuss in Chapter 1, you may be interested in and benefit from directly investing in things such as real estate, your own business, and many other investments. While beyond the scope of this book, some other types of privately managed investment accounts exist that have some things in common with mutual funds. Here's the straight scoop for you if you're considering using them:

Wrap (or managed) accounts

Many of the brokerage firms that used to sell investment products only on commission (for example, Prudential, Merrill Lynch, Smith Barney Shearson, Paine Webber, and Dean Witter) are moving into fee-based investment management. This change is an improvement for investors because it reduces some of the conflicts of interest caused by commissions.

On the other hand, these brokers charge extraordinarily high fees (which are usually quoted as a percentage of assets under management) on their *managed* (or *wrap*) investment accounts.

These accounts go under a variety of names. Smith Barney Shearson calls them "Traks." Merrill Lynch calls them "Consults." But they're all the same in one crucial way: for the privilege of investing your money through their money managers, they all charge you a fixed percentage of the assets they're managing for you.

Wrap accounts have two major problems. First, their management expenses are extraordinarily high, often up to 3 percent (or more) per year of assets under management. Remember that historically, stocks have returned about 10 percent per year before taxes. So if you're paying 3 percent per year to have the money managed in stocks, 30 percent of your return (before taxes) is siphoned off. But don't forget (the government certainly won't) that you pay a good chunk of money in taxes on your 10 percent return as well. So the 3 percent wrap actually ends up depleting 40 to 50 percent of the profits you get to keep after you pay taxes!

Forbes magazine said it best in a recent article on wrap accounts: "Brokerage firms love wrap accounts because they're so lucrative — for them."

No-load (commission-free) mutual funds offer investors access to the nation's best investment managers for a fraction of the cost of wrap accounts. You can invest in dozens of top-performing funds for an annual expense of 1 percent per year or less. Many excellent funds are available for far less — 0.2 to 0.5 percent annually.

So how do brokerage firms hoodwink investors into paying 3 to 15 times as much for access to investment managers? Marketing. Slick, seductive, deceptive, misleading pitches that include some outright lies. Here are the key components of the brokers' pitch for wrap accounts — and then the real truth behind their pitch:

"You're getting access to investment managers who don't take money from small-fry investors like you (that is, investors who have less than a million)."

First off, not a single study shows that the performance of money managers has anything to do with the minimum account they handle. Second, no-load mutual funds hire many of the same managers who work at other money management firms. In fact, Vanguard, the nation's largest exclusively commission-free investment firm, contracts out to hire money managers who typically handle only million-dollar-plus accounts to run many of their funds. A number of other mutual funds are managed by private money managers with high entrance requirements.

"You'll earn a higher rate of return, so the extra cost is worth it."

Part of the bait brokers use to hook you into a wrap account is the wonderful rates of returns they supposedly generate. You could have earned 18 to 25 percent per year, they say, had you invested with the "Star of Yesterday" investment management company. The key words here are "could have." History is history. Many of yesterday's winners become tomorrow's losers or mediocre performers.

You also must remember that, unlike mutual funds, whose performance records are audited by the SEC, wrap account performance records may include marketing hype: *wrap accounts are not audited by the SEC.* The most common ploy is showing only the performance of selected accounts — which turn out to be (you got it) only the ones that performed the best!

The expenses you pay to have your investments managed have an enormous impact on the long-term growth of your money. If you can have your money managed for 0.5 to 1 percent per year instead for 2.5 to 3 percent, you've got a 2 percent-per-year performance advantage already.

"There's little difference in cost between wrap accounts and no-load mutual funds."

Baloney! True, the worst and most inefficient mutual funds can have total costs approaching that of a typical wrap account. But you're no dummy — you're not going to invest in the highest-cost funds. Chapters 6 through 8 detail which mutual funds offer both top performance and low cost.

Private money managers

Mutual funds seem rather pedestrian because every Tom, Dick, and Jane can invest their paltry savings in them. People who drive expensive cars, fly first class when they travel, stay in expensive hotels, and order $100 bottles of wine in four-star restaurants tend to demand some exclusivity and are used to paying more to get "better" quality.

In the world of money management, there's added benefit — snob appeal and ego stroking — that comes with having your own private money manager. First of all, you generally need big bucks, often $1 million or more to gain entrance, although it never ceases to amaze me how often this minimum account size is lowered if you have a friend who recommends you and already has an account with the firm. "You only have $200,000, no problem."

A private money management company allows you to sit down and visit with a personal representative and perhaps even the investment manager. They'll lavish you with lots of attention and glossy brochures. You'll hear how your money will not only receive individualized and personalized treatment but also how superb the investment manager's performance has been in prior years.

Even if you've got big bucks, you probably don't need a private money manager for two simple reasons. First, the best, average, and worst private money managers earn returns comparable to their counterparts in the mutual fund business. And, as mentioned earlier, some mutual fund firms contract out to or are themselves private money managers. This gives you the best of both worlds: the SEC oversight of a mutual fund and access to some money managers you may not otherwise be able to use.

If you're considering investing through private investment firms, make sure that you

✔ Ask to see independently audited rates of return.

✔ Check lots of references.

✔ Compare with the best mutual funds.

For more ideas about evaluating money managers, see the criteria for selecting mutual funds in Chapter 3.

Hedge funds

Hedge funds are also only for big ticket investors, but they have the added glamour and allure of taking significant risk and gambles with their investments. They may do this by purchasing derivatives (options, futures, and the like, discussed in Chapter 1). They may also bet on the fall in price of particular securities by selling them short. *Short selling* entails selling a security first by borrowing it from a broker and then hoping to buy it back later at a lower price. When they happen to guess right, they can produce high returns. When they don't, however, the fund manager can have his head handed to him on a very expensive silver platter. Since the security sold short can rise an unlimited amount, the potential loss from buying it back at a much higher price can be horrendous.

A number of hedge funds have gone belly up, kaput, bankrupt when they guessed wrong. In other words, their investments did so poorly, investors in the fund lost all of their money. The odds of this happening with a mutual fund, particularly from one of the larger, more established companies, are nil.

If you want more risk, there are aggressive mutual funds. You can also buy mutual funds on *margin* (meaning you make a down payment, such as when you purchase a home, but control a larger investment) through a brokerage account if you like more risk (see Chapter 10).

Chapter 3

How to Pick Great Funds and Avoid Losers

• •

In This Chapter

▶ Fund costs

▶ Risk and return and how funds hide their true colors

▶ Fund manager and fund family expertise

▶ Warning signs of a loser fund

▶ Understanding prospectuses and annual reports

• •

*I*nvesting in stocks and bonds through mutual funds can help your financial status. But it also involves some risks.

When you go camping in the wilderness, you can do a number of things to maximize your odds of happiness and success. You can take maps to keep you on course, food to keep you from starving, proper clothing to stay dry and warm, and some first-aid stuff in case something awful happens such as an outbreak of mosquitoes. But no matter how much advance preparation you do, you still may not have the time of your life. You may get sick, trip over a rock and break your ankle, or face unpredictable weather, like the time it snowed on Memorial Day weekend all over northern California.

And so it is with mutual funds. They come with no guarantees. You can, however, use a number of simple, common sense criteria to greatly increase your chances of investment success. The following issues are the main ones you should consider. The mutual funds that I recommend in Chapters 6 through 9 meet these criteria.

Cost

For a particular type of mutual fund (short-term bonds, for example), from dozens to in some cases hundreds of choices are available. The charges you pay to buy or sell a fund, as well as the ongoing fund operating expenses, can have a big impact on the rate of return you earn on your investments.

The biggest mistake that novice investors make when buying mutual funds is looking first (and sometimes only) at the prior performance of the fund. Another mistake is paying too much attention to the current bond fund yield. As you see in Chapter 7, doing so is dangerous because a fund can inflate its return or yield in many (risky) ways. Besides, what worked yesterday may flop tomorrow.

Fund costs are an important factor in the return that you earn from a mutual fund. Fees are deducted from your investment returns and can attack a fund from many angles. All other things being equal, high fees and other charges depress your returns.

Sales loads

Sales loads are commissions paid to "financial planners" and brokers who sell mutual funds. Typically, commissions range from 4 percent to as high as 8.5 percent of the amount you invest.

Sales loads have their problems. First of all, they are an additional and unnecessary cost that is deducted from your investment money.

Not surprisingly, those who have a vested interest in sales loads have made a number of misleading arguments in favor of funds that carry sales loads. Some of their statements are downright silly.

Over the years, I've heard quite a number of arguments from brokers and, in counseling clients who come to me for advice, I frequently hear them repeat arguments they've heard from investment salespeople to get them to pay a sales charge when buying a mutual fund. Here are the common arguments and the facts:

"Don't concern yourself with my commission — I get paid by the mutual fund company."

It's true that the mutual fund company pays the investment salesperson a commission. However, and this is an important however, the commission comes out of your investment dollars. Brokers like to imply that you're effectively not paying for the commission since it comes from the mutual fund company. Not so.

"You get what you pay for— load funds have better fund managers."

Balderdash! Five out of five studies, as well as common sense, suggest there is absolutely no relationship between paying a sales charge to buy a fund and gaining access to better investment managers. Some funds (load funds) pay sales commissions as the incentive to get brokers to sell their funds. The commission goes to the selling broker, not to the management of the fund. Objective studies have shown that load funds not only don't outperform but in fact underperform no-loads. Why? It's simple. When you factor in the higher commission and the higher average ongoing operating expenses charged on load funds, you pay more to own one so your returns are less.

Many of the published mutual fund rankings and ratings services completely ignore the sales commissions in their calculations of what an investor's return would be in a fund (see Chapter 14).

"No-loads have higher ongoing fees."

Not! Investment salespeople will try to imply or actually say that no-loads have to make it up somewhere if they aren't charging you a sales commission. This may sound logical, but remember that sales commissions go to the broker, not toward the expenses of managing the fund.

Brokers will also say that no-loads have to spend gobs of money marketing themselves to investors, and that these higher costs, inevitably, are reflected in no-loads' annual operating expenses. This sounds good from a broker's perspective, but it is false. Load funds also have to spend money to market themselves, both to brokers and to the investing public like you and me. And the better no-load companies, such as those recommended in the next chapter, benefit from the thousands of investors who call, based on word-of-mouth or other recommendations (such as through this book!), seeking to invest.

"No-loads have hidden fees."

Another nice try, Mr. Broker. This is a case where a half-truth does not make a whole. Both no-load *and* load funds incur brokerage transaction costs when securities are bought and sold in the fund. These costs are not really "hidden." They are disclosed in a fund's prospectus (statement of additional information); however, they are not included in the calculated annual operating costs for any type of mutual fund, either load or no-load (see discussion later in this chapter).

"No-loads are for do-it-yourself types. People who need help buy load funds."

This either/or mentality permeates not only investment brokers but also some of the financial writing in the mass media, where writers sometimes parrot what brokers say to them. If you need advice, you have other options. (Many brokers would like you to believe that they are your only option.) One other option is to hire a financial advisor and pay a fee for his or her time to recommend specific no-load mutual funds. No-loads are hardly just for do-it-yourself types (see Chapter 5 for the different types of advisors you might hire).

"I'll do a financial plan for you to determine your needs."

Try as they might, investment salespeople simply cannot perform objective, conflict-free financial planning. You should never pay for a "financial plan" produced by an investment salesperson. Such financial plans end up being nothing more than sales tools.

The problem with sales loads is the power of self-interest that we'll talk about in the next chapter. This issue is rarely talked about, but it is even more important than the extra costs you pay. When you buy a load fund through a salesperson, you miss out on the chance to decide for yourself whether you should buy a mutual fund at all. Maybe you'd be better off paying debts or investing in something entirely different. But salespeople almost never advise you to pay off your credit cards or your mortgage — or to invest through your company's retirement plan — instead of buying an investment through them.

I've seen too many people get into an investment without understanding what they're buying and what the risks are. People who sell mutual funds usually sell other investments, too. And some of those other products hold the allure (for the salespeople) of high commissions — vehicles such as limited partnerships, cash-value life insurance, annuities, futures, and options. Salespeople tend to exaggerate the potential benefits and obscure the risks and drawbacks of what they sell; they don't seem to take the time to educate investors.

"I can get you funds from the same no-load companies, such as Fidelity..."

Another half truth. Brokers like to imply that they can sell you basically the same funds that you could buy on your own through no-load companies. Top no-load companies, such as Vanguard, for example, do not sell any load funds through brokers. Fidelity sells a limited number of load funds but charges substantially more for their Fidelity Advisor funds, which are sold through commission-based brokers. These funds carry 4.75 percent sales charges and much higher ongoing fees — up to a full 1 percent more per year for many of their stock funds.

"On a busy day, you won't be able to get through on the phone lines to the no-loads."

When the financial markets make wide swings or there is a major news event, it's true that many investment firms see a pick-up in calls. Brokers will imply that you won't be able to place your trade at a no-load company on such days. This is one of the more ludicrous arguments I've heard. Since you can't time the financial markets, odds are quite high that you'll be making an emotionally based, knee-jerk reaction if you trade on days of turmoil. For example, the investors who sold when the market crashed in October 1987 ended up bailing out at bargain, "on sale now" prices. Those who wanted to buy had plenty of weeks of low prices in which to do so.

Most of the major no-load mutual fund companies and discount brokers maintain business hours far greater than brokerage firms that sell load funds. Some even offer 24-hour-a-day phone assistance.

"The no-loads won't call you to tell you when to get out of the market or switch funds."

True, but this isn't a disadvantage. It's actually a plus. Although mutual funds offer daily liquidity, funds are meant to be a longer-term investment. Of course, if you win the lottery or lose your job, it makes sense to reassess your financial circumstances and perhaps alter your investment mix.

As for switching funds, use the same criteria discussed in this chapter for selecting funds to evaluate your current funds and ensure that they are still up to snuff. A broker, who stands to gain financially when you trade, is hard pressed to be a source of objective advice.

"No-loads have worse performance because investors on their own are more likely to panic and bail out when the financial markets turn volatile."

This is another myth perpetuated by investment salespeople. A broker, who was surfing one of the bulletin boards incognito on America Online, dishing out investment advice, said that funds sold through brokers are better to hold in a downturn because, "Scared money tends to flow fast out of no-advice funds, while brokered funds tend to lose less assets and don't force the hand of the reluctant fund manager."

No data support this. In fact, there's a danger that, if your load fund goes in the tank, your broker may use this as an excuse to call and recommend selling at a time when prices are low, not high. The majority of mutual funds experiencing large redemptions in recent years have been load funds.

"No-loads are impersonal organizations."

When you call a no-load fund's 800 line, you will surely get a different representative every time. If it's important to you to have a relationship with someone at these firms, some representatives will give you their names and extensions (just ask) so you can reach them in the future.

A broker can be a personal contact who asks you about your golf game, how your family is doing, and phone numbers of relatives with money to invest. Independent financial counselors who charge a fee for their time can serve the same role. Likewise, firms such as Charles Schwab and Fidelity maintain branch offices that offer a personal, local touch if you need and want it.

Note: some funds sold at companies such as Fidelity and Dreyfus charge a commission even though you purchase the fund directly from them without a broker's involvement. I recommend that you avoid these funds as well. (I'll make sure that you do when I recommend specific funds later in Part II. I'll even show you how to buy some of the better funds at Fidelity without paying the loads).

Invest in no-loads and avoid load funds and investment salespeople. The only way to be sure that a fund is truly no-load is to look at the prospectus for the fund. Only there, in black and white and absent all marketing hype, must the organization tell the truth about its sales charges and other fund fees.

Be wary of brokers or planners pitching house brands: for example a Dean Witter broker recommending only Dean Witter mutual funds or an American Express financial planner only extolling the virtues of American Express mutual funds. Salespeople often get a higher commission by pushing house brands. Many of the better load mutual funds, such as American, Franklin/Templeton, are managed by companies independent of brokerage firms. Brokerage firms are Johnny-come-latelys to the mutual fund field, and the performance of their funds reflects their lack of experience. They also suffer from developing and selling funds when the funds are likely to be most popular, which often coincides with the worst time for investors to buy them.

Alphabet soup — Do we have a (hidden) load for you...ABCD shares

Over the years, investors have learned about the sales loads that are deducted from their investments in load mutual funds. Perhaps you just learned this yourself. Well, the companies that specialize in selling load funds have, with the unwitting assistance of government regulators, developed new types of funds that make finding the load much harder.

Just as some jewelers flog fake diamonds on late-night TV commercials, increasing numbers of brokers and financial planners are selling funds that they *call* no-loads, but these funds are *not* no-loads. By any other name, these funds are load funds: the only difference is that, with these funds, someone has taken the time to hide the sales commission.

The commission is hidden thanks to the different classes of shares, known as A, B, C, and D classes. Up-front load funds that historically have been sold are A shares. B, C, and D are the classes that the mutual fund marketers like to push today since the load is hidden as a back-end or ongoing charge that is more transparent. These charges may include 12b-1 fees, ongoing marketing expenses, which may be paid out as commissions to investment salespeople.

You're told something along the lines that, as long as you stay in a fund for five to seven years, you need not pay the back-end sales charge that would apply when you sell the investment. This claim may be true, but it's also true that these funds pay investment salespeople a hefty commission. The salespeople can receive their commissions because the fund company charges you exorbitant continuing operating expenses (which are usually 1 percent more per year than the best funds). So, one way or another, they get their pound of flesh (their commissions) from your investment dollars.

How can you avoid all these different types of load fund? Don't buy funds through salespeople, and do buy the no-loads recommended in this book.

Figure 3-1 is a sample of a typical fee table from a fund prospectus for a load fund. Note that the "Class A Shares" have an up-front 6.5 percent sales commission that's deducted when you invest your money.

The "Class B Shares" don't have an up-front commission but instead have a deferred sales charge, which reduces over time. *However,* note that it charges you an extra 1.00 percent per year (12b-1 marketing expense fees). Class B Shares in this example (as in most real cases) will cost you more in the long run and in the short run if you need to redeem them.

TYPICAL FEE TABLE
From a Load-Fund Prospectus

	Class A Shares	**Class B Shares**
Shareholder Transaction Expenses:		
Maximum Sales Charge Imposed on Purchases (as a percentage of offering price)	6.50%	None
Sales Charge Imposed on Dividend Reinvestments	None	None
Deferred Sales Charge	None	4.0% during the first year, decreasing 1.0% annually to 0.0% after the fourth year
Exchange Fee	None	None

Annual Fund Operating Expenses
(as a percentage of average net assets):

	Class A Shares	**Class B Shares**
Management Fee	1.00%	1.00%
12b-1 Fees	None	1.00%
Other Expenses	0.25%	0.35%
Total Fund Operating Expenses	1.25%	2.35%

Example:

Cumulative Expenses Paid for the Period of:			
1 Year	**3 Years**	**5 Years**	**10 Years**

You would pay the following expenses on a $1,000 investment, assuming a 5% annual return, and redemption at the end of the period:

	1 Year	3 Years	5 Years	10 Years
Class A	$52	$78	$106	$185
Class B	$64	$93	$124	$265

You would pay the following expenses on the same $1,000 investment assuming no redemption at the end of the period:

	1 Year	3 Years	5 Years	10 Years
Class A	$52	$78	$106	$185
Class B	$24	$73	$124	$265

Figure 3-1:
How to spot load funds.

The incredible invisible brokerage costs

One of a fund's truly invisible expenses is the annual brokerage fees the fund pays to buy and sell securities for the fund. These costs are *not* included in the fund annual operating expense numbers that a fund reports. They reduce a fund's returns just the same. Don't worry — the annual rate of return — which appears in the performance numbers that a fund reports to the public — does reflect the brokerage charges paid.

Funds that frequently trade or "turn over" the securities they hold generally spend more on brokerage fees because the fund has to pay the broker on every trade. More trades mean more costs draining your returns. This may also lead to more taxable distributions. The brokerage costs on a fund can range from practically nothing to as much as 2 percent or more.

Later in this chapter, I'll tell you where to find this type of information (it's in a fund's "Statement of Additional Information") if you're the type who likes treasure hunts.

Operating expenses

We covered one of two costs of buying and owning funds, loads. Don't pay them: buy no-load funds. Another cost is the *operating expense.* All mutual funds charge fees as long as you keep your money in the fund. The fees pay for the operational costs of running a fund: employees' salaries, marketing, servicing the toll-free phone lines, printing and mailing prospectuses, buying super-duper computers to track all those investments and customer account balances, and so on. Running a business costs money!

A fund's operating expenses are quoted as a percentage of your investment. The percentage represents an annual fee or charge. You can find this number in a fund's prospectus, in the fund expenses section, where there should be a line that says something like "Total Fund Operating Expenses." Or you can call the mutual fund's 800 number and ask a representative. I'll give you, for no extra charge, such information on the funds recommended in this book.

A mutual fund's operating expenses are essentially invisible to you. That's because they're deducted before you're paid any return. The expenses are charged on a daily basis, so there's no need to worry about trying to get out of a fund before these fees are deducted. They're invisible but the impact on your returns is very real.

Funds with lower operating costs can more easily produce high returns for you than a comparable type of fund with high costs. Higher expenses mean a lower return to you.

Expenses matter on all types of funds, but more on some and less on others. Expenses are critical on a money market mutual fund and very important on bond funds because these funds are buying securities that are so similar and so efficiently priced in the financial markets. With stock funds, expenses are a less important (but still important) factor in picking a fund. Don't forget that, over time, stocks have averaged returns of about 10 percent per year. So if one stock fund charges 1.5 percent *more* in operating expenses than another, you're already giving up an extra 15 percent of your expected annual returns.

Some people argue that stock funds that charge high expenses may be justified in doing so — *if* they are able to generate higher rates of return. *But there's no evidence that high-expense stock funds do generate higher returns.* In fact, funds with higher operating expenses, on average, tend to produce *lower* rates of return. This makes sense because operating expenses are deducted from the returns that a fund generates.

Consistently high operating expenses at a mutual fund relative to its peers usually indicate one of two situations. Either the fund has little money under management — and therefore has a smaller group of investors to bear the management costs — or the fund owners are greedy. In either case, you don't want to be a shareholder at such a fund. Another possibility could be that the fund company is inefficiently managed (maybe their telephone reps spend half the day making long distance phone calls to friends!).

There's no reason to pay a lot for the best funds. Many excellent commission-free money market, bond, and stock funds from fund companies such as Vanguard, Fidelity, USAA, and T. Rowe Price "cost" under 1 percent per year, with plenty available for less than 0.5 percent per year in terms of their annual operating expense ratio.

Stick with funds that maintain low total operating expenses and that don't charge sales loads (commissions). Both types of fees come out of your pocket and reduce your rate of return. Make sure that a fund doesn't appear to have low expenses simply because it is temporarily waiving them (see Chapter 6).

Performance and Risk

A fund's *performance,* its historic rate of return, is another important factor to weigh when selecting a mutual fund. As all mutual fund materials tell you, past performance is no guarantee of future results. Analysis of historic mutual fund performance proves that some of yesterday's stars turn into tomorrow's skid-row bums (as I discuss in the next section, "Star today, also-ran tomorrow").

Many former high-return funds achieved their results by taking on high risk. Funds that assume higher risk should produce higher rates of return. But high-risk funds usually decline in price faster during major market declines. Thus, in order for a fund to be considered a *best* fund, it must consistently deliver a favorable rate of return given the risk that it takes.

Star today, also-ran tomorrow

The single biggest mistake investors make when choosing a mutual fund is over-emphasizing the importance of historic returns or past performance numbers. The shorter the time period, the greater the danger of using performance as an indicator of a good fund.

Although past performance *can* be a good sign, high returns for a fund, relative to its peers, are largely possible only if a fund is taking more risk. The danger of taking more risk is that it doesn't always work the way you'd like. The odds are very high that you won't be able to pick the next star before it vaults to prominence in the investing sky. There's a far greater chance that you'll board that star when it's ready to plummet back to Earth.

In fact, if you had invested in the annual #1 top performing stock and bond funds over the last 15 years, 80 percent subsequently performed worse, over the next three to ten years, than the average fund in their peer group! Two of these former #1 funds are actually the worst performing funds in their particular category.

The following is a sampling of the many examples of short-term stars becoming tomorrow's also-rans (and in some cases losers):

Managers Intermediate Mortgage

Managed by portfolio manager Worth Bruntjen, this fund was the darling-of-the-moment for almost every mutual fund rating service in 1993. It earned kudos because, in its seemingly boring investment universe — government-backed mortgage securities — it was able to produce a rate of return 3 percent per year higher than its peers (who came in it at just 10 percent per year) over the five-year period ending 1993. By earning 13 percent per year instead of 10 percent, MIM's performance was about 30 percent better than that of its peers.

This fund received some of the highest ratings that most mutual fund rating companies allowed for performance — and supposedly MIM had "below average" risk. It earned Morningstar's coveted "5-star" rating. (Partly to its credit, in its analysis of the fund on January 21, 1994, Morningstar said of MIM, "Its portfolio is made up entirely of volatile derivative securities," and went on to add, "If rates move back up, this fund will find it hard to maintain its great record.")

When interest rates finally did rise sharply in early 1994, this fund not only found it difficult to continue its past performance, it got clobbered. It produced a total return of -22 percent in the first half of 1993. This little six-month disaster brought the fund in dead last among 50 other mortgage bond funds for the five-year period ending 6/30/94.

Turns out this fund was able to achieve such a high return for a while by taking a ton of risk. Whence came all the danger, you ask? The fund invested in complex *collateralized mortgage obligations*. Believe it or not, there's a simple way to explain this mouthful. Complex collateralized mortgage obligations (CMOs) are pieces of a mortgage; when you buy them, it's like buying chicken parts instead of a whole chicken at the supermarket. A mortgage gets chopped into the different years of principal and/or interest repayments. CMOs are incredibly complicated to understand, even if you surround yourself with computers and investment bankers.

Forbes magazine, which had written a glowing article praising fund manager Bruntjen on January 17, 1994, admitted that its earlier enthusiasm had been excessive — a rare and honorable thing for a financial magazine to do. *Forbes* said that they had learned from the episode "not to be overly confident in historical statistics, especially those attached to complex investment products. In this case, a volatility measure calculated from a mostly bullish period turned out to be meaningless during a period when the market turned bearish."

United Services Gold

Among no-load funds, this fund has been the #1 overall performer four out of the last 15 years!

Sounds like a real winner, right? Wrong!

Not only did this fund significantly underperform the broad stock market (averaging 6.8 percent per year versus 14.8 percent), but it also ranked in the bottom half among precious metals funds!

Currently burdened with a high annual expense ratio of 1.9 percent per year, this fund is handicapped from ever producing solid long-term returns.

44 Wall Street

This aggressive stock fund skyrocketed 184 percent in 1975, the year following the end of one of the worst declines for the stock market since the Great Depression. Since the 1970s, this fund has been in the dog house. It holds the distinction for being the worst stock fund during the 1980s, one of the best decades for the stock market this century. And over the most recent ten-year period ending December 31st, it has returned a paltry 7.5 percent per year versus more than 13 percent for comparable funds.

As money has poured out of the fund, its annual operating expenses as a percentage of assets have ballooned and now stand in excess of an astounding 5 percent per year!

Apples to apples

Remember back in school when the teacher handed back the exams and you were delighted to have gotten a 92 (unless you're from an overachieving family). But then you learned that the average on the exam was a 95. You still might have been pleased, but much of the air likely was let out of your balloon.

Well, a few too many mutual fund companies love to compare their fund's performance to a supposed benchmark for comparable funds. And — you guessed it — in the great American advertising tradition, funds sometimes pick benchmarks that make it easy for themselves to look good.

The greatest truthbending and hucksterism takes place in advertisements for mutual funds. Here are some examples of the games funds play to make themselves look a lot better than they really are.

During 1994, the Strong Short-Term Bond Fund ran ads claiming to be the #1 short-term bond fund. (I'd show you the ad but Strong refused permission to reprint it.) The ads showed a 12-month comparison graph that compared the average yield on other short-term bond funds to the yield on its own short-term bond fund. The Strong Short-Term Bond Fund, according to the graph, consistently yielded 2 to 2.5 percent more than the competition! And, gosh, with a vibrant, solid name like Strong, how can you go wrong?

As you see in Chapter 7, a bond fund has to be taking a *lot* more risk to generate a dividend this much higher than the competition's. And if it is taking that much more risk, then we're certainly not comparing this fund to its true competition — which, in Strong's case, would be other funds whose investments take similarly high risks. This fund isn't a bad fund, but it isn't anywhere near as good as this ad would have you think.

How can you go wrong? Because this fund is on steroids! The Strong Short-Term Bond Fund is not comparable to most other short-term bonds because

- **A high percentage of its bonds are not high-quality:** historically, about 40 percent of its bonds are rated BBB or below.

- **Many of its bonds are not short-term bonds:** it invests in mortgage bonds that are more like intermediate-term bonds.

You also should be suspicious of any bond fund claiming to be this good which has annual operating expenses of 0.80 percent. With expenses that high (as you see in Chapter 7), you know that it's taking higher risks than other supposedly comparable funds just to keep its yield pumped up.

Strong's ad also claimed that Strong was ranked number one for the year ending 3/31/94. If a fund takes more risk than the funds it compares itself to, during particular, brief periods, it is can easily to end up at the top (and bottom) of the charts. But how strong a performer is this "number one"? Over the five years ending 3/31/94, Strong had *under*performed most short-term bond funds.

As you see in Chapter 7, short-term bond funds managed by companies such as Fidelity, PIMCO, and Vanguard charge far lower operating expenses, take less risk, and generate equal or better returns than this fund does.

During much of 1994, ads for the Warburg Pincus Growth & Income Fund similarly trumpeted its superior performance — claiming to be the #1 growth and income fund for the year ending 3/31/94 and #4 out of 180 funds for the five years ending 3/31/94. Sounds great, doesn't it? (I'd show you the ad, but they refused to give permission to reproduce it.)

Most growth and income funds invest in U.S. companies, primarily larger ones. This fund, however, would actually be more appropriately called the Warburg Pincus Global Growth fund, since this fund had invested about 20 percent overseas and 40 percent in small company stocks in the spring of 1994.

The average growth and income pays dividends of around 3 percent, whereas this fund pays only 0.2 percent. Thus, a huge amount of this fund must be focused on relatively growth-oriented, rather than dividend-oriented, securities.

As with the Strong Short-Term Bond fund, the Warburg Pincus Global Growth (I mean Growth and Income) fund is not a bad fund. But it's hardly as superior as the ad implies.

Some mutual funds choose comparative benchmarks for the sole purpose of making themselves look good. More than a few investment advisors who manage money in a variety of mutual funds do the same, as you'll learn in Chapter 19. In Chapter 11, I discuss relevant benchmarks for different types of funds.

Fund Manager and Fund Family Expertise

Much is made of who manages a specific mutual fund. Although the individual fund manager is important, a manager is not an island unto himself. The resources and capabilities of the parent company are equally important.

For example, the departure of a portfolio manager with a good track record usually makes headlines. Peter Lynch's departure from the Fidelity Magellan fund is a good example. Some analysts said, "The star is gone. Dump the fund." Now, if you were managing Fidelity's mutual funds, wouldn't you put another capable manager at the helm of the Magellan fund? Of course you would — you're not in mourning, and you're not stupid. And that's why Magellan has done just fine since Lynch's departure. Fidelity is an outstanding company in terms of its capability at managing money in U.S. stock funds. It has a pool of talented managers to draw upon when one manager leaves the firm or moves to another fund.

Different companies have different capabilities and levels of expertise with different types of funds. Vanguard, for example, is terrific at money market, bond, and conservative stock funds, thanks to their low operating expenses. Fidelity has a ton of experience and success with investing in U.S. stocks.

A fund company has more or less experience than others not only from the direct management of certain fund types but also by "hiring out." For example, some fund families contract with private money management firms that have significant experience.

In other cases, private money management firms with long histories in money management offer mutual funds. If you look at their mutual fund assets, you might think they are small players. Examples of firms like this include PIMCO bond funds, Neuberger & Berman, Warburg Pincus, and Dodge & Cox.

Warning Signs for (Likely) Loser Funds

You've seen how a star fund can flare for its moment of investor glory and then easily twinkle down to become just another average or worse-than-average fund. An unfortunate fact of the human condition is that more than a few people want to believe that a chosen few, in each field of endeavor, can walk on water and achieve extraordinary performance. In sports, in the entertainment world, even in business, some like to think that everything revolves around a few superhumans.

It's true that those who are best at what they do are better than the average performer and vastly superior to the worse. In the investment and mutual fund arena, however, the gap between the best and the average (assuming an apples-to-apples comparison) over longer time periods is incredibly small.

If the stocks of U.S. large companies, for example, have advanced 13 percent per year over a decade, the money manager focusing on such securities may vault to god-like status if his fund earns 15 percent per year investing in such securities. Don't get me wrong: an extra 2 percent per year ain't nothin' to sneeze at — especially if you've got 5 or 10 million bucks to invest. Compounded over a decade, an additional 2 percent return would mean that you end up with an extra 22 percent return on your investment (before taxes). On $10 million, that's $2.2 million — at least enough for that ranch in Montana you've always wanted. But how will you know who the next star will be?

We can try to pick the stars, but there's actually far more value — and far greater likelihood that you are right — in avoiding the losers. It's not hard at all for you to avoid loser funds, whether they're big losers, little losers, or run-of-the-mill losers. All you have to do is follow these few simple rules with maniacal and religious zeal:

➤ **Avoid funds with high annual operating fees.** How high is high? Depends on the type of fund, but you should *never* own a money market or bond fund that charges more than 0.5 percent per year, a U.S. stock fund that charges more than 1 percent per year, or an international or specialty fund that charges more than 1.3 percent per year. Steel yourself against clever marketing brochures and charming salespeople. Read the fine print and walk the other way.

➤ **Avoid fund companies with little mutual fund management experience and success.** If you need surgery, would you rather turn your body over to a surgeon who has successfully performed this operation hundreds of times — or to a rookie who has only seen it on the local cable station and tried it out on his cat?

➤ **Avoid novelty funds.** Mutual funds have been around for decades. Yet not a week goes by without some newfangled fund coming out with a new concept. Some of these ideas come out of the fund company's marketing department, which in some companies has too much clout. Rather than come up with investments that meet investors' needs, they come up with gimmicky funds that involve extra risk and that almost always cost extra in their high annual operating expenses.

Prospectuses

Securities laws require all funds to issue a *prospectus.* The U.S. Securities and Exchange Commission reviews every last fund (which probably keeps plenty of coffee and eyeglass companies in business). Prospectuses are usually written by very expensive lawyers who wouldn't know a lively and comprehensible sentence if it hit them on the head with a law dictionary. You can safely skip most of what's said in any prospectus, but prospectuses do contain a few things you should check out.

The most valuable information — the fund's investment objectives, costs, and performance history — is summarized in the first few pages of the prospectus. Read these. Skip most of the rest. The rest only tells you more than you could possibly want to know about how the fund is administered. Do you really want to know whether employees are paid monthly or weekly? Which brand of computers they recently bought for the accounting department? Which pizza place they call for late-night deliveries? I don't think so.

Because prospectuses are positively lethal in their tediousness, let me suggest a friendlier alternative: just jump ahead to the fund recommendations in Chapters 6 to 9 of this very book.

In the pages that follow, I'll walk you through the more useful and relevant parts of a typical prospectus for one of Vanguard's funds, the Vanguard Wellesley Income Fund.

Cover page

Some prospectuses (though not this one) describe more than one fund in a particular fund family. This can save a fund company's printing and mailing charges where they have funds with very similar investment objectives and/or funds managed under the same management.

As I said before, it's dangerous to select a fund just because someone says it's good. This particular fund, for example, pays a high level of taxable dividends. That means that this fund most likely is not suitable for you if you're investing money outside a tax-sheltered retirement account and are in a higher tax bracket.

The information on the first page is duplicated inside the prospectus, but the page provides a synopsis of pertinent facts (see Figure 3-2). The prospectus is dated so that you know how recent its information is. Don't sweat it if the prospectus is a number of months old; in general, fund companies update prospectuses annually. Phone numbers are handy to have in case you forget or lose them. What applications do you need to establish an account, and how much money do you need to open an account?

The table of contents is a sure sign the prospectus is too long — but then lawyers (the people who wrote this prospectus) seldom use one word where 50 will work as well. The table of contents helps you navigate the prospectus for whatever information you want. To illustrate here, I cover only the first few pages of this prospectus; they're the pages that contain the best stuff, anyway.

Vanguard
WELLESLEY
INCOME FUND

A Member of The Vanguard Group

PROSPECTUS—April 13, 1994

NEW ACCOUNT INFORMATION: Investor Information Department—1-800-662-7447 (SHIP)

SHAREHOLDER ACCOUNT SERVICES: Client Services Department—1-800-662-2739 (CREW)

INVESTMENT OBJECTIVES & POLICIES	Vanguard/Wellesley Income Fund, Inc. (the "Fund") is an open-end diversified investment company that seeks to provide as much current income as is consistent with reasonable risk. The Fund also offers the potential for moderate growth of capital. The Fund invests primarily in U.S. Government and corporate fixed income securities of investment grade quality and dividend-paying common stocks. There is no assurance that the Fund will achieve its stated objectives.
OPENING AN ACCOUNT	To open a regular (non-retirement) account, please complete and return the Account Registration Form. If you need assistance in completing this Form, please call the Investor Information Department. To open an Individual Retirement Account (IRA), please use a Vanguard IRA Adoption Agreement. To obtain a copy of this form, call 1-800-662-7447, Monday through Friday, from 8:00 a.m. to 8:00 p.m. (Eastern time). The minimum initial investment is $3,000 ($500 for Individual Retirement Accounts and Uniform Gifts/Transfers to Minors Act accounts). The Fund is offered on a no-load basis (i.e., there are no sales commissions or 12b-1 fees). However, the Fund incurs expenses for investment advisory, management, administrative, and distribution services.
ABOUT THIS PROSPECTUS	This Prospectus is designed to set forth concisely the information you should know about the Fund before you invest. It should be retained for future reference. A "Statement of Additional Information" containing additional information about the Fund has been filed with the Securities and Exchange Commission. This Statement is dated April 13, 1994, and has been incorporated by reference into this Prospectus. It may be obtained, without charge, by writing to the Fund or by calling the Investor Information Department.

TABLE OF CONTENTS

Figure 3-2:
The cover page starts you off right.

THESE SECURITIES HAVE NOT BEEN APPROVED OR DISAPPROVED BY THE SECURITIES AND EXCHANGE COMMISSION OR ANY STATE SECURITIES COMMISSION, NOR HAS THE SECURITIES AND EXCHANGE COMMISSION OR ANY STATE COMMISSION PASSED UPON THE ACCURACY OR ADEQUACY OF THIS PROSPECTUS. ANY REPRESENTATION TO THE CONTRARY IS A CRIMINAL OFFENSE.

Source: The Vanguard Group

Fund expenses

Thankfully, funds are required to present, in a standardized format (see Figure 3-3), the costs you'll incur for the privilege of owning their fund. The first list of expenses shows *transaction fees*, the fees you pay when you buy and sell shares. These fees are deducted at the time a transaction occurs; unfortunately, they're rarely itemized. A no-load fund such as the Wellesley Income Fund does not charge any sales commissions.

FUND EXPENSES

The following table illustrates all expenses and fees that you would incur as a shareholder of the Fund. The expenses and fees set forth below are for the 1993 fiscal year.

Shareholder Transaction Expenses

Sales Load Imposed on Purchases	None
Sales Load Imposed on Reinvested Dividends	None
Redemption Fees	None
Exchange Fees	None

Annual Fund Operating Expenses

Management & Administrative Expenses		0.21%
Investment Advisory Fees		0.08
12b-1 Fees		None
Other Expenses		
Distribution Costs	0.02%	
Miscellaneous Expenses	0.02	
Total Other Expenses		0.04
Total Operating Expenses		**0.33%**

The purpose of this table is to assist you in understanding the various costs and expenses that you would bear directly or indirectly as an investor in the Fund.

The following example illustrates the expenses that you would incur on a $1,000 investment over various periods, assuming (1) a 5% annual rate of return and (2) redemption at the end of each period. As noted in the table above, the Fund charges no redemption fees of any kind.

1 Year	3 Years	5 Years	10 Years
$3	$11	$19	$42

This example should not be considered a representation of past or future expenses or performance. Actual expenses may be higher or lower than those shown.

Figure 3-3:
Fund
expenses.

Source: The Vanguard Group

If a so-called financial advisor is pitching a fund but you're not sure if they get paid for selling you the fund, always, always, *always* get a prospectus and check out the fund expenses section. That way, you can see if commissions will erode your returns. In this case you would see that if an advisor recommended this fund, he or she is not being paid any commission — always a good sign. See the example earlier in the chapter of a typical load-fund fee table.

As discussed earlier in the chapter, operating expenses are the fees that are charged on a continuous basis for all mutual funds. In this case, they total a reasonable 0.33% Because these fees are deducted from the fund's returns before your returns are paid to you, lower operating expenses translate into higher returns for you. These fees cover the expenses of running a fund and include profits for the fund.

Financial highlights

If you get a headache looking at all these numbers, you're not alone. Figure 3-4 looks forbidding, but this table is just a yearly summary of the value of the fund's shares and the distributions the fund has made (I cover these subjects in detail in Chapters 11 and 12).

The *Net Asset Value* (NAV) is the price per share of the fund. Tracking this value is a *terrible* measure of what you would have earned in the fund. Why? Just look at the distributions section that details all the money paid out to shareholders each year. This fund has paid out total distributions of $14.46 per share over this ten-year period. This per-share figure is an enormous amount when you consider that the share price has only increased from $12.66 to $19.24 during the period — a modest 52 percent increase. But if you add in the distributions

FINANCIAL HIGHLIGHTS

The following financial highlights for a share outstanding throughout each period, insofar as they relate to each of the five years in the period ended December 31, 1993, have been audited by Price Waterhouse, independent accountants, whose report thereon was unqualified. This information should be read in conjunction with the Fund's financial statements and notes thereto, which are incorporated by reference in the Statement of Additional Information and in this Prospectus, and which appear, along with the report of Price Waterhouse, in the Fund's 1993 Annual Report to Shareholders. For a more complete discussion of the Fund's performance, please see the Fund's 1993 Annual Report to Shareholders which may be obtained without charge by writing to the Fund or by calling our Investor Information Department at 1-800-662-7447.

	Year Ended December 31,									
	1993	1992	1991	1990	1989	1988	1987	1986	1985	1984
Net Asset Value, Beginning of Year	$18.16	$18.08	$16.02	$16.82	$15.26	$14.57	$16.27	$15.31	$13.28	$12.66
Investment Operations										
Net Investment Income	1.14	1.21	1.27	1.30	1.32	1.23	1.24	1.33	1.38	1.37
Net Realized and Unrealized Gain (Loss) on Investments	1.48	.29	2.06	(.72)	1.79	.69	(1.52)	1.43	2.13	.62
Total from Investment Operations	2.62	1.50	3.33	.58	3.11	1.92	(.28)	2.76	3.51	1.99
Distributions										
Dividends from Net Investment Income	(1.14)	(1.21)	(1.27)	(1.30)	(1.31)	(1.23)	(1.04)	(1.33)	(1.38)	(1.37)
Distributions from Realized Capital Gains	(.40)	(.21)	—	(.08)	(.24)	—	(.38)	(.47)	(.10)	—
Total Distributions	(1.54)	(1.42)	(1.27)	(1.38)	(1.55)	(1.23)	(1.42)	(1.80)	(1.48)	(1.37)
Net Asset Value, End of Year	$19.24	$18.16	$18.08	$16.02	$16.82	$15.26	$14.57	$16.27	$15.31	$13.28
Total Return	14.65%	8.67%	21.57%	3.76%	20.93%	13.61%	(1.92)%	18.34%	27.41%	16.64%
Ratios/Supplemental Data										
Net Assets, End of Year (Millions)	$6,011	$3,178	$1,934	$1,022	$788	$567	$495	$510	$224	$115
Ratio of Expenses to Average Net Assets	.33%	.35%	.40%	.45%	.45%	.51%	.49%	.58%	.60%	.71%
Ratio of Net Investment Income to Average Net Assets	5.79%	6.50%	7.08%	7.77%	7.68%	8.14%	7.83%	7.74%	9.36%	10.68%
Portfolio Turnover Rates:										
Common Stocks	26%	16%	19%	12%	10%	19%	27%	18%	32%	35%
Bonds	18%	24%	34%	23%	11%	21%	48%	39%	14%	37%

Figure 3-4: Financial highlights.

Source: The Vanguard Group

to the change in share price, now you're talking about a 166 percent increase (if you had reinvested these distributions, you would have had an even greater return).

Presenting the NAV on line one might strike you as odd and deceptive. If it does, talk to the fund regulators at the SEC to understand why they think this sort of presentation makes sense. It would make more sense to put the total return numbers here.

The total return is an important number since it represents what investors in the fund have earned historically. The returns on this type of fund, which invests in stocks and bonds, bounce around from year to year.

You can see how the total investments (*net assets*) in the fund have changed over time. Assets can increase from new money flowing into the fund as well as from an increase in the value of a fund's shares.

This section of a prospectus also shows you how a fund's annual operating expenses have changed over time. They should decrease when a fund like this one has grown. If operating expenses do not decrease, their persistence may signal a company that maximizes its profits because of the fund's popularity. For funds only a few years old, expenses may remain higher because the fund is building its base of investors.

The *investment income ratio* represents the annual dividends or yield that the fund has paid. (This figure is especially important for retired people, who need income to live on.) In this example, the downward trend merely reflects the overall decline in interest rates during the period. If you looked at this ratio for a similar fund, you would see the same trend for this period. It's not Vanguard's fault that income has gone down. This has happened because of the reduction in interest rates over most of this period.

Turnover measures the amount of trading taking place in a fund. High numbers, such as 100 percent plus, indicate a fund manager who shifts things around alot. Rapid trading is riskier and may increase the taxable distributions that a fund produces.

Investment objectives and policies

The first section, on objectives, explains what the fund is trying to do (see Figure 3-5). The Wellesley Income Fund is an open-end fund, which means that the fund will issue however many shares the fund has buyers for (as opposed to a closed-end fund, where only a fixed number of shares are issued and traded; see Chapter 2 for more details on the difference). For its goal, the Wellesley Income Fund is seeking both current income and moderate growth of capital with much greater emphasis on income. It's trying to accomplish these objectives by investing in bonds (fixed-income securities) and common stocks (large, blue-chip companies) that pay decent dividends.

The investment policies or objectives can be thought of as a broad set of "rules" or guidelines (for example, the major type of securities the fund invests in) that the fund operates under when investing your money. This hopefully protects you from most major surprises. And if a fund violates these guidelines — for instance, if this fund puts all its money into international stocks — the SEC would spank, reprimand, and penalize Vanguard. Less ethical fund companies may be willing to pay this "small price" if they can seduce more people into their fund by jacking up returns by taking poorly disclosed risks.

INVESTMENT OBJECTIVES The Fund seeks to provide a current income and moderate capital growth	The Fund is an open-end diversified investment company. The objective of the Fund is to provide as much current income as is consistent with reasonable risk. The Fund also offers the potential for moderate growth of capital. The Fund invests primarily in U.S. Government and corporate fixed income securities of investment grade quality and dividend-paying common stocks. There is no assurance that the Fund will achieve its stated objectives.
INVESTMENT POLICIES The Fund invests in bonds and common stocks	Fund invests in fixed income securities and dividend-paying common stocks. Under normal circumstances, it is expected that fixed income securities will represent approximately 60% of the Fund's net assets. The remainder of the Fund's assets will be invested primarily in common stocks chosen largely for their income characteristics. The Fund will invest at least 65% of its assets in income-producing securities under normal circumstances. The Fund is managed without regard to tax ramifications.
	The fixed income securities owned by the Fund will include U.S. Government and corporate bonds and mortgage-backed securities (such as Government National Mortgage Association pass-through certificates), as well as bonds or preferred stocks which are convertible into common stock. Fixed income securities will be primarily of investment grade quality—i.e., those rated at least Baa by Moody's Investors Service, Inc. or BBB by Standard & Poor's Corporation.
	The mix of bonds and stocks held by the Fund may be varied from time-to-time depending on the investment adviser's assessment of business, economic and investment conditions. However, fixed income securities can be expected to represent the majority of the Fund's assets so long as the general level of interest rates remains well in excess of dividend yields available on common stocks.
*	In addition to investing in fixed income securities and dividend-paying common stocks, the Fund may also invest in certain short-term fixed income securities as cash reserves. The Fund is also authorized to invest in stock and bond futures contracts and options to a limited extent. See "Implementation of Policies" for a description of these and other investment practices of the Fund.
	The investment objectives and policies of the Fund are not fundamental and so may be changed by the Board of Directors without shareholder approval. However, shareholders would be notified prior to a material change in either.

Figure 3-5:
Investment objectives and policies.

Source: The Vanguard Group

*Note that this fund, like almost all others, may invest some money in futures and options. Most funds, like this one, use these sparingly and generally do it to reduce risk (see Chapter 14 for how to get more details about a fund's investment practices with these riskier securities).

Investment risks

If you've taken the time to look at how much money this fund has made for investors, you owe it to yourself to understand this fund's risks, too. This prospectus does an excellent job of discussing the Wellesley Income Fund's risks, using examples from earlier in this century rather than just from the past ten years, which were unusually good years for the financial markets (see Figure 3-6).

If you're investing for a short period of time, say for only a few months, this section would steer you clear of this fund.

INVESTMENT RISKS

The Fund is subject to interest rate and stock market risk

Like any investment program, the Fund entails certain risks. The Fund is subject to the risk that bond or stock prices will decline during short or even extended periods.

The Fund is expected to invest the preponderance of its assets (63% as of December 31, 1993) in longer-term fixed income securities, such as government and corporate bonds. Bond prices are influenced primarily by changes in the level of interest rates. When interest rates rise, bond prices generally fall; conversely, when interest rates fall, bond prices generally rise. While bonds normally fluctuate less than stocks, there have been extended periods of increases in interest rates that have caused significant price declines. For example, bond prices fell 48% from December 1976 to September 1981. The risk of bond holdings declining in value, however, may be offset in whole or in part by the high level of income that bonds provide.

A smaller portion of the Fund's assets will be invested in stocks (37% of assets as of December 31, 1993). The stock market tends to be cyclical, with periods when stock prices generally rise and periods when stock prices generally decline. During the period from 1926 to 1993, stocks have provided a positive annual rate of return (capital change plus income) of +12.3%, as measured by the Standard & Poor's 500 Composite Stock Price Index (the "S&P 500 Index"). This level of return can be used as a guide for setting reasonable expectations for future stock market returns, but may not be useful for forecasting future returns in any particular period, as stock returns are quite volatile from year-to-year. For example, in the period from 1926 to 1993, the range of annual returns on the S&P 500 Index was +53.9% to –43.3%. Over longer-term holding periods, stocks tend to be less volatile. For five-year periods since 1926, the annualized rates of return for the S&P 500 Index ranged from +23.9% to –12.5%.

In large part, the common stocks held by the Fund will be selected for their current income and potential growth in income. The aggregate characteristics of such stocks will tend to be quite different from those exhibited by the S&P 500 Index. As a result, investors should anticipate that the common stocks in the Fund may perform differently than those in the Index.

Bond and stock prices may tend to move differently. For instance, bond prices may rise when stock prices fall. As a "balanced" mutual fund investing in bonds and stocks, the Fund may be expected to entail less risk than a mutual fund investing solely in common stocks or solely in bonds.

From the Fund's inception on July 1, 1970 to December 31, 1993, the Fund has provided an average annual return of +11.7%. During this period, the Fund has experienced 20 years of positive returns and three years of negative returns. Annual returns have ranged from +27.4% to –6.4%. These return characteristics are provided to illustrate the risks and returns that the Fund has provided in the past and may not be indicative of future results.

Figure 3-6
Investment
risks.

Source: The Vanguard Group

Statement of additional information

The statement of additional information contains more details about the fund, such as the types of securities and investment strategies it will employ. If you want the statement of additional information, you gotta ask for it; the company won't automatically send it to you along with a fund's prospectus.

This report will give you other juicy tidbits, too — such as how much the fund's directors and officers were paid for their work with this fund, or how much in total brokerage fees the fund has paid. **Note:** As I mentioned earlier in the chapter (in the little section on "Operating expenses"), a fund's total brokerage expenses is the one cost that is not included in a fund's reported annual operating expense ratio.

Annual Reports

Funds also produce annual reports that discuss how the fund has been doing and provide details on the specific investments that a fund holds. Look here if, for instance, you want to know which countries an international fund currently is invested in.

You can get answers to questions like that one by calling a fund's 800 number. Some of the mutual fund information sources recommended in Chapter 14 also report this type of information. Or you could say, "Details, details. Just tell me what funds to buy for different needs." That's just what is done in Chapters 6 to 9.

In this section, I'll review the pages from the annual report on the Vanguard Wellesley Income Fund, the same fund whose prospectus I just introduced you to. In addition to producing an annual report, each fund produces a semiannual report that (guess what?) comes out halfway between annual reports. The semiannual reports are usually a bit shorter than the full-year reports. Their advantage over the previous annual report is that they contain the most up-to-date information on the fund's current investment holdings and performance.

When you call a fund company to ask for applications, you specifically request a fund's recent annual or semi-annual reports. Unlike with a prospectus, most funds don't automatically send annual reports along.

Chairman's letter

The "Chairman's Letter" is supposed to explain how well the fund has performed recently and why (see Figure 3-7). In far too many reports, the fund's chief executive uses his or her letter to the stockholders merely as an opportunity to overhype how well the fund has done — during *good* periods in the financial markets. In tougher times, too many fund execs blame subpar performance on the market. It's like fishing. On a successful day, you talk about your uncanny casting ability, your brilliant choice of lures, and your ability to keep still and quiet. When you come home empty-handed, the fish just weren't biting.

 CHAIRMAN'S LETTER

Fellow Shareholder:

With a "double-digit" total return of +14.6% during 1993, Vanguard/Wellesley Income Fund enjoyed yet another year of excellent performance. Overall, it was a fine year for bonds and, as it happened, a pretty good year for stocks. Our income-oriented strategy enabled us to capitalize on the best elements of both markets.

The table that follows compares the Fund's total return (capital change plus income) with the returns of the two unmanaged indexes of the markets in which we invest: for bonds, the Salomon Brothers High-Grade Bond Index; for stocks, the Standard & Poor's 500 Composite Stock Price Index. Over the past year, bonds represented about 65% of our portfolio and stocks the remaining 35%. We are pleased to have handily beaten both Indexes during the past year.

	Total Return Year Ended December 31, 1993
Vanguard/Wellesley Income Fund	+14.6%
Salomon Brothers High-Grade Bond Index	+13.2%
Standard & Poor's 500 Stock Index	+10.1

The Fund's total return is based on net asset values of $18.16 per share on December 31, 1992, and $19.24 on December 31, 1993, with the latter figure adjusted to take into account our four quarterly dividends totaling $1.14 per share from net investment income and two distributions totaling $.40 per share from net realized capital gains, which largely resulted from our operations during the past twelve months. (I would note that, in March 1994, the Fund will be making a distribution of about $.05 per share from net capital gains realized from 1993 operations, but taxable to shareholders in 1994.) Wellesley's annualized dividend yield at December 31, 1993, was 5.7%.

■ **THE FINANCIAL MARKETS IN 1993**
As noted at the outset, bonds—which have consistently composed the predominant portion of

our portfolio—gave a great account of themselves during the past year. The yield on long-term corporate bonds opened the year at 8.0%; within a few weeks, corporate yields began to drop swiftly, resulting in a dramatic rally in bond prices. By the end of February, yields had fallen to 7.5%, reflected in a 6% increase in the price of the average long-term corporate bond. The rally in prices continued apace—with a few interruptions—through the end of the year, when the yield touched 7.3%, engendering an additional 2% price gain.

This sharp rate decline seemed to be driven by continuing evidence that inflation remained under control. The U.S. consumer price index (CPI) increased 2.7% during 1993, down from 2.9% in 1992. As a result, despite the decline in interest rates, "real" yields (nominal yields less the inflation rate) on long-term bonds remain at healthy levels.

Since one factor that investors consider in setting their asset allocations is the relative yield of stocks versus bonds, lower bond yields provided impetus to stock prices. During 1993, the dividend yield on stocks (as measured by the Standard & Poor's 500 Index) declined marginally, from 2.8%

Figure 3-7: Chairman's letter.

Source: The Vanguard Group

A good annual report like Vanguard's will detail the performance of the fund and compare it to relevant benchmarks and comparable funds. You hope that your fund will meet or exceed the performance of comparable funds (and perhaps even of the benchmark, too) in most periods. Don't worry if your fund periodically underperforms a little. Especially with stock and bond funds, you're investing for the long haul, not just for six months or a year.

Unfortunately, more than a few fund companies use benchmarks (indexes) as comparisons for their funds' performance so that their funds look as if they performed better than they really did. (Such as the Warburg Pincus Growth & Income fund, discussed earlier, comparing itself to the S&P 500 Index of large company U.S. stocks despite the fact that this fund had much of its assets invested overseas and in small company U.S. stocks). This ruse is similar to a financially savvy adult like, say, me comparing his mutual fund selection abilities to those of, say, a child. I'm at something of an unfair advantage (at any rate, I'd better be). As you review a fund's annual report, keep in mind this tendency of some funds to fudge comparisons. I'll discuss ways you can make sure that you're comparing a fund's performance to an appropriate benchmark in Chapter 11.

In addition to discussing the fund's performance during the year, an annual report also covers how the overall financial markets were feeling. If you're used to a steady diet of the daily news, an overview like this can help you to better see and understand the big picture (and maybe you won't be so shocked that the fund lost 2 percent last year when you see that the benchmark index most relevant to that fund lost 2.5 percent).

Performance discussion

A good annual report is educational and honest. Vanguard's is both. Note that rather than taking credit for their shrewd investment decisions, Vanguard tells you that the overall market environment favored the exact types of securities that this fund is chartered to invest in (see Figure 3-8). Such a lack of self-promotion and focus on an objective assessment of market realities is not common in the investment world.

The report also does a nice job providing a historical context for understanding this fund's performance. It explains that bonds normally are less volatile than stocks. The comparative stability of bonds means that a portfolio composed of stocks *and* bonds, like this one, is less volatile than one made up of just stocks.

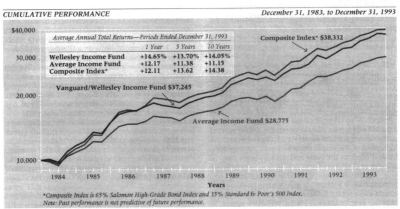

CUMULATIVE PERFORMANCE   December 31, 1983, to December 31, 1993

Average Annual Total Returns—Periods Ended December 31, 1993			
	1 Year	5 Years	10 Years
Wellesley Income Fund	+14.65%	+13.70%	+14.05%
Average Income Fund	+12.17	+11.38	+11.15
Composite Index*	+12.11	+13.62	+14.38

Composite Index* $38,332

Vanguard/Wellesley Income Fund $37,245

Average Income Fund $28,775

*Composite Index is 65% Salomon High-Grade Bond Index and 35% Standard & Poor's 500 Index.
Note: Past performance is not predictive of future performance.

■ WELLESLEY INCOME FUND IN 1993

We are of course pleased that we outpaced both of the market indexes that we use as benchmarks for our performance. At year-end 1993, bonds (including a small position in short-term reserves) composed about 63% of the Fund's net assets and stocks about 37%. A similarly weighted "index portfolio" would have enjoyed a return of +12.0%, *before* the deduction of any operating expenses or portfolio transaction costs. Our return of +14.6%, *after* taking into account such expenses and costs, was clearly a signal accomplishment.

Unlike the "paper world" of market indexes, the "real world" is reflected in our second performance benchmark: the average income mutual fund. As a group, our peers turned in a return of +12.2%, giving us a comparative advantage of more than two percentage points. This margin was engendered by both our bond strategy and our stock strategy.

On the bond side, not only do we have a larger commitment to bonds (61% of net assets at year-end versus 56% for our competitors), but we generally hold longer maturities. In the declining interest rate environment of 1993, "longer was stronger" in terms of performance. I would also note that we maintain a much higher quality bond portfolio than our competitors, with 100% of our bond position rated "investment grade" (AAA to BBB) compared to just 75% on average for our peers.

On the equity side, our 37% position (including 2% in convertible preferreds) at year-end compared with but 29% for our peers. With value stocks—including the yield-oriented stocks we emphasize—giving such a good account of themselves during the year, our larger position was a positive factor. In addition, we were more heavily invested in the high-performing utility and energy sectors of the market (about 50% of our stock position compared to 34% for our competitors) and were under-represented in two of the year's poorer-performing market sectors—health and consumer staples—which represented but 9% of our stock position compared to a 17% position for our competitors.

You may be wondering about our math! Wellesley's combined bond and stock commitment totals 98% of net assets; for our competitors, the total is but 85%. The remaining 2% segment of our net assets was invested in short-term reserves. For our competitors, their remaining 15% of net assets included cash reserves (7%), convertible bonds (5%), and "other" (3%), whatever exactly that may include. In other words, the portfolios of other income-oriented mutual funds are a sort of "mixed bag" and, in the final analysis, difficult to evaluate relative to our "plain vanilla" bond-stock strategy.

To give you a more detailed evaluation of the year's fine results, a report from the Fund's investment adviser, Wellington Management Company, is presented on pages 7 and 8.

Figure 3-8: Performance discussion.

Source: The Vanguard Group

■ A TEN-YEAR PERSPECTIVE

Investors should place only so much weight on *any* mutual fund's results during a single year. It is the long-term record that really matters. The chart at the top of this page shows our cumulative total returns over the past decade, compared with the returns of our composite market index (65% Salomon High-Grade Bond Index and 35% Standard & Poor's 500 Stock Index), as well as those of the average income mutual fund. This table presents the results.

	Total Return Ten Years Ended December 31, 1993	
	Cumulative	Annual Rate
Wellesley Income Fund	+272%	**+14.1%**
Average Income Fund	+188%	**+11.1%**
Composite Index*	+283	**+14.4**

**The annual rates of return for the Salomon Bond Index and S&P 500 Stock Index, respectively, were +14.0% and +14.9%.*

I should emphasize that these returns reflect past performance, and are in no way intended as an indication of the results that the Fund, the average income fund, or the bond and stock indexes may achieve in the future.

In the competitive world of mutual fund performance, it is of course gratifying to have churned out such a substantial cumulative margin over our peer group (+272% for Wellesley versus +188% for the competitors) during this period. It is also, to some degree at least, gratifying to virtually match the cumulative return of our Composite Index. While Wellesley fell slightly short of this hurdle, I would add that any market index is *always* a tough "bogey," not only because it operates in a theoretical world bereft of the frictional costs of investing, but also because any index used for comparative purposes inevitably has significant structural differences from those of any given mutual fund. In Wellesley's case, for example, the bond index normally has longer-term maturities than the Fund; the stock index includes growth stocks as well as yield stocks. Sometimes these disparities will favor the Fund, as they did in 1993, sometimes not.

Since Wellesley is, after all, an income-oriented mutual fund, it is important to consider, well, income. During 1993, in part because of our emphasis on high-quality bonds, our *gross* income yield was 6.1% of assets. For our peers, reaching out a bit, in our view, for higher yields at the expense of quality, the *gross* yield was 7.2%. But on a *net* yield basis, despite our quality "handicap," our income yield was 5.8%, virtually identical with the 6.0% yield of our competitors. Shareholders, to state the obvious, receive income dividends based on a fund's net yield.

The difference between a fund's *gross* yield and *net* yield is, of course, accounted for by its expenses. Our competitive net yield comes after the deduction of an expense ratio of 0.33%; for our competitors, the expense ratio averaged 1.20%—almost four times as large as ours. Put another way, our competitors' costs consumed nearly 17% of gross income; for Wellesley Income Fund, costs consumed but 5% of gross income. Particularly for investors seeking an optimal blend of high net yield and high portfolio quality, one of the most rewarding aspects of investing in Wellesley Income Fund is our low expense ratio. As far as we can tell, our expenses are by far the lowest among our entire field of competitors.

Figure 3-9:
Long-term performance discussion.

Source: The Vanguard Group

You also see a description of how this fund invested its money during 1993. You can see that Wellesley had 61 percent of its fund invested in bonds, whereas other income-oriented funds invested 56 percent of their shareholders' money in bonds. The comparisons to "competitors" help you make sure that you're comparing your fund to Wellesley's true peers — apples to apples.

These comparisons are even more valuable and useful when applied over longer periods, as in this annual report's "Ten-Year Perspective" section (see Figure 3-9). Remember: in the world of stocks and bonds, one year is too short a period to evaluate a fund. In this section, the chairman also looks forward and prudently reminds us that the future will likely contain both good and bad periods.

In Figure 3-10 you can see how Wellesley performed against its competitors' "average income funds" and the benchmark "composite index." Wellesley beat the pants off of its competition, but ever so slightly underperformed — by just 0.3 percent per year — the benchmark index. The "Composite Index" is a mythical investment, which has the advantage of not having any costs deducted from it.

Figure 3-10:
Comparative
performance.

	Total Return	
	Ten Years Ended December 31, 1993	
	Cumulative	Annual Rate
Wellesley Income Fund	+272%	+14.1%
Average Income Fund	+188%	+11.1%
Composite Index*	+283	+14.4

*The annual rates of return for the Salomon Bond Index and S&P 500 Stock Index, respectively, were +14.0% and +14.9%.

Source: The Vanguard Group

Performance and its components

This page looks like a terrible overload of numbers, but it actually contains valuable information (see Figure 3-11).

For example, this table shows you, on a year-by-year basis, how the Wellesley Income Fund has performed. As the table shows you, although the fund has produced an *average* annual return of 11.7 percent per year, its return varies much from year to year. In 1986, for instance, it returned 18.3 percent — but then lost 1.9 percent in the next year. (If a swing in returns such as in this example makes you reach for your motion sickness prescription, better skip investing in it. Remember, to earn better returns, you gotta take risk.)

TOTAL INVESTMENT RETURN

This table illustrates the results of an investment in *Vanguard/Wellesley Income Fund* during the period from July 1, 1970, to December 31, 1993. During this period, stock and bond prices fluctuated widely. The results shown should not be considered as a representation of the dividend income or capital gain or loss that may be realized from an investment made in the Fund today.

Year ended December 31	All Income Dividends and Capital Gain Distributions in Cash			Dividends in Cash: Capital Gain Distributions Reinvested		All Dividends and Capital Gain Distributions Reinvested			
	Net Asset Value	Annual Capital Gain Distributions	Annual Income Dividends	Net Asset Value	Annual Income Dividends	Net Asset Value	Capital Return	Income Return	Total Return
Initial (7/70)	$11.66	—	—	$11.66	—	$ 11.66	—	—	—
1970	12.03	—	$ .46	12.03	$ .46	12.49	+ 3.2%	+ 3.9%	+ 7.1%
1971	12.56	$ .38	.85	12.94	.85	14.37	+ 7.6	+ 7.4	+15.0
1972	12.66	.26	.82	13.31	.84	15.77	+ 2.9	+ 6.9	+ 9.8
1973	11.40	—	.83	11.99	.87	15.22	−10.0	+ 6.5	− 3.5
1974	9.84	—	.82	10.35	.86	14.24	−13.7	+ 7.3	− 6.4
1975	10.69	—	.82	11.24	.86	16.73	+ 8.6	+ 8.9	+17.5
1976	12.23	—	.88	12.86	.93	20.62	+14.4	+ 8.9	+23.3
1977	11.81	—	.93	12.42	.98	21.50	− 3.4	+ 7.7	+ 4.3
1978	11.27	—	.96	11.85	1.01	22.28	− 4.6	+ 8.1	+ 3.5
1979	10.98	—	1.00	11.54	1.05	23.66	− 2.6	+ 8.9	+ 6.3
1980	11.08	—	1.14	11.65	1.20	26.47	+ 0.9	+11.0	+11.9
1981	10.74	—	1.25	11.29	1.31	28.76	− 3.1	+11.8	+ 8.7
1982	11.82	—	1.26	12.43	1.32	35.46	+10.1	+13.2	+23.3
1983	12.66	—	1.31	13.31	1.38	42.06	+ 7.1	+11.5	+18.6
1984	13.28	—	1.37	13.96	1.44	49.06	+ 4.9	+11.7	+16.6
1985	15.31	.10	1.38	16.20	1.45	62.51	+16.0	+11.4	+27.4
1986	16.27	.47	1.33	17.70	1.41	73.97	+ 9.2	+ 9.1	+18.3
1987	14.57	.38	1.04	16.27	1.13	72.55	− 8.1	+ 6.2	− 1.9
1988	15.26	—	1.23	17.04	1.37	82.42	+ 4.7	+ 8.9	+13.6
1989	16.82	.24	1.31	19.05	1.46	99.67	+11.8	+ 9.1	+20.9
1990	16.02	.08	1.30	18.23	1.47	103.42	− 4.3	+ 8.1	+ 3.8
1991	18.08	—	1.27	20.58	1.45	125.73	+12.9	+ 8.7	+21.6
1992	18.16	.21	1.21	20.91	1.38	136.63	+ 1.6	+ 7.1	+ 8.7
1993	19.24	.40	1.14	22.62	1.31	156.64	+ 8.2	+ 6.4	+14.6
Total		$2.52	$25.91		$27.79				
Average Annual Total Return							+ 2.9%	+ 8.8%	+11.7%

Note: No adjustment has been made for income taxes payable by shareholders on reinvested income dividends and capital gains distributions.

Figure 3-11:
Total
Investment
Return.

Source: The Vanguard Group

You also can see how much the fund paid out in dividends and capital gains each year. I cover all of these details in Chapter 11 when I discuss a fund's returns.

Take note here that a fund's share price (the second column labeled "Net Asset Value") is a terrible barometer of how well the fund is rewarding you. For the Wellesley Income Fund, for example, since 1970 the share price has moved only from $11.66 per share to $19.24 at the end of 1993. These figures represent an annual return of a paltry 2.2 percent per year! But, as you'll see in Chapter 12, the change in the share price, or *net asset value* of a fund, is just one of three ways that you can earn money investing in a stock or bond mutual fund. The other two are through dividend and capital gains payments. (Money market funds earn you money only through paying dividends.)

Investment adviser's thoughts

The "Report From the Investment Adviser" is where the portfolio managers of the fund (in this case, the Wellington Management Group) explain as best they can how the economic environment affected the fund's performance. They also look ahead and discuss what the future may hold and what investment strategy they plan to take in the near future (see Figure 3-12).

REPORT FROM THE INVESTMENT ADVISER

During the second half of 1993, long-term interest rates fell to levels not seen in two decades. For the entire year, long-term Treasury yields declined more than one hundred basis points (1.00%). Largely because of this decline in rates, Vanguard/Wellesley Income Fund had a respectable absolute total return of +14.6%.

Due in part to the long average maturity of our bond position and in part to a meaningful weighting in interest-rate-sensitive stocks, the performance of Wellesley Income Fund is very sensitive to the general direction of interest rates. Nonetheless, the Fund maintained its traditional posture of 60% to 65% of assets invested in longer-term bonds of investment-grade quality, and 35% to 40% of assets invested in dividend-paying equities.

We seek to invest the equity portion of the Fund in the stocks of high-quality companies which we believe have the opportunity to maintain and grow their dividends over time. However, primarily because of declining interest rates, the Fund's dividend declined from the $1.21 earned in 1992 to $1.14 in 1993.

■ INVESTMENT OUTLOOK FOR 1994
The U.S. economy is improving in a measured and sustainable fashion. Inflation should remain subdued, although, with further economic growth, inflation expectations may begin to increase, which might prompt the Federal Reserve to raise interest rates. While the capital markets will anxiously monitor the Federal Reserve's resolve to prevent sharp increases in prices, we do not expect the anticipated modest rise in short-term rates to upset the stock market. In fact, a token gesture towards monetary restraint may encourage the stock market and the long-term bond market. Yield premiums for lower-rated bonds are likely to continue to shrink as the economy rebounds.

■ INVESTMENT STRATEGY IN 1994
Our strategy remains consistent with previous years. We will maintain our allocation to stocks at 35% to 40% of net assets. The dominant theme which guides the investment strategy for Wellesley Income Fund is our ongoing obligation to shareholders to achieve an attractive absolute level of income with high-quality securities. We do not invest in below-investment-grade bonds, nor do we buy stocks with ultra-high dividends, which may not be sustainable over the longer term.

Our long-term goal is to achieve increases in Wellesley's dividend by purchasing the stocks of strong, well-recognized companies which are able to pass along to shareholders the higher dividends generated from rising earnings spurred by successful business strategies. We expect to be able to obtain our objective of growing Wellesley's dividend when interest rates stabilize or increase.

The majority of Wellesley's stocks are New York Stock Exchange-listed issues and generally have above-average yields. We seek securities of well-financed companies with attractive growth prospects. Our largest sector concentrations are in the areas of utilities (12% of net assets) and finance companies (6%). However, the percentage invested in utility stocks was reduced by 3% during the last six months and is at its lowest point in at least eight years. The drop in interest rates over the last two years has pushed utility valuations up to unattractive levels.

Wellesley's common stocks sell at an average price/earnings ratio of 12.5 times our 1994 earnings estimates, substantially below the level of 16.4 times earnings that we estimate for the S&P 500 Index. The dividend yield of the Fund's equity holdings as of December 31, 1993, was 4.8%, which is 78% above the 2.7% yield of the S&P 500 Index.

The Fund's bond investments will continue to have a long average maturity, which should lend sustainability to the Fund's income stream. These assets currently have an average maturity of 15.9 years, an average coupon of 7.3%, and an average quality rating of "Aa." As rates fell during the year, we reduced gradually the average maturity. Over the long term, we still believe that high-quality, long-term bonds with call protection will provide reasonably attractive real (after inflation) returns. Mortgage-backed securities continue to represent the second largest sector of the bond portfolio. Despite

■ SUMMARY
After the large decline in rates last year, we do not envision achieving as strong a return in 1994 as we did in 1993. We will, however, employ the same investment disciplines in 1994 as have been followed by the Fund over the past two decades. In large part, we believe it is the solid consistency of this approach that has enabled us to achieve attractive results for shareholders.

Respectfully,

Earl E. McEvoy
Senior Vice President

John R. Ryan
Senior Vice President

Wellington Management Company

January 10, 1994

Figure 3-12: Investment adviser's thoughts.

Source: The Vanguard Group

Investment holdings

The "Statement of Net Assets" section lists every single solitary investment the fund owns. Here's where you get the details that tell you exactly where your money is invested. You can see here the incredible diversification your money gets in a mutual fund; you actually own a teeny, tiny sliver of each of these securities if you invest in this fund (see Figure 3-13).

STATEMENT OF NET ASSETS

FINANCIAL STATEMENTS

December 31, 1993

	Face Amount (000)	Market Value (000)†		Face Amount (000)	Market Value (000)†
CORPORATE BONDS (41.6%)			J. P. Morgan Co.		
Banks & Finance (10.2%)			5.75%, 10/15/08	$20,000	$18,739
Allstate Corp.			Morgan Guaranty Trust		
7.5%, 6/15/13	$20,000	$20,415	7.375%, 2/1/02	20,000	21,618
Associates Corp.			National City Cleveland Bank		
8.75%, 2/1/96	5,000	5,335	6.5%, 5/1/03	10,000	10,001
5.25%, 9/1/98	10,000	9,836	National City Corp.		
Banc One Corp.			8.375%, 3/15/96	5,000	5,354
8.74%, 9/15/03	5,000	5,797	NationsBank CR 93-2		
BankAmerica Corp.			6.0%, 12/15/05	20,000	19,569
7.5%, 3/15/97	10,000	10,637	NBD Bank		
7.5%, 10/15/02	10,000	10,559	6.25%, 8/15/03	20,000	19,862
Bank of Boston			Norwest Financial Corp.		
8.375%, 12/15/02	3,000	3,352	6.0%, 3/15/00	15,000	15,125
6.875%, 7/15/03	15,000	15,186	7.95%, 5/15/02	10,000	11,062
6.625%, 12/1/05	15,000	14,851	Republic New York Corp.		
Bank of New York			5.875%, 10/15/08	15,000	14,054
7.875%, 11/15/02	15,000	16,269	State Street Bank & Trust Co.		
Boatmen's Banchares, Inc.			5.95%, 9/15/03	10,000	9,715
7.625%, 10/1/04	10,000	10,781	Suntrust Banks		
British Telecom Finance			7.375%, 7/1/02	16,000	17,067
9.625%, 2/15/19	5,000	5,844	Torchmark Corp.		
Chemical Bank			7.875%, 5/15/23	15,000	15,483
8.625%, 5/1/02	20,000	22,910	Wachovia Corp.		
Cigna Corp.			6.375%, 4/15/03	20,000	20,107
7.65%, 3/1/23	4,000	4,024	Wells Fargo & Co.		
Comerica, Inc.			6.125%, 11/1/03	15,000	14,389
7.125%, 12/1/13	15,000	14,812	**Group Total**		611,972
Continental Corp.					
7.25%, 3/1/03	20,000	20,472	**Industrial (13.4%)**		
CoreStates Capital			Amoco Canada Petroleum Co.		
6.625%, 3/15/05	20,000	20,090	6.75%, 9/1/23	25,000	24,379
Discover Card			ARCO Chemical		
6.25%, 8/16/00	20,000	20,612	10.25%, 11/1/10	3,000	3,937
First Bank System			Bristol-Meyers Squibb Co.		
6.625%, 5/15/03	10,000	10,053	7.15%, 6/15/23	25,000	25,852
First Chicago Corp.			British Petroleum Co.		
7.625%, 1/15/03	15,000	16,036	7.875%, 5/15/02	20,000	22,028
First Union Corp.			Chevron Corp.		
6.0%, 10/30/08	15,000	13,766	9.375%, 6/1/16	10,000	11,192
Fleet Financial Group			Chevron Profit Sharing Trust		
7.625%, 12/1/99	15,000	16,094	8.11%, 12/1/04	3,750	4,218
6.875%, 3/1/03	30,000	30,359	Clorox Co.		
Ford Motor Credit Corp.			8.8%, 7/15/01	10,000	11,531
5.625%, 12/15/98	20,000	19,869	Coastal Corp.		
General Motors			9.75%, 8/1/03	3,865	4,510
Acceptance Corp.			Coca Cola Co.		
7.0%, 9/15/02	20,000	20,262	7.75%, 2/15/96	10,000	10,526
International Bank for			6.0%, 7/15/03	10,000	9,917
Reconstruction &			Coca Cola Enterprises, Inc.		
Development			7.875%, 2/1/02	10,000	11,057
8.25%, 9/1/16	15,000	17,493	Crown Cork & Seal Co., Inc.		
8.625%, 10/15/16	20,000	24,113	6.75%, 4/15/03	10,300	10,429
			8.0%, 4/15/23	25,000	26,387

Figure 3-13: Investment holdings.

Source: *The Vanguard Group*

For example, in this first section, you can see that this fund (as of December 31, 1993) was 41.6 percent invested in bonds issued by corporations. The corporate bond slice of the fund's pie divides further into which industries and specific companies the fund holds bonds from.

For each security, you also can see how much the fund originally invested and what each investment was worth at the end of the most recent year. (Do you need to know, should you care, will it be on the test? No, no, and no!)

More investment holdings

More of the investments that the fund owns. Here you can see some of the stocks the fund owns (see Figure 3-14).

	Shares	Market Value (000)†
COMMON STOCKS (34.2%)		
Consumer (1.3%)		
Fleming Cos., Inc.	175,900	$ 4,354
Flowers Industries, Inc.	963,300	18,423
Kimberly-Clark Corp.	539,000	27,961
Tambrands, Inc.	230,200	10,186
Universal Corp.	596,100	15,275
Group Total		76,199
Energy (5.6%)		
Amoco Corp.	1,181,100	62,451
Atlantic Richfield Co.	160,000	16,840
Exxon Corp.	447,700	28,205
Mobil Corp.	856,900	67,695
Royal Dutch Petroleum Co.	659,500	68,835
Shell Transport & Trading Co. PLC	187,000	12,108
Texaco, Inc.	1,222,200	78,985
Group Total		335,119
Finance (6.1%)		
Alexander & Baldwin, Inc.	577,800	15,023
American Express Co.	262,500	8,105
Bankers Trust New York Corp.	380,700	30,123
Boatmen's Bancshares, Inc.	2,154,000	64,351
Comerica, Inc.	414,000	11,023
CoreStates Financial Corp.	2,962,100	77,385
First Bank System, Inc.	294,000	9,040
First Hawaiian, Inc.	30,000	727
Independence Bancorp, Inc.	80,000	2,960
Keycorp	1,000,000	35,375
J.P. Morgan & Co., Inc.	719,430	49,910
PNC Bank Corp.	1,431,800	41,522
Society Corp.	668,900	19,900
Group Total		365,444
Healthcare (3.2%)		
American Home Products Corp.	1,025,000	66,369
Baxter International, Inc.	845,200	20,602
Bristol-Myers Squibb Co.	877,000	50,976
Eli Lilly & Co.	700,100	41,568
Upjohn Co.	518,000	15,087
Group Total		194,602
Industrial (4.3%)		
Dow Chemical Co.	347,000	19,692
E.I. du Pont de Nemours & Co.	1,822,400	87,931
Eastman Kodak Co.	404,800	22,669
Olin Corp.	234,200	11,564
Union Camp Corp.	242,900	11,568
Weyerhaeuser Co.	464,000	20,706
Witco Chemical Corp.	848,600	27,049
Xerox Corp.	676,700	60,480
Group Total		261,659

	Shares	Market Value (000)†
Real Estate Investment Trusts (2.2%)		
CBL & Associates Properties, Inc.	780,000	$14,137
*Colonial Properties	415,000	8,922
Duke Realty Investments	799,700	17,793
Equity Res. Properties Trust	308,200	9,824
General Growth Properties	396,800	8,531
Holly Residential Properties	361,700	7,234
Post Properties, Inc.	407,400	12,527
Roc Communities, Inc.	382,300	8,267
*Simon Property Group	581,500	13,156
Spieker Properties	445,400	8,351
Town & Country Trust	547,000	11,145
*Urban Shopping Centers	532,800	11,722
Group Total		131,609
Utility (11.5%)		
BCE, Inc.	1,286,200	44,856
BellSouth Corp.	348,600	20,175
Carolina Power & Light Co.	235,000	7,079
Cincinnati Gas & Electric Co.	753,550	20,723
Commonwealth Edison Co.	952,407	26,905
Consolidated Edison Co.		
of New York	527,400	16,943
DQE Inc.	760,100	26,223
Detroit Edison Co.	1,148,200	34,446
Entergy Corp.	464,000	16,704
GTE Corp.	1,021,800	35,763
General Public Utilities Corp.	479,000	14,789
Houston Industries, Inc.	499,700	23,798
MCN Corp.	253,800	8,820
Montana Power Co.	1,166,400	30,035
National Fuel & Gas Co.	283,700	9,646
Niagara Mohawk Power Corp.	655,000	13,264
NICOR, Inc.	917,100	25,679
Nova Scotia Power	1,035,000	10,162
NYNEX Corp.	1,198,472	48,089
PSI Resources, Inc.	256,400	6,795
Pacific Gas & Electric Co.	1,480,700	52,010
Pennsylvania Power & Light Co.	513,000	13,851
Philadelphia Electric Co.	1,514,900	45,826
Rochester Gas & Electric Corp.	548,600	14,401
SCE Corp.	1,377,000	27,540
Sierra Pacific Resources	737,800	15,125
Southern Co.	988,000	43,596
Texas Utilities Co.	371,937	16,086
US West Corp.	482,092	22,116
Group Total		691,445
TOTAL COMMON STOCKS		
(Cost $1,849,771)		2,056,077

Figure 3-14: Stock holdings.

Source: The Vanguard Group

Accountant-speak

The remainder of a fund's annual report is accounting stuff that will make your eyes glaze over (see Figure 3-15). The good news is that it's not relevant to owning the fund. Spare yourself the pain and agony.

These reports are reviewed and signed by an accounting firm. If the annual report's good enough for them, it's good enough for you. If you feel an irrepressible desire to read this stuff, start studying for the CPA exam!

REPORT OF INDEPENDENT ACCOUNTANTS

To the Shareholders and Board of Directors
Vanguard/Wellesley Income Fund

In our opinion, the accompanying statement of net assets and the related statements of operations and of changes in net assets and the financial highlights present fairly, in all material respects, the financial position of Vanguard/Wellesley Income Fund (the "Fund") at December 31, 1993, the results of its operations, the changes in its net assets and the financial highlights for each of the respective periods presented, in conformity with generally accepted accounting principles. These financial statements and financial highlights (hereafter referred to as "financial statements") are the responsibility of the Fund's management; our responsibility is to express an opinion on these financial statements based on our audits. We conducted our audits of these financial statements in accordance with generally accepted auditing standards which require that we plan and perform the audit to obtain reasonable assurance about whether the financial statements are free of material misstatement. An audit includes examining, on a test basis, evidence supporting the amounts and disclosures in the financial statements, assessing the accounting principles used and significant estimates made by management, and evaluating the overall financial statement presentation. We believe that our audits, which included confirmation of securities by correspondence with the custodian and brokers and the application of alternative auditing procedures where confirmations from brokers were not received, provide a reasonable basis for the opinion expressed above.

PRICE WATERHOUSE

Thirty South Seventeenth Street
Philadelphia, Pennsylvania 19103
January 24, 1994

Figure 3-15:
Accountant-
speak.

Source: The Vanguard Group

Chapter 4
Where to Buy Funds

● ●

In This Chapter
▶ What to watch out for
▶ Best places to buy funds
▶ What discount brokers can do for you

● ●

So you want to buy some mutual funds? Well, get ready for a confusing maze. Unlike when you purchase a train ticket or get a driver's license, you have far too many options for buying mutual funds.

Eventually, this will change — not where to get a train ticket or a driver's license — as the shopping mart for mutual funds is bound to get smaller. So many companies have rushed into the mutual fund business because of the lure of enormous profits that there will soon be a shakeout, with consolidations and mergers as competition stiffens. Fear not, though; mutual fund companies won't fail or go belly-up (see Chapter 2). In fact, the battle for your investment dollars should be good for you because it will eliminate the worst companies and make the best even better.

For now, however, hundreds of investment companies offer thousands of fund options. (Remember that a parent company such as T. Rowe Price offers many individual funds such as money market, bond, balanced, and stock funds.) This chapter will help you to understand what companies are the best places for your fund investing. In Part II of this book, I recommend some specific funds at the best companies that you may want to try.

(Modern) History of Selling Investments

In the earlier decades of the 20th century, most people invested their money in what now appears a Neanderthalic way: many investors of modest means who didn't keep all their money in bank accounts and who wanted to invest in stocks and bonds hired a stockbroker. In those days, stockbrokers were actually called stockbrokers (today, they operate under the marketing guises of financial consultants, advisors, and planners).

Stockbrokers made their living buying and selling shares of individual stocks and bonds to you the investor. For this they earned commissions. Before the early 1970s, all brokers were forced by law to charge individual investors identical commissions. You couldn't shop around for a better deal, and "discount brokers" didn't exist.

In 1975, the Securities and Exchange Commission deregulated commissions so that brokers could discount and compete on price. In that same year, total assets invested in mutual funds were less than $50 billion, only a fraction of the more than $3 trillion invested today. The vast majority — more than 85 percent — of all funds invested in 1973 were in mutual funds sold through brokers. These funds are known as "load" funds. Load simply means commission. When you purchase a load fund through a broker, the broker is paid a commission that ranges typically from 4 percent to 8.5 percent of the amount that you invest.

What propelled the growth of the mutual fund industry was the technological revolution of the 1980s and its accompanying explosion of low-cost computer equipment. This provided fund companies with a cost-effective way to handle thousands of accounts from folks like you who didn't have millions of dollars to invest. This also enabled fund companies to sell funds directly to people like you and me.

As discussed in Chapter 3, today you can stick with the no-load (commission-free) funds — those that cut brokers and their commissions out of the picture. Today, no-load funds account for the majority of investors' mutual fund holdings. Here's a list of the major no-load and load players so that you can more easily tell who's who.

The Major No-Load and Load Companies

Major No-Load Fund Companies	Major Load Fund Companies
Acorn	AIM
Benham	Alliance
Columbia	American
Federated	American Capital
Harbor	Dean Witter
Invesco	Franklin/Templeton
Janus	IDS
Mutual Series	Kemper
Neuberger & Berman	Merrill Lynch
Nicholas	MFS (Mass. Financial Services)
PIMCO	Nuveen
Schwab	Oppenheimer
Scudder	PaineWebber
SteinRoe	Prudential
Strong	Putnam
T. Rowe Price	Smith Barney Shearson
20th Century	
USAA	**Companies That Do Both No-Load and Load Funds**
Vanguard	
Warburg Pincus	Dreyfus
	Fidelity

Not So Smart Ways to Buy Funds

Now, if someone sets up what looks like a hot dog stand on the street corner and starts peddling mutual funds, you would not buy a fund from that person, right? Why not? Probably because it does not seem like a legitimate investment management company to you. Where are the computers, the telephone equipment, and the fax machine? What about the conference room and mahogany table?

You can research this-and-that mutual fund until the cows come home. In the end, however, if you're like most people, you'll make your final investing decisions based on your gut emotions — that is, based on what makes you comfortable. Some of life's most important decisions can and must be made this way. Unfortunately, if you make invesment decisions this way, you'll often end up purchasing investments, such as mutual funds, from the wrong sources.

What types of places are likely to make you feel comfortable but lead you astray? Here's a short list of the wrong places where many people do their fund investing:

- The First Faithful Community Bank. Many people feel comfortable turning their money over to the friendly neighborhood banker. You've done it for years with your checking and savings accounts. The bank has a solid-looking branch close to your home, complete with parking, security cameras, and an impressive-looking vault. And then there's that FDIC insurance that guarantees your deposits. So now that your bank offers mutual funds, you feel comfortable taking a little advice from the "investment specialist" or "consultant" in the branch. Besides, it's so convenient.

    What could be wrong? Odds are that the branch representative is actually a broker who is earning commissions from the mutual funds he's selling you. And since banks are relatively new to the mutual fund game, he may have spent last year helping customers establish new checking accounts, having little experience with fund selection. Remember, if he's working on commission, he's a salesperson, not an advisor.

- Plunder and Pillage Brokerage Firm. Brokers work on commission, so they can and will sell you only load funds. They may even try to hoodwink you into believing that they can do financial planning for you. Don't believe it. As discussed in the last chapter, there's no benefit for you to purchase a load fund; you have much better alternatives.

- Joe the Friendly Financial Planner. You may have met Joe through a "free seminar," "adult education class," or a cold call that he made to you. Joe may not really be a financial planner at all, but rather a salesperson/broker who sells load funds. (If you want to hire a real planner or advisor for help with investing in funds, be sure to read Chapter 5.)

- Bob Your Insurance Broker. Bob's not just selling insurance anymore. Bob now may be selling mutual funds as well and may even be calling himself a financial consultant. Ditto the above remarks for brokers.

- Your Airline, Alma Mater, and other friendly, nonfinancial folks. The mutual fund field has attracted a lot of new competitors who are tempted by the riches that early winners have accumulated. Banks, insurance companies, and even airlines have joined the parade. Unfortunately, most of these newcomers sell load funds, and they may have little experience with money management. Let them learn the ropes with someone else's nest egg.

BEWARE

Banks fight back but lack best ammunition

For the past two decades, banks have been losing a ton of assets from investors. Back in the late 1970s and early 1980s, banks were regulated to limit the amount of interest they could pay depositors. When interest rates surged as inflation took hold, bank depositors looked longingly at money market funds, which were virtually identical to bank savings accounts with one major difference: The yield on money market accounts was much higher since money market funds were not subject to rate ceilings.

When other types of mutual fund investments boomed in the 1980s — bond and stock funds — banks again got left behind. Other government regulations (the Glass-Steagall Act, for you

history buffs), dating back to the 1930s, prevented banks from getting into the mutual fund business. Thanks to some lobbying and fancy organizational footwork, banks now are able to jump into the mutual fund fray and offer their current depositors more choices for investment.

Unfortunately for you as the fund investor, as did many earlier entrants in the industry, bank funds generally charge sales fees. Studies have also indicated problems with investors not understanding that bank funds don't carry FDIC insurance. The banking industry is working on better disclosure, and some banks have been coming out with no-load funds. But the bank is still not the best place to purchase mutual funds.

The Best Fund Companies: Just Dial Toll-Free, 1-800 . . .

Here are the best places to invest and the best ways to buy funds:

The best and least costly way to purchase top performing mutual funds also happens to be the preferred choice of couch potato remote control users. Just pick up your phone and dial an 800 number.

From the convenience of your home, you can order fund educational materials, request applications to set up accounts, and move money from one fund into another. You can even ask that a check be sent to you if you need money. Some accounts, primarily money market funds, come with check-writing privileges, so you can draw on money in your account that way, too.

Don't worry; other folks can't gain access to your money. If money is ever redeemed out of your account, fund companies always make the check payable to you, the account holder, and will only mail checks to your address as listed on the account. If you still think that someone can steal your mail or change your address and intercept a check, stop worrying. Even if they get their paws on your check, they won't be able to cash it since it's made payable to you.

The Vanguard Group

Vanguard is probably the most underrated mutual fund company in America today. It's not that some people don't think it's good; it's simply that, by most measures, Vanguard is the best mutual fund company but isn't recognized as such.

One of the reasons for Vanguard's underrating is the fact that its funds are almost never at the top of the performance charts for their respective categories. As discussed in Chapter 3, this is really a *good* sign, since many Number 1 performing funds are rarely even above average over the long haul. Although Vanguard offers a spectrum of funds from low risk to high risk and everything in between, Vanguard doesn't take excessive risks with the funds it offers.

In the early 1970s, when Vanguard was formed, John Bogle, its founder and former CEO, made the big decision that to this day clearly differentiates Vanguard from its competition. Vanguard distributes funds and provides shareholder administration on an "at cost" basis — that is, with no mark-up or profit.

The seed for the founding of Vanguard was planted when Bogle was fired (over philosophical differences) in 1974 from his position as chairman by the board of directors of Wellington Management Company, an investment management firm. The Wellington Fund, the country's oldest balanced mutual fund, had a separate board of directors that decided to keep Bogle as the Fund's chairman, despite his termination by the parent company.

Bogle was given the latitude and authority to decide how the new fund company, which he named Vanguard, would operate. He insisted that the management of most of the individual funds be contracted out to private money management firms, from whom Vanguard would negotiate the best deal. Thus, Vanguard's mutual fund investors (now numbering five million) would own the company. At traditional fund companies, the parent company owns the individual mutual funds and receives the profits from managing their funds.

The best of both worlds? Funds with branch offices.

Many mutual fund companies have their offices in one location. If you happen to live in the town or city where they're located and want to do business with them, you can visit them in person. Odds are that, unless you maintain several homes, you don't live near the companies with which you want to do your fund investing business.

Some fund companies, such as Fidelity, have branch offices located primarily in densely populated and more affluent areas. You may feel more comfortable droping a check off or speaking to a live person face to face instead of being navigated through an automated voice message system. However, there's no sound financial reason that you need to go in person — everything you need to do can be done by phone and mail.

In most cases, you pay a financial cost for doing your fund investing through firms with branch offices. No, you don't pay tolls to be allowed through the front door, but operating all of those branch offices in areas where rent and employees don't come cheaply costs a good chunk of money. Ultimately, firms that maintain a large branch network need to build these extra costs into their fund's fees. Higher fees lower your investment returns.

A counter-argument in favor of the branch offices is that if they succeed in enticing more investors to use the funds offered by the company, more total money is brought in. Having more money under management helps to lower the average cost of managing each dollar invested.

Bogle felt that this unique corporate structure ensured that fund shareholders would obtain the best deal possible on money managers. "Funds ought to be run for the benefit of shareholders, not for the fund managers," Bogle reasoned. History has proven Bogle not only to be right, but also to be a mutual fund investor's best advocate.

Unlike many other mutual fund companies, Vanguard contracts out with top outside money managers to manage many of its funds — especially stock funds. This, coupled with the fact that their funds charge the lowest average operating expenses of any fund group in the country, has maximized Vanguard's chances for success.

Vanguard's fund operating expenses average just 0.30 percent per year versus an average of more than three times that amount at other fund companies. With money market and bond funds, the Vanguard expense advantage is significant because these markets are highly efficient (even the best fund managers can add relatively little performance value).

Vanguard is best at the funds that appeal to safety-minded investors — those who want to invest in money market, bond, and conservative stock funds. However, Vanguard offers a sufficient number of aggressive funds with top-notch performance and rock-bottom expense ratios that will appeal to the gambler in you. Vanguard offers many excellent stock funds as well (see Chapter 8). In managing stock funds, where performance is supposed to be more closely tied to the genius of the fund manager, Vanguard's parsimony has not harmed performance.

Vanguard is also the innovator of index mutual funds, which are unmanaged portfolios of the representative securities that comprise an index, such as the Standard & Poor's 500 (500 large companies' stock). Vanguard offers the broadest selection of index funds, and these have the lowest operating expense average (0.18 percent) in the business.

What Vanguard doesn't offer should also appeal to you. Vanguard won't jump on the fad-of-the-month bandwagon and develop some newfangled fund designed primarily by slick marketers to line the company's coffers. Vanguard uses a customer-first approach and designs funds with the chief focus on meeting the customer's needs.

Vanguard has two branch offices (their headquarters are near Valley Forge, PA, and the branch offices are in Philadelphia and Phoenix). Their representatives are available weekdays from 8 A.M. to 9 P.M. EST and on Saturday from 9 A.M. to 4 P.M. EST. Vanguard does offer an automated 24-hour phone service that enables customers to call for fund prices and yields and even to enter transactions.

Fidelity Investments

Fidelity Investments, The Behemoth of Bean Town, is the largest mutual fund company in America (although Vanguard is the largest exclusively commission-free fund company). Fidelity is huge — it manages about $400 billion in mutual funds and handles half a million phone calls per day!

Fidelity's roots trace back to the 1940s, when Edward C. Johnson II took over the then-fledgling Fidelity Fund from its president, who felt that he couldn't make enough money as the head of an investment fund! Johnson's son, Ned (Edward C. Johnson III), assumed management of Fidelity in 1972 and has clearly proven that you can make a truckload of money operating mutual funds. Ned is now the fourth wealthiest person in America, according to *Forbes* magazine, with a fortune estimated at $5 billion.

Fidelity offers a number of excellent mutual funds, particularly those that invest in U.S. stocks. A mutual fund Goliath, Fidelity offers more mutual funds (200+) than any other mutual fund company. If your company offers Fidelity mutual funds for the company retirement plan, you can sleep well at night knowing you've got mostly good investment options.

If you're venturing to do business with Fidelity on your own, you've got your work cut out for you. One of the biggest problems novice investors have at Fidelity is discerning the good funds from the not-so-good. Relative to the best of the competition, Fidelity is weakest with the following:

- **Bond funds**. Fidelity's bond funds charge high operating expenses that depress an investor's returns. Bond fund management is an area where Fidelity's fund managers have not displayed particular investment prowess. If you want bond funds, Vanguard is a superior alternative.

  Note: Fidelity offers a decent series of bond funds known as Spartan funds that have lower operating expense ratios. These funds' minimum investment is typically $10,000, and they charge additional fees for check writing and redemptions (see Chapter 7).

- **International stock funds**. Fidelity was late in entering this field and made many hiring mistakes. Its international funds are also burdened by high fees, both sales loads and ongoing operating expenses. See Chapter 8 for alternative companies.

- **Non-retirement investing**. Many of Fidelity's best U.S. stock funds charge 2 to 3 percent sales loads when used for non-retirement investing. (This sales charge is waived for most Fidelity funds when purchased inside of retirement accounts — for example, individual retirement accounts.) Fidelity funds also have a tendency to produce more capital gains distributions, which increase the tax burden for non-retirement account investors (see Chapter 5).

Fidelity decided to cultivate the support of the armies of commission-based securities brokers by offering them Fidelity funds that they could sell. Thus was born the Fidelity Advisor funds, a load family of funds that Fidelity sells through investment salespeople and that carry high sales and ongoing fees. I would avoid these funds.

Fidelity's sector funds (Select), which invest in just one industry, such as air transportation, insurance, or retailing, should also be avoided. These funds charge sales commissions of 3 percent and have high ongoing operating expenses (often in excess of 1.5 percent per year) and exchange fees. Being industry focused, these funds are poorly diversified and thus highly risky for investors. Unfortunately, Fidelity encourages a trader mentality with these funds by pricing them hourly instead of daily.

One of Fidelity's strengths as a mutual fund company also explains its higher costs — it operates nearly 100 branch offices throughout the U.S. and staffs its phones 24 hours a day, 365 days a year. So if you want to have personalized attention and conduct business face to face, check your local phone directory or call Fidelity's 800 number for the office location nearest you.

Like Charles Schwab and other discount brokers, Fidelity also offers a service where you can buy and sell mutual funds from a variety of other companies (see "Using Discount Brokers" later in this chapter).

Other noteworthy fund companies

In addition to the larger families already discussed, here's a short list of some fund companies with strengths in more focused areas. I recommend specific funds at these companies in Chapters 6 through 8.

Benham is a small but high-quality mutual fund company based in Mountain View, CA, with a branch office in Denver. It specializes in conservative funds, particularly bond funds with low expense ratios (comparable to USAA's but still higher than Vanguard's). Benham also offers a gold fund (see Chapter 8).

Mutual Series offers stock funds that focus on investing in undervalued companies. Mutual's four stock funds (Beacon, Discovery, Qualified, and Shares) managed under Michael Price have produced excellent returns (see Chapter 8).

PIMCO is a family of primarily bond funds that normally are available only to investors who have at least $500,000 to invest. However, for as little as $1,000, you can purchase its excellent bond funds through discount brokerage firms discussed in the next chapter. These funds are managed by William Gross, who is considered to be one of the best bond fund managers in the country (see Chapter 7). Beware of PIMCO Advisor Funds — as with Fidelity's broker-sold funds, these have high fees and should be avoided.

Schwab offers its own family of mutual funds as well as funds from other companies (this service is discussed in the next section). The Schwab family of funds is quite small but noted for its recently developed series of tax-friendly stock index funds that have low minimum initial investments compared to Vanguard's (see Chapter 8).

T. Rowe Price is one of the oldest mutual fund companies. It is named after its founder, T. (Thomas) Rowe Price, who is generally credited with popularizing investing in growth-oriented companies. The Price family of funds is diverse and good. Price has been a pioneer in and has a long track record with international fund investing. It also offers 401(k) retirement plans specifically for smaller companies.

Price offers some fund concepts similar to Vanguard's and Fidelity's. Specifically, it offers some funds (known as Spectrum) that are mutual funds comprising several other Price stock or bond mutual funds. It also offers a series of money market and bond funds (Summit) with low operating expenses. Summit funds, however, have $25,000 minimum investments, and their expenses are generally 0.5 to 0.6 percent, well above Vanguard's.

USAA (as it's now called — the acronym officially replaces its dated name of United States Automobile Association) has a lot in common with Vanguard. USAA is a solid company that offers a small family of no-load mutual funds as well as low-cost, high-quality insurance. Although you (or a family member) need to be a military officer to gain access to its homeowner's and auto insurance, anyone can buy into its mutual funds.

Like Vanguard, USAA is a conservative company. All of its mutual funds are no-load, and its operating fees are well below average. And there's no hype, slick advertising, or newfangled fund ideas that don't make sense for you as an investor. You just won't find many choices within most categories of funds, particularly among growth-oriented funds. USAA does have six branch offices scattered throughout the country.

Using Discount Brokers

For many years, you could only purchase no-load mutual funds directly from mutual fund companies. If you wanted to buy some funds at, say, Vanguard, Fidelity, T. Rowe Price, USAA, and Benham, you needed to call these five different companies and request each firm's application. So you ended up filling out five different sets of forms and mailing them with five envelopes, five stamps, and five separate checks.

Soon, you'd start receiving separate statements from each of the five fund companies reporting how your investments were doing. (Some fund companies make this even more of a paperwork nightmare by sending you a separate statement for each individual mutual fund you bought through them.)

What about . . . ?

There are hundreds of mutual fund companies offering thousands of funds. Many aren't worth your consideration because they don't meet the common sense selection criteria I outline in Chapter 3. So if you're wondering why I didn't mention Prudential or some other fund family, it's because their funds are either high cost, low performance, managed in a schizophrenic fashion, or all of the above.

One of the beauties of all the fund choices out there is that there's no need to settle for lousy or mediocre funds. If you're wondering what to do with poor funds you already own, read Chapter 11.

Now suppose that you wanted to sell one of your Benham funds and invest the proceeds at Fidelity. This was also a time-consuming pain in the hindquarters, since you needed to contact Benham to sell, waited days for them to send you the money, and then you needed to send the money with instructions to Fidelity.

In 1984, Charles Schwab, founder of the discount brokerage firm that bears his name, thought it would be useful to provide investors a more convenient way to invest in mutual funds from multiple firms. He created a mutual fund supermarket, which other discount brokers have since copied, where you can purchase hundreds of individual funds from dozens of fund companies.

The major benefit of such a service is that it greatly simplifies the paperwork involved in buying and selling different companies' mutual funds. No matter how many mutual fund companies you wish to invest in, all you need to do is complete just one application for the discount broker. And instead of getting a separate statement from each company, you get one statement from the discount broker that summarizes all of your mutual fund holdings. (**Note:** you still must maintain separate non-retirement and IRA accounts).

Moving from one company's fund into another's (for example, where the investor wants to sell a Benham fund and purchase a Fidelity fund) is a snap as well. The discount broker can usually take care of all this with one phone call from you. Come tax time, you'll also receive just one 1099 statement summarizing your fund's taxable distributions that must be recorded on your tax return.

You weren't born yesterday, so you know that there must be a catch for all this convenience. Here's a hint: since discount brokers are serving as intermediaries (or middle-persons, for those who are politically correct) for the buying and selling of funds and the time and money spent sending you statements, they expect to make some money in return. Guess what! It costs you more to use the discount broker's services.

Discount brokers charge you a transaction fee whenever you buy or sell most of the better funds that they offer. While the transaction fee has the same impact as a sales commission — it is deducted from your investment — discount brokers' transaction fees (typically in the neighborhood of 0.7 percent or less) are substantially less than the sales commissions that you would pay to buy a load fund (usually 4 to 8.5 percent).

For investments of less than $5,000, the discounters' minimum transaction fees gobble a large percentage of the amount that you invest. You're better off buying directly from a fund company and bypassing discounters and their transaction fees or buying a no-transaction-fee fund (discussed later in this section) from the discounter.

Not all discounters are created equal

The discount brokerage industry has done much good for investors since its birth in the 1970s in response to the long-overdue deregulation of brokerage commissions by the Securities and Exchange Commission. By employing salary-based representatives, discounters have eliminated the inherent conflicts of interest that traditional brokers such as Prudential, Dean Witter, Smith Barney Shearson, and others still have today (see Chapter 3).

One major problem for mutual fund investors who blindly pick a discounter is the fact that some discount brokers sell load mutual funds. A handful of discounters (for example, Olde Discount, Kennedy Cabot), in fact, only sell load (commission) funds.

Discounters such as Olde Discount also engage in the practice of saying that you can purchase stocks free of any brokerage commissions. This is not quite true because, in many cases, the firm is making a *spread* — the difference between the buy and sell price — on the trade since they "make a market in" many securities. When you call them for information, Olde's brokers, who earn commissions, even ask for your phone number, which they use for follow-up sales calls.

One feature available through the discount broker's mutual fund services is the ability to purchase some funds not normally available to smaller investors. There aren't a lot of funds that you can do this with (PIMCO is an example).

Buying direct versus using discount brokers

Using discount brokers is a little bit like having a prepared meal delivered to your home. Discounters offer convenience — one application, one account, and one statement for all your funds. But you pay extra for this convenience.

So how do you decide if a discount brokerage account is for you? Several factors should influence your choice. If most of the following comments apply to you, you may be a candidate for happily using a discounter:

- ✔ You hate paperwork.
- ✔ You want to invest in funds at many companies.
- ✔ You have a fair amount of money to invest ($5,000 or more per fund).
- ✔ You don't trade a lot.
- ✔ You aren't a penny pincher.

If you're primarily going to do bond fund and money market fund investing, you're better off skipping discounters. Deal directly with a mutual fund company that excels in this area (such as Vanguard) so that you can minimize your fees and maximize your investment returns. Discounters generally pay lower yields on their money market funds than do mutual fund companies.

Another interesting but rarely used feature that comes with a brokerage account is that you can borrow on margin (taking out a loan from the brokerage firm) against mutual funds and other securities held in a non-retirement account which are then used as collateral. Borrowing against your funds is generally lower-cost than your other loan options, and it's potentially tax-deductible.

There is a way to buy and sell your funds and use a discounter but reduce the total transaction fees that you pay: purchase your funds initially from the mutual fund company and then transfer the shares at no charge into a discount brokerage account. Conversely, when you're ready to sell shares, you can transfer shares from the discounter to the mutual fund company before you're ready to sell (see Chapter 10 for details about transfer forms).

"No Transaction Fee" funds — free funds?

After several years of the distribution of funds from all of these different companies, it was just a matter of time before the discount brokers came up with another innovation. Discount brokers were doing a lot for mutual fund companies (for instance, handling the purchase and sale of funds as well as the ongoing account record keeping and reporting), but they were not being paid for all their work. In 1992, Charles Schwab & Company changed all that with its Mutual Fund OneSource program.

Under OneSource, Schwab negotiated with some mutual funds to pay his firm an ongoing fee to service and handle customer accounts. Initially, this was a hard sell because the fund companies were used to receiving this shareholder servicing for free. Eventually, however, Schwab succeeded.

Today, through Schwab and other discount brokers who copied this service, you can purchase several hundred funds without paying any transaction fees (that is, you pay the same cost as if you had bought the funds through the mutual fund company itself). These are called *No Transaction Fee* (NTF) funds.

Schwab and other discount brokers can afford to offer these NTF funds to you seemingly for free because the participating fund companies share a small percentage (usually 0.25 percent of their annual operating expense fees) with the discount broker for servicing the customers' accounts.

Some discount brokers and their employees push these funds as better than other funds, emphasizing the "free" aspect. While it's true that you may purchase NTF funds without paying an explicit transaction fee, these funds are hardly free. Remember, these NTF funds must have enough fat in their annual operating expenses (discussed in Chapter 3) to be able to afford to pay the discounter a share. In their rush to sign up more NTF funds, some discounters have ignored the quality of the NTF funds they offer. (In addition, some financial publications encourage and effectively endorse this lack of quality control by giving higher ratings to those discounters offering more free funds to customers. As with food, more isn't always better — quality counts as well!)

As a group and in general, NTF funds are inferior to the no-load funds that you pay the discounters a transaction fee to purchase. NTF bond funds in particular are usually pretty doggy, since they carry higher operating expenses.

Whenever you're making a mutual fund investment decision through a discount broker, try not to be influenced by the prospect, or lack thereof, of a transaction fee. In your efforts to avoid paying a small fee today, you could end up buying a fund with high ongoing fees and subpar performance. If you're so concerned about paying additional fees, you're better off dealing directly with mutual fund companies and bypassing the discount brokers and their transaction fees.

More discount brokers open shop all the time. Here is a short list of the better firms. Decide which firm is best for you based on your needs and what is and is not important to you.

Charles Schwab & Company

Charles Schwab was the pioneer in offering no-load mutual funds in the discount brokerage field. Among discounters, Schwab is one of the most expensive firms when it comes to the transaction fees charged to buy and sell no-load mutual funds (see Table 4-1 later in the chapter). So why would you want to do business with this pricier firm?

- Schwab offers an extensive array of quality no-load mutual funds. (That's not to say that all the funds they sell are good.)

- Schwab has a bunch of branch offices (more than 200) if you want to deal face-to-face with a real person instead of calling an 800 number or sending stuff in the mail.

- Schwab is always open when you have free time to think about your investments. At 10 P.M. on Sunday night or at 8 A.M. on New Year's Day, Schwab is open — in fact, it's open 24 hours a day, 365 days a year.

- If you like using technology, you'll love Schwab. It has software, called StreetSmart (see Chapter 15), that enables you to access your account information on-line and place trades (you get a 10 percent discount, too). Another automated way to trades through Schwab and receive the 10 percent discount is by using a touch-tone telephone.

If you're fee-sensitive and don't need fancy technology and a firm with branch offices, don't use Schwab. Read on to find better choices.

Jack White & Company

Jack White & Company is a deep discount broker: its fees are discounted from a traditional discount broker's charges. For example, White's mutual fund transaction fees on typically sized trades are 50 to 70 percent *less* than what the larger discounters (Schwab, Fidelity, Quick & Reilly, Waterhouse) charge. On really large trades ($100,000+), White's fees can be up to 90 percent less than the competition's!

You know that you usually don't get something for nothing. So you may be asking if White has telephones and computers, and will it be in business tomorrow. You may also be wondering who in the heck is Jack White — he's not exactly a household name.

There really is a Jack White. He's a nice fellow, like Chuck Schwab, and ethical. His firm does a terrific job doing what they do, but White isn't a giant. The main difference is the level of hand-holding and service options the two firms offer. White offers little, Schwab quite a bit. White doesn't have branch offices (although you're welcome to visit the one if you're in the San Diego area).

If you like technology and you like obtaining information or trading without involving a human being, then White's not for you. There's no on-line trading software, nor is there the ability to access account information with a touch-tone telephone; however, representatives are available around the clock.

White also is not quite as low cost as it might appear on the surface. For example, self-employed folks who establish a Keogh plan (discussed in Chapter 5) with White should know that the annual fee charged can be substantially higher than at the competition. White's money market funds also have lousy yields.

Get paid to dump your load funds and buy load funds without the load

Another minor benefit of using discounters is that they offer you the ability to purchase some load funds without the load.

Jack White has a service, *Connect*, that allows holders of load mutual funds to sell their shares to another buyer. The buyer pays a flat $200 fee instead of the normal 4 to 8.5 percent commission that an investment salesperson earns. For purchases of $5,000 or more, this service can save a buyer hundreds or thousands of dollars. The seller benefits, too — getting paid $100 to sell a load fund through White's service.

Fidelity

Fidelity Brokerage offers discount brokerage services through which, if you're so inclined, you can trade individual securities or buy mutual funds from other fund companies (a service similar to Schwab's and White's).

Fidelity's service has lagged behind Schwab's and White's in the breadth and quality of the funds they offer. Their level of service leaves something to be desired, but hopefully, they'll get better as they gain more experience in this line of work.

The best and main reason to use Fidelity's discount brokerage services is if you plan on investing a fair portion of your mutual fund assets in Fidelity funds. You can buy Fidelity funds without paying transaction fees through Fidelity — something you cannot do through other discount brokers.

Table 4-1	Discount Brokers' Mutual Fund Transaction Fees		
Investment Size	*Fidelity* *	*Schwab* *	*White*
$ 5,000	$ 35	$ 39	$ 27
$ 10,000	$ 35	$ 70	$ 35
$ 30,000	$ 35	$135	$ 50
$100,000	$ 35	$275	$ 50

*Both Schwab and Fidelity offer 10 percent discounts if you use their respective computer software packages (see Chapter 15) or trade by touch-tone phone. If, when you sell one fund, you place an order to invest that money in another fund, you pay the fee on the sell order only and a reduced fee ($15) for the buy order.

Other discounters

Increasing numbers of discount brokers offer mutual funds from a variety of companies. Muriel Siebert & Company, for example, offers significant numbers of funds as well as low transaction fees (although not as low as Jack White's). Most discounters don't offer mutual fund services — they simply do individual securities transactions.

Stay tuned for more options, but Schwab, White, and Fidelity are the best currently available. Vanguard and T. Rowe Price offer discount brokerage services, and they offer their own mutual funds as well. Vanguard's discount brokerage offers consolidated statements that list your security holdings as well as your Vanguard fund holdings. T. Rowe Price will soon offer this, too.

Chapter 5

Fitting Mutual Funds into Your Financial Plans

In This Chapter

▶ Common planning mistakes made with funds

▶ Smart things to do before investing

▶ Retirement planning and tax considerations

▶ When to hire an advisor

*E*verywhere you turn today, you're inundated with investment advice. The financial magazines and daily business sections of newspapers are glutted with articles and advertisements for investing.

Your mailbox is flowing with newsletter and other solicitations from the guru du jour. "Subscribe now and save 67 percent off our normal (overpriced) subscription rates and you too can earn 40 percent per year while the common folk who aren't on our exclusive (bulk mail) mailing list are floundering around earning a paltry 10 percent per year." (You read the truth about newsletters in Chapter 14, where I name the few that are good for something besides recycling.)

One of the problems created by this information explosion is that it causes many people to lose sight of the big picture: for what purpose, besides earning a decent return, are they investing in the first place?

Common Financial Planning Mistakes with Funds

Because people invest in mutual funds for so many different reasons, there are many ways that you can make wrong moves that can mitigate your selection of an otherwise good investment. Take the case of Justine and Max. They went to a seminar taught by a financial planner who admonished them, and the other students, to plan ahead for retirement. If they wanted to retire by, say, age 65, Justine and Max learned that they needed to save around 12 percent of their income every year until age 65. They were in their late 20s, so this was a long way away.

The longer they waited to start saving, the seminar leader taught them, the more painful it would be. Just postponing the start of saving a mere ten years would almost double the amount of their annual income that they needed to save.

On the drive home from the seminar, Justine and Max had an intense and focused discussion. They were going to get on the phone the very next day and call two mutual fund companies for applications. And so it was resolved: a serious investment program must begin right away. They weren't too excited about the prospect of working through age 65.

Justine and Max also were frightened about the need to save a healthy chunk of their income *every* year. They hoped to begin a family in a few years. Surely, they thought, there would be years when they would not want to work full-time so that they could spend more time with their children. Justine and Max wondered how they would save the necessary money to reach their goals during these times if saving money now was a challenge. They figured at best they were currently saving 5 percent of their income, if that.

Within a week, they had set up accounts in five different mutual funds at two firms. No more 3-percent-return bank savings accounts — the funds they chose had been returning 10 to 12 percent per year over the prior years!

Justine and Max had the best of intentions but made some major mistakes by investing in the funds they chose. The funds themselves weren't poor choices — in fact, the funds they chose were quite good: they had competent managers, good historic performance, and reasonable fees.

The problems with Justine and Max's investments were several. First, Justine and Max completely neglected investing in their employers' retirement savings plans. Thus, they were missing out on making tax-deductible contributions. By investing outside of their employers' plans, they received no tax deductions.

To add tax insult to injury, many of the mutual funds that Justine and Max were investing in paid significant, taxable dividends. The last thing Justine and Max needed was more taxable income. It's not that they were rolling in money — neither one had a high salary. But because they were a two-income couple, they were in a high tax bracket.

Besides, Justine and Max were trying to *save* money, not produce more current income from their investments. Investments that produce more income have less growth potential. Since Justine and Max were in their late 20s and investing for retirement, they should have been doing more growth-oriented investing.

In their enthusiasm to get serious about their savings, Justine and Max made another major error: they didn't adjust their spending habits to allow for greater savings. They *thought* they were saving more — 12 percent of their income was going into the mutual funds versus the 5 percent they had been saving in a bank account. However, as the months rolled by, their outstanding balances on credit cards grew.

In fact, when they started to invest in mutual funds, Justine and Max had $1,000 of revolving debt on a credit card at 14 percent. Six months later, the debt had grown to $2,000. They needed to stop investing money and pay down their debt first. Then they needed to examine where they could trim their spending in order to free up more money to invest. The extra money for investment had to come from somewhere — in Justine and Max's case, it was coming from building up their credit card debt. Since it was highly unlikely that their investments would return 14 percent per year, they were losing money in the process. There was no real additional saving going on — just borrowing from VISA to invest in the mutual funds.

Ten Smart Things to Do Before Investing

It's great to be motivated. For some people finding motivation is the first hurdle to overcome. So, if you've been thinking about investing but haven't yet begun, congratulations on taking the next step and reading to learn more.

Unfortunately, motivation isn't enough. You'll save yourself a lot of financial heartache and money if you make some important financial assessments and moves before you begin channeling money into mutual funds.

Here are the ten most important things to do so that you get the most from your mutual fund investments:

Pay off your debts

Investing money makes you feel good, and paying off debt is somehow boring and unexciting. But I'm not going to be able to recommend mutual funds for you that will consistently generate a rate of return high enough to exceed what you're paying on consumer debt such as your credit cards and auto loans.

Some financial gurus claim that they can make you 15 to 20 percent per year. They can't. Besides, in order to try and earn these high returns, you have to take much risk. If you have consumer debt and little savings, you're not in a position to take that much risk. Get rid of the debt and establish a safety reserve that can sustain you through at least three months without having an income.

Figure out your financial goals

Although you may be saving money only because it makes you feel good, odds are that you're saving with some other purpose in mind. Common financial goals include saving for retirement, a home purchase, an emergency reserve, and stuff like that. You'll be better able to make the most of your money if you figure out how much you should be saving and set some goals.

Your goals and needs will change over time, so these determinations need not be carved in stone. Until you've ascertained what you're going to do with the savings down the road, however, you won't really be able to thoughtfully choose suitable mutual funds.

Another benefit of going through this exercise is that you'll know better how much risk you need to take to accomplish your goals. Seeing the amount you need to save to achieve your dreams may encourage you to invest in more growth-oriented funds. Conversely, if you find that your nest egg is substantial given what your aspirations are, you might scale back on the riskiness of your fund investments.

The younger you are, the more of your longer-term investment money should be in growth mutual funds. See Chapter 9 for a discussion about dividing, or allocating, your investment money among the different types of funds.

Determine how much you are currently saving

If you're like most people, you're more likely to know the name of the 13th U.S. President than the amount of income you're now saving. By saving, I mean, over the past year, how did your spending compare with your income? For example, if you earned $40,000, and $38,000 of it got "spent" on taxes, food, clothing, rent, insurance, and other fun things, you saved $2,000. Your savings rate then would be 5 percent ($2,000 of savings divided by your income of $40,000).

The vast majority of Americans haven't a clue what their savings rate is. If you already know that your rate is low, non-existent, or negative, you can safely skip this step since you also already know that you need to save much more. But figuring out your savings rate can be a real eye opener and wallet closer. (Incidentally, in case you forgot, Millard Fillmore was the 13th U.S. President.)

Examine your current spending and ability to earn more income

If you're saving enough to meet your goals, you can skip this step and move ahead. For the rest of the class, however, some additional work needs to be done. To save more, you need to reduce your spending, increase your income, or both. This isn't rocket science, but it's not easy to do.

For most people, reducing spending is the more feasible option. But where do you begin? First, figure out where your money's going. You may have some general idea, but you need to have facts. Get out your checkbook register, credit card bills, and any other documentation of your spending history and tally up how much you spend on dining out, operating your car(s), paying your taxes, and everything else. Once you have this information, you can begin to prioritize and make the necessary tradeoffs to reduce your spending and increase your savings rate.

Earning more income may work as well if you can get a higher paying job or increase the number of hours you're willing to work. But if you're already working a lot, reining in your spending will be better for your emotional and social well-being.

Maximize tax-deferred retirement account savings

It's difficult for most people to save money. Don't make a tough job impossible by forsaking the terrific tax benefits that come from investing through retirement savings accounts. Employer-based 401(k) and 403(b) retirement plans offer substantial tax benefits. Contributions into these plans are federally and state tax-deductible. And once the money is invested inside these plans, the growth on your contributions is tax-sheltered as well.

The common mistake fund investors make is that they neglect to take advantage of these accounts in their enthusiasm to invest in funds in "non-retirement" accounts. This can cost you hundreds, perhaps thousands, of dollars per year in lost tax savings and tens of thousands to hundreds of thousands of dollars over your working years.

Fund companies are happy to encourage this financially detrimental behavior. It's not detrimental to them. They'll lure you into their funds without educating you about using your employer's retirement plan first. Why? Because the more you invest through your employer's plan, the less you have available to invest in their mutual funds. (See the section "Retirement Planning, Taxes, and Mutual Funds" later in this chapter to learn about the different retirement accounts you may contribute to, including plans for self-employment income.)

Don't neglect to fund retirement accounts in an effort to save money for your kids' college expenses. If you do, you'll not only pay more in taxes, but your children will have a more difficult time qualifying for financial aid, including loans that are not based on financial need (see Chapter 18). If you're affluent enough that you can afford to pay for your children's college costs and fund your retirement needs, you can safely ignore this concern.

Consider other "investment" possibilities

Mutual funds are a fine way to invest your money, but they're hardly the only way. You can also invest in real estate, in your own business or someone else's, or you can pay down mortgage debt more quickly.

Again, what makes sense for you depends on your goals and personal preferences. If you hate taking risks and detest volatile investments, paying down your mortgage may make better sense than investing in mutual funds.

Determine your tax bracket

When you're investing in mutual funds outside of tax-sheltered retirement accounts, the profits and distributions that your funds produce are subject to taxation. So the type of fund that makes sense for you depends at least partly on your tax situation.

If you're in a high bracket, you should give preference to mutual funds such as tax-free bond funds and stock funds with low levels of distributions, particularly dividends. If you're not in a high bracket, you want to avoid tax-free bond funds because you'll end up with less of a return than in taxable bond funds. (In Part II, I explain how to select the best types of money market, bond, and stock funds that fit your tax status.)

Be honest with yourself about what risk you're comfortable with

Think back over your investing career. I know you're not a star money manager, but you've already made some investing decisions. For instance, leaving your excess money in a bank savings or checking account is a decision — it might indicate you're afraid of volatile investments.

How would you deal with an investment that drops 10, 20, 30, 40, or even 50 percent in a year? Some of the more aggressive mutual funds that specialize in volatile securities like growth stocks, small company stocks, emerging market stocks, and long-term and low-quality bonds can fall in a hurry.

If you can't stomach big waves on the seas of the financial markets, don't get in a small boat that you'll want to bail out of in a big storm. Selling after a big drop is the equivalent of jumping into the frothing sea at the peak of a pounding storm — you're sealing your doom.

You can invest in the riskier types of securities by selecting mutual funds that mix riskier securities with more stable investments. For example, you can purchase an international fund that invests in companies of varying sizes in established as well as emerging economies. That would be better for you than investing money in the Not-Quite-Yet-On-Our-Feet Tahitian Small Company Stock Fund.

Review current investment holdings

Many people have a tendency to compartmentalize their investments — IRA money here, 401(k) there, brokerage account somewhere else. Part of making sound investment decisions is to examine how the pieces fit together to make up the whole. That's where fancy-schmancy terms like "asset allocation" come from. Asset allocation simply means how your investments are divvied up among the major types of securities or funds, such as money market, bond, U.S. stocks, international stocks, precious metals, and others.

Another reason to take stock of your current investments before you buy into new mutual funds is that some house cleaning may be in order. You may discover investments that don't fit with your objectives or tax situation. Perhaps you'll decide to clear out some of the individual securities that you know you can't adequately follow and that clutter your life.

Review your insurance coverage

Insurance? What's that got to do with mutual funds? Take this as my friendly little paternalistic reminder to get all of your financial house in order. Saving and investing is psychologically rewarding and makes many people feel more secure. But, ironically, even some good savers and investors are in precarious positions because they have gaps in their insurance coverage.

Do you have:

- Adequate life insurance to provide for your dependents?
- Long-term disability insurance to replace your income in case a disability prevents you from working?
- Sufficient liability protection on your home and car to guard your assets against lawsuits?

In reviewing your insurance, you may also discover unnecessary policies or ways to spend less on insurance, freeing up more money to invest in mutual funds. (See *Personal Finance For Dummies* to learn about the right and wrong ways to buy insurance and whip the rest of your finances into shape.)

Don't become so obsessed with making, saving, and investing money that you neglect the things that money can't buy: your health, friends, family, and exploration of new career options and hobbies.

Retirement Planning, Taxes, and Mutual Funds

We've already discussed a little about taxes and retirement accounts. You want to minimize your taxes when you make financial moves and are investing your money. If you hope to retire someday, you need to be investing for that goal.

You can actually reduce your taxes and prepare financially for retirement by funding retirement accounts to the maximum possible. This reduces your taxes and helps you work toward building your retirement reserves.

In the sections that follow, I give you a crash course on the importance of planning for retirement, determining methods of investing, and understanding the tax consequences of your mutual fund investing decisions.

The sooner the better — investing for retirement

In order to take advantage of the tax savings that come with retirement savings plans, you must first spend less than you earn. Only then can you afford to contribute to these plans.

The mistake people at all income levels make with retirement accounts is not taking advantage of them — thereby delaying the age at which they start to sock money away. The sooner you start to save, the less painful it is each year, because your contributions have more years to compound.

Each decade you delay approximately doubles the percentage of your earnings you should save to meet your goals. For example, if saving 5 percent per year in your early 20s would get you to your retirement goal, waiting until your 30s may mean socking away 10 percent; waiting until your 40s, 20 percent; beyond that, the numbers get troubling.

As much as you want to invest in mutual funds, however, taking advantage of saving and investing in tax-deductible retirement accounts should be your number one priority (unless you're still paying off high-interest consumer debt on credit cards or an auto loan). If you can invest in mutual funds inside of your retirement accounts, so much the better.

Here are the main benefits of investing in retirement accounts first:

- **Tax-deductibility**. Retirement accounts should be called tax-reduction accounts. If they were called that, people might be more excited about contributing to them. For many people, avoiding higher taxes is the motivating force that opens the account and starts the contributions.

  Suppose that you are paying about 35 percent between federal and state income taxes on your last dollars of income (see discussion later in the chapter to determine your tax bracket). For most of the retirement accounts described in this chapter, for every $1,000 you contribute, you save yourself about $350 in taxes in the year that you make the contribution.

- **Tax-deferred growth of your investments.** Once money is in a retirement account, any interest, dividends, and appreciation add to the amount of your account without being taxed. You defer taxes on all the accumulating gains and profits until you withdraw the money down the road. Thus, more money is working for you over a longer period of time.

- **They save you from yourself.** Retirement accounts are separate from your other personal money. The IRS also penalizes you if you want the money out of your accounts prior to age $59^1/_2$. Don't let this deter you from contributing — the penalties will keep you from raiding your accounts to go to the Bahamas!

On average, most people need about 70 to 80 percent of their preretirement income throughout retirement to maintain their standard of living. If you've never thought about what your retirement goals are, looked into what you can expect from Social Security (stop laughing), or calculated how much you should be saving for retirement, now's the time to do it. *Personal Finance For Dummies* goes through all the necessary details and even tells you how to come up with more money to invest and how to do it wisely.

Your retirement investing options

If you earn employment income (or receive alimony), you have the option of putting money away in a retirement-type account that compounds without taxation until you withdraw the money. With many retirement accounts, you can elect to use mutual funds as your retirement account investment option. And if you have retirement money in some other investment option, you may be able to transfer it into a mutual fund company (see Chapter 10).

In most cases, your contributions into retirement accounts are tax-deductible. The following list includes the major types of accounts and explains how to determine whether you are eligible for them.

401 (k) plans

For-profit companies offer 401(k) plans, which typically allow you to save up to $9,500 per year (for 1996). Your contributions to a 401(k) are excluded from your reported income and thus are free from federal and state income taxes but not FICA (Social Security) taxes.

Absolutely don't miss out on contributing to your employer's 401(k) plan if your employer matches a portion of your contributions. Your company, for example, may match half of your first 6 percent of contributions (so in addition to saving a lot of taxes, you get a bonus from the company). Check with your company's benefits department for your plan's details.

Thanks to technological innovations and the growth of the mutual fund industry, smaller companies (those with fewer than 100 employees) can consider offering 401(k) plans, too. In the past, it was prohibitively expensive for smaller companies to administer 401(k)s. If your company is interested in this option, have them contact a mutual fund organization such as T. Rowe Price, Vanguard, or Fidelity, or a discount brokerage house, such as Charles Schwab or Jack White.

403 (b) plans

Many nonprofit organizations offer 403(b) plans to their employees. As with a 401(k), your contributions to these plans are federal and state tax-deductible. The 403(b) plans often are referred to as tax-sheltered annuities, the name for insurance-company investments that satisfy the requirements for 403(b) plans.

For the benefit of 403(b) retirement-plan participants, no-load (commission-free) mutual funds can now be used in 403(b) plans. Check which mutual fund companies your employer offers you to invest through — hopefully you have access to the better ones covered in Chapter 4.

Nonprofit employees generally are allowed to contribute up to 20 percent or $9,500 of their salaries, whichever is less. Employees who have 15 or more years of service may be allowed to contribute a few thousand dollars beyond the $9,500 limit. Ask your employee benefits department or the investment provider for the 403(b) plan (or your tax advisor) about eligibility requirements and details about your personal contribution limit.

If you work for a nonprofit or public-sector organization that doesn't offer this benefit, make a fuss and insist on it. Nonprofit organizations have no excuse not to offer a 403(b) plan to their employees. This type of plan includes virtually no out-of-pocket set-up expenses or ongoing accounting fees like a 401(k). The only requirement is that the organization must deduct the appropriate contribution from employees' paychecks and send the money to the investment company that handles the 403(b) plan.

SEP-IRAs

If you're self-employed, you can establish your own retirement savings plans. You can and should do this through the excellent no-load mutual fund companies discussed in this book.

Simplified employee pension individual retirement account (SEP-IRA) plans require little paperwork to set up. They allow you to sock away from about 13 percent (13.04 percent, to be exact) of your self-employment income (business revenue minus expenses) up to a maximum of $22,500 (1994) per year. Each year, you decide the amount you want to contribute — there are no minimums. Your contributions to a SEP-IRA are deducted from your taxable income, saving you big-time on federal and state taxes. As with other retirement plans, your money compounds without taxation until withdrawal.

Keoghs

Keogh plans are another retirement savings option for the self-employed. And also can and should be established through the no-load fund providers recommended in this book.

Keogh plans require a bit more paperwork to set up and administer than SEP-IRAs (I show you the differences in Chapter 10). The appeal of certain types of Keoghs is that they allow you to put away a greater percentage (20 percent) of your self-employment income (revenue less your expenses), up to a maximum of $30,000 per year.

Another appeal of Keogh plans is that they allow business owners to maximize the contributions to which they are entitled relative to employees in two ways that they can't with SEP-IRAs. First, all types of Keogh plans allow vesting schedules, which require employees to remain with the company a number of years before they earn the right to their retirement account balances. If an employee leaves prior to being fully vested, the unvested balance reverts to the remaining plan participants.

Second, Keogh plans allow for Social Security integration. Integration effectively allows those in the company who are high-income earners (usually the owners) to receive larger percentage contributions for their accounts than the less highly compensated employees. The logic behind this idea is that Social Security taxes top out once you earn more than $60,600 (for 1994). Social Security integration allows you to make up for this ceiling.

When establishing your Keogh plan at a mutual fund or discount brokerage company, ask what features their plan allows — especially if you have employees and are interested in vesting schedules and Social Security integration.

Select the Keogh that fits you best

Anything that involves the IRS is never simple. Keoghs are no exception. You've got several options. While these options make understanding Keoghs a bit of a headache, they allow you to choose a Keogh plan that best meets your needs.

A profit-sharing plan allows for the same contribution limits as SEP-IRA and is suitable for small business owners who want to use vesting schedules and Social Security integration, which cannot be done with SEP-IRA plans. You can vary your contribution (and even contribute nothing if you'd like) each year.

Another option is a money-purchase pension plan, which appeals to self-employed people who want to contribute more to a retirement account than can be done with a profit-sharing plan or SEP-IRA. The maximum tax-deductible contribution here is the lesser of 20 percent of your self-employment income or $30,000 per year. While allowing for a larger contribution, there is no flexibility allowed on the percentage contribution you make each year — it's fixed. Thus, these plans make the most sense for high-income earners who are comfortable enough financially to know that they can continue making large contributions.

If you don't like the rigidity of a money purchase plan but like the ability it gives you to contribute more, check out a paired plan, which combines the best features of the profit-sharing and money-purchase plans. You can attain the maximum contribution possible (20 percent) that you get with the money-purchase pension plan but have some of the flexibility that comes with a profit-sharing plan. You can fix your money-purchase pension plan contribution at 8 percent and contribute anywhere from 0 to 12 percent of your net income to your profit-sharing plan.

If you are a consistently high-income earner between the ages of 45 to 50 who wants to save more than $30,000 per year in a retirement account, you have still another option: a defined-benefit plan.

Individual Retirement Accounts (IRAs)

Anyone with employment (or alimony) income can contribute to IRA accounts. You may contribute up to $2,000 each year or the amount of your employment or alimony income if it's less than $2,000 in a year. If you are a nonworking spouse, you're eligible to put $250 per year into a so-called spousal IRA.

Your contributions to an IRA may or may not be tax deductible. If you're single and your adjusted gross income is $25,000 or less for the year, you can deduct your IRA contribution. If you're married and file your taxes jointly, you're entitled to a full IRA deduction if your AGI (adjusted gross income) is $40,000 per year or less.

If you make more than these amounts, you can take a full IRA deduction if and only if you (or your spouse) are not an active participant in any retirement plan. The only way to know for certain whether you're an active participant is to look at the W-2 form that your employer sends you early in the year to file with your tax returns. Little boxes indicate whether or not you are an active participant in a pension or deferred-compensation plan. If either of these boxes is checked, you're an active participant.

If you are a single-income earner with an adjusted gross income (AGI) above $25,000 but below $35,000, or part of a couple with an AGI above $40,000 but below $50,000, you're eligible for a partial IRA deduction, even if you're an active participant. The size of the IRA deduction that you may claim depends on where you fall in the income range. For example, a single-income earner at $30,000 is entitled to half ($1,000) of the full IRA deduction because his or her income falls halfway between $25,000 and $35,000.

Even if you can't deduct a portion or all of a $2,000 IRA contribution, you can still contribute the full $2,000 to an IRA as long as you had that much employment income during the year. An IRA contribution that is not tax deductible is called, not surprisingly, a *nondeductible* IRA contribution. The benefit of this type of contribution is that the money can still compound and grow without taxation. For a person who plans to leave contributions in the IRA for a long time (a decade or more), this tax-deferred compounding makes even nondeductible contributions worthwhile.

Consider a nondeductible IRA only *after* you have exhausted the possibilities of contributing to retirement accounts that do provide an immediate tax deduction, such as 401(k)s, SEP IRAs, Keoghs, and so on.

Annuities

Annuities are peculiar investment products. They are contracts that are backed by insurance companies. If you, the annuity holder (investor), should die during the so-called accumulation phase (that is, prior to receiving payments from the annuity), your designated beneficiary is guaranteed to be reimbursed the amount of your original investment. This is not life insurance!

Annuities, like IRAs, allow your capital to grow and compound without taxation. You defer taxes until withdrawal. However, unlike an IRA that has a $2,000 annual contribution limit, you can deposit as much as you want in any year into an annuity — even a million dollars if you've got it! As with a so-called nondeductible IRA, you get no up-front tax deduction for your contributions. See Chapter 9 for examples of when these may make sense. (Some fund companies offer annuity plans.)

Prioritizing your retirement contributions

If you have access to more than one type of retirement account, prioritize which accounts to use by what they give you in return. Your first contributions should be to employer-based plans that match your contributions. After that, contribute to any other employer or self-employed plans that allow tax-deductible contributions. If you've contributed the maximum possible to tax-deductible plans or do not have access to such plans, contribute to an IRA.

If you've maxed out on contributions to an IRA or don't have this choice because you lack employment income, consider an annuity or tax-friendly investments (discussed in the next section). Annuities get the lowest priority since your contributions are not tax-deductible and because annuities carry higher annual operating fees due to the small insurance that comes with them.

Taxes and mutual funds

Many people invest their money in ways that increase their tax burdens. In many cases, they (and sometimes their advisors) don't consider the tax impact of their investment strategies.

For investments that you hold in *tax-sheltered* retirement accounts such as IRAs and 401(k) plans, you don't need to worry about taxes. This money is not taxed until you actually withdraw funds from the retirement accounts. Thus, you should never invest money that is inside retirement accounts in tax-favored investments such as tax-free money market funds and bonds (discussed later in this chapter).

You are far more likely to make tax mistakes investing assets held outside retirement accounts. Distributions, such as dividends, and capital gains (explained in Chapter 11), produced by non-retirement account mutual funds and other investments are all exposed to taxation.

Make sure that you take advantage of opportunities to direct your employment earnings into retirement accounts. That way, you don't need to concern yourself with the taxability of mutual fund distributions.

If you are investing money outside of retirement accounts, here are some investing tax issues to be aware of based on your tax bracket:

- ✔ **31 percent or higher federal tax bracket.** If you're in this bracket, you should definitely avoid mutual funds and other investments that produce much taxable income. For tax year 1996, the 31 percent federal bracket started at $58,150 for singles and $96,900 for married couples filing jointly.

- ✔ **28 percent federal tax bracket.** In most cases, you should be as well or better off in mutual funds that do not produce major taxable income when investing outside retirement accounts.

- ✔ **15 percent federal bracket.** Investments that produce taxable income are just fine for you. You will likely end up with *less* if you purchase mutual fund investments that produce tax-free income.

In this section are some of the best methods to reduce the taxes on mutual funds held outside of a retirement account. In Chapter 12, I explain how to read mutual fund tax forms (yuck).

Use tax-free money market and bond funds

If you're in a high enough tax bracket (federal 28 percent to 31 percent or higher), you may find that you come out ahead with tax-free investments. Tax-free investments yield less than comparable investments that produce taxable earnings. But because of the difference in taxes, the earnings from tax-free investments *can* end up being greater than what you're left with from taxable investments. (See Chapters 6 and 7.)

Invest in tax-friendly stock mutual funds

Too often, when selecting non-retirement account investments, people mistakenly focus on past rates of return. We all know that the past is no guarantee for the future. But an even worse mistake is choosing an investment with a reportedly high rate of return without considering tax consequences.

Investors often make this mistake when investing in stock mutual funds. Historically, however, many mutual fund investors and publications have not focused on the tax-friendliness of some mutual funds versus others. Just as you should avoid investing in funds with high sales commissions, high annual operating expenses, and poor relative performance, you should also avoid tax-unfriendly funds.

What's my tax bracket?

Your tax bracket is actually known as your *marginal tax rate*, which is the rate you pay on the last dollar you earn. For example, if you earned $35,000 last year, the marginal rate is the rate you paid on the dollar that brought you from $34,999 to $35,000. The reason this subject comes up in the first place is that the government charges you different tax rates for different parts of your annual income.

You pay less tax on your *first* dollars of earnings and more tax on your *last* dollars of earnings. For example, if you're single and your taxable income totaled $30,000 during 1996, you paid federal tax at the rate of 15 percent on the first $24,000 of taxable income and 28 percent on income above $24,000 up to $30,000.

Your marginal tax rate is the rate of tax that you pay on your *last* or so-called *highest* dollars of income. In the example of a single person with taxable income of $30,000, that person's federal marginal tax rate is 28 percent. In other words, he or she effectively pays a 28 percent federal tax on his or her last dollars of income — those dollars earned between $24,000 and $30,000.

Your marginal tax rate allows you to quickly calculate additional taxes that you would pay on additional income or the amount of taxes that you save by contributing more into retirement accounts or by reducing your taxable income (for example, by investing in tax-friendly mutual funds).

Here are federal tax rates for singles and for married households filing jointly.

1996 Federal Income Tax Brackets and Rates

Singles *Taxable Income*	*Married-Filing-Jointly* *Taxable Income*	*Federal Tax Rate*
Less than $24,000	Less than $40,100	15%
$24,000 to $58,150	$40,100 to $96,900	28%
$58,150 to $121,300	$96,900 to $147,700	31%
$121,300 to $263,750	$147,700 to $263,750	36%
More than $263,750	More than $263,750	39.6%

When comparing two similar funds, most people would prefer a fund earning returns of 14 percent per year to a fund earning 12 percent. But what if the 14-percent-per-year fund causes you to pay a lot more in taxes? What if, after factoring in taxes, the 14-percent-per-year fund nets just 9 percent, while the 12-percent-per-year fund nets an effective 10 percent return? In such a case, you'd be unwise to choose a fund solely on the basis of the higher reported rate of return.

Numerous mutual funds effectively reduce their shareholders' returns because of their tendency to produce more taxable distributions (capital gains and dividends). Many mutual fund investors are affected by taxable distributions, because more than half the money in mutual funds resides outside tax-sheltered retirement accounts.

All mutual fund managers buy and sell stocks during the course of a year. Whenever a mutual fund manager sells securities, any gain or loss from those securities must be distributed to fund shareholders. Securities sold at a loss can offset those liquidated at a profit. If a fund manager has a tendency to often cash in winners rather than holding them, significant capital gains distributions can result.

Choosing mutual funds that minimize capital gains distributions helps investors defer taxes on their profits. Index mutual funds, which maintain more stable investment portfolios, tend to produce fewer capital gains distributions since they hold their securities longer. By allowing their capital to continue compounding as it would in an IRA or other retirement account, fund shareholders receive a higher total return. (See Chapter 8 for more details on stock index funds.)

Investors who purchase mutual funds outside tax-sheltered retirement accounts should also consider the time of year they purchase shares in funds. December is the most common month in which mutual funds make capital gains distributions. When making purchases late in the year, investors may want to find out whether and when the fund may make a significant capital gains distribution. The December payout generally happens when a fund has had a good performance year. For funds I recommend, the month of distribution is listed in the Appendix.

Should You Hire an Advisor?

You may decide that it's too much trouble to research mutual funds and plan the rest of your finances. So you'll be tempted to find a financial advisor to relieve you of the burden.

Don't do it!

Actually, what I mean to say is, don't do it until you've explored the real reasons why you want to hire help. If you're like many people, you may hire an advisor for the wrong reasons. Or you'll hire the wrong type of advisor, an incompetent one or one with major conflicts of interest.

The wrong reason to hire an advisor

Don't hire an advisor because of what I call the *crystal ball phenomenon*. Although you know that you're not a dummy, you may feel that you can't possibly make informed and intelligent investing decisions because you don't closely follow or even understand the financial markets and what makes them move.

No one that you're going to hire has a crystal ball. No one can predict future movements in the financial markets, which investments will do well, and which won't. Besides, the financial markets are pretty darn efficient — meaning that lots of smart folks are following the markets, so it's highly unlikely that you or an advisor, myself included, could outfox them. The few extraordinary money managers beat the market averages by a couple percent per year over the long haul. The few that have been able to do this — Peter Lynch, John Neff, Warren Buffet — are or were so busy managing money that they barely had time for publicity-getting media interviews, let alone rendering personal financial advice.

Besides, investing intelligently in mutual funds isn't that complicated. You bought this book. Read it, and you'll learn what you need to know to invest in funds.

The right reasons to hire an advisor

Consider hiring an advisor if you're

- ✔ Too busy to do your investing yourself
- ✔ Always putting it off because you don't enjoy doing it
- ✔ Uncomfortable making investing decisions on your own
- ✔ Wanting a second opinion
- ✔ Needing help with establishing and prioritizing financial goals

Beware of conflicts of interest

Early in this chapter, I reviewed ten things to do before investing. If you're thinking about hiring a financial planner to help plan your financial future as well as make mutual fund investing decisions, read on to learn how to avoid another major mistake that Justine and Max made — listening to the wrong advisor.

There are numerous land mines and conflicts of interest awaiting the naive investor venturing into the investment and financial planning fields. A major one is the enormous conflict of interest that is created when "advisors" sell products that bring them commissions to people they purport to advise.

The Consumer Federation of America said it best in its review of the investment industry: "Today's investors go up against a deadly combination of abusive securities industry practices and regulatory inattentiveness when investing their money."

The vast majority of *financial planners* and *financial consultants* sell products and work on commission, creating the type of conflict of interest I described here. As discussed in Chapter 3, there's no good reason to purchase load funds; if you do, you're paying unnecessary sales commissions, and you won't get objective advice from the person selling you the funds.

Selling a product that provides a commission tends to skew a planner's recommendations. Products that carry commissions mean that you have fewer dollars working in the investments you buy. Because a commission is earned only when a product is sold, such a product or service almost inevitably becomes more attractive in the planner's eyes than any other option.

Don't be lulled into a false sense of security and hire someone just because call themselves a financial planner. If a planner is selling products and working on commission, he's a salesperson, not a planner. There's nothing wrong with salespeople — you just don't want one spouting suggestions when you're looking for objective investment and financial planning advice.

Another danger of trusting the recommendation of a commission-based planner is that he may steer you toward products that have the biggest payback for him. These are among the *worst* for you because they siphon off even more of your money up front to pay the commission. They also tend to be among the costliest and riskiest financial products available.

Planners who are commission-greedy may also try to *churn* your investments. They'll encourage you to buy and sell frequently, attributing the need to changes in the economy or in the companies you've invested in. More trading means — big surprise — more commissions for the broker.

Because of how they earn their money, many planners are biased in favor of certain strategies and products. As a result, they typically do not keep your overall financial needs in mind. For example, if you have a problem with accumulated credit card debts, some planners may never know (or care) because they're focused on selling you an investment product.

Sometimes, your best investment is to pay off loans you have, be they credit card, auto, or even mortgage debts. Some financial planners don't recommend this strategy, however, because paying down debts depletes capital that you could invest. Paying off debts reduces your need to buy investments or turn your money over to the planner to manage.

One of your best financial options is to take advantage of saving through your employer's retirement savings plan because it's tax-deductible. Planners are reluctant to recommend taking full advantage of this option because most people lack the monthly income to save and invest in addition to what they may contribute through their employer's plans.

Another conflict of interest is that of planners creating dependency. They may try to make things seem so complicated that you believe you can't possibly manage your finances or make major financial decisions without them.

Your best options for help

You must do your homework *before* hiring any financial advisor. The first step is to try your best to learn as much as you can about what you're seeking help with. That way, if you do hire someone to help you make investment and other financial decisions, you'll be in a better position to evaluate their capabilities and expertise.

Realizing that you need to hire someone to help you make and implement financial decisions can be a valuable insight. Even if you have a modest income or modest assets, spending a few hours of your time and a few hundred dollars to hire a professional can be a good investment. The services that advisors and planners offer, their fees, and their competence vary tremendously.

Financial advisors make money in one of three ways: from commissions based on sales of financial products, from fees based on a percentage of your assets that they are investing, or from hourly consultation charges. I've already discussed why the first option is the least preferred option (if you really want to or are forced to work with an investment broker who works on commission, be sure to read the last section in this chapter).

A better choice than a commission-based planner is one who works on what's called a *fee-basis*. In other words, they are paid by fees from clients such as yourself rather than from the investments and other financial products that they recommend you buy. This compensation system removes the incentives to sell you products with high commissions and churn your investments through lots of transactions to generate more commissions.

The most cost-effective method is to hire an advisor who charges an hourly fee and doesn't sell investment and other financial products. Because he doesn't sell any financial products, his objectivity is maintained. He doesn't perform money management, so he can help you get your financial house in order and make comprehensive financial decisions, including selecting good mutual funds.

Your primary risk in selecting a planner, hourly-based or otherwise, is hiring one who is competent. You can address this by checking references and learning enough yourself to discern between good and bad financial advice. There is further risk if you and the advisor don't clearly define the work to be done and the approximate total cost before you begin. Don't forget to set your parameters up front.

A drawback of an entirely different kind occurs when you don't follow through on the recommendations of your advisor. You paid for this work but didn't act on it, the potential benefit is lost. Your hourly-based planner should therefore make provisions to ensure that she is there to help with implementation. If part of the reason that you're hiring an advisor in the first place is because you're too busy or not interested enough to make changes to your financial situation, then you should look for this support in the services you buy from the planner.

If you just need someone as a sounding board for ideas or to recommend some specific no-load mutual funds, hire an hourly-based planner for only one or two sessions of advice. You save money doing the legwork and implementation on your own. Just make sure the planner is willing to give you specific enough advice that you can implement it on your own. Some planners will intentionally withhold specific advice and recommendations to create the need for you to hire them to do more, perhaps even to manage your money.

If you have a lot of money you want managed among a variety of mutual fund investments, you can hire a financial advisor who charges a percentage of your assets under management. Some of these advisors also offer financial planning services. Some just manage money in mutual funds and other investments.

In the chapters ahead, you should learn enough to make wise mutual fund investing decisions. You owe it to yourself to read the rest of the book *before* deciding whether to hire some financial help. Chapter 19 covers the ten issues to consider and questions to ask when hiring an advisor to help with mutual fund investing.

If you must have a salesperson

Despite the additional (and hence, avoidable) sales charges that apply when you purchase a load fund instead of a no-load fund, you might be forced to, or actually want to, buy a load fund through a salesperson working on commission. Perhaps you work for an employer that set up a retirement plan with only load funds as the investment option. Or your Uncle Ernie, who's a stockbroker, will put you in the family doghouse if you transfer your money out of his firm and into no-load funds. Maybe you really trust your broker because of a long-standing and productive investment relationship (is it because of the broker or the financial markets?).

If you're comfortable and willing to pay 4 percent to as much as 8.5 percent to invest in mutual funds, there are a number of ways that you should protect your money and well-being. In the best of worlds, your money should grow and multiply and help you to achieve your personal and financial goals. But in the worst of worlds, you could be sold poor or inappropriate investments that handicap your ability to retire when you want, buy a home, or meet some other important financial obligation.

Many sales occupations pay commissions on the basis of the amount and type of product sold. As you may imagine, this creates an inherent conflict of interest since the salesperson, all things being equal, has a financial incentive that's at odds with yours: to sell you a higher commission product. Another conflict is that the salesperson only gets paid if he sells you something.

Unlike the real estate profession in which an employee's title — real estate broker or agent — clearly conveys how they make their money, many investment salespeople today have appellations that obscure what they do and how they make money. A common misnomer: financial planner, financial consultant, or financial advisor as a name for salespeople who used to be called stock, securities, or insurance brokers.

Herein lies one of the most important things to watch out for if you're going to invest through a commission-based investment salesperson: make sure you've already decided what money you want to invest and how it fits into your overall financial plans. This example will illustrate the dangers of not doing this.

Joe, an intelligent travel executive, began to feel the need to get serious about investing for his retirement after he turned 40. He and his wife received a call from a "financial planner" who recommended some load mutual funds that they should invest in monthly. When Joe asked the planner's opinion about contributing to his company retirement plan, the planner said that Joe's employer's investment options were poor and that he was better off investing in the funds that the planner recommended.

Actually, through his company's retirement plan, Joe had access to some of the best no-load mutual funds via the Fidelity fund options that he could use. More importantly, however, was the fact that if Joe invested through his company retirement plan instead of through the financial planner, his contributions would be immediately tax-deductible. And once the money was inside Joe's employer's retirement plan, the money would compound and grow without taxation until the money was withdrawn in the future.

Joe's planner didn't recommend this course of action because he was selling mutual funds to earn a commission. The more money Joe invested through his company's retirement plan, the less was available to invest with the financial planner. Joe's planner did him a terrible disservice — the planner had a big financial incentive to do so.

If you've optimized the structuring of your finances and you have a chunk of money that you're willing to pay as a sales charge to invest in load funds, you want to make sure that you're getting the best funds for your investment dollars. The criteria to use in selecting those load funds are no different from what you use to select no-load funds. You want to invest in funds managed by mutual fund companies and portfolio managers that have track records of expertise, that take a level of risk that fits your needs, and that charge reasonable annual operating expenses.

Some investors overlook the annual operating expenses that funds, both load and no-load, charge. The annual operating fees are deducted from your funds' investment returns in much the same way that IRS taxes are deducted from your paycheck — with one critical difference. Your paystub shows how much you pay in taxes, whereas your mutual fund account statement will never show the fund's operating expense charges.

Never invest in a mutual fund without knowing all the charges — sales charges, annual operating expenses, and any annual maintenance or account fees. You can find these in a fund's prospectus or by calling the fund company's 800 number.

Part II
The Main Course:
Nothing but the Best

In this part...

Here you learn all the details, differences, and nuances of the major types of funds and how and when to use them. I recommend the best money market, bond, and stock funds to meet the needs of the most finicky and particular of fund investors. And just to make sure I don't leave you hanging, I pull 'em all together for you in the last chapter to show you how real, live people fit funds into their overall financial plans. To make it all as clear as possible, I go through lots of helpful specific examples to show you how to construct a mutual fund portfolio.

Chapter 6

Funds That Beat the Bank — Money Market Funds

. . . .

In This Chapter

▶ What are money market funds?

▶ How do money market funds invest your money?

▶ How do you choose the right fund for you?

▶ The best money market funds

. . . .

*J*ust a generation ago, you had hundreds of alternatives for safely investing your spare cash — you could schlep around town and shop among banks, banks, and still more banks. Although it may seem that safe money investors had many alternatives, they really didn't. As a result, yields weren't all that great compared with what a large institutional investor with hundreds of thousands to millions of dollars could obtain by investing in ultra-safe short-term securities.

Back in the early 1970s, money market mutual funds were born. The concept was fairly simple. The money market mutual fund would invest in the same safe, higher-yielding financial instruments that only those with big bucks could buy. The money fund would then sell shares to investors who didn't have the big bucks to invest. By pooling together the money from thousands of investors, the money fund could offer investors a decent yield (after charging a fee to cover the fund's operational expenses and a profit).

In their first years of operation, these "people's" money funds had little cash flowing in. By 1977, less than $4 billion were in money market funds. But then interest rates rose precipitously as inflation took hold. Soon, bank depositors found that the rates of interest they could earn could rise no more, since banks were limited by federal regulations to paying 5 percent interest.

As interest rates skyrocketed in the late 1970s and investors learned that they could earn more percentage points (see Figure 6-1) by switching from bank accounts to money market funds, money flooded into money market mutual funds. Within just four years, money market fund assets mushroomed more than 50-fold to $200 billion.

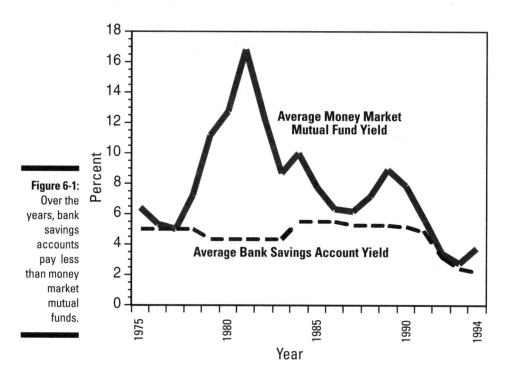

Figure 6-1:
Over the years, bank savings accounts pay less than money market mutual funds.

Money Market Funds Defined

Money market funds are a type of mutual fund. This fact often gets lost in discussions and writings about mutual funds in which many people equate mutual funds with stocks. In addition to stocks and money market securities, mutual funds can also invest in bonds.

Money market mutual funds are a large (assets totaling around $750 billion) and unique part of the mutual fund industry's offering. Money market funds are the only type of mutual fund that do not fluctuate in value. All mutual funds quote their price in dollars per share. Bond and stock mutual fund share prices fluctuate from day to day depending on how the stock and bond markets are doing. Money market funds, in stark contrast, are locked in at a $1 per share price.

Money markets funds may appear to be the most boring of mutual fund investments, and in a sense they are. As with a bank savings account, your principal investment in a money market fund will not change in value all the while you're earning dividends (same as the interest on a bank account). However, money market mutual funds offer several significant benefits over bank savings accounts:

- **Higher yields.** What first caught investors' attention — the higher yields available on money market mutual funds versus bank accounts back when interest rates zoomed up in the late 1970s and early 1980s — still holds true today. Money market mutual funds today still pay a higher yield than equivalent bank accounts, despite the deregulation of the banking industry (refer to Figure 6-1).

  How and why do banks continue to pay less interest? Two reasons. First, banks have a lot of overhead due to all of the branch offices they operate. Second, banks know that they can get away with paying less since many of their depositors, perhaps including you, believe that the FDIC insurance that comes with a bank savings account makes it safer than a money market mutual fund. A section later in the chapter dispels this myth.

- **Multiple tax flavors.** Besides the lower rate of return, another problem with bank savings accounts is that they come in one — and only one — tax flavor: taxable. There is no such thing as a bank savings account that pays you tax-free interest. Money market funds, however, come in a variety of tax-free versions, paying dividends free of federal or state tax or both.

- **Check writing.** Another useful feature that comes with money market mutual funds is the ability to write checks, without charge, against your account. Most mutual fund companies require that the checks that you write be for larger amounts — typically at least $250. They don't want you using these accounts to pay all of your small household bills because checks cost money to process.

- **Convenient access to invest in other funds.** Money market funds are your home base. Once you've established a money market mutual fund, you can usually do exchanges into the fund company's other mutual funds by calling the fund company's 800 line. This eliminates the need to complete additional application forms every time you want to invest in a new fund. Paperwork nirvana!

- **No lines and traffic jams.** Because you can invest and transact in mutual funds over the phone and through the mail, you can save yourself considerable time. No more waiting in long lines at a bank branch or wasting gas and your free time driving to the bank.

  Sometimes, you'll get stuck on hold for a short time when you call a mutual fund company. The better companies (recommended in this book) generally won't leave you hanging for more than 15 to 30 seconds. If they do, please write me in care of the publisher and let me know so that together we can hassle (or delete!) them for the next edition.

Banks have developed their own money market deposit accounts (MMDAs) that are money fund wannabees. Banks set the interest rate over time, and the interest rate is generally lower than on the better money market mutual funds. Check writing, if it's available, is usually restricted to three or some number of checks per month.

Scrambling now as late-comers in the mutual fund business, some banks are offering real money market mutual funds, including tax-free ones. Again, the better money market mutual funds offered by mutual fund companies are generally superior (see recommendations later in the chapter) to those offered by banks.

What money funds can be used for

Earning a higher yield gets most people interested in a money market mutual fund. Money market mutual funds are an ideal, higher yielding substitute for bank savings and bank money market deposit accounts. If you've got too much cash dozing away in your checking account, you can plow some of that into your money fund too. Of course, not all money market mutual funds are created equal. But soon I'll explain how to pick your funds and where to find the best.

Money market funds are a good place to keep your emergency cash reserve. Because you don't know what the future holds in store, it's wise to prepare for the unexpected — such as the job loss, large expenses, and the like. Six months of living expenses is a good emergency reserve target for most people (for example, if you spend $2,000 in an average month, keep $12,000 reserved).

You may be able to skinny by with just three months' expenses if you have other accounts such as a 401(k) or family members and close friends that you could tap for a loan. Consider keeping up to one year's expenses handy if your income fluctuates wildly from year to year. If your profession involves a high risk of job loss and if it could take you a long while to find another job, you also need a significant cash safety net.

Money funds are also a suitable place to keep money that you plan to use for these other purposes:

> ✔ **Money awaiting investment in the near future.** If you're saving money for a home that you expect to purchase soon (next year or so), a money fund can be a safe place to accumulate and grow the down payment. Some people may feel this is boring and wasteful, but remember: earning a healthy enough return to keep your money growing about as fast or slightly faster than the rate of inflation without the potential for market fluctuations that come with bond and stock investments is much underrated.

If you have a chunk of money that you want to invest for longer-term purposes but that you don't want to invest all at once for fear that you may buy into stocks and bonds just before a big drop, a money market fund can be a friendly home to the money awaiting investment as you purchase into your chosen investment gradually over time (see Chapter 9).

✔ **Business accounts.** Just as you can use a money market fund for your personal purposes, you can open a money market fund for your business. This account can be used for depositing checks received from customers and holding excess funds as well as for paying bills via the check-writing feature. Some money funds allow checks to be written for any size amount and can be completely replace a bank checking account. I've had my business checking account for years in a money market mutual fund.

✔ **Personal checking accounts.** Money market funds that allow for unlimited check writing can be established and used for household checking purposes as well. The discount brokerage firms that offer accounts with this capability downplay your ability to do this. You can leave your bank altogether — some money funds even come with debit cards that can be used at bank ATMs for a nominal fee! See the recommended funds later in this chapter for which ones allow checks to be written for any amount.

You may also be interested to know that you can establish direct deposit with most money market funds. You can have your paycheck, monthly Social Security benefit check, or most other regular payments you receive from larger organizations zapped electronically to your money market mutual fund account. Some people I know use this feature so that their extra money month-to-month resides in their money fund rather than in a bank account.

Money fund worries you may have

Investors new to money market mutual funds sometimes worry about what they're getting themselves into. It's good to be concerned and educated *before* you move your money into something you've never before invested in.

Most people don't worry about the money they keep in the bank. They should — well, at least a tiny bit. First of all, banks get burglarized and defrauded more than mutual funds! Although crooks and white collar criminals won't take your bank account money, keeping money in a bank account, as in any investment, carries some risks. There's the risk that the purchasing power of your bank deposit will be eroded by inflation because of the paltry interest your money is earning. And the FDIC insurance system is a government insurance system — that's hardly an ironclad, 100 percent safety guarantee.

When the bank or credit union may be better for you

If you have less than a thousand or two dollars to invest, the easiest path may be to keep this excess savings in a local bank or credit union. Your local bank may also appeal to you if you like being able to do business face to face. Perhaps you operate a business where a lot of cash is processed; in this case, the convenience and other services that a local bank office offers can't be beat.

For investing short-term excess cash, look first to the institution where you keep your checking account. Keeping this savings in your checking account may make financial sense if the extra money helps you avoid monthly service charges because your balance occasionally dips below the minimum. In fact, keeping money in a separate savings account instead of in your checking account may *not* benefit you if service charges wipe out your interest earnings.

Don't forget to shop around for better deals on your checking account since minimum balance requirements, service fees, and interest rates vary quite a bit among banks. Credit unions offer some of the best deals, although they usually don't offer extensive access to free ATMs. The largest banks with the most ATM machines in the most areas — you know, the ones that spend gobs of money on advertising jingles and billboards — usually offer the worst terms on checking and savings accounts.

Here are the concerns that I hear from people like you about money market funds, and the reasons I think you should all stop worrying so much:

Lack of FDIC insurance

Money market mutual funds are not insured. Bank accounts come with insurance that protects up to $100,000 you have deposited in a bank. So, if a bank fails because it lends too much money to people and companies that go bankrupt or abscond with the funds, you should get your money back. Mutual fund companies can't fail because they have a dollar invested in securities for every dollar you deposited in their money fund. (Banks, by the way, are required to have available just 12 cents for every dollar you hand over to them.)

It is possible that a money market fund's investments may decline slightly in value — thus reducing the share price of the money market fund below a dollar. There have been a few cases where money market funds bought some bad investments. However, in each and every case except one, the money market fund was "bailed out" — that is, cash was infused into the money fund by the mutual fund company, thus enabling the fund to maintain a price of $1 per share.

One money market fund did "break the buck." One newspaper article dramatically headlined, "Investors Stunned as a Money Fund Folds." The article went on to say, "The fund's collapse is the latest blunder to shake investors' confidence in the nation's mutual fund industry." While such hype may help to fill readers with anxiety (and perhaps sell more newspapers), it obscures several important facts. The fund didn't collapse but rather was liquidated because its investors, who were all small banks, were the owners of the fund and they decided they wanted to disband it. The fund did not have money in it from investors like you and me. If it had, the fund owners surely would have bailed it out. You should also know that only 6 percent of the investing banks' money was lost. Hardly a collapse — and I doubt anyone was stunned!

If you have more than $100,000 in one bank and that bank fails, you can lose the money over the $100,000 insurance limit. I've seen more than a few cases where people had several hundred thousand — in one case, a person who came to me for advice had nearly $2 million — sitting in a bank account! Now that's risk! Since 1980, more than 1,000 banks have failed. In recent years, because the government has taken a hard line on not going beyond the $100,000 insurance limit, bank depositors have lost hundreds of millions of dollars.

Stick with larger mutual fund companies if you're worried about the lack of FDIC insurance. They have the financial wherewithal and the largest incentive to save a floundering money fund. Fortunately, the larger fund companies have the best money funds anyway.

The check may get lost or stolen

If you have the kind of mail delivery that I do in San Francisco, I can understand your concerns. However, if you're worried about a deposit being lost in the mail, don't. If it does happen (it rarely does), all you do is have the check(s) reissued.

No one can legally cash a check made payable to you. Don't mistakenly think that going to your local bank in person is any safer — you could slip on some dog droppings or get carjacked.

If you're really concerned about the mail, use a fund company or discount broker with branch offices. I would not recommend spending the extra money and time required to send your check via registered or certified mail. You'll know if your check got there when you get the statement from the fund company processing the deposit. If you're depositing a check made payable to you, just be sure to endorse the check with the notation "for deposit only" under your signature.

How can I access my money?

Although it may appear that you can't easily and quickly access your money market fund holdings, you can, in fact, efficiently tap your money market fund in a variety of ways. (**Note:** You can use these methods at most fund companies, particularly the larger ones.)

- ✔ **Write a check**. The most efficient way to access your money market fund is to write a check. Suppose you have an unexpectedly large expense that you can't afford to pay out of your bank checking account. Just write a check on your money market mutual fund.

- ✔ **Telephone redemption.** Another handy way to access your money (which may be useful if your money fund checkbook is hidden under a mountain of papers somewhere in the vicinity of your desk) is to call the fund company and ask them to mail you a check for whatever amount you'd like from your money fund.

    Many money funds also allow you to call in to have money sent electronically from the money market fund to your bank account or vice-versa.

- ✔ **Automatic withdrawal plans.** If you need money sent from your money market fund to, say, your local bank checking account, you can establish an automatic electronic funds transfer with your fund company. On a particular day of the month, you can have a set amount of money transferred to your bank account. These transfers can also be done on an as-needed basis.

- ✔ **Wiring.** If you need cash in a flash, an optional feature available on many money market funds is the ability to wire money to and from your bank. There will usually be a small charge on both ends for this. Most companies will also send you money via an overnight express carrier such as Federal Express if you provide them with an account number.

- ✔ **Debit Cards.** Brokerage account money funds that offer debit cards allow access to your money via ATMs (see later in the chapter).

Chapter 10 explains how to establish these account features. Unlike when you visit a bank, visiting the local branch office of a mutual fund company or discount broker that deals in mutual funds won't do you any good in obtaining money from your account. They don't keep money in branch offices because they're not banks. However, you can establish the above account features through the fund's branch office if you didn't when you originally set up your account.

What do money funds invest your money in?

In a moment, I'll describe the different types of securities that a money market fund invests your money in. First, a quick overview. Under SEC regulations, money market funds can invest only in the most credit-worthy securities, and their investments must have an average maturity of less than 120 days. The short-term nature of these securities effectively eliminates the risk of money funds being sensitive to changes in interest rates.

The securities that money market funds use are extremely safe. General-purpose money market funds invest in government-backed securities, bank certificates of deposits, and short-term corporate debt issued by the largest and most credit-worthy companies and the U.S. government (although that may not be much comfort to some of you). Here's the rundown on the major types of securities that money funds hold:

Commercial paper

Companies, particularly large ones, often need to borrow money to help make their businesses grow and prosper. It used to be the case that most companies needing a short-term loan would have to borrow money from a bank. In recent decades, it has become easier to issue short-term debt or IOUs — commercial paper — directly to interested investors.

Money market funds buy high-quality commercial paper that matures typically within 60 to 90 days and is issued by large companies (such as AT&T, Hewlett-Packard, Intel, Kellogg, Texaco), finance firms (such as Ford Motor Credit), banks, and foreign governments.

If you had hundreds of thousands of dollars to invest, you could purchase commercial paper yourself rather than buying it indirectly through a money market fund. I don't recommend this, however, because you incur fees when you do this and you probably don't have the expertise to know what's good to purchase, what's not, and what's a fair price to pay. The best money funds do all this for you plus offer check writing, charging a very small fee in return.

Certificates of deposit

You can go to your local bank and invest some money in a certificate of deposit (CD). A CD is nothing more than a specific-term loan that you make to your banker — ranging anywhere from a month to some number of years.

Money market funds can buy CDs as well. The only difference is that they invest a lot more money — usually millions — in a bank's CD. Thus, they can command a higher interest rate than you can obtain on your own. Money funds buy CDs that mature within one to three months. The money fund is only insured up to $100,000 per bank CD, just like the bank insurance that you and I receive. As with other money fund investments, the money fund does research to determine the credit quality of banks and other institutions that it invests in. Remember that money funds' other investments are not insured.

Derivatives and money funds

Derivatives, which I describe in Chapter 1, should not be a concern if you stick with the better and larger money market funds. There's unfortunately no way to really know if a particular money fund holds risky derivatives, which is done in an attempt to pump up yield. Money fund managers I've talked to have said even they can't discern the degree of risk by examining other money funds' annual reports that list detailed information on the securities held by those funds.

Historically, some managers didn't disclose derivative information because, until derivatives lost money for some investors in 1994, no one cared (or understood them). Now, responsible managers know people care, yet some managers are still not disclosing — some may have something to hide. The SEC should be tougher and require greater uniformity of disclosure.

There are some other types of CDs that money market funds may hold. Yankee CDs are CDs issued by U.S. branches of foreign banks. Eurodollar CDs are simply CDs issued by foreign banks or U.S. banks' foreign branches.

Government debt

McDonald's, the burgermeisters, in many locations have signs saying billions and billions served. (They used to tell you the exact number, but perhaps it was too costly to change as often as necessary). Well, our federal government serves up billions and billions — of debt, that is — in the form of Treasury securities. There's a truckload of federal government debt outstanding— about $ 5 trillion (a trillion is a thousand billion, for those of you who missed that math class).

Most money market funds invest a small portion of their money in Treasuries soon to mature. Money funds also invest in short-term debt issued by government-run and-sponsored agencies such as the Federal Home Loan Bank, which provides funds to the nation's savings and loans, and the Federal National Mortgage Association, which packages and sells government-backed mortgages.

Government agency debt, unlike Treasuries, is not backed by the "full faith and credit of the U.S. government." However, no federal agency has ever defaulted on its debt. While one should never say never, it's unlikely that this would ever happen; the folks back in Washington are certain to avoid the loss of faith in government-issued debt that would surely follow such a default.

As I discuss in more detail later in the chapter, some money market funds specialize in the type of government securities they hold. Treasury money market funds, for example, buy Treasuries and pay dividends that are state tax-free, but federally taxable. State-specific municipal money market funds invest in debt issued by state and local governments in one state. The dividends on state money funds are federal and state tax-free (if you're a resident of that state).

Other stuff

There are bunches of other types of securities that typically make up small portions of a money fund's holdings. *Repurchase agreements (repos)* are overnight investments that money funds send to "dealers" (banks and investment banks' securities divisions), and the money fund receives treasury securities overnight as collateral.

Bankers' acceptances are more complex — they are issued by banks guaranteeing corporation debt incurred from trade. For example, if Sony sends televisions to the U.S. by freight but doesn't want to wait for its money until the ship comes in and stores pay them for the televisions, Sony can get paid right away by borrowing from a bank based on the expected delivery of the televisions a loan to Sony. When the stores get the televisions and pay for them, then Sony's loan gets repaid.

Selecting the Best Money Fund for You

A money market is probably the easiest type of fund to choose. The downside to not making a good choice is not horrendous — you may lose out on some interest, be a little irritated by mediocre customer service, and need to fill out more paperwork later to access better mutual funds through other companies. To save you time and make you the most money, here are the major issues to consider in selecting the best money fund to meet your needs:

Yield and expenses go hand in hand

The main motivation for investing in a money market fund instead of a bank savings account is to earn a greater rate of return, or yield. Within a given category of money market funds (general, Treasury, municipal), money fund managers are investing in the same basic securities. The market for these securities is pretty darn efficient, so "superstar" money fund managers may eke out an extra 0.1 percent per year in yield but not much more.

Select a money fund that does a good job with controlling its expenses. The operating expenses deducted before payment of dividends is the single biggest determinant of yield. All other things being equal (which they usually are with different money market funds), lower operating expenses translate into higher yields for you.

There's no need or reason to tolerate annual operating expenses of greater than 0.5 percent. Top quality funds charge a quarter of one percent or less annually. Remember, lower expenses don't mean that a fund company is cutting corners or providing poor service. Lower expenses are possible in most cases because a fund company has been successful in attracting so much money to invest. As you see in Chapter 7, fund companies with consistently low expenses on their money funds also happen to offer many good bond funds as well.

Money funds 20% off!

Some mutual funds aren't above resorting to the marketing tricks that retailers use. Beware of money market mutual funds running specials or sales. They do this by temporarily waiving (also known as *absorbing*) operating expenses. Like the effect on a steroid-popping athlete's muscles, a money fund's expense tricks artificially pump up a fund's yield.

When the fund managers thirst for profits — and with time they will, since these aren't charities — the operating expenses charged to the fund deflate the too-good-to-be-true yield. Some bond mutual funds (see Chapter 7) engage in this practice as well.

Unlike when you buy from a retailer, the decision to invest in a money fund is usually a long-term proposition. Fund companies like Dreyfus run sales because they know that a good percentage of the fund buyers lured in won't bother leaving (or knowing) when the prices (operating expenses)

are jacked up. Why the SEC allows this poor disclosure is beyond me.

You're better off sticking with funds that maintain "everyday low prices" (for operating expenses) to get the highest long-term yield. You can ensure that your fund isn't running a special by asking what the current operating expense ratio is and whether the fund is waiving some portion of the expenses. You may also discern this by checking the annual operating expense ratio in the fund's prospectus (see Chapter 3).

If you want to move your money to companies having specials and then move it back out when the special's over, you may come out a little ahead in your yield. If you have lots of money and don't mind paperwork, it may actually be worth the bother. But don't forget the value of your time and the chance that you may not stay on top of the fund's expense changes.

Tax considerations

You've probably heard the expression, "It's not what you make, it's what you keep." What you keep on your investment returns is what is left over after the federal and state governments take their cut of your investment income. If you're investing money held outside of a retirement account and you're in a high tax bracket (particularly the federal 31 percent or higher bracket), you should come out ahead by investing in *tax-free* money market funds. If you're in a high-tax state, a *state* money market fund, if good ones exist for your state (see recommended funds in the next section), may be a sound move.

Tax-free refers to the taxability of the dividends paid by the fund. You don't get a tax deduction for money you put into the fund as you do with 401(k) or other retirement-type accounts.

Determining whether tax-free money market funds net you more

If you're in the federal 31 percent tax bracket (which starts at $58,150 of taxable income for singles and $96,900 for married couples filing jointly for tax year 1996), you will *usually* come out ahead in tax-free investments. If you're in the federal 28 percent tax bracket, you may or may not earn more in tax-free money funds.

In order to do the comparison properly, factor in federal as well as state taxes. Suppose, for example, that you call Vanguard, which tells you that its Prime Portfolio money market fund currently yields 4.5 percent. The yield or dividend on this fund is fully taxable.

Suppose further that you are a resident of California and that Vanguard's CA money market fund currently yields 3.0 percent. The California tax-free money market fund pays dividends that are free from federal *and* California state tax. Thus, you get to keep all 3.0 percent that you earn. The income you earn on the Prime Portfolio, on the other hand, is taxed. So here's how you compare the two:

yield on tax-free fund ÷ yield on taxable fund

.03 (3 percent) ÷ .045 (4.5 percent) = 0.67

In other words, the tax-free fund pays a yield of 67 percent of that on the taxable fund. Thus, if you must pay more than 33 percent (1 minus 0.67) in federal and California state tax, you net more in the tax-free fund.

If you do this analysis comparing some funds today, be aware that yields bounce around. The difference in yields between tax-free and taxable funds widens and narrows a bit over time.

A place to call home

Another factor that may be important to you is other investing you plan to do at the fund company where you establish a money market fund. For example, if you decide to do other mutual fund investing in stocks and bonds at T. Rowe Price, then keeping a money market fund at a different firm that offers a slightly higher yield may not be worth the time and administrative hassle, especially if you don't plan on keeping much cash in the money fund.

 If you don't mind the extra paperwork, why not net the extra yield? Calculate based on the yield difference what it's costing you to keep a lower-yielding money fund. Every tenth (0.1) of a percent per $10,000 invested costs you $10 in lost dividends annually.

Seeing eye to eye

Most mutual fund companies don't have many local branch offices. Generally, this helps fund companies to keep their expenses low and pay you greater yields on their money market funds. As discussed previously, you may open and maintain your money market mutual fund through the fund's toll-free 800 phone line and the mail.

There's really not much benefit, expect psychological, for you to select a fund company with an office in your area. But I don't want to diminish the importance of your emotional comfort level. Fund providers Fidelity and Schwab have the largest branch networks. Depending on where you live, you may be near one of the other fund companies I recommend (see Appendix for locations).

Other considerations

Most, but not all, money market funds offer other useful services, such as free check writing, telephone exchange and redemptions, and automated, electronic exchange services with your bank account. The best and larger fund companies I recommend offer all this so you need not generally concern yourself with these issues when debating among money fund options.

As mentioned earlier, most money market funds require that you write checks for at least $250 or $500. Some don't have this restriction, which may be important to you if you want to pay smaller bills out of the account.

Another potentially important issue is the initial minimum investment required to open an account. Most have minimums around $3,000 or so, although some require heftier amounts. If you drop below the minimum at most money market funds, it's no big deal and no charge. Some money funds do, however, charge small fees for use of certain features. I discuss this in the next section.

The best money market funds

Using the criteria I just discussed, this section recommends the best money market funds: those that offer competitive yields, check writing, access to other excellent mutual funds, and other commonly needed money market services. Vanguard funds predominate the list since they offer rock-bottom expenses as well as most of the other goodies. Vanguard's funds generally have minimums of $3,000 to open (their Admiral U.S. Treasury fund with its $50,000 minimum is an exception), and allow check writing as long as the check is for at least $250.

Taxable money market funds

Money market funds that pay taxable dividends are appropriate for retirement account funds awaiting investment as well as non-retirement account money when you're not in a high federal tax bracket (less than 31 percent federal) *and* are not in a high state tax bracket (less than 5 percent). Here are the best taxable money market funds to consider. (At the time this book went to press, the following funds were yielding around 5 percent. Call the fund companies for current yields.)

Vanguard's Money Market Reserves Prime Portfolio has a microscopic operating expense ratio of 0.3 percent per year. This fund has been managed on a daily basis since 1989 by John Hollyer. The fund and the entire "fixed income group" at Vanguard is overseen by Ian MacKinnon, who has been in his position since the group's birth in 1981. ☎ 800-662-7447.

What's my yield now?

To determine the current yield on money funds, simply call the fund's 800 number. Alternatively, check out newspaper yield summaries. The business sections of many larger newspapers carry this data.

Yields on money market funds will fluctuate with overall market yields. A mutual fund's operating-expense percentages may change over time as well. Just to make things challenging for you when you do call, fund representatives don't always have up-to-date information. Fidelity's Spartan fund expenses are more likely to change than other companies' fund expenses. Fidelity Spartan funds can charge operating expense ratios of up to 0.5 percent or so. Historically, it hasn't.

Fidelity's Spartan Money Market has a much higher minimum than Vanguard's. This fund's minimum initial investment is $20,000 for non-retirement accounts, $10,000 for retirement accounts. Its expense ratio, like Vanguard's, is also 0.3 percent. This fund has been managed by John Todd since 1989. Fidelity Spartan money funds charge $2 per check written, $5 for a redemption, exchange, or closing of the account. These fees are waived if your balance is greater than $50,000. So if you're seeking maximum money market returns and don't keep big balances, Vanguard's a better choice. ☎ 800 544-8888.

If you can't afford Spartan's high minimums, Fidelity has other taxable fund options for the proletariat: **Fidelity Cash Reserves** and **Fidelity Daily Income Trust**. These two funds differ from one another in that Daily Income has no minimum check amount requirement (Cash Reserves' check-writing minimum is $500), charges $1 per check written for less than $500, and has a higher minimum initial investment requirement of $5,000 for non-retirement accounts (Cash Reserves has a $2,500 minimum). Both funds have an operating expense ratio of 0.5 percent.

Looking at discount brokerage accounts, **Schwab Value Advantage Money Market** also has a high minimum: $25,000 for non-retirement accounts, $15,000 for retirement accounts. Its expense ratio of 0.4 percent is a bit higher than Fidelity's and Vanguard's best taxable money funds. This fund is managed by Linda Klingman. There's a $5 fee assessed in any month in which the balance drops below $20,000 for non-retirement accounts and $15,000 for retirement accounts and a $5 fee if you sell less than $5,000 in non-retirement and $2,000 in retirement accounts. ☎ (800) 526-8600.

Do I need these extra bells and whistles?

Fidelity's USA account, as some other brokerage accounts, offers things such as a VISA debit card, VISA credit card, and a bill-paying service. The main benefit of these items is that you get more of your financial stuff consolidated onto one statement and simplified administration. For example, your VISA credit card bill balance due is drawn against your core money market account balance, saving you the time and hassle of writing a check to pay your monthly bill.

A debit card looks just like a credit card — it's got the VISA logo on it — but the money is deducted from the money fund within a day or so of your purchases made on the card. If you're used to receiving a credit card bill at month's end and paying it in full, you enjoy free use of that money (called float) for a while. You'll give this up if you use a debit card.

Fidelity's bill-paying service may save you time by automatically paying bills that are the same amount each month as well as saving you from licking and addressing envelopes. Checkbook software programs such as Quicken offer this service as well. Most charge a monthly fee of around $10 for 20 checks.

If you want to use Schwab but don't have big bucks, their lower minimum money market fund is the **Schwab Money Market**. It has a minimum initial investment amount of $1,000 for non-retirement accounts. It weighs in with a hefty 0.7 percent annual operating expense ratio.

If you're using Schwab for discount brokerage services, keep as little as necessary in this money fund. If you want check writing, you'll need to open what's called a SchwabOne account, which offers unlimited check writing of any denomination. However, you'll be assessed a $5 monthly fee any month your balance drops below $5,000. This account offers a VISA debit card as well. SchwabOne comes with 50 free checks and then charges you $9 per 100 additional checks ordered.

If you use Fidelity's brokerage services, so that you can invest in mutual funds from other fund companies, your money awaiting investment goes into the Fidelity Cash account, which isn't a money fund — it's actually an interest-bearing bank account. This pays a horrible yield — it's typically a full percentage point less than the yield on Cash Reserves. If you keep larger balances, you can, however, purchase the other higher-yielding money market funds instead, such as Spartan Money Market and Cash Reserves, through your Fidelity brokerage account.

The Fidelity brokerage account (known as the **Plus account**) can be opened with balances of $2,500 or more. It limits your free check writing to 20 checks per year and charges $10 per check reorder of 25 checks.

The **Fidelity USA account** requires a higher initial minimum, $10,000, but offers unlimited check writing for checks of any size. There's a $10 check reorder fee for 100 checks. USA can come with a VISA debit card and a credit card ($24 annual fee). You won't get copies of your checks back with this account.

The **Fidelity Enhanced USA account** requires a higher minimum balance to open ($25,000), offers a bill payment service for $5 month ($25 set-up fee), and does not charge check reorder fees. This account also charges a $5 monthly fee. You do get actual copies of checks returned to you, and a no-fee VISA or MasterCard charge card.

If you use **Jack White** for your discount brokerage services, be advised that it has terrible money market fund offerings. The taxable **Alliance Capital Reserves** has an outrageous 1.00 percent annual operating fee. If you use White to take advantage of the lower transaction fees its mutual fund service offers (described in Chapter 4), keep your money market balance to the absolute minimum.

If you want to invest in other fund companies' stock and bond funds, it's your call whether or not you should open a money fund with them. USAA offers competitive yields. Their taxable money market fund, **USAA Mutual Money Market,** has an annual operating expense ratio of 0.5 percent, a $3,000 minimum for all types of accounts, and check writing for amounts above $250. ☎800-531-8181. **T. Rowe Price Summit Cash Reserves** has a minimum initial investment of $25,000, a thin expense ratio of 0.5 percent per year, and check writing for amounts of $500 or more. ☎800-638-5660.

U.S. Treasury money market funds

U.S. Treasury money market funds are appropriate if you prefer a money fund that invests in U.S. Treasuries, which have the safety of government backing, or if you're not in a high federal tax bracket (less than 31 percent) but *are* in a high state tax bracket (5 percent or higher). (At the time this book went to press, the following funds were yielding just under 5 percent. Call the fund companies for current yields.)

Vanguard Money Market Reserves U.S. Treasury Portfolio has a $3,000 minimum and 0.3 percent operating expense ratio. **Vanguard's Admiral U.S. Treasury Money Market Portfolio** offers big-ticket investors who can handle the $50,000 minimum initial balance requirement a higher yield, thanks to this fund's 0.15 percent annual expense ratio. ☎ 800-662-7447.

Benham has two U.S. government money market funds — **Capital Preservation** and **Government Agency,** which both have $1,000 minimums and 0.5 percent expense ratios. ☎ 800-472-3389. **USAA's Treasury Money Market** has a 0.4 percent operating cost and a $3,000 minimum. ☎ 800-531-8181.

Fidelity's Spartan U.S. Treasury Money Market has an expense ratio of 0.4 percent. This fund's minimum initial investment is $20,000 for non-retirement accounts. Fidelity Spartan money funds charge $2 per check written, $5 for a redemption, exchange, or closing of the account. These fees are waived if your balance is greater than $50,000. So if you're seeking maximum money market returns and don't keep big balances, use Vanguard. ☎ 800-544-8888.

If you don't need or want to draw on your U.S. Treasury money fund money, you should know that you can purchase Treasury bills directly from your local Federal Reserve bank for no fee, thus saving yourself the annual operating fee that money funds charge. These can be bought in three-, six-, twelve-month, and longer maturities. You have to weigh whether or not you need liquidity and check writing access to the money since you give this up when you leave a money fund. If you need money from your Treasuries before they mature, you must bother with getting and depositing them into a brokerage account. With Vanguard's expense ratios on their Treasury money funds, it's "costing" you $30 per year with a $10,000 balance; $75 per year with a $50,000 balance in Admiral.

Municipal tax-free money market funds

Municipal (a.k.a. muni) money market funds invest in short-term debt issued by state and local governments. A municipal money fund, which pays you federally tax-free dividends, invests in munis issued by state and local governments throughout the country. A state-specific municipal fund invests in state-and local government-issued munis for one state, such as New York. So if you live in New York and buy a New York municipal fund, the dividends on that fund will be federal and NY state tax-free.

So how do you decide whether to buy a nationwide or state-specific municipal money market fund? Federally-tax-free-only money market funds are appropriate when you're in a high federal (31 percent and up) but *not* a high state bracket (less than 5 percent).

If you're in a higher state tax bracket, your state may not have good (or any) state tax-free money market funds available. If you live in any of those states, you're likely best off with one of the following national money market funds. (At the time this book went to press, the following funds were yielding around 3 percent. Call the fund companies for current yields.)

Vanguard Municipal Money Market has a 0.2 percent annual expense ratio and requires $3,000 minimum to open. ☎800-662-7447. **Fidelity Spartan Municipal Money Market** has a 0.4 percent annual expense ratio and requires $25,000 minimum to open. Fidelity Spartan money funds charge $2 per check written and $5 for a redemption, exchange, or closing of the account. These fees are waived if your balance is greater than $50,000. So if you're seeking maximum money market returns and don't keep big balances, use Vanguard. ☎800-544-8888.

USAA Tax-Exempt Money Market, has a 0.4 percent annual expense ratio and requires $3,000 minimum to open. ☎ 800-531-8181.

When you sign up for any of the municipal money market funds, make sure you fill out the correct part of the application for the money market fund or be sure that you say *money market* (and that the telephone representative gets it) if you're doing an exchange over the phone!! Otherwise, you may end up in a municipal bond fund (discussed in the next chapter) that fluctuates in value and is intended as a longer-term investment. See Chapter 10 for how to complete application forms correctly.

The state tax-free money market funds in Table 6-1 are appropriate when you're in a high federal (31 percent and up) *and* a high state tax bracket (5 percent or higher). If none is listed for your state or you're only in a high federal tax bracket, remember that you need to use one of the nationwide muni money markets just described.

Table 6-1	State and Federally Tax-Free Money Market Funds	
Fund	**Operating Expense**	**Minimum to Open**
Vanguard CA Tax-Free Money Market	0.2%	$ 3,000
Fidelity Spartan CA Muni Money Market	0.3%	$ 25,000
Fidelity Spartan CT Muni Money Market	0.5%	$ 25,000
Fidelity Spartan FL Muni Money Market	0.5%	$ 25,000
USAA Tax-Exempt FL Money Market	0.5%	$ 3,000
Benham CA Tax-Free Money Market	0.5%	$ 1,000
Fidelity Spartan MA Muni Money Market	0.5%	$ 25,000
Vanguard NJ Tax-Free Money Market	0.2%	$ 3,000
Fidelity Spartan NY Muni Money Market	0.5%	$ 25,000
USAA Tax-Exempt NY Money Market	0.5%	$ 3,000
Vanguard OH Tax-Free Money Market	0.2%	$ 3,000
Vanguard PA Tax-Free Money Market	0.2%	$ 3,000
Fidelity Spartan PA Muni Money Market	0.5%	$ 25,000
USAA Tax-Exempt VA Money Market	0.5%	$ 3,000

Chapter 7

Funds for Shorter-Term Needs — Bond Funds

*M*any investors, both novice and expert, think that the "b" in bonds is for boring. And they're partly correct. No one gets off on bonds — unless they're an investment banker or broker who gets to sell them and work on commission.

But you should take the time to learn about bonds. They may seem boring but they offer higher yields than bank accounts without subjecting you to as high a risk of wide price swings as stocks do.

So what the heck is a bond? Let me try to explain with an analogy. If a money market fund is like a savings account, then a bond is similar to a certificate of deposit (CD). With a five-year CD, for example, a bank agrees to pay you a predetermined rate of interest — such as, say, 6 percent. If all goes according to plan, at the end of five years of earning the 6 percent interest, you get back the principal that you originally invested. (Actually, the bank likely will send you a form letter just days before your CD is due to mature. Such a letter would announce that if the bank doesn't hear from you very soon, it'll roll your CD over "for your convenience"!)

Bonds work about the same way. For example, you can purchase a bond, scheduled to mature five years from now, that is just being issued by a company such as the computer software giant Microsoft. A Microsoft five-year bond may pay you, oh, 8 percent. As long as Microsoft doesn't have a financial catastrophe, after five years of receiving interest payments (a.k.a. *coupon rate*) on the bond, Microsoft will return your original investment to you. (Note: "Zero coupon" bonds pay no interest but are sold at a discounted price to make up for it.)

The worst that can happen to your bond investment is that Microsoft's newest software devours the hard drives in users' computers, causing Microsoft to suffocate under a class-action lawsuit and file bankruptcy. If that were to happen, you may not get back *any* of your original investment, let alone the remaining interest.

For several important reasons, though, you shouldn't let this unlikely but plausible scenario scare you away from bonds:

- **Bonds can be safer than you think — many companies need to borrow money (issue bonds) and are good credit risks.** If you own bonds in enough companies — say, in several hundred of them — if one or even a few of them unexpectedly takes a fall, it would affect only a sliver of your portfolio and wouldn't be a financial catastrophe. This is what a bond mutual fund and its management team can do for you. A bond fund is a collection of many bonds.

- **You'll be rewarded with higher interest rates versus comparable bank investments because the financial markets and those who participate in them — people like you and me — aren't dumb.** If you take extra risk and forsake that FDIC insurance, you should receive a higher rate of interest investing in bonds. Guess what? All the Nervous Nellie savers who are comforted by the executive desks, the vault door, the guard in the lobby, and the FDIC insurance logo at their local bank should remember that they're being paid less interest at the bank because of all of those "comforts."

   If you like the government backing afforded by the FDIC program, you can replicate that in bond mutual funds that specialize in government-backed securities. (See the recommended funds later in this chapter.)

- **Bond alternatives aren't as safe as you might like to believe.** Any investment that involves lending your money to someone else or to some organization carries risk. That includes putting your money into a bank or buying a Treasury bond issued by the federal government. Although I'm not a doomsayer, any student of history over the centuries knows that governments and civilizations fail. It's not a matter of whether they will fail; it's a question of when.

Sizing Up a Bond Fund's Personality

Bond funds aren't as complicated and unique as people, but they're certainly more complex than money market funds. And, thanks to some shady marketing practices by some mutual fund companies and some salespeople who sell funds, you have your work cut out for you in getting a handle on what many bond funds really are and how they differ from their peers. But don't worry: I take the time to explain to you the good funds that I recommend later in this chapter.

Maturity

In everyday conversation, *maturity* refers to that quiet, blessed state of grace and wisdom that we all develop as we get older (ahem). But that's not the kind of maturity I'm talking about here. Maturity, as it applies to bonds, simply means: when does the bond pay you back? — next year, five years from now, 30 years from now, or longer. The major and most important dimension on which bond funds differ from one another is the answer to how short-, long-, or intermediate-term are the bonds that a fund invests in. In other words, what's the *maturity* of the fund's bonds?

You should care *plenty* about how long it takes a bond to mature. Why? Because a bond's maturity gives you a good (although far from perfect) sense of how volatile a bond will be if interest rates change (see Table 7-1).

Table 7-1	Interest Rate Increases Depress Bond Prices
Price Changes of Bonds of Differing Maturities if Rates Were to Suddenly Rise 1 Percent*	
Short-Term bond (2-year maturity)	- 2%
Intermediate-Term bond (7-year maturity)	- 5%
Long-Term bond (20-year maturity)	- 10%

* Assumes bonds are yielding approximately 7 percent. If bonds were assumed to be yielding more, then a 1 percent increase in interest rates would have less of an impact. For example, if interest rates are at 10 percent and rise to 11 percent, the price change of the 20-year bond is - 8%.

If interest rates fall, bond prices rise. See Chapter 1 for an explanation of why interest rates and bond prices move in opposite directions.

Bond funds are portfolios of dozens — and in some cases hundreds — of bonds. That means that you won't want to know the maturity of every bond in a bond mutual fund. A useful summarizing statistic to know for a bond fund is its *average maturity*. In their marketing literature and prospectuses, bond funds typically tell you something like, "The Turbocharged Intermediate-Term Bond fund invests in high-quality bonds with an average maturity of 7 to 12 years."

Bond fund objectives and names usually fit one of three maturity categories — short-, intermediate-, and long-term. Why only three categories? Why not five? Or a dozen? I'm suspicious that it's a conspiracy on the part of all the bond fund companies that have less-than-stellar bond funds; there's more than a few of those! Fewer maturity categories makes it harder for fund investors to be sure that they're comparing comparable funds. For example, one intermediate bond fund can have bonds that mature on average in seven years while another contains bonds with a 12-year average maturity. The first fund is a "shorter" intermediate-term fund, and the other is a "longer" intermediate-term fund.

Typically, the three most common classifications of funds hold bonds that have the following average maturities:

- **Short-term bond funds** concentrate their investments in bonds maturing in the next few years.

- **Intermediate-term bond funds** generally hold bonds that typically come due within seven to ten years.

- **Long-term bond funds** usually hold bonds that typically mature in 15 to 20 years or so.

These definitions are not hard and fast. One "long-term" bond fund may have an average maturity of 14 years while another has an average of 25 years.

So much for maturity and average maturities. Here's a statistic that you'll find even more useful if you're trying to determine how sensitive bonds and bond funds are likely to be to changes in interest rates: duration. *Duration* is a splendid statistic that better enables you to grasp how sensitive a bond fund is to a change in interest rates. A duration of ten years implies that if interest rates rise by 1 percent, then the value of the bond fund should drop by 10 percent. (Conversely, if rates fall 1 percent, the fund should rise 10 percent.)

Trying to use average maturities to determine what impact a 1 percent rise or fall in interest rates will have on bond prices forces you to slog through all sorts of ugly calculations. Duration gives you no fuss, no muss — and it gives you one big plus, too. Besides saving on number crunching, duration allows you to compare the interest rate sensitivity of one bond fund to another's. If a long-term bond fund has a duration of, say, 12 years, and an intermediate fund has a duration of 6 years, then the long-term fund should be about twice as volatile to changes in interest rates.

Okay, if duration is easier to work with *and* a better indicator than average maturity, why do so many financial types talk about average maturity so much? Simply because average maturity is easier for most people to relate to. A fund's duration isn't that easy to understand. Mathematically, it represents the point at which a bondholder receives half (50 percent) of the present value of their total expected payments (interest plus payoff of principal at maturity) from a bond. Present value adjusts payments to be received in the future for changes in the cost of living.

Once you know a bond fund's duration, you know almost all you need to know about the interest rate sensitivity of different funds. (In fact, durations are such handy numbers for you to have around the house that I'll share recent duration numbers for my recommended funds with you later in the chapter.)

Duration hasn't been a foolproof indicator: some funds have dropped more when interest rates have risen than the funds' durations predicted. But bear in mind that it took some heavy investing in unusual securities (such as derivatives) to make duration unreliable — so the duration values of the better funds in this chapter should work as a guide just fine. You also should be aware that other factors — such as how the credit quality of the bonds in a fund changes — may affect the price changes of a bond fund over time.

Credit quality: Would you lend them your money?

Bond funds also differ from one another in terms of the creditworthiness of the bonds that they hold. That's just a fancy way of saying, "Hey, are they gonna stiff me or what?"

Every year, bondholders get left holding nothing but the bag for billions of dollars when the bonds they own default. So what should you do? Common sense suggests that you should purchase high-credit quality bonds. Credit rating agencies exist — Moody's, Standard & Poor's, Duff & Phelps, and so on — that do nothing except rate the credit quality and likelihood of default of bonds.

The credit rating of a security depends on the company's (or the government entity's) ability to pay back its debt. Bond credit ratings are usually done on some sort of a letter- grade scale where AAA is the highest rating, with ratings descending through AA and A, followed by BBB, BB, B, CCC, CC , C, and so on. A fund that focuses on AAA and AA rated bonds is considered a high-grade or high-credit quality bond fund; such a fund's bonds have little chance of default. A fund concentrating its investments in A and BBB rated bonds is considered a general bond fund (moderate credit quality). Junk bond funds (known more by their marketed name, *high yield*) hold bonds mostly rated BB or lower. These funds expect to suffer more defaults — perhaps as many as a couple of percent per year.

The financial markets attract bond investors to buy lower quality bonds by paying them a higher interest rate. The lower the credit quality of a fund's holdings, the higher the yield you can expect a fund to pay.

In addition to their credit ratings, bonds differ from each other according to what type of organization is issuing them — that is, according to what kind of organization you're lending your money to. Here are the major options:

- **Treasuries.** These are IOUs from the biggest debtor of them all, the federal government. There are Treasury bills (which mature within a year), Treasury notes (which mature between one and ten years), and Treasury bonds (which mature in more than ten years). Treasuries pay interest that is state tax-free but federally taxable.

- **Municipals.** Munis are state and local government bonds that pay interest that's federally tax-free and state tax-free to the residents in the state of issue. The governments that issue municipal bonds know that the investors who buy municipals don't have to pay most or any of the income tax that normally would be required on other bonds — which means that the issuing governments can get away with paying a lower rate of interest. Later in this chapter, I explain how to determine if you're in a high enough tax bracket to benefit from these bonds when you're investing money outside of retirement accounts.

- **Corporates.** Issued by companies such as Microsoft and Toys R Us, corporate bonds pay interest that's fully taxable.

- **Mortgages.** You remember that mortgage you took out when you purchased a home? Well, you can actually invest in that mortgage through purchasing a bond fund that holds it! The repayment of principal on such bonds is usually guaranteed at the bond's maturity by a government agency such as the Government National Mortgage Association (GNMA, or Ginnie Mae — cute, huh?) or the Federal National Mortgage Association (FNMA, or Fannie Mae — what cuteness *won't* our friends in government think of next!).

- **Convertibles.** These are hybrid securities — they're bonds that you can convert into a preset number of shares of stock in the company that issued the bond. Although these bonds do pay interest, their yield is lower than non-convertible bonds because convertibles offer you the upside potential of being able to make more money if the underlying stock rises.

- **International bonds.** Most of the bonds just described can be bought from foreign issuers as well. In fact, international corporate and government bonds are the primary bonds that international bond mutual funds may hold. Internationals are riskier bonds since their interest payments can be offset by currency price changes.

So now you know three *very* important things about bond funds: you know about maturities, what entities issue bonds, and the credit rating system for bonds. Now you can put the three together to understand how mutual fund outfits came up with so many different types of bond funds. For example, corporate bond funds may be high quality or what's known as investment grade, general (moderate), or high yield (junk). They may also be short-, intermediate-, or long-term in nature.

The riskier the bonds a fund holds, the higher the yield of that fund should be. Generally speaking, bonds are riskier the longer their maturity and the lower the credit rating of their issuer. A higher yield is the bond market's way of compensating you for taking greater risk.

Passive versus active management

Some bond funds are managed like an airplane on autopilot. They stick to investing in a particular type of bond (such as high-grade corporate), with a target maturity (for example, an average of ten years). Index funds that invest in a relatively fixed basket of bonds — so as to track a market index of bond prices — are a good example of this passive approach.

At the other end of the spectrum are aggressively managed funds. Managers of these funds have a fair degree of latitude to purchase bonds that they think will perform best in the future. For example, if a fund manager thinks that interest rates will rise, he usually buys shorter-term bonds (remember we discussed earlier in the chapter that shorter-term bonds are less sensitive to interest rate changes) and keeps more of a fund's assets in cash. The fund manager may be willing to invest more in lower-credit-quality bonds if he thinks that the economy is going to improve and that more companies will prosper and improve their credit standing.

Aggressively managed funds gamble. If interest rates fall instead of rise, the fund manager who moved into shorter-term bonds and cash suffers worse performance. If interest rates fall because the economy sinks into recession, the lower credit quality bonds likely will suffer from a higher default rate and depress the fund's performance even further.

Some people think that it's fairly easy to predict which direction interest rates or the economy is heading. The truth is that economic predictions *are* difficult. Over long periods of time (10+ years), in fact, meaningful predictions are almost impossible. In 1993, for example, few investors expected interest rates to plummet as far as they did. On the highest quality bonds, short-term interest rates plunged to 3 percent, long-term rates under 6 percent. A few figured that this was the bottom. But then almost no one expected rates to rise as high as they did over the next year as short-term and long-term rates grew about 3 percent by late 1994. The few who figured that this was going to happen were largely a different group than those who guessed right in 1993.

It's fine to invest some of your bond fund money in funds that try to be best positioned for changes in the economy and interest rates. But remember that if these fund managers are wrong, you can lose more. Over the long term, you'll do best in efficiently managed funds that stick with an investment objective — such as holding intermediate-term, high-quality bonds — and that don't try to time and predict the bond market. If you or a bond fund manager consistently knew which way interest rates were headed, you could make a fortune trading interest rate futures that leverage your investment. But none of us can know — so don't even try!

Trying to beat the market can lead to getting beat. There have been increasing numbers of examples in recent years of bond funds falling on their face after risky investing strategies have backfired (see Chapter 3). Interestingly, bond funds that charge sales commissions (loads) and higher ongoing operating fees are the ones more likely to have blow-ups. This may be because these fund managers are under more pressure to try and pump up returns to make up for these higher fees.

Bond Fund Considerations

Now that you know a fair amount about bonds and bond funds and how they differ, it's time to get down to how and why you might use bonds. Bonds may be boring, but they can be more profitable for you than super-boring bank savings accounts and money market funds. Bonds pay you more than these investments because they involve more risk: you're purchasing an investment that is meant to be held for a relatively longer period of time. As I discussed earlier, bond funds are riskier than money market funds and savings accounts because their value can fall if interest rates rise. However, bonds tend to be more stable in value than stocks (a fact I cover in detail in Chapter 9).

Bonds (and the funds that hold them) don't have to be held for a longer period of time because there is an active market for them — the bond market — where you can sell your bond to someone else (which is exactly what a bond fund manager does for you if you want out of your bond fund). You may receive more — or less — for the bond than you paid for it depending upon what has happened since then.

Bond fund uses and abuses

Investing in bonds is a time-honored way to earn a better rate of return on money that you don't plan to use within the next couple of years or more. As with other mutual funds, bond funds are completely liquid on a day's notice. Because their value fluctuates, though, you're more likely to lose money if you are forced to sell the bond fund sooner rather than later. In the short term, the bond market can bounce every which way; in the longer term, you're more likely to receive your money back with interest.

Don't invest money in bond funds that represents all you've got; don't put your emergency cash reserve into bond funds — that's what a money fund is for (see Chapter 6). I also recommend against using the check writing option that comes with many bond funds. Every time you sell shares (which is what you're doing when you write a check), this transaction must be reported on your annual income tax return. Even though selling shares may increase your need to purchase *Taxes For Dummies*, I know that you don't need more tax headaches.

But don't put too much of your longer-term investment money in bond funds, either. With the exception of those rare periods where interest rates drop significantly, bond funds are lousy ways to make your money grow. Growth-oriented investments such as stocks, real estate, and your own business are where you have the potential to build real wealth.

Here are some common financial goals and reasons why investing some money in bond funds can make sense:

- **A major purchase** that won't happen for at least two years, such as the purchase of a home or some other major expenditure. Shorter-term bond funds may work for you as a higher-yielding and slightly riskier alternative to money market funds.

- **Diversification.** Bonds don't move in tandem with the performance of other types of fund investments such as stocks. In fact, in a terrible economic environment such as the Great Depression, bonds may appreciate in value if inflation is declining.

- **Retirement investments.** Funds that invest in bonds that have longer-term maturities may be appropriate while you're still working. You can choose among funds that invest in intermediate- and longer-term bonds and diversified hybrid funds, which invest in bonds, stocks, and other securities (see Chapter 8).

  When you invest in bonds as part of a longer-term investment strategy (such as for retirement), you should have an overall plan about how to invest your money, sometimes referred to as an *asset allocation strategy*. Aggressive, younger investors should keep less of their retirement money in bond funds than older folks who are nearing retirement (see Chapter 9).

- **Income-producing investments.** If you're retired or not working, bonds can be useful because they are better at producing current income than many other investments.

Aren't higher interest rates better if I need income?

In late 1993, after a multiyear plunge, interest rates were at what seemed like rock-bottom levels compared to those of the previous decade. High-quality short-term bonds of six months were paying 3.5 percent, intermediate-term bonds were yielding around 5 percent, and long-term bonds were paying about 6 percent. These rates represented less than half of what rates had been a decade earlier.

Generally speaking, lower interest rates are great for the economy because they encourage consumers and businesses to borrow and spend more money. But if you were a retiree trying to live off of the income being produced by your bonds, low interest rates seemed like the worst of all possible economic worlds.

For each $100,000 that a retiree invested in intermediate-term bonds, CDs, or whatever when interest rates were 10 percent, the retiree received $10,000 per year in interest or dividends. A retiree purchasing intermediate-term bonds in the fall of 1993, however, saw her dividend income slashed by 50 percent because rates on the same bonds and CDs were just 5 percent. So for every $100,000 invested, only $5,000 in dividend or interest income was paid.

If you're trying to live off the income being produced by your investments, a 50 percent drop in that income may — just may, mind you — tend to cramp your lifestyle. So higher interest rates are better if you're living off of your investment income, right? Wrong!

Never forget that the primary driver of interest rates is the rate of inflation. Interest rates were much higher in the early 1980s because we had double-digit inflation. If the cost of living was increasing at the rate of 10 percent per year, why would you as an investor lend your money out (which is what you're doing when you purchase a bond or CD) at 5 percent? Of course, you *wouldn't* do this — which is exactly why interest rates were so high in the early 1980s.

In late 1993, interest rates were so low because the inflation dragon seemed to have been slain. So the rate of interest that investors could earn by lending their money dropped accordingly. Although low interest rates reduce the interest income coming in, the corresponding low rate of inflation doesn't devour the purchasing power of your principal balance as quickly.

So what's an investor to do when she lives off of the income from her investments but can't generate enough income because present interest rates are too low? A financially simple but psychologically difficult solution is to use up some of your principal to supplement your interest and dividend income. In effect, this is what happens anyway when inflation is higher — the purchasing power of your principal erodes more quickly.

I'm gonna make how much?

Bond fund investors often are led astray as to how much they can expect to make in a bond fund. The first mistake is to look at recent performance and assume that that's what you're going to get in the future. Investing in bond funds based only on recent performance is tempting right after a period where interest rates have declined because declines in interest rates pump up bond fund total returns. Remember that there's an equal but opposite force waiting to counteract pumped-up bond returns — bond prices fall when interest rates rise, which they eventually will.

Don't get me wrong: past performance is an important issue to consider. But in order for performance numbers to be meaningful and useful, you must compare comparable bond funds to each other (such as intermediate-term funds that invest exclusively in high-grade corporate bonds) and against the correct bond market index or benchmark (see Chapter 11).

The market for bonds is pretty efficient; it's difficult for a bond fund manager to beat the market averages significantly over time. Much better numbers to look at when selecting a bond fund are the fund's *yield* — how much the fund currently pays in dividends — and the fund's annual *operating expense ratio*. Bond mutual funds calculate their yield after subtracting their operating expenses, so you would expect that simply looking at a bond fund's yield is all you need to examine. Unfortunately, if you select bond funds based on yield, you're almost guaranteed to purchase the wrong bond funds.

Bond funds and the mutual fund companies that sell them can play more than a few games of creative accounting to fatten a fund's yield. Such sleight of hand makes a fund's marketing and advertising departments happy because higher yields make it easier for salespeople and funds to hawk the bond funds. But always remember that yield-enhancing shenanigans can leave you poorer. Here's what to watch out for and beware of:

- ✔ **Lower quality.** You may compare one short-term bond fund to another and discover that one pays 0.5 percent more and therefore looks better. However, if you look a little further, you discover that the higher-yielding fund invests 20 percent of its assets in junk bonds, whereas the other fund is fully invested in high-quality bonds.

- ✔ **Lengthen maturities.** A bond fund can be true to itself as a bond fund with a particular maturity objective — short-, intermediate-, or long-term — but bond funds usually can increase their yield just by increasing maturity a bit. (Insiders call this gambit *going further out on the yield curve*.) So if one intermediate bond fund invests in bonds maturing on average in seven years, while another fund is at ten years for its average maturity, comparing the two is a classic case of comparing apples to oranges.

- ✔ **Giving your money back without your knowing it.** Some funds return a portion of your principal in the form of dividends. This move artificially pumps up a fund's yield but depresses its total return.

When comparing bond funds to each other, make sure that you compare their total return over time (in addition to making sure that the funds have comparable portfolios of bonds and durations).

✔ **Waiving of expenses.** Some bond funds, particularly newer ones, waive a portion or even all of their operating expenses to temporarily inflate the fund's yield. Yes, you *could* invest in a fund that is having a sale on its operating fees, but you'd also buy yourself the bother of having to monitor things to determine when the sale is over. Bond funds engaging in this practice often end sales quietly when the bond market is doing well. Don't forget that if you go to sell a bond fund (held outside of a retirement account) that has appreciated in value, you owe taxes on your profits.

You can earn a higher yield from a bond fund in one of three major ways — by investing in funds that hold longer-term bonds, by investing in funds that hold lower-credit-quality bonds, or by investing in funds that have lower operating expenses. Once you've settled on the type of bonds you want, a bond fund's costs — its sales commissions and annual operating fees — are a huge consideration. Stick with no-load funds that have lower annual operating expenses.

Where on the yield curve

Most of the time, longer-term bonds pay higher yields than do short-term bonds. You can look at a chart of the current yield of bonds plotted against when they mature — such a chart is known as a *yield curve*. At most times, this curve slopes upward (see Figure 7-1). Most financial newspapers and magazines carry a current chart of the yield curve.

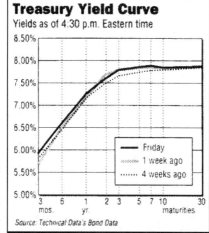

Figure 7-1:
Yield curve
chart.

Reprinted by permission of Wall Street Journal © 1995. Dow Jones & Company, Inc. All Rights Reserved Worldwide.

How bond funds calculate their yields

When you call a mutual fund company to ask for a fund's current yield, make sure that you understand what time period the yield covers. Fund companies are supposed to report to you the *SEC yield,* which is a standard yield calculation that allows for fairer comparisons among bond funds.

The SEC yield reflects the bond fund's so-called *yield to maturity.* This is the best yield to utilize when comparing funds since it captures the effective rate of interest an investor will receive looking forward.

Funds also calculate a *current yield,* which only looks at the recently distributed dividends relative to the share price of the fund. It's easier for funds to pump up this number by purchasing particular types of bonds. For just that reason, current yield is not nearly as useful a yield number to look at (although brokers love to use it because it makes some funds look better than they really are).

Higher yields compensate you for taking more risk. Earlier in the chapter, you saw the greater risk of longer-term bonds, which suffer price declines greater than do short-term bonds when rates rise.

To muni or not to muni

Just as money market funds can produce taxable or tax-free dividends, so too can bond funds. In order to produce tax-free income, a bond fund must invest in municipal bonds issued by state or local governments.

As long as you live in the U.S., municipal bond funds are federally tax-free to you. Muni bond funds that specialize in investing in bonds issued just in your state pay dividend income that's free of your state's taxes as well.

If you're in a high tax bracket (31 percent or higher for federal tax) and you want to invest in bonds outside of tax-sheltered retirement accounts, you should end up with more dividends in a muni fund than in a bond fund that pays taxable dividends (see Chapter 5 to determine your tax bracket). If you're in the 28 percent federal bracket, it's borderline whether you'll come out ahead with munis. At less than 28 percent, don't muni.

Recommended Bond Funds

Now that you know more about bond funds than you probably ever wanted to know, it's time to get down to brass tacks: recommending great bond funds for a variety of investing needs. Using the logic laid out so far in this chapter, I'll present you with a menu of choices. Although there are hundreds of bond funds — an overwhelming number of choices — there are not that many to consider once you eliminate high-cost funds (those with loads and ongoing fees), low-performance funds (which are often your friends and mine, the high-cost funds), and funds managed by fund companies and fund managers with minimal experience investing in bonds. What's left are the best that I present you with now.

The funds in the sections that follow are the best of the best for meeting specific needs. The funds are organized by the average maturity and duration of the bonds that they invest in, as well as by the taxability of the dividends that they pay. If you're investing in bonds inside retirement accounts, then you want taxable bonds. If you're investing in bonds outside retirement accounts, the choice between taxable versus tax-free depends on your tax bracket.

You should use the following funds only if you have reserved sufficient money in an emergency reserve (see Chapter 6). If you're investing money for longer-term purposes, particularly retirement, you should come up with an overall plan for allocating your money among a variety of different funds, including bond funds. For more on allocating your money, be sure to read Chapter 9.

Short-term bond funds

Short-term bond funds invest in — surprise, surprise — short-term bonds. Of all bond funds, these are the least sensitive to interest rate fluctuations. Their stability makes them the most appropriate bond funds for money that you want to earn a better rate of return on than a money market fund could produce for you. But, with short-term bond funds, you also have to tolerate the risk of losing a percent or two in principal value if rates rise.

Short-term bonds work well for major purchases that you expect to make in a few years — purchases such as a home, a car, or a portion of your retirement account investments that you expect to tap in the near future.

Taxable short-term bond funds

Bond funds that pay taxable dividends are appropriate when you're not in a high tax bracket (less than 28 percent federal) and for investing inside retirement accounts. (At the time this book went to press, the following funds were yielding around 6 percent. Call the fund companies for current yields.)

Vanguard Short-Term Corporate Portfolio invests about 85 percent of its portfolio in high- and moderate-quality short-term corporate bonds (average credit rating = A to AA); typically, it keeps the rest of its portfolio in U.S. Treasuries. It may even stray a bit overseas and invest several percent of the fund's assets in promising foreign bonds. This fund maintains an average maturity of two to three years and duration currently is 2 years. Ian MacKinnon and Robert Auwaerter have co-managed Vanguard's Short-Term Corporate fund since the early 1980s (between them, MacKinnon and Auwaerter boast four decades of bond investing experience). All told, this fund invests in about 200 bonds (imagine you keeping track of all of them by your poor little old lonesome!). This fund maintains a wafer-thin 0.3 percent operating expense ratio and has a $3,000 minimum initial investment ($1,000 for retirement accounts). ☎ 800-662-7447.

PIMCO Low Duration is a more aggressive short-term bond fund than Vanguard's Short-Term Corporate. The fund invests mostly in corporate bonds, as well as in mortgage bonds with maturities that typically range from one to five years depending on fund manager William Gross's outlook for inflation and the economy. Gross, who has managed this fund since 1987, has two decades of experience managing money in the bond market. He makes relatively wide swings in strategy and has had periods where the fund has kept much in money market securities (more than 40 percent at times) when Gross saw interest rates rising and wanted to protect principal. He's also ventured up to 20 percent into foreign bonds, some junk bonds (around 10 percent), and even a sprinkling of derivatives, such as futures and options, to slightly leverage returns. Despite this aggressiveness, the fund has had very low volatility and an absence of disasters and bad periods. The fund's duration is a low 2 years. PIMCO Low Duration maintains a low 0.4 percent annual operating expense ratio. Although this fund may seem intended for heavy hitters, given its normally stratospheric $500,000 minimum initial investment, the rest of us non-wealthy folks can buy it through discount brokers with as little as $1,000 (I cover this subject in detail in Chapter 4).

U.S. Treasury short-term bond funds

U.S. Treasury bond funds are appropriate if you prefer a bond fund that invests in U.S. Treasuries (which have the safety of government backing) or if you're not in a high federal tax bracket (less than 28 percent), but you *are* in a high state tax bracket (5 percent or higher). I don't recommend Treasuries for retirement accounts because they pay less interest than fully taxable bond funds. (At the time this book went to press, the following funds were yielding around 6 percent. Call the fund companies for current yields.)

Vanguard Short-Term Treasury invests in U.S. Treasuries maturing within two to three years — can't get much safer than that for the credit safety. Duration currently is 2 years. Like short-term corporate, this fund is managed by the bond dynamic duo of MacKinnon and Auwaerter. While the fund's got that cheap Vanguard expense ratio of 0.3 percent annually, don't forget if you don't need liquidity, you can buy Treasuries direct from your local Federal Reserve bank. $3,000 minimum initial investment.

Vanguard Admiral Short-Term U.S. Treasury does what the Short-Term Treasury fund does, except it does it even cheaper: its annual expense ratio is 0.15 percent. But — and, yes, this is a *big* but — you need $50,000 minimum to get in the door. ☎ 800-662-7447.

Municipal tax-free short-term bond funds

State and federally tax-free short-term bond funds are scarce. If you want shorter-term bonds, invest in these *federally* tax-free bond funds (the dividends on them are state taxable) if you're in a high federal bracket (28 percent and up) but in a low state bracket (less than 5 percent).

If you live in a state with high taxes, also consider checking out the state and federally tax-free intermediate-term bond funds if you can withstand their volatility (see the next section); another option is to use a state money market fund (which I cover in Chapter 6). (At the time this book went to press, the following funds were yielding around 3.75 percent. Call the fund companies for current yields.)

Vanguard Municipal Short-Term Portfolio invests in the *creme de la creme* of the federally tax-free muni bonds issued by state and local governments around the country (its average credit rating = AAA). The fund's average maturity ranges from one to two years and duration currently is about 1 year. Christopher Ryan, with more than a decade's tenure in the bond fund business, has managed this fund since 1988.

Vanguard Municipal Limited-Term does just what the short-term fund does (and has the same manager), except that it does it a while longer. Its average muni bond matures in two to five years, although its average credit rating is a lower-but-still-respectable AA. Average duration is 2.2 years. Both funds have a parsimonious annual operating expense ratio of 0.2 percent and require a $3,000 minimum initial investment. ☎ 800-662-7447.

Intermediate-term bond funds

Intermediate-term bond funds hold bonds that typically mature in a decade or so. They are more volatile than shorter-term bonds but should be more rewarding. The longer you can own an intermediate-term bond fund, the more likely you are to earn a higher return on it than on a short-term fund, unless interest rates keep rising over many years.

As an absolute minimum, you should not purchase an intermediate-term fund unless you expect to hold it for three to five years — or even longer, if you can. Therefore, the money you put into such a fund should be money that you don't expect to use during that period. Also, when investing in such funds in a non-retirement account, be sure you're not in a high tax bracket (28 percent or more federal). (At the time this book went to press, the following funds were yielding around 6.75 percent. Call the fund companies for current yields.)

Taxable intermediate-term bond funds

Vanguard Index Total Bond Market is an index that tracks the index of the entire bond market, the Lehman Brothers Aggregate Bond Index. The fund is managed by Ian MacKinnon, Kenneth Volpert, and a computer. The index that this fund seeks to replicate has almost 5,000 bonds, but this fund typically holds only about 10 percent of those bonds by using a sampling to mirror the index. Average maturity of the fund's bonds is around nine years, with a current duration of about 5 years. Investment-grade corporate bonds and mortgages make up half of the investments, while the other half are U.S. government and agency securities (average credit rating = AAA). Annual operating expenses are a paltry 0.2 percent and the fund charges a $10 annual account maintenance fee (for balances under $10,000) to encourage longer-term investors and discourage trading. $3,000 minimum to open ($1,000 for retirement accounts.) ☎ 800-662-7447.

PIMCO Total Return is managed in much the same way as the PIMCO Low Duration fund (which I describe in the section on short-term bonds), and the two funds even share the same fund manager, William Gross. The Total Return fund's main distinction is that it invests in bonds that mature in roughly ten years (plus or minus a few years). The fund's duration is more than twice that of Low Duration and is currently about 5 years. Annual operating expense ratio is 0.4 percent. See my description of PIMCO Low Duration earlier in the chapter for more details on PIMCO Total Return and how to purchase it. **PIMCO Total Return III** is almost identical to Total Return, except that III invests in bonds issued by companies deemed to be socially responsible (a class of funds that Chapter 8 covers). As with the other PIMCO funds, purchase these funds through discount brokers (see Chapter 4) which have $1,000 minimums; otherwise the minimum is half a million dollars.

Vanguard GNMA invests in residential mortgages that people just like you take out when they purchase a home and borrow money from a bank. Like other GNMA funds, this one has very low credit risk (its average credit rating = AAA). Why? Because the principal and interest on GNMAs is guaranteed by the federal government (which makes most people — Americans, anyway — feel downright warm and fuzzy). All GNMA funds have prepayment risk (if interest rates fall, mortgage holders refinance). But this GNMA fund has less risk than most because it minimizes the purchase of mortgage bonds that were issued at higher interest rates — and are therefore more likely to be refinanced and paid back early. This fund is managed by Paul Kaplan at Wellington Management, a private money management firm that Vanguard uses for many of their other funds. GNMA doesn't invest in some of the more exotic mortgage securities and derivatives abused by other firms' bond funds. Like all other bond funds, this one has interest rate risk, though it's comparable to other intermediate-term bond funds despite the longer maturity of most of this fund's holdings. Duration is currently 5.5 years and the fund's yearly operating expense ratio is 0.3 percent. $3,000 minimum; $1,000 for retirement accounts. ☎ 800-662-7447.

Other noteworthy GNMA bond funds include these delectable morsels:

- ✔ **Benham GNMA**. Boasts an excellent track record back to 1985, although it has suffered numerous manager changes in recent years. It has a 0.5 percent annual operating expense ratio and $1,000 minimum investment for all account types. Often, it can be purchased through discount brokers without additional fees. ☎ 800-472-3389.

- ✔ **USAA Federal Securities GNMA**. One of the many solid funds offered by USAA. Its track record, however, dates back only to 1991. This fund is odd in that it holds so few bonds — often fewer than ten. Annual operating expense ratio is 0.3 percent. $3,000 minimum initial investment; $250 for retirement accounts. ☎ 800-531-8100.

U.S. Treasury intermediate-term bond funds

U.S. Treasury bond funds are appropriate if you prefer a bond fund that invests in U.S. Treasuries (which have the safety of government backing) or if you're not in a high federal tax bracket (less than 28 percent), but you *are* in a high state tax bracket (5 percent or higher). I don't recommend Treasuries for retirement accounts because they pay less interest than fully taxable bond funds. (At the time this book went to press, the following funds were yielding around 6.5 percent. Call the fund company for current yields.)

Vanguard Intermediate-Term Treasury invests in U.S. Treasuries maturing in five to ten years with a currently duration of 5 years. **Vanguard Admiral Intermediate-Term U.S. Treasury** is for higher balance customers (see the descriptions for the short-term U.S. treasury funds for minimum initial investments and expense ratios). ☎ 800-662-7447.

Municipal tax-free intermediate-term bond funds

You should consider *federally* tax-free bond funds if you're in a high federal bracket (28 percent and up) but a relatively low state bracket (less than 5 percent). If you're in a high federal and state tax bracket, see the state and federally tax-free bonds later in this section. (At the time this book went to press, the following funds were yielding around 4.5 percent. Call the fund company for current yields.)

Vanguard Municipal Intermediate-Term does what Vanguard's short-term muni funds do, except that it invests in slightly longer-term muni bonds (average credit rating = AA). This fund maintains an average maturity of around eight to ten years, and its duration is currently about 6 years. Annual operating expense ratio of 0.2 percent; $3,000 minimum initial investment. ☎ 800-662-7447.

The *state and federally* tax-free bond funds listed in Table 7-2 may be appropriate when you're in high federal (28 percent and up) *and* state (5 percent or higher) tax brackets. (If one is not listed for your state or if you're only in a high federal tax bracket, remember to use the nationwide Vanguard municipal bond fund that I described just in the last paragraphs.)

Table 7-2	State and Federally Tax-Free Intermediate-Term Bond Funds	
Fund	**Operating Expense**	**Minimum to Open**
Benham CA Tax-Free Intermediate-Term	0.5%	$1,000
Fidelity Spartan CA Intermediate Muni	0.3%	$10,000
Schwab CA Short-Intermediate Tax-Free	0.5%	$1,000
Vanguard CA Tax-Free Insured Intermediate Term	0.2%	$3,000
Fidelity Spartan NY Intermediate	0.2%	$10,000

Long-term bond funds

Long-term bond funds are the most aggressive and volatile bond funds around. If interest rates on long-term bond funds increase substantially, you can easily see the principal value of your investment decline ten percent or more.

Long-term bond funds generally are used for retirement investing in one of two situations: (1) where investors don't expect to tap their investment money ideally for a decade or more or (2) where they want to maximize current dividend income and are willing to tolerate volatility. Definitely don't use these funds for investing money you plan to use within the next five years because a bond market drop could leave your portfolio with a bit of a hangover. And don't use them in a non-retirement account if you're in a high tax bracket (28 percent or more federal). (At the time this book went to press, the following funds were yielding around 7+ percent. Call the fund companies for current yields.)

Taxable long-term bond funds

Vanguard Long-Term Corporate is comprised mostly of high-grade corporate bonds, but it also holds around 10 percent in Treasuries and foreign and convertible bonds (average credit rating = AA). The fund's volatility is driven by the high average maturity of 20 years (duration equals about 8 years). Long-term bonds such as these can produce wide swings in volatility. For example, this fund lost more than 9 percent of its principal value in 1987, its worst year in a decade. The dividends of 9.2 percent paid that year brought the fund back to produce a total return of 0.2 percent. The fund is managed by Wellington Management's Earl McEvoy, who was new to the fund in 1994, but Wellington itself has managed this fund since its inception in 1973. It has an annual operating expense ratio of 0.3 percent, with a $3,000 minimum investment ($1,000 for retirement accounts).

Vanguard High Yield Corporate does what Long-Term Corporate does, except that it invests in lower-quality (a.k.a. junk) corporate bonds. These pay more and are for more aggressive investors stretching for greater yield. Remember that long-term junk bonds are among the most volatile funds available: they not only are interest-rate-sensitive, but they're also susceptible to changes in the economy. For example, this fund lost *nearly 18 percent* of its principal value in 1990. The average credit rating of the bonds held by this fund is typically BB. Unlike other high-yield funds, this fund invests little (if any) of its funds in bonds rated lower than B; it invests in the best of the junk! Duration is around 6 years. This fund has been managed since 1984 by Earl McEvoy at Wellington Management; the fund has been around since 1978, a degree of longevity that makes it one of the longest- and best-performing junk bond funds. Yearly operating expenses are 0.3 percent. $3,000 minimum ($1,000 for retirement accounts). ☎ 800-662-7447.

U.S. treasury long-term bond funds

U.S. Treasury bond funds are appropriate if you prefer a bond fund that invests in U.S. Treasuries (which have the safety of government backing) or if you're not in a high federal tax bracket (less than 28 percent), but you *are* in a high state tax bracket (5 percent or higher). I don't recommend Treasuries for retirement accounts because they pay less interest than fully taxable bond funds. (At the time this book went to press, the following funds were yielding around 6.75 percent. Call the fund companies for current yields.)

Vanguard Long-Term Treasury invests in U.S. Treasuries with average maturities around 20 years. Currently, duration is about 10 years. **Vanguard Admiral Long-Term U.S. Treasury** is for higher balance customers (see the descriptions for the short-term U.S. Treasury funds for minimum initial investments and expense ratios.) ☎ 800-662-7447.

Municipal tax-free long-term bond funds

Vanguard Municipal Long-Term does what Vanguard's short-term muni funds do, except that it invests in long-term muni bonds (average credit rating = AA). It maintains an average maturity of around 20 years and its duration is currently 10 years. Another twist on Vanguard's Long-Term muni fund is the **Vanguard Municipal Insured Long-Term** fund, which also buys long-term munis, but only those that are insured (average credit rating = AAA). Both of these funds have annual operating expense ratios of 0.2 percent and $3,000 minimum initial investments. ☎ 800-662-7447.

The state and federally tax-free bond funds listed in Table 7-3 may be appropriate when you're in high federal (28 percent and up) *and* high state (5 percent or higher) tax brackets. (If a fund is not listed in Table 7-3 for your state or if you're only in a high federal tax bracket, remember to use the nationwide Vanguard Municipal bond funds just described.) (At the time this book went to press, the following funds were yielding around 5 percent. Call the fund companies for current yields.)

Table 7-3   State and Federally Tax-Free Long-Term Bond Funds

Fund	Investments	Operating Expenses	Minimum to Open
Benham CA Tax-Free Long-Term	CA Municipals	0.5%	$ 1,000
Fidelity Spartan CA Muni Income	Lower-quality CA Municipals	0.5%	$10,000
Vanguard CA Tax-Free Insured Long-Term	Insured CA Municipals	0.2%	$ 3,000
Fidelity Spartan CT Muni Income	Lower-quality CT Municipals	0.5%	$10,000

(continued)

Table 7-3 (continued)

Fund	Investments	Operating Expenses	Minimum to Open
Fidelity MA Muni Income	Lower-quality MA Municipals	0.5%	$ 2,500
Fidelity MI Muni Income	Lower-quality MI Municipals	0.6%	$ 2,500
Fidelity MN Muni Income	MN Municipals	0.6%	$ 2,500
Vanguard NJ Tax-Free Insured Long-Term	Insured NJ Municipals	0.2%	$ 3,000
Vanguard NY Insured Tax-Free	Insured NY Municipals	0.2%	$ 3,000
USAA NY Bond	NY Municipals	0.5%	$ 3,000
Vanguard OH Tax-Free Insured Long-Term	Insured OH Municipals	0.2%	$ 3,000
Vanguard PA Tax-Free Insured Long-Term	Insured PA Municipals	0.2%	$ 3,000
USAA VA Bond	VA Municipals	0.5%	$ 3,000

Alternatives to Bond Funds

Bond mutual funds are hardly the only way to "lend" your money and get paid a decent yield. I'll talk you through the pros and cons of other alternatives, some of which have acronyms you can impress your friends and family with — or confirm that you really are a hopeless investments geek. Regardless of what investment type(s) you end up purchasing, remember to do the big-picture thinking first: What do you plan to use the money for down the road? How much risk can you take — and how much are you willing to take? What's your tax situation?

Most of these bond fund alternatives have one thing in common: they offer psychological solace to those who can't stomach fluctuations in the value of their investments. Once you understand more about these alternatives (including things I'll tell you that you're not likely to hear in a marketing pitch from the company or person who's trying to sell you on them), those low-cost bond funds will probably look more attractive.

CDs

For many decades, bank certificates of deposit (CDs) have been the investment of choice for folks with some extra cash that is not needed in the near-term. The attraction is that you get a higher rate of return on a CD than on a bank savings account or money market fund. And unlike a bond fund, a CD's principal value does not fluctuate. Of course, there's also the peace of mind afforded by the government's FDIC insurance program.

All of these advantages of CDs are not nearly as attractive as they may seem on the surface. Let's start first with the FDIC insurance issue. Bonds and bond mutual funds are not FDIC-insured. The lack of this insurance, however, shouldn't trouble you on high-quality bonds because such bonds rarely default. Even if a fund held a bond that defaulted, it probably would be a tiny fraction (less than 1 percent) of the value of the fund, so it would have little overall impact.

You may feel that's there's no chance that you'll lose money on a CD — but banks have failed and will continue to fail. Although you're insured for $100,000 in a bank, if the bank crashes, you'll likely wait quite a while to get your money back — and you'll probably settle for less interest than you thought you would get, too.

Here's another myth about CDs: the principal value of your CD really does fluctuate; you just don't see the fluctuations! Just as the market value of a bond drops when interest rates rise, so too does the "market value" of a CD and for the same reasons. At higher interest rates, investors expect a discounted price on your fixed-interest rate CD because they always have the alternative of purchasing a new CD at the higher prevailing rates. Some CDs are actually bought and sold among investors on what's known as a secondary market and they trade and behave just like bonds.

So a lot of those advantages CDs seem to have aren't as impressive as some may believe. And CDs also carry a number of drawbacks specifically in comparison to bonds:

- ✔ **Early withdrawal penalties.** The first is that your money is not accessible unless you cough up a fairly big penalty — typically, six months' interest. With a no-load (commission-free) bond fund, if you need some or all of your money next week, next month, or next year, you can access it without penalty.

- ✔ **Restricting tax options.** Another seldom-noted drawback of CDs is that they come in only one tax flavor — taxable. Bonds, on the other hand, come both in tax-free (federal and/or state) and taxable flavors. So if you're a higher-tax bracket investor, bonds offer you a tax-friendly option that CDs can't.

✔ **Lower yield.** For a comparable maturity (such as two years or five years), CDs yield less than a high-quality bond. Often, the yield difference is 1 percent or more. If you don't shop around — if you lazily purchase CDs from the bank that you use for your checking account, for example — you may be sacrificing 2 percent or more in yield.

Don't forget about the unfriendly forces of inflation and taxes. They may gobble up all of the yield that your CD is paying, thus leaving you no real growth on your investment. A couple of extra percentage points from a bond can make a big difference in the long-term.

In the long run, you earn more and have better access to your money in bond funds than in CDs. And bond funds make particular sense when you're in a higher tax bracket and would benefit from tax-free income on your investments. If you're not in a high tax bracket (federal rate of less than 28 percent), and you get gloomy whenever your bond fund's value dips, then consider CDs.

CDs may make the most sense when you know, for example, that you can invest your money for one year, after which you'll need the money for some purchase you expect to make. Just make sure that you shop around to get the best interest rate.

If having the U.S. government back your investments through FDIC insurance gives you the peace of mind to sleep better, then you can invest in Treasuries, which are government-backed bonds. Treasuries often pay more interest than the better CDs available. And there are always the insured municipal bond funds for high tax-bracket investors.

Individual bonds

"Why buy a bond fund and pay all those ongoing management fees, year after year, when you can buy high-rated bonds that pay a higher yield than that fund you're looking at?"

"You can create your own portfolio of bonds and purchase bonds with different maturities. That way, you're not gambling on where interest rates are headed and you won't lose principal as you can in a bond fund."

Maybe you've thought thoughts like these. More likely, you've had a broker who was trying to sell individual bonds to you say these sorts of things. Does the purchase of individual bonds make sense for you? Although the decision depends on a few factors, it's safe to say that most types of individual bonds probably are *not* for you. (Treasuries that you can buy directly from a local Federal Reserve bank without charge are notable exceptions to the comments that follow.) Here are some strong reasons why you're probably better off with a good bond fund instead:

✔ **Diversification.** You don't want to put all of your investment money into a small number of bonds that are issued by companies in the same industry or that mature at the same time. It's difficult to build a diversified bond portfolio with individual issues unless you've got a hefty chunk (at least $100,000) that you desire to invest in bonds.

✔ **Commissions.** If you purchase individual bonds through a broker, you're going to pay a commission. In most cases, it's hidden; the broker quotes you a price of the bond that includes the commission. Even if you use a discount broker, though, these fees take a healthy bite out of your investment. The smaller the amount invested, the bigger the bite. On a $1,000 bond, the fee can equal up to 5 percent through a discounter. Commissions take a smaller bite out of larger bonds — perhaps less than 0.5 percent if you use discount brokers.

✔ **Life's too short.** You've got better things to do with your time. Do you really want to research bonds and go bond shopping? Bonds and the companies that stand behind them aren't that simple to understand. For example, did you know that some bonds can be "called" before their maturity date? Companies often do this to save money if interest rates drop significantly. Once you purchase a bond, you need to do the same things that a good portfolio manager would need to do, such as tracking the issuer's creditworthiness and monitoring other important financial developments.

In terms of costs, you can purchase terrific bond funds with yearly operating expense ratios of just 0.2 percent. And remember, a bond mutual fund buys you tons of diversification and professional management so that you can spend your time doing what you're good at and enjoy doing. You can increase your diversification through purchasing bond funds with different maturity objectives (short, intermediate, and long).

If you already own individual bonds and they fit your financial objectives and tax situation, you can hold them until maturity because you've already incurred a commission when they were purchased; selling them now would just create an additional fee. When the bond(s) mature(s), you can check out bond funds at that time if you'd like to continue owning bonds.

Don't mistakenly think that your current individual bonds are paying the yield they had when they were originally issued (that yield is the number listed on your brokerage account statement in the name of the bond). As the market level of interest rates changes, the yield that's on your bonds fluctuates as well to rise and fall with the market level of rates. So if rates have fallen since you bought your bonds, the value of those bonds has increased — which in turn reduces the effective yield that you're currently earning.

GICs

Guaranteed-investment contracts (GICs) are sold and backed by an insurance company. Typically, they quote you a rate of return projected one or a few years forward. So, like that of a CD, a GIC's return is always positive and certain. With a GIC, there's none of the uncertainty that you normally face with a bond fund that fluctuates with changes in interest rates and other major economic upheavals.

The attraction of these investments is that your account value does not fluctuate (at least, not that you can see). As a rule, the insurance company invests your money mostly in bonds and maybe a bit in stocks. The difference between what these investments generate for the insurer and what they pay you in interest is profit to the insurer. The yield is usually comparable to that of a bond fund. Typically, once a year, you'll receive a new statement showing that your GIC is worth more thanks to the newly added interest.

Some companies offer GICs in their retirement savings plans as a butt-covering option or because an insurance company is involved in the company's retirement plan. More and more companies are eliminating GICs as investment options because of greater awareness of GIC's drawbacks. First, insurance companies (like banks) have failed and will continue to fail. Although failed insurers almost always get bailed out — usually through a merger into a healthy company — you can take a haircut on the promised interest rate if your GIC is with a failed insurance company. By having a return guaranteed in advance, you pay for the peace of mind in the form of lower long-term returns.

For people who would panic the moment a bond fund's value slips, GICs soothe the nerves. And they usually provide a higher yield than a money market or savings account.

Mortgages

Another way that you can invest your money for greater dividend income is to lend your money via mortgages and second mortgages. Such "deals" are often arranged by mortgage brokers. They appeal to investors who don't like the volatility of the stock and bond markets. With a mortgage, you can't look up the value every day in the newspaper; a mortgage seems safer because you can't watch your principal fluctuate in value.

What's amazing is that people who invest in these types of mortgages don't realize that they're getting a relatively high interest rate *only because they are accepting relatively high risk.* The risk is that the borrower can default — which would leave you holding the bag. More specifically, you could get stuck with a property that you may need to foreclose on. If you don't hold the first mortgage, you're not first in line with a claim on the property.

If a property buyer or owner could obtain a mortgage through a conventional lender, such as a bank, they usually would go through the bank because banks generally give better interest rates. So if a mortgage broker is offering you a deal where you can lend your money at 12 percent when the going bank rate is 9 percent, the deal must carry a fair amount of risk. Your mortgage investment also carries interest rate risk: if you needed to "sell" it early, you'd have to discount it, perhaps substantially if interest rates had increased since you purchased it.

If you're willing to lend your money to borrowers who carry a relatively high risk of defaulting, check out the high-yield bond funds discussed earlier in the chapter. With these funds, you at least diversify your money across many borrowers, and you benefit from the professional review and due diligence of the fund management team. If the normal volatility of a bond fund's principal value makes you queasy, then don't follow your investments so closely!

If you're selling some real estate and are willing to act as the bank and provide the financing to the buyer in the form of a first mortgage, that can be a viable investment. Be careful to check the borrower's credit, get a large down payment (at least 20 percent), and try not to lend so much money that it represents more than, say, 10 percent of your total investments.

Chapter 8

Funds for Longer-Term Needs — Stock Funds

. . . .

In This Chapter

▶ How, when, and why to invest in stock funds

▶ The different types of stock funds

▶ Recommended hybrid, index, and U.S. funds

▶ Recommended international funds

▶ Specialty funds — real estate, precious metals, and the like

▶ Socially responsible funds

. . . .

*T*o some, the stock market is nothing more than legalized gambling. To others it is a ticket to great wealth if they can figure what makes it tick.

So as you enter this perhaps most important of investing chapters, I need to set some expectations so that you and I can see eye to eye. I don't want you to come home battered and wounded by the stock market, which can be punishing and unrelenting during bad times. Nor do I want you to fear the market because (as FDR once said under slightly different circumstances) there's nothing to fear except fear itself.

Here's what you and I need to agree on:

✔ People who make money in the stock market make money not because they're smarter than anyone else and not because they know when to buy or sell. Those who build wealth from the stock market make their money grow by using three simple methods available to people of all economic means and intellectual horsepower: (1) invest in a diversified portfolio of stocks, (2) continue to save money and add to your investments, and (3) don't try to time the market. In other words, save, invest, and sit on your hands!

About 1 percent of professional investors appear to be "smarter" than the rest of us. They make a couple percent more per year on average (some say they're just lucky or statistical aberrations). You (and I) aren't going to be part of this 1 percent. If you were, you wouldn't need this book!

✔ People who make a lot less money in the stock market or get soaked are those who make easily avoidable mistakes. I define *investment mistake* as *a bad decision that you could or should have avoided,* either because better options were available, or because the odds were heavily stacked against your making money. Investment mistakes result from not understanding risk and how to minimize it, ignoring taxes and how your investments fit into your overall financial plans, paying unnecessary and exorbitant commissions and fees to buy and hold your investments, surrendering to a sales pitch (or salesperson), and trading in and out of the market. Give up the search for a secret code — there isn't one. Focus on avoiding major gaffes.

✔ The stock market is not the place to invest money that you will need to tap in the near future (certainly not money you'll need to use within the next five years). If the market gets into one of its cranky moods, you don't want to be forced to sell when your investments have lost value. So come along for the ride — but only if you can stay for a while!

If you're looking for magic ways to build a vast fortune without peril, you've come to the wrong book. But, gentle reader, if you want insights for how you can tap into one of the best investment funds to make your money *grow,* read on.

Stocks and Funds

Mutual funds are the way to go when you want to invest in stocks. Stock funds offer you tons of diversification and a low-cost way to hire a professional money manager. (In Chapter 2, I talk about why purchasing individual stocks on your own doesn't make good financial sense. If you haven't read Chapter 2 yet — and you're not convinced that buying individual stocks isn't the best route for you to take — please read it.)

As I explain in Chapter 1, stocks represent a share of ownership in a company and its profits. As companies, and the economy in general, grow and expand, stocks represent a way for investors to share in that growth and success.

Who should invest in stock funds?

Stock mutual funds, funds that invest some or all of their portfolios in stocks, are for you if you want your money to grow. Over the last two centuries, investors who held diversified stock portfolios earned a rate of return averaging 7 percent higher than the rate of inflation.

Your investment's return relative to the rate of inflation determines the growth in purchasing power of your portfolio. What's called the *real growth rate* on your investments is the rate of return your investments earn per year minus the yearly rate of inflation. If the cost of living is increasing at 3 percent per year and your money is invested in a bank savings account paying you 3 percent per year, you're treading water — your *real* rate of return is zero. If you invest your savings account money outside a tax-sheltered retirement account, you end up paying taxes on your piddly 3 percent interest earnings — thus leading to a *negative* real "growth" in the purchasing power of your money!

If you can invest your money in tax-sheltered retirement accounts, all of the increased value on your investments continues to work for you. Earning 7 percent per year more than the rate of inflation may not seem like much (especially in a world with gurus and brokers telling you they can make you 20 percent, 50 percent, or more per year). But don't forget the power of compound interest: The purchasing power of your invested money will double about every ten years if you're investing in stocks that provide you a return of 7 percent per year above inflation.

While enhancing the rate of return that your money earns makes it grow faster, the real key to making your money grow is saving more to invest. If you save $1,000 a year for the next ten years and invest each $1,000 saved into stock funds that generate the historic return of 7 percent per year more than the rate of inflation, you'll have nearly $14,000 at the end of ten years. If you had invested just $1,000 in the first year, and then not saved any more, remember that you'd have only about $2,000 in ten years — or about 85 percent less!

You simply must link these two simple but powerful financial concepts: *regular savings* and *investing in growth-oriented investments* such as stocks leads to simply amazing long-term results. For every $1,000 you can save and invest yearly into stocks (or other growth) investments that return 7 percent more than the rate of inflation, you'll have the purchasing power of $41,000 in 20 years — more than double the money you invested!

Disclaimer: Historic rates of return are not guaranteed to be the same in the future. The stock market can get hammered over short periods of time. Consider these plummets from the past century (see Table 8-1):

Table 8-1	Great Plunges (20 percent or more) in the Dow Jones Industrial Average Index of 30, (used to be 20), large company stocks		
Years	Percent Decline*	Years	Percent Decline*
1890-1896	47%	1946-1949	24%
1899-1900	32%	1961-1962	27%
1901-1903	46%	1966	25%
1906-1907	49%	1968-1970	36%
1909-1914	29%	1973-1974	45%
1916-1917	40%	1976-1978	27%
1919-1921	47%	1981-1982	24%
1929-1932	89%	1987	36%
1937-1942	52%		

*Please note that the returns that stock market investors earned during these periods would differ slightly from the above figures, which ignore dividends paid by stocks. The returns also ignore changes in the cost of living, which normally increases over time and thus makes these drops seem even worse. The Great Depression is the exception to that rule: then the cost of living dropped.

Stock funds make sense for people who've got time on their hands — specifically, the time to wait out a major market decline. If you may need to use your invested money in a year or two, stocks are most definitely not the place for you to be. It's not that you won't be able to sell — you can; stocks (and stock funds) are salable at the drop of a hat. But you may be forced to sell at a great loss if you must sell after holding such a short time.

Don't keep your emergency money in stock funds. Consider earmarking for stock funds money that you don't plan to use for a decade or more. Investing in stocks inside retirement accounts would be ideal if retirement is a long way away for you. Even if you're soon to retire or already retired, some of that money you've got squirreled away probably won't be used for many years.

Time and regular investing heals stock investors' wounds

As you see in Table 8-1, the stock market can sometimes fall out of bed. Look at the time periods during which those great plunges occurred. Notice how short most of those periods are. During the last century, major stock market declines have lasted less than two years on average. Some of the 20-percent-plus declines lasted less than one year. The longest declines — 1890-1896, 1909-1914, 1929-1932, 1937-1942, and 1946-1949 — lasted six, five, three, five, and three years, respectively.

Now, consider the powerful advances that happened after each of these long market declines. From 1896 to 1899, the Dow rocketed ahead 173 percent, from 1914 to 1916 it rose 114 percent, from 1932 to 1937 it soared 372 percent, from 1942 to 1946 it jumped 129 percent, and from 1949 to 1956 it leaped 222 percent. Wait long enough and time will bail you out!

Because it's almost impossible to predict when major drops will happen, how long they'll last, and how strong they'll be, another strategy is to keep buying more every year. An investor who buys in regular chunks (some call this strategy *dollar cost averaging,* a subject I cover in Chapter 9) feels less of the effects of a major decline. Why? Because you'll make some of your stock investments as the market is heading south; perhaps you'll even buy at or near the very bottom. Once the market rebounds, you'll show a profit on some of those last purchases you made, which will help to soothe the rest of your portfolio — as well as your bad feelings about the stock market.

Three ways you make money on stock funds

When you invest in stock mutual funds, you can make money in three ways! They are:

✔ **Dividends.** Stocks pay dividends. Companies hopefully make some profits during the year. Some high-growth companies reinvest most or all of their profits right back into the business. Many companies, however, pay out some of their profits to shareholders in the form of dividends. As a mutual fund investor, you can choose to receive these dividends as cash or reinvest them yourself by purchasing more shares in the mutual fund.

Unless you need the income to live on (if, for example, you've already retired), reinvest your dividends into buying more shares in the fund. If you do this outside a retirement account, keep a record of those reinvestments because those additional purchases should be factored into the tax calculations you'll make when you sell the shares. (You'll find the lowdown on the relationship between fund investments and taxes in Chapter 12.)

✔ **Capital gains distributions.** When a fund manager sells stocks for more than he or she paid for them, the resulting profits, known as capital gains, must be netted against losses and paid out to the fund's shareholders. Just as with dividends, your capital gains distributions can be reinvested in the fund.

✔ **Appreciation.** The fund manager isn't going to sell all the stocks that have gone up in value. Thus, the price per share of the fund increases to reflect the gains in the stocks. For you, these profits are on paper until you sell the fund and lock them in. Of course, if a fund's stocks decline in value, the share price will depreciate.

If you add together dividends, capital gains distributions, and appreciation — you arrive at the *total return* of a fund. Stocks (and the funds that invest in them) differ in the dimensions of these three possible returns, particularly with respect to dividends. Utility companies, for example, tend to pay out more of their profits as dividends. But don't buy utility stocks thinking you'll make more money because of the heftier dividends. Utilities and other companies paying high dividends tend not to appreciate as much over time because they aren't reinvesting as much in their businesses and growing.

Stock fund choices

Stock mutual funds, as their name implies, invest in stocks. These funds are often referred to as *equity* funds. Equity (not to be confused with equity in real estate) is another word for stocks.

Stock funds and the stocks that they invest in usually are pigeonholed into particular categories based on the types of stocks they focus on. Categorizing stock funds often is tidier in theory than in practice, though, because some funds invest in an eclectic mix of stocks. Here are the major ways that funds and the stocks that they hold differ from one another:

✔ **Size of company.** Just as you can purchase shirts or sweaters in small, medium, and large sizes, you can purchase stock in small, medium, and large companies. The categories with stocks are defined by the total market value (capitalization) of a company's outstanding stock. Small-company stocks, for example, are usually defined as stocks of companies that have total market capitalization of less than $1 billion. Medium-capitalization stocks have market values between $1 billion and $5 billion. Large-capitalization stocks are those of companies with market values greater than $5 billion. These dollar amounts are somewhat arbitrary.

Why care what size of companies a fund holds? Historically, smaller companies pay smaller dividends but appreciate more. They have more volatile share prices but tend to produce greater total returns. Larger companies' stocks tend to pay greater dividends and on average be less volatile and produce slightly lower total returns than small company stocks. Medium size, as you might suspect, falls between the two.

✔ **Growth or value?** Stock fund managers and their funds are further categorized by those who invest in growth or value stocks. *Growth* stocks are companies that are experiencing rapidly expanding revenues and profits. These companies tend to reinvest most of their earnings in the company to fuel future expansion; thus, these stocks pay low dividends. For example, IDG Books (the company that published the book you're reading) reinvests much of its profits back into doing more good books. (You can't buy stock in IDG though, since the company is private.)

Value stocks are priced cheaply in relation to the company's assets, profits, and potential profits. It's possible that such a company is a growth company, but that's unlikely because growth companies' stock prices tend to sell at a premium compared to what the company's assets are worth.

✔ **Geography.** Stocks and the companies that issue them are generally divided as well by the location of their main operations and headquarters. Is it in the U.S. or overseas? Funds that specialize in U.S. stocks are (surprise, surprise) called U.S. stock funds; those focusing overseas are typically called "international" or "overseas" funds.

Putting together two or three of these major classifications, you can start to appreciate all those silly and lengthy names mutual funds give to their stock funds. You can have funds that focus on large-company value stocks or small-company growth stocks. These categories can be further subdivided into more fund types by adding in U.S., international, and worldwide funds. So you can have international stock funds focusing on small company stocks or growth stocks.

How stock funds reduce risk and increase returns

Now that you're aware of all the different major types of stock funds, you need to get comfortable with the concept of risk. Risk is simply how often and how much money you invest in stock funds that you will lose. It's not that the mutual fund companies are careless and might misplace your money or are dishonest and abscond with it — it's just that stocks go up and they also go down.

What do all those other names mean?

If small and large, value and growth, U.S. and international haven't created enough mind-numbing combinations of stock fund options, here are a few more names that you'll confront.

Let's start with all the variations on growth. *Aggressive growth* funds are, well, more aggressive than the other growth funds. They not only tend to invest in the most growth-oriented companies, but the fund itself may also engage in riskier investing practices, such as making major shifts in strategy and trading in and out of stocks frequently (turning over the fund's investments several times or more during the year).

Then you've got *growth and income* funds and *equity-income* funds. Both of these fund types invest in stocks (equities) that pay decent dividends, thus offering the investor the potential for growth and income. Growth and income and equity-income are basically one and the same. The only real difference between them is trivial: equity-income funds tend to pay slightly higher dividends (although some growth and income funds have higher dividends than equity-income funds!). They may pay higher dividends because they invest a small portion of their portfolios in higher-dividend securities such as bonds and convertible bonds.

Income funds tend to invest a healthy portion (but by no means all) of their money in higher-yielding stocks. Bonds usually make up the other portion of income funds. As you'll see later in this chapter, other fund names designate those funds investing in both stocks and bonds — names such as *balanced* funds. Income funds are really quite similar and in some cases near twins of some balanced funds.

The term *international* typically means that a fund can invest anywhere in the world except the U.S. The term *worldwide* or *global* generally implies that a fund can invest anywhere in the world, including the U.S. I generally recommend avoiding worldwide or global funds for two reasons. First, it's difficult for a fund manager to thoroughly follow the companies and financial markets across a truly global investment landscape. (It's hard enough to follow either solely-U.S. or solely-international markets.) Second, most of these funds charge high operating expenses — often well in excess of 1 percent per year — which only drags down investors' returns.

Don't get bogged down in the names of funds. Remember that funds sometimes have misleading names and don't necessarily do what their names may imply. What matters are the investment strategies of the fund and the fund's typical investments — I'll tell you what these are for the funds recommended in this book.

Unless you have a lot of money to invest, you're likely to buy only a handful of stocks. If you end up with a lemon in your portfolio, it could devastate your other good choices. Companies are quite capable of going bankrupt. Even those that survive a rough period can see their stock prices plummet by huge amounts — 50 percent or more. Consider what once was considered to be among the more reliable and safe blue chip stocks, IBM. After trading as high as 175 in the early 1980s, it plunged 77 percent to a low of almost 40 in 1993.

Of course, any stock in a company that goes bankrupt and stays that way means that you'll lose 100 percent of your investment. If such a stock represents, say, 20 percent of your holdings, the rest of your stock selections will need to increase about 25 percent in value just to get you back to even.

Stock mutual funds reduce your risk by investing in many stocks, often 50 or more. If a fund holds 50 stocks and one goes to zero, you've lost only 2 percent of the value of the fund if the stock was an average holding. If the fund held 100 stocks, you would've lost 1 percent, while a 200-stock fund would have lost only 0.5 percent if one stock were to go under. And don't forget another advantage of stock mutual funds: a good fund manager is more likely to sidestep investment disasters than you are.

Another way that stock funds reduce risk (and thus their volatility) is that they invest in different types of stocks, such as those we discussed in the last section: growth, value, small, and large. Some funds also invest in U.S. and international stocks (even though the fund name may hide this fact).

Different types of stocks don't always move in tandem. So if smaller-company stocks are being beaten up, larger-company stocks may be faring better. If growth companies are sluggish, value companies may be in vogue. If U.S. stocks are in the tank, international ones may not be.

You can diversify into different types of stocks by purchasing several stock funds, each of which focuses on different types of stocks. There are two potential advantages to doing this. First, not all of your money is riding in one stock fund and with one fund manager. Second, each of the different fund managers can look at and track particular stock investing possibilities.

How stock funds make themselves look good

One of the ways that increasing numbers of stock funds have made themselves look better than their peers is by not investing in the types of stocks that their supposed peers do. For example, some U.S. stock funds invest significant portions of their funds in international stocks, yet compare their performance to the Standard and Poor's 500 Index of large-company U.S. stocks. Or a fund that appears to focus on large-company stocks actually might be holding major positions in small-company stocks, yet compare its performance to the S&P 500.

Fidelity is notorious for such tactics. Although there's nothing wrong with a fund investing in different types of stocks (and Fidelity certainly offers some good stock funds), the use of bogus benchmarks is nothing more than a marketing ploy. You as an investor should be aware of the investment strategies of the funds you're considering or holding.

The Best Stock Funds

Using the selection criteria outlined in Chapter 3, the following sections describe the best stock funds worthy of your consideration. The funds differ from one another primarily in terms of the types of stocks they invest in. Keep in mind as you read through these funds that they also differ from each other in their "tax-friendliness" (see Chapter 5). If you're investing inside a retirement account, you don't need to care about this issue.

Because stock funds are used for longer-term purposes, the subject of stock funds usually raises another important issue: how do you divvy up your loot into the different types of investments for purposes of diversification and to make your money grow? Chapter 9 answers that very question.

Mixing it up: recommended hybrid funds

Hybrid funds invest in a mixture of different types of securities. Most commonly, they invest in both bonds and stocks. These funds are usually less risky and less volatile than funds that invest exclusively in stocks; in an economic downturn, bonds usually hold up better in value than stocks do.

Hybrid funds make it easier for investors who are skittish about investing in stocks to hold stocks while they avoid the high volatility that normally comes with pure stock funds. Oh, you *could* place 60 percent of your investment monies into a stock fund and the other 40 percent into a bond fund — but you can do just that by investing in one hybrid fund that has the same overall 60/40 mix. Because bonds and stocks often don't fluctuate in unison, movements of one can offset those of the other. Hybrid funds are excellent choices for retirement account investing, particularly where an investor doesn't have much money to start with.

The two main types of hybrid mutual funds are *balanced* funds and *asset allocation* funds. Balanced funds try to maintain a fairly constant percentage of investment in stocks and bonds. Some funds, such as the Fidelity Balanced fund, are exceptions to this rule.

Asset allocation funds adjust the mix of different investments according to the portfolio manager's expectations. Essentially, the fund manager keeps an eye on the big picture — watching both the stock and bond markets — and moves money between them in an *attempt* to get the best value. The manager's efforts mean that you don't have to worry about whether to move some money from your bond mutual fund to your stock fund, or vice versa. You can spend more time in your garden.

You should note, however, that most managers have done a dismal job in beating the market averages by shifting money around rather than staying put in sensible investments (see the next section on the Rodney Dangerfield of mutual funds: index funds).

One of the brighter spots on the mutual fund landscape is the increasing numbers of mutual funds that invest in a variety of different funds within their own company. Think of these as "funds of funds," the ultimate couch-potato way to invest! The Vanguard Star fund, for example, (which I'll describe in more detail shortly) invests portions of its assets in nine different Vanguard stock and bond funds that focus on different types of securities.

So, without further ado, here are some stupendous hybrid funds. They are loosely ordered from those that generally take less risk to those that take more. Higher-risk hybrid funds tend to hold greater positions in stocks and/or make wider swings and changes in their investments and strategies over time.

Taxes and hybrid funds

Because hybrid funds pay decent dividends from the bonds that they hold, they are not appropriate for many investors who are purchasing funds outside tax-sheltered retirement accounts. If you're in a higher tax bracket (federal 31 percent and higher), bonds that you purchase outside a retirement account should be tax-free. With the exception of the Vanguard Tax-Managed Balanced fund (which I discuss in a few seconds), you should avoid the hybrid funds if you're in this situation. Buy separate tax-friendly stock funds (which I cover later this chapter) and tax-free bond funds (which put in their appearance in Chapter 7).

Vanguard Tax-Managed Balanced is the one hybrid fund that is tax-friendly enough to be considered for investments held outside tax-sheltered retirement accounts. Why? Because bonds typically make up half (or more) of this fund's investments, and its bonds are federally tax-free municipal bonds. Be forewarned, though, that this fund has a steep initial minimum of $10,000 and is intended for investors who will hold for at least five years. Otherwise, a 1-to-2 percent transaction fee is charged against your sale proceeds and paid into the fund.

The bond portion of the portfolio is managed by Vanguard's bond fund king, Ian MacKinnon; the bonds are high-quality (average credit rating = AA) and intermediate to longer-term in nature (duration = 6 years). The stocks in this fund try to replicate the Russell 1000 Index of the 1000 largest company stocks in the country, although the fund emphasizes stocks with lower dividends to reduce taxable dividends. Selling of stocks with capital gains is also minimized to reduce those taxable distributions as well. As with Vanguard's other index funds, this portion of the fund is managed by Gus Sauter and his army of computers.

If you live in a high-tax state, instead of buying this Vanguard fund, you may be better off buying a state and federally tax-free municipal bond fund if a good one's available for your state (see Chapter 7 to find out) and pairing it with a tax-friendly stock fund.

Vanguard Wellesley Income

This is among the most conservative and income-oriented of the hybrids. This fund typically has about two-thirds of its assets in high-quality bonds, with the other third in high-yielding, large-company stocks. Since its inception in 1970, about 75 percent of this fund's returns have come from dividends. Like many of the other conservative Vanguard funds, this one is managed by Wellington Management and the dynamic duo of Earl McEvoy and John Ryan, who have nearly 50 years of investment experience between them.

This fund is ideal for people who have either retired or are on the verge of retiring — or anyone else who wants a high rate of current income but also some potential for growth from their investments. The main drawback of this fund is that it is somewhat interest rate-sensitive because it tends to hold intermediate to longer-term bonds (its duration is 7 years) and higher-yielding stocks. Its stocks, however, are more value-oriented large-company stocks, and are among the more stable of stocks. Its high-quality bonds (average credit rating = AA) also don't go through the gyrations that junk bonds do. Expense ratio is 0.4 percent. $3,000 initial minimum, $1,000 for retirement accounts. ☎ 800-662-7447.

Vanguard Star

Begun in 1985 — and thus the oldest of the funds of funds — Star invests in *nine* different Vanguard funds: six stock, two bond, and a money market fund. Each of the nine funds is managed by its respective fund manager. Star keeps 63 percent in stock funds (Windsor and Windsor II, U.S. Growth, Morgan Growth, Explorer, Primecap) that cover the range of small-, medium-, and large-company and growth and value styles of investing. This fund emphasizes value more than growth because the value-oriented Windsor and Windsor II funds account for about half of the fund. The fund's funds are all U.S.-focused, although the stock funds sometimes hold a couple percent or so in foreign stocks. About 25 percent of Star is kept in bond funds (split between GNMA and Long-Term Corporate) with 12 percent in the Prime Portfolio money market fund.

In addition to the incredible diversification this fund offers, it has a low initial investment requirement of just $1,000 for both retirement and non-retirement accounts. But note the minor, potential drawbacks of this fund: Vanguard's experience with growth investing hasn't been the best (though they have improved greatly in recent years) — and the growth funds used sparingly in this fund are Vanguard's *best*. Keeping an eighth of the fund in money market securities is bothersome to longer-term investors who want the risk and expected higher returns that come from being fully invested in bonds and stocks. On the other hand, that strategy serves as a steady anchor during stormy times in the financial markets. Expense ratio is 0.4 percent of all underlying funds, and there's no additional charge for packaging them together. ☎ 800-662-7447.

Vanguard has attempted to improve on the original Star fund of funds concept by launching its LifeStrategy funds in 1994. Don't be concerned about a lack of a long-term track record for these funds since they also invest in underlying Vanguard funds in relatively fixed proportions. The major differences from Star are that they include Vanguard's index international funds, European and Pacific, and they vary in how aggressive they are from Life Strategy Growth, which is 80 percent stocks, to Life Strategy Income, which is 20 percent stocks.

Dodge & Cox Balanced

Dodge & Cox is an old San Francisco money management firm and has been managing money for large private accounts since 1930. This particular fund is one of the older balanced funds, having started in 1931. It wasn't until the 1980s that Dodge & Cox started marketing and registering the fund for sale in more states. They've never been all that aggressive or interested in building a huge mutual fund (the fund is available in about half of the states, mostly larger ones). Although never at the top of the fund heap, this fund has not had a down year since 1981.

Like Dodge & Cox itself, this fund is conservatively run, investing primarily in large-company value stocks and high-quality intermediate-term bonds (average credit rating = AA, duration is six years). Typically, it invests 60 percent in stocks and the rest in bonds. A small portion of the fund (less than 10 percent) may be invested overseas and less than 5 percent in junk bonds. This fund has always been managed using a team approach, so if you like to be able to rattle off the name of a star fund manager who's investing your money, this is not the fund for you (although you can impress others by saying that the minimum account size that Dodge & Cox normally accepts is several million dollars). This fund has an almost Vanguard-like 0.6 percent expense ratio. $2,500 initial minimum, $1,000 for retirement accounts. ☎ 800-621-3979.

Vanguard Wellington

Wellington is the oldest hybrid fund: it dates back to the summer of 1929 (which means that it even survived the Great Depression!). It typically invests about two-thirds in large-company stocks, very similar to the S&P 500 index, with the other third in high-quality intermediate- to longer-term bonds (average credit quality of AA and duration of eight years).

This fund is co-managed by Wellington Management's Ernst H. von Metzsch and Paul Kaplan, who together have five decades of investment experience. Up to 10 percent of this fund's assets can be and often are invested internationally. Its expense ratio is 0.3 percent. $3,000 initial minimum, $1,000 for retirement accounts. ☎ 800-662-7447.

Fidelity Balanced

Fidelity offers a number of hybrid funds that invest overseas as well as in the U.S. They also differ from Vanguard's offering in making more radical shifts in strategies and investments held. Fidelity is one of the few companies that has the research capabilities to allow a fund manager to invest intelligently in many different markets.

Managed by Stephen Petersen, this fund has done a decent job of diversifying in stocks and bonds around the globe. The fund can have as little as 25 percent to as much as 75 percent in stocks, with the rest in bonds (although the average bond credit quality is AA, often 20 percent of this fund's bonds are junk). The fund also invests much of its assets overseas, sometimes holding as much as half of its stocks in international companies. Like many of the other Fidelity funds, Balanced has a high rate of trading — typically turning over its portfolio about 200 percent per year. Expense ratio is 1.0 percent. $2,500 initial minimum, $500 for retirement accounts.☎ 800-544-8888.

Fidelity Asset Manager

This fund has much in common with Fidelity Balanced. Managed by Richard Habermann, Asset Manager typically has one-third to one-half of its assets in stocks, with a healthy portion of those overseas. Most of the rest of the fund is invested in bonds (average credit quality = BBB; often half of the bonds are junk).

Expense ratio is a little on the high side at 1.1 percent annually; like many other Fidelity funds, they're making a boatload of profits on this fund's more than $12 billion asset base. $2,500 initial minimum, $500 for retirement accounts. ☎ 800-544-8888.

Fidelity Puritan

One of Fidelity's oldest funds (it began in 1947), this fund is managed by Bettina Doulton. Like Fidelity's Balanced and Asset Manager funds, Puritan is a world-wide hybrid fund. Puritan typically has more money invested in stocks, 50 to 60 percent, and these stocks tend to be more value-oriented. Foreign stocks are heavily used as well, comprising around a third of this fund in recent years.

The bonds in this fund are similar to those in Asset Manager and Balanced in that 20 to 25 percent of this fund is invested in junk bonds (average credit quality = A). Most of the bonds are intermediate-term (duration is generally around five years). Beware the sales charge of 2 percent on this fund if purchased outside of a retirement account beginning on 1/1/96. $2,500 initial minimum, $500 for retirement accounts. ☎ 800-544-8888.

Other noteworthy hybrids

Lindner Dividend most closely resembles Vanguard Wellesley in that it focuses on maximizing income. Lindner does this by investing in higher-yielding stocks (including international) and bonds (including convertibles). Expense ratio of 0.6 percent. $2,000 initial minimum, $250 for retirement accounts. It's irritating but these guys don't have an 800 number. You can reach them at ☎ 314-727-5305.

T. Rowe Price Balanced is a decent fund if you're investing through that company. It's sort of like a conservative version of Fidelity's hybrid funds, as it invests about 20 percent of its stocks overseas and 20 percent of its bonds in junk. Smaller size causes it to carry an expense ratio of 1.0 percent. $2,500 initial minimum, $1,000 for retirement accounts. ☎ 800-638-5660.

SteinRoe Balanced almost seems a clone of Price's Balanced fund. Typically, half its assets are in bonds, mostly convertibles, with the balance in stocks, including healthy helpings of smaller-company and international stocks. Annual operating fee is 0.8 percent per year. $2,500 initial minimum, $500 for retirement accounts. This fund can be purchased through discount brokers (normally without a fee) or through SteinRoe at ☎ 800-338-2550.

Computers amok: recommended index funds

Unlike other mutual funds, in which the portfolio manager and a team of analysts scour the market for the best securities, an index fund manager simply invests to match the performance of an index. Index funds are funds that can be (and, for the most part, are) managed by a computer. Managers invest an index fund's assets so as to replicate an underlying index, such as Standard & Poor's 500 Index — the 500 companies with the greatest market value of stock outstanding in the U.S. In fact, an S&P 500 Index fund buys and holds exactly the same 500 stocks, and in exactly the same amounts, as comprise the S&P 500 Index.

These are perhaps the most underrated stock funds in existence. Like the offensive linemen in football or people who do a lot of good and don't seek or receive publicity, index funds don't get the credit they deserve. Index funds are a little bit like Jaime Escalante, that Garfield High School math teacher of poor Hispanic children in the ghettos of Los Angeles. In a school where kids often dropped out and were lucky to learn some algebra, Escalante got his kids to learn calculus. In fact, he got *entire classes* to work hard and pass the college advanced placement exam for calculus. (The College Board that administers the AP test couldn't believe so many kids from this school could pass this exam so the kids were investigated for cheating — that's how Escalante's story was learned and he finally got credit for all the great work he did.)

Index funds "work hard" by keeping expenses to the minimum, staying invested, and not trying to jump around. So, like Escalante's kids, index funds are virtually guaranteed to be at the top of their class. Over long periods (ten years or more), index funds outperform about three-quarters of their peers! Most other so-called actively managed funds cannot overcome the handicap of high operating expenses that pulls down their funds' rates of return. Because significant ongoing research need not be conducted to identify companies to invest in, index funds can be run with far lower operating expenses.

The average U.S. stock fund has an operating expense ratio of 1.3 percent per year (some funds charge expenses as high as 2 percent or more per year). That being the case, a U.S. stock index fund with an expense ratio of just 0.2 percent per year has an average advantage of 1.1 percent per year. A 1.1 percent difference may not seem like much, but in fact it is a significant difference. Because stocks tend to return about 10 percent per year, you're throwing away about 11 percent of your expected stock fund returns. If you factor in the taxes you pay on your fund profits, these higher expenses gobble perhaps a quarter of your after-tax profits.

Another overlooked drawback to actively managed stock funds: your fund manager can make costly mistakes, such as not being invested when the market goes up, being too aggressive when the market plummets, or just being in the wrong stocks. An actively managed fund can easily underperform the overall market index that it is competing against. An index fund, by definition, can't.

Vanguard is the largest mutual fund provider of index funds. Schwab's index funds are tax-friendly: whenever its fund managers need to sell securities because of changes in the index or shareholder redemptions, they make sure to offset capital gains with losses. The fund can achieve this result by having the flexibility to temporarily deviate from index weightings by small amounts. Vanguard also recently introduced a series of "Tax-Managed" mutual funds, which are index funds that seek to maintain low capital gains distributions (see the hybrid section and U.S. stock fund sections of this chapter).

Schwab's index funds make sense for non-retirement investing because of their tax-friendliness and lower initial minimum investment requirements of $1,000 (Vanguard's is $3,000). However, Schwab's index funds have slightly higher expenses, which tilt the scale towards using Vanguard index funds for retirement account investing. For retirement accounts, Schwab's initial minimum is $500; Vanguard's is $1,000. Vanguard ☎ 800-662-7447; Schwab ☎ 800-526-8600.

Table 8-2 lists the worst-performing U.S. Stock Funds over the past decade. Note how much worse these bowser funds performed versus the S&P 500 Index.

Table 8-2 Worst Performing U.S. Stock Funds Over Past Decade*

	Annualized Total Return (load adjusted)
Steadman Technology Growth	-16.4% per year
Steadman American Industry	-13.8% per year
Steadman Investment	-3.7% per year
Centurion T.A.A.	-3.2% per year
Steadman Associated	-2.3% per year
American Heritage	-1.9% per year
Stock market indexes	
Standard & Poor's 500 Index	+14.0% per year
Wilshire 5000 Index	+13.2% per year

* Ending July 31, 1996

Table 8-3 lists the better index funds.

Table 8-3	Good Index Funds	
Fund	*Index (investments)*	*Annual Expenses**
Vanguard Balanced Index	Hybrid fund - 60% in Wilshire 500 Index and 40% in Bond Index (see chapter 7)	0.2%
Vanguard Index 500	S&P 500 Index of 500 large-company U.S. stocks	0.2%
Schwab 1000 (tax-friendly)	Schwab 1000 Index of 1000 large-company U.S. stocks	0.5%
Vanguard Index Total Stock Market (tax-friendly)	Wilshire 5000 Index of (almost) the entire U.S. market of large-, medium-, and small-company stocks	0.2%
Schwab International Index (tax-friendly)	Invests in a Schwab-created index of 350 large-company stocks outside the U.S.	0.6%
Vanguard Total International (tax-friendly)	Established and emerging markets	0.4%

* Vanguard's index funds assess nominal annual account fees ($10 per year) for account balances of less than $10,000, and some charge transaction fees upon purchase (0.25% for Total Stock Market). They assess these fees to discourage short-term investors and traders. Such fees do increase the costs of owning these funds, but total index fund fees still run far lower than those of actively managed funds.

Index mutual funds are tax-friendlier

Mutual fund mangers of actively managed portfolios, in their attempts to increase their shareholders' returns, buy and sell individual securities more frequently. This process increases the chances of a fund needing to make significant capital gains distributions.

Thus, for money invested outside retirement accounts, index funds have an added advantage: fewer taxable distributions are made to shareholders because less trading of securities is conducted and a more stable portfolio is maintained. For mutual funds held outside tax-sheltered retirement accounts, this reduced trading effectively increases an investor's total rate of return.

When you invest in index funds, you never see your funds in the list of the top ten funds — but then you never see your funds in the list of the bottom ten funds, either. Don't overestimate your ability to pick *in advance* the few elite money managers who manage to beat the market averages by a few percentage points per year in the long run. And then don't overestimate the pros' ability to consistently pick the right stocks. Index funds make sense for a portion of your investments, especially when investing in bonds and larger, more conservative stocks, where it's very difficult for portfolio managers to beat the market. Index funds also make sense for investors who are terrified that fund managers might make big mistakes and greatly underperform the market.

Recommended U.S.-focused stock funds

I've already covered stock index funds, so this section focuses on the better actively managed funds that invest primarily in the U.S. stock market. I say *primarily* because some "U.S." funds venture into overseas investments.

Of the all the different types of funds offered, U.S. stock funds are the largest category. To see the forest amidst the trees, remember the classifications we covered earlier in the chapter. Stock funds differ mainly in terms of the size of the companies that they invest in and in whether the funds focus on growth or value companies. Some funds do all of the above.

Some of these funds may invest a little overseas. The only way to know for sure where a fund is currently invested (or where the fund may invest in the future) is to ask. You can start by calling the 800 number of the mutual fund company that you're interested in. You also can read the fund's annual report (which I explain how to do in Chapter 3). A prospectus, unfortunately, won't give you anything beyond general parameters that guide the range of investments; it won't tell you what the fund is currently investing in or has invested in.

I've tried to order these funds from those that are more conservative to those that are more aggressive.

Dodge & Cox Stock

Another of the fine but few funds offered by Dodge & Cox, this fund focuses on large- company value stocks. Unlike most U.S. stock funds today, it does little trading, often less than 10 percent of its portfolio annually. Like the Dodge & Cox Balanced fund, this fund is managed by a team and does not try to time the markets. It has held around 5 percent or so invested overseas. It's annual expense ratio is a plus as well, coming in at 0.6 percent. $2,500 initial minimum, $1,000 for retirement accounts. ☎ Call 800-621-3979 to see if it's available in your state.

Mutual Qualified, Shares, and Beacon

These three nearly identical funds all invest in value companies of all sizes. These funds are unusual in that they successfully take this approach to an extreme by investing heavily in "turnaround situations," sometimes in companies that are on the ropes and even in bankruptcy. This strategy is not as dangerous as it sounds. Consider that most investors are scared away from these situations, so there are bargains to be had; with such investments, a fund manager has time to tell whether a company has the financial wherewithal to make a comeback. If occasionally the manager is wrong on an issue or two, it's no big deal because the fund invests in 200-plus stocks. This type of investment approach doesn't always fare well, as this fund's lagging performance in the mid-80s and from 1989 to 1991 indicates. It also invests a little (around 10 percent) in junk bonds and 10 to 20 percent overseas.

All three of these funds are managed by Michael Price, who has managed money at Mutual for the past two decades. Although he's not a market timer, Price won't invest cash if he can't find good places to put it and has even closed these funds when too much cash was accumulating from the increasing numbers of new investors. Why have three nearly identical funds — and how do you choose among them? Part of the reason for having similar funds stems from the fact that they were marketed to different customers. Qualified was sold mostly to retirement plans, including pension funds. Beacon tends to invest a little more in small companies. Qualified has lower minimums ($1,000 for all account types), whereas Shares and Beacon have minimums of $5,000 for non-retirement and $2,000 for retirement accounts. ☎ 800-553-3014.

At the time this book went to press, Michael Price had reopened the Mutual Discovery fund, which is a good choice for investors looking for a small company focused fund.

T. Rowe Price Spectrum Growth

T. Rowe Price offers a number of good stock funds, both U.S. and international, and this fund of funds offers a simplified way to invest in six of them. Four of them are U.S. stock funds that cover the "spectrum" of company sizes, one's an international stock fund, and the New Era fund invests in natural resource stocks and provides a good inflation hedge. Typically, international stocks comprise about 30 percent of this fund's holdings.

This fund of funds is managed through monthly meetings of a committee made up of fund managers within the company. Slight changes in allocations among the different funds are made based on expectations of how a particular sector will fare in the future. The expense ratio of the funds in this fund averages out to 0.9 percent generally and there's no additional fee charged for the fund's packaging. $2,500 initial minimum, $1,000 for retirement accounts. ☎ 800-638-5560.

Fidelity's gaggle of funds

No mutual fund company in the world has more experience and success with investing in U.S. stocks than Fidelity. One of the secrets to the performance success of Fidelity's U.S. stock funds is that they not only invest often in small-, medium-, and large-company stocks in the U.S., but they also invest modest (and in some cases significant) portions of assets overseas. For some peculiar reason, the international investments in these funds have worked better than those in Fidelity's pure international funds, perhaps because their U.S. fund managers have many other options and presumably are investing in the best overseas opportunities. Another reason that Fidelity's U.S.-focused funds work better is that they aren't nearly as burdened with high fees, which ultimately depress an investor's return.

Fidelity is the Procter & Gamble of mutual funds. Just as P&G comes up with scores of different brands of laundry detergent that are pretty much the same, Fidelity offers a maddening array of more-or-less similar funds. In selecting among these better offerings within the Fidelity family, pay close attention to fees, both ongoing and up-front sales charges. On all of the following funds that have sales charges, those charges can be avoided by purchasing the fund inside a tax-sheltered retirement account. *If you're investing outside of a tax-sheltered retirement account, avoid the funds with sales charges. They ain't worth it — you have plenty of other alternatives available. Also beware that Fidelity funds do lots of trading, so they tend to produce high rates of capital gains distributions — which increases the tax burden for non-retirement account investors.*

For investors looking for stock funds that pay modest dividends, Fidelity offers several good choices. **Fidelity Equity-Income** fund invests in larger company value stocks and tends to pay a decent dividend, currently in the range of 4 percent. One of the ways that this fund gooses its dividend is through investing about 20 percent of its portfolio in bonds, including convertibles. The fund also invests overseas and lately has had about 20 percent of its stock investments there.

This fund is managed by Stephen Petersen. Petersen has managed this fund only since 1993, but before he came to this fund he had managed a similar fund plus another for large institutions in Fidelity's institutional division since 1987. Equity-Income will re-institute its sales charge of 2 percent for non-retirement accounts beginning 1/1/96. Annual expenses equal 0.7 percent.

Fidelity-Equity Income II is a clone of Equity-Income with some minor differences. II is less concerned with dividends (yield is currently around 2.5 percent). It also focuses primarily on large-company value stocks, but it invests less in bonds (10 percent) and a little bit more in smaller-company and international stocks than Equity-Income does. This fund expects to produce a slightly higher total return (during up markets, of course) and has met this expectation in recent years.

Equity-Income II's investments are under the capable guidance of Brian Posner, who has managed this fund since 1992. Prior to that he managed several other funds at Fidelity. This fund has no sales charge and charges annual expenses of 0.7 percent.

Fidelity is Fidelity's original fund, dating back to the Depression years — 1930. This is not "the Fidelity fund without a name," although if you say "I want to invest in the Fidelity fund," most people will say something like, "That's great . . . which one?" This fund is similar to Equity-Income II. It pays a modest dividend of around 2 percent, invests less than 10 percent in bonds, and invests, in recent times, around 15 percent overseas.

This fund is managed by one of the few but increasing number of women in the mutual fund field, Beth Terrana, who has more than a decade of experience managing similar funds (Growth & Income and Equity-Income funds) at Fidelity. Until the Reagan years, investors had to pay a whopping 8.5 percent load to get into this fund, but today it's load-free and charges a 0.7 percent per year operating fee.

Taxes on stock funds

For mutual funds held outside of retirement accounts, you gotta pay current income tax on dividends and capital gains that are distributed. This is another reason that most investors are best off sheltering more money into retirement accounts (see Chapter 5).

If your circumstances lead you to have money that you want to invest in stock funds outside retirement accounts, then by all means do it. But pay close attention to the dividend and capital gains distributions that funds make. I've indicated which funds are "tax-friendly."

In addition to the tax-friendly index funds discussed earlier in the chapter, also check out the **Vanguard Tax-Managed Capital Appreciation**, fund which, like the Schwab 1000 fund, invests in the universe of the 1,000 largest company stocks

in the U.S. stock market. Unlike the Schwab 1000 fund, though, Vanguard's offering selects and samples from among the 1,000 companies. Like the Schwab fund, it seeks to minimize capital gains distributions by holding onto appreciating stock and, if it needs to sell some stocks at a profit, offsetting those sales by selling other stocks at a loss.

As with the Vanguard Tax-Managed Balanced fund, you shouldn't go into this fund unless you plan to hold for five years. Why? Because you'll get clipped with a transaction fee of 1 to 2 percent for such an early exit. The minimum initial investment is also a hefty $10,000. If you want the flexibility of selling within five years without cost, or if you don't have 10 grand burnin' a hole in your wallet, use the Schwab 1000 fund.

Fidelity Disciplined Equity, unlike the other Fidelity funds I've discussed so far, is a growth fund. You can tell it's a growth fund by noting that it invests in stocks with low dividends — the fund's dividend yield is just 1 percent. This is one of the few Fidelity U.S. stock funds that stays focused on U.S. stocks; recently it had *no* foreign holdings. It invests in a mixture of mostly large- but also medium- and small-company stocks. These stocks are selected largely by a computer model developed by fund manager Brad Lewis for the specific purpose of selecting stocks that seem underpriced in relationship to a company's overall financial picture.

Lewis has managed this fund since 1988. The fund's operating expenses are a reasonable 0.9 percent. If you like this fund's and Lewis's approach and want some foreign stock exposure, you're in luck: since 1990, Lewis has managed a near-clone of this fund called *Fidelity Stock Selector*, which has around 15 to 20 percent overseas.

Fidelity Contrafund is another good growth fund at Fidelity. In 1990, its management passed into the hands of Will Danoff, who invests in companies somewhat out of favor but poised for a positive change (not unlike Michael Price's approach with the Mutual Series funds). Contrafund invests in an eclectic mix of U.S. stocks of all sizes and will invest 10 to 20 percent overseas.

Danoff has been with Fidelity since 1986. For a few months in 1990, he worked with the now-infamous Peter Lynch on the Magellan fund before Lynch retired. This fund charges a 3 percent sales charge for non-retirement accounts and has frenetic rates of trading (reaching as high as 300 percent of the fund's assets yearly) which leads to capital gains distributions; for both of these reasons, you should *buy this fund only inside a retirement account.* At 1 percent per year, annual expense ratio is a little high given the huge asset base (around $19 billion) that this fund carries.

Fidelity Low Priced Stock specializes in investing in small-company, value stocks. As you might guess from its name, it buys stocks that have low share prices. At least two-thirds of the fund's investments will be in such stocks. Lower-priced stocks tend to coincide with smaller companies. The price per share of a stock may bear little resemblance to the size of the issuing company because companies can "split" their stock and issue more shares, which cuts the price per share.

This fund has been managed since its inception in 1989 by Joel Tillinghast who also worked as an analyst and assistant on several other Fidelity funds beginning in 1986. Avoid this fund's 3 percent sales charge by purchasing this fund *inside a retirement account.* Annual operating expenses are 1.1 percent. All the Fidelity funds mentioned in this section have $2,500 initial minimum investment requirements, $500 for retirement accounts. ☎ 800-544-8888.

Hello, Fidelity??? - DO a fund of funds!

Fidelity would make everyone's life easier if they just came out with a fund of funds, similar to the T. Rowe Price Spectrum Growth or Vanguard Star funds. It could invest in a handful of the better stock funds at Fidelity and would be ideal for retirement account investors who don't want the headache of picking and choosing among their far-too-numerous offerings.

So why don't they do it?

Well, they won't really say. Getting SEC approval on funds of funds is a bit of a pain, but T. Rowe Price and Vanguard have done it. My theory is that Fidelity doesn't want to be forced to choose which of their many funds they think is "best" because the rest, by definition, will be "worse."

Warburg Pincus Growth & Income & Warburg Pincus Emerging Growth

These two funds' names suggest that the funds are different — but don't be fooled. They're both growth funds and they both can and do invest overseas even though they focus primarily on U.S. investments. Both funds also make major bets on select industries that are performing well; if they are wrong, these funds can suffer more than most. To date, though, this hasn't happened. The Warburg, Pincus company was in the private money management business first and then jumped into the mutual fund fray in the mid-80s.

Warburg Pincus Growth & Income fund invests in a diverse array of companies that pay low dividends, despite the fact that the fund's charter is to invest in stocks that pay decent dividends! It also invests significant assets overseas, although the amount varies over time. The fund manager is Anthony Orphanos, who has been with Warburg since 1977.

Warburg Pincus Emerging Growth focuses on small company stocks and invests smaller amounts overseas; less than 10 percent. It's managed by Elizabeth Dater, who has been managing this fund since its inception in 1988, and Stephen Lurito, who joined Dater in 1993 as co-manager. Expense ratios on these funds are a bit high — 1.2 percent for Growth & Income and 1.3 percent for Emerging Growth — partly due to the smaller size of these funds (both have less than $1 billion under management). If you go through discount brokers, normally you can purchase these funds without transaction fees. $1,000 initial minimum for Growth & Income, $2,500 for Emerging Growth, $500 for each with retirement accounts. ☎ 800-257-5614.

Other noteworthy U.S.-focused stock funds

Neuberger & Berman: Guardian, Partners, and Selected Sectors are three stock funds run by Neuberger & Berman, a New York-based private money manager that's also been in the mutual fund business for decades. The firm was founded by Roy Neuberger, who in his ninth decade of life still works at the company. These three funds are similar in that they invest in a mixture of small to large stocks. The Selected Sectors and Partners funds tend to focus more on small- and medium-size company stocks, whereas Guardian holds more large-company stocks. Annual operating expense ratio on all three is a very competitive 0.8 percent, and they can be purchased through discount brokers, normally without a transaction fee. Note the low $1,000 initial minimums, $250 for retirement accounts. ☎ 800-877-9700.

Should I invest in the Warren Buffett fund?

It's widely known now that Warren Buffett is a heck of an investor. As Chairman and CEO of the Nebraska-based firm Berkshire Hathaway, which invests in other companies' stocks and also owns several other businesses, Buffett's stock market investments have earned in excess of 20 percent per year on average over recent decades.

Because Buffett and his firm invests in many other companies' stocks, investing in his firm's stock is sort of like investing in a mutual fund. So if he's so shrewd a money manager, should you buy into his stock? Probably not. Here's why.

Unlike a true mutual fund, because of Buffett's renowned stock-picking acumen, Berkshire Hathaway stock sells at a hefty premium to the value of the underlying stocks that Buffett and crew invest in. This stock commonly sells at more than 30-plus times its annual earnings, which is high even for a growth company. In addition, one share of Berkshire Hathaway stock costs about $20,000 because Buffett doesn't like stock splits.

He thinks that splits would encourage people with a short-term focus (although this is debatable).

Although normally I don't advocate buying individual stocks, here's what you can do if you want to invest with Buffett but not pay the inflated premium to buy his "stock fund." Write to his firm at 1440 Kiewet Plaza, Omaha, NE 68131, and obtain its annual report each year (it comes out in early March). In it, you can find a list of the stocks Buffett is currently invested in. Go ahead and buy these stocks yourself to replicate Buffett's portfolio. This is easy to do because Buffett invests in a relatively small number of other companies' stocks (typically a dozen or less), and holds them for the long term.

If you're wondering if I would do this with my own money, the answer is no. It's not worth the bother and I can (and do) put my money into the hands of many capable mutual fund managers presented in this chapter.

Vanguard Primecap is one of the few growth-oriented stock funds that doesn't trade its portfolio heavily, trading typically 15 percent of its fund per year. It invests in companies of all sizes and even invests a bit overseas. This fund has been managed since its inception by Howard Schow and Theo Kolokotrones (say that name five times real fast!) of Primecap Management, a Southern California investment management company. Schow and Kolokotrones have more than six decades of investment experience between them. Expense ratio is a competitive 0.7 percent. Reasonably tax-friendly. $3,000 initial minimum, $1,000 for retirement accounts. ☎ 800-662-7447. (At the time this revised printing went to press, this fund was temporarily closed.)

Columbia Growth and **Columbia Special**, like some of the other solid mutual funds offered by companies such as Dodge & Cox and Warburg Pincus, are managed by a firm that got into the mutual fund business after managing money for the already-rich-and-famous. Both of these funds are fairly aggressive and tend to take their lumps in down markets. Columbia Growth invests in a broad array of primarily larger- and medium-size U.S. stocks. Columbia Special focuses more on smaller- to medium-size company growth stocks that have low to no dividends; it is the more volatile and aggressive of the two funds. Both may invest small amounts overseas, typically less than 10 percent. These funds, as the other Columbia funds, are managed using a team management approach. Growth's annual operating expenses total about 0.8 percent per year, Special's 1.1 percent. Growth's initial minimum is $1,000 for all accounts, Special's $2,000. ☎ 800-547-1707.

Brandywine invests in high-growth companies of all sizes. If you can't afford to invest $25,000 in one fund, you can skip this high-minimum fund. This fund has done well over the years, but it suffers in down markets. It is managed by a team management approach led by Foster Friess, with three other managers scattered throughout the country, each of whom manages a portion of the fund's assets. Friess has been with the fund since it began in 1985. Annual operating fees are 1.1 percent per year. ☎ 800-656-3017.

Recommended international funds

As I discuss in Chapter 1, for diversification and growth potential, funds that invest overseas should be part of an investor's portfolio that is invested in stocks. Normally, you can tell you're looking at a fund that focuses its investments overseas if its name contains words such as *international, global, worldwide,* or *world.*

As a general rule, you should avoid foreign funds that invest just in one country, such as India or Indonesia or Italy. As with investing in a sector fund that specializes in a particular industry, this lack of diversification defeats the whole purpose of investing in funds. Funds that focus on specific regions, such as Southeast Asia, are better but still problematic because of poor diversification and higher expenses than other, more-diversified international funds.

If you want to invest in more geographically limiting international funds, take a look at T. Rowe Price's and Vanguard's offerings, which invest in broader regions, such as those investing just in Europe, Asia, and the volatile but higher-growth-potential emerging markets in Southeast Asia and Latin America.

In addition to the risks normally inherent in stock fund investing, international securities and funds are also subject to buffeting by changes in the value of foreign currencies relative to the U.S. dollar. If the dollar declines in value, that helps the value of foreign stock funds. Some foreign stock funds hedge against currency changes. While this helps to reduce volatility a bit, it costs money to do it. I wouldn't worry about these things. Remember, you're investing in stock funds for the long haul. And in the long haul, your international stock funds' performance will largely be driven by the returns generated on foreign stock exchanges, not currency price changes.

Here are my picks for diversified international funds that may meet your needs. Compared to U.S. funds, there are fewer established international funds, and they tend to have higher annual expense ratios. So I've listed fewer options for you (don't forget the Schwab International Index fund discussed in the index section earlier in the chapter). Beware of unproven managers and fund companies that are advertising the heck out of newly developed international funds. Newer funds in this area also tend to have high expenses, which will depress your returns.

T. Rowe Price International Stock

The international stock fund of T. Rowe Price, a pioneer in international investing, has performed well since its inception in 1980. It invests primarily in larger companies in the larger, established economies, but it also invests modest amounts (10 to 20 percent) in emerging international stock markets.

This fund is team-managed by the firm of Rowe Price-Fleming (a joint venture with Fleming, a London-headquartered private money management firm). The team is led by Martin Wade, who has three decades' experience in international stock investing. It uses numerous managers around the globe, each of whom is responsible for researching stocks in specific countries. Annual operating fee is an internationally reasonable 1.0 percent. $2,500 initial minimum, $1,000 for retirement accounts. ☎ 800-638-5660.

Vanguard International Growth

Like T. Rowe Price International Stock, Vanguard International Growth invests primarily in large companies with growth potential, mainly in established countries. It also invests about 10 to 20 percent in emerging markets.

International Growth is managed by London-headquartered Schroder Capital Management, which has research offices around the world focused on specific countries. The team is led by Richard Foulkes, who has managed this fund since its inception in 1981. This fund has a Vanguard-thin expense ratio of 0.5 percent. Reasonably tax-friendly in recent years. $3,000 initial minimum, $1,000 for retirement accounts. ☎ 800-662-7447.

Warburg Pincus International Equity

This fund invests in an eclectic mix of small-, medium-, and large-company value stocks in both established economies and emerging markets (which often make up a third or so of the fund).

This fund is managed by Richard King, who has three decades of international investment experience and has managed this fund since it began in 1989. At 1.4 percent, expenses are slightly higher than those for some of the fund's peers, but expenses have continued to come down as the fund's assets have grown. This fund is available through most discount brokers without transaction fees. Tax-friendly. $2,500 initial minimum, $500 for retirement accounts. ☎ 800-257-5614.

Other noteworthy international funds

USAA Investment International is well-diversified internationally and focuses on larger company stocks. This fund has been managed since its inception in 1988 by David Peebles. Expenses are a tad high at 1.2 percent but they're coming down as assets grow. Tax-friendly. $3,000 initial purchase for non-retirement accounts, $250 minimum for retirement accounts. ☎ 800-531-8100.

Tweedy Browne Global Value invests mainly in smaller- and medium-size value stocks worldwide, primarily in established countries. Although it can invest in the U.S., its U.S. holdings are expected to be small (less than 20 percent of the fund). The parent company has an excellent reputation, managing money privately since the 1920s; this fund itself has been in existence only since 1993 but has done well. Expenses are high at 1.6 percent but should decline as the fund grows in size. $2,500 initial minimum, $500 for retirement accounts. ☎ 800-432-4789.

One of a kind: recommended specialty funds

Specialty funds don't fit neatly into the previously discussed categories. These funds are often known as *sector* funds because they tend to invest in securities in specific industries.

Specialty or sector funds should be avoided in most cases. Investing in stocks of a single industry defeats a major purpose of investing in mutual funds — you give up the benefits of diversification. Also, just because the fund may from time to time be dedicated to a "hot" sector (different ones of these funds are often at the top of short-term performance charts), you can't assume that the fund will pick the right stocks and/or bonds within that sector.

Another good reason to avoid sector funds is that they tend to carry much higher fees than other mutual funds do. Many sector funds also tend to have rates of trading or turnover of their investment holdings. Investors using these funds outside of retirement accounts will have to face the IRS for the likely greater capital gains distributions this trading produces.

The only types of specialty funds that may make sense for a small portion (say, 10 percent or less) of your investment portfolio are funds that invest in real estate or precious metals. These types of funds can help diversify your portfolio because they can do better during times of higher inflation — which often depresses general bond and stock prices. You could comfortably skip these funds since diversified stock funds tend to hold some of the same stocks as held by these specialty stock funds.

Utility funds are popular with investors who want more conservative stock investments and I'll discuss these funds in this section, too. Here's the background you need to know on useful sector funds.

Real estate funds

Want to invest in real estate without the hassle of being a landlord? Invest in real estate investment trusts (REITs), which are stocks of companies that invest in real estate. These typically invest in properties such as apartment buildings, shopping centers, and other rental properties. Just as it's a hassle to evaluate REIT stocks, you can always (you guessed it) invest in a mutual fund of REITs!

REITs are small-company stocks and usually pay decent dividends. As such, they are not appropriate for higher-tax-bracket investors investing money outside retirement accounts.

Fidelity Real Estate is managed by Barry Greenfield, as it has been since its inception in 1986. This is the oldest REIT fund. Greenfield is an investing veteran and has been with Fidelity since 1968. It has expenses of 1.1 percent per year. $2,500 initial minimum, $500 for retirement accounts. ☎ 800-544-8888.

Cohen & Steers Realty Shares has been managed by Martin Cohen and Robert Steers since the fund began in 1991. This fund is best purchased through most discount brokers, where the minimum initial investment is much lower (typically $2,000) instead of the normal $10,000. Discounters also offer it without transaction charges. Annual expenses are 1.1 percent. ☎ 800-437-9912.

Gold & silver - precious metals funds

Over the millennia, gold and silver have served as medium of exchange or currency because they cannot be debased and have intrinsic value. These precious metals are used not only in jewelry but also in less-frivolous things such as manufacturing.

As investments, gold and silver do well during bouts of inflation. For example, during the period from 1972 to 1980, when inflation zoomed up in the U.S. and stocks and bonds went into the tank, gold and silver company stocks skyrocketed more than 500 percent. People were concerned that our government was going on a money-printing binge.

Over a *very* long term, precious metals are lousy investments. They don't pay any dividends and their price increases just keep you up with, but not ahead of, increases in the cost of living. Although this is better than keeping cash in a piggy bank or stuffed in a mattress, it's not as good as bonds, stocks, and real estate.

If you want to invest in precious metals, don't buy the bullion itself; storage costs and the concerns over whether you're dealing with a reputable company make buying bullion a pain. Also avoid futures and options (see Chapter 1), which are gambles on short-term price movements.

Among the better funds are the **Vanguard Gold Fund,** which, like most gold funds, invests in stocks worldwide because many mining companies are outside the U.S. in countries such as South Africa and Australia. This fund has one of the best track records among precious metals funds and has been around since 1984. Since 1987, David Hutchins of M&G Investment Management has managed the fund. Annual operating expenses are 0.6 percent. Tax-friendly. $3,000 initial minimum, $1,000 for retirement accounts. ☎ 800-662-7447.

Benham Global Gold Fund invests only in gold companies in North America. Around since 1988, this fund has been managed by Bill Martin since 1992. Annual expenses are a reasonable 0.6 percent. This fund can be purchased through most discount brokers without a transaction charge. $1,000 initial minimum for all accounts. ☎ 800-331-8331.

If you expect high inflation, or if you just want an inflation hedge in case you expect the end of civilization as we know it, stick with a gold fund. But these funds have wild swings and are not for the faint of heart or for the majority of your portfolio. To illustrate why, consider this: In 1993, the Vanguard Gold fund rocketed up 93 percent, whereas in both 1992 and 1990 it lost almost 20 percent and was down more than 14 percent in 1988.

Utility funds

Utility funds tend to attract older folks who want to earn good dividends and not have the risk of most stock investments. And that's what utility funds are good for. But this once-staid industry is being shaken up by increased competition caused by deregulation.

In a sense, these funds are superfluous. Most diversified stock funds contain some utilities, and those investors who want income can focus on better income-producing funds such as Wellesley Income in the hybrid group.

But if you want a pure play on this relatively stable industry, consider **Fidelity Utilities**, which has been around since 1987 and sports a good track record investing in utilities of all shapes and sizes, including some overseas stocks, which now comprise about 15 to 20 percent of the fund. The fund has been managed by John Muresianu since 1992 who has been with Fidelity since 1986. Its expense ratio is a 0.9 percent annually. $2,500 initial minimum, $500 for retirement accounts. ☎ 800-544-8888.

For the Cause: "Socially Responsible" Funds

Increasing numbers of mutual funds are popping up that label themselves *socially responsible.* If you blindly plunk down your money on such a fund, you may be disappointed with what you're actually getting. Bear with me while I explain.

First, the term *socially responsible* means different things to different people. In most cases, though, it implies that the fund avoids investing in companies, such as tobacco manufacturers, that are considered by many to be harming people or the world at large. Because cigarettes and other tobacco products are associated with the deaths of hundreds of thousands of people annually and add billions of dollars to health-care costs, most socially responsible funds shun tobacco companies.

Socially responsible funds appeal to some investors who desire to marry their investments to their social principles and who want to avoid supporting causes that they feel are harmful. Although some of the socially responsible funds attempt to "do the right thing," doing good and agreeing on what is good aren't as easy as the funds' marketing materials and the socially responsible label may imply. And, although there's nothing wrong with making a profit, some of these funds are slickly marketed to exaggerate the good that these funds actually do.

Your definition of social responsibility may not match the definition of the investment manager who's running a fund. And even if you can agree on what's socially irresponsible (such as selling tobacco products), funds aren't always as clean as you would think or hope. Although a fund may avoid tobacco manufacturers, it may invest in retailers that sell tobacco products, or the paper supplier to the tobacco manufacturer, or the advertising agency that helps pitch tobacco to consumers. (These kinds of definitional problems have caused the major mutual fund companies to steer clear of offering a socially responsible fund. Neither Vanguard nor Fidelity offers such funds.)

The relatively small size of socially responsible funds also means that you'll pay more to invest your money in these funds — yet your performance probably won't place you among the above-average performing funds. Socially conscious funds, which have been around since the early 1970s, have developed a relatively small following despite the continued boom in mutual funds. Today there are about 30 such mutual funds, but their total assets under management are less than 1 percent of all fund assets.

Janet's journey

I once had a client, Janet, who investigated these funds seriously, and her journey highlights the numerous challenges to socially responsible investing. The idea of socially responsible investing appealed to her: over the years, she had volunteered and participated in the civil rights and women's rights movements, among others. She didn't want her money invested in companies engaged in practices she didn't agree with.

Janet did not want to invest in companies that have a poor track record for hiring women and minorities. Because she believes in universal health coverage and thinks that no company should profit from people's need for health care, Janet's definition of social responsibility also included avoiding investing in funds that hold for-profit health care enterprises. After perusing the holdings of many socially responsible funds, Janet had few choices left — only one fund met her definition and also had a decent track record.

Socially responsible funds attempt to look at more than a company's bottom line before deciding to commit their investors' capital. Many of these funds consider such factors as environmental protection, equal employment opportunity, the manner in which a company's employees are treated, and the level of honesty a company displays in its advertising. They also typically exclude specific industries such as defense contractors who manufacture weapons. Some people question what's socially irresponsible about investing in defense stocks, reasoning that defense is needed for the protection of a country and its people.

Your definition of social responsibility may differ from mine or Janet's. Whether it does or not, you may be concerned about the *Domini Social Equity Index* fund, which invests in 400 companies of all sizes that meet their social screens. Among that portfolio's holdings is McDonald's, the world's largest fast-food (hamburger) company. Domini considers McDonald's socially responsible because of its support of children's charities, participation in recycling programs, hiring and promotion of women and minorities, and purchasing of hundreds of millions of dollars in goods and services from woman- and minority-owned businesses.

But, if you think about it, the social responsibility of a company whose business depends on beef is questionable because of its impact on people's health and how tremendously land- and water-intensive cattle raising is. Some might also question the screening and awarding of contracts based on gender and ethnicity.

Like many other funds, Domini also invests in Ben & Jerry's, the ice cream company. Even a company like Ben & Jerry's, with a reputation for social responsibility, can have its ethics questioned. Like McDonald's, Ben & Jerry's products are considered by some to be detrimental to personal health and the environment. In 1992, the Food and Drug Administration forced Ben & Jerry's to relabel one of its "low-fat" frozen yogurts because it was not actually low in fat.

A number of socially conscious funds invest in Toys R Us. This company is the giant toy retailer that sells, among other things, widely criticized video games that are quite violent and keep kids away from homework. Gun control supporters argue that selling toy guns encourages kids to use the real thing. Investors who agree should consider Toys R Us as a socially *irresponsible* company — and that's before we consider the heaps of plastic (made from petroleum) and the drive toward over-consumption that the toy industry encourages.

Ways to express your social concerns

Some funds that are not labeled "socially responsible" still meet many investors' definition of socially responsible. These other funds usually carry lower fees and produce better returns. For example, GNMA bond funds invest in mortgages that allow people to purchase their own homes. Municipal bond funds buy bonds issued by local governments to fund projects that most would consider good — such as building public transportation, libraries, and schools. See Chapter 7 for my specific bond fund recommendations.

Among the funds that label themselves as socially responsible, as I said earlier, the pickings are slim. Here are some that are worth your time if you really want to try to be socially responsible in your investing:

- ✔ **PIMCO Total Return III** invests mainly in U.S. bonds using the same philosophy as PIMCO Total Return (which I describe in Chapter 7). Annual expense ratio is 0.5 percent. It must be purchased through discount brokers.

- ✔ **Domini Social Equity Index** is a quasi-index fund that invests in S&P 500 stocks that meet its definition of socially responsible. Annual expense ratio is rather high for an index fund at 0.90 percent. This fund is small, with less than $100 million under management. ☎ 800-762-6814.

If you consider investing in socially responsible funds, make sure you look well beyond a fund's marketing materials. If you find a socially responsible fund that interests you, call the mutual fund company and ask it to send you a recent report that lists the specific investments that the fund owns. Otherwise, you may be blissfully ignorant, but not as socially responsible as you might like to believe.

As my client Janet eventually did, you can always consider alternative methods of effecting social change, such as through volunteer work and donations to causes that you support. Janet also exercises a means of change that people the world over are dying for, a means that is guaranteed to all American citizens by the Constitution — THE RIGHT TO VOTE!

Chapter 9

Great Recipes — Funds for All Occasions

In This Chapter

▶ Allocating those assets among funds and families

▶ Working out the percentages

▶ Great recipes — starting out and starting over

▶ Managing a windfall

*I*n Chapters 6, 7, and 8, I covered the details of money market, bond, and stock funds and everything in between. I named names and recommended specific funds to you. The concepts and individual funds may be swirling around your brain like random pieces of paper in a city alley during a 60-mile-an-hour windstorm.

Now comes the fun part, which is also the necessary part if you're still confused about so many different types of funds: assembling a portfolio of funds that fits with your overall financial situation. As I highlight throughout the book, particularly in Chapter 5, your mutual fund and other investing decisions should fit into your overall financial picture. In some cases, you may need to make other financial moves prior to (and maybe even instead of) investing in mutual funds. Sometimes you won't know what your priorities are or should be; so, in this chapter, I try to touch base on many possible financial scenarios.

Here's another way to look at this chapter. If you go to see a medical doctor about your health, a good physician will highlight things you should and should not be doing. For example, if you drink too much, smoke, and eat unhealthy foods, doc may tell you that you need to make some changes. If you're a woman about to try to conceive, your physician may recommend a diet most favorable to your and your baby's health. In the real world, of course, your physician may never ask about your health habits or take the time to provide important health advice. But education and taking care of your health is a two-way street, so maybe part of the problem is that you never ask your physician for advice in these areas.

As a "financial doctor," it's my job to help make people aware of how their investing decisions fit together and interact with the rest of their financial situation. I also see it as my responsibility to emphasize and explain what you should and should not do to improve your financial health. In the pages ahead, you soon get to read about different people's circumstances and how they can reposition their investments in mutual funds to make the most of their money and accomplish their goals.

Big Picture Stuff

Before you jump into the examples of putting together portfolios of funds, we need to cover some important issues that affect the overall strategies you will use to invest in funds. Bear with me. It won't take long and you'll be better able to digest and make sense of the cases.

Note: If you haven't read Chapter 5, "Fitting Funds into Your Financial Plan," now is a prime time to read it. It covers important financial planning considerations you should be aware of when you invest in mutual funds.

Add one cup sugar, two cups flour . . .

So here you are ready to whip up a great mix of mutual funds, but you don't have a recipe. This chapter is filled with winning, proven recipes. Some recipes may not match your needs or tastes at the moment. Most of them apply to longer-term investing — investing over, say, about seven to ten or more years. However, as you learn in Chapter 6 on money market mutual funds and in Chapter 7 on bond mutual funds, some of these funds also work for shorter time periods. (Don't forget: all funds are liquid on a day's notice — the risk is that you're investing money you may need in the short-term into funds that are more volatile).

When investing money for the longer term, such as for retirement, you can choose among all the different types of funds discussed in this book. Most people get a big headache when they try to decide how to spread their money across those choices. The specific amount that you decide to invest in the different options is known as *asset allocation.* All this means is that you decide what percentage of your investments you place — or *allocate* — into bonds versus stocks and into international versus U.S stocks.

Now that you've read at least some of Part I (you *have* read at least some of Part I on investing basics — haven't you?), you know the benefits of investing for growth and the importance of diversification. If you're like most people, though, you still may be concerned about placing your retirement money or other long-term money into investments that can decline in value. You may feel that you're gambling with dollars intended for the security of your golden years.

Many working folks have time on their side, and they need to *use* time to make their money grow. You may have two or more decades before you need to draw on some portion of your retirement account assets. If some of your investments drop a bit over a year or two — or even over five years — the value of your investments has plenty of time to recover before you retire.

Your current age and the number of years you must wait until you retire should be the biggest factors in your allocation decision. The younger you are and the more years you have before retirement, the more comfortable you should be with growth-oriented (and more volatile) investments, such as stock funds.

Table 9-1 lists some guidelines for allocating money you've earmarked for long-term purposes such as retirement. All you need to figure out is how old you are (I told you investing was easier than you thought!) and the level of risk you're comfortable with.

Table 9-1	Asset Allocation for the Long Haul	
Your Investment Attitude	*Bond Allocation (%)*	*Stock Allocation (%)*
"Play it safe"	= Age	= 100 – age
"Middle of the road"	= Age – 10	= 110 – age
"Aggressive"	= Age – 20	= 120 – age

What's it all mean, you ask? Consider this example: If you're a conservative sort who doesn't like a lot of risk, but you recognize the value of striving for some growth to make your money work harder, you're a *middle-of-the-road* type. Using Table 9-1 if you're 35 years old, you might consider putting 25 percent (35 - 10) into bonds and 75 percent (110 - 35) into stocks.

Now let's divvy up your stock investment money between U.S. and international funds. Here's what portion of your "stock allocation" I would recommend investing overseas:

   20 percent (for *play it safe*)

   35 percent (for *middle-of-the-road)*

   50 percent (for *aggressive*)

If, for example, in Table 9-1, the 35-year-old, middle-of-the-road type is investing 75 percent in stocks, then about 35 percent of the stock fund investments (which works out to be around 25 percent of the total) could be invested in international stock funds.

So here's what the 35-year-old, middle-of-the-road investor's portfolio asset allocation looks like so far:

Bonds	25 %
U.S. Stocks	50 %
International Stocks	25 %

So there you have it. Now all this person needs to do is divvy up his money according to these percentages using appropriate mutual funds. Sounds easy, right? Well, it is — but then again it isn't. Some common problems arise that inevitably complicate your divvying. Here they are, along with my advice for quickly and intelligently getting around them:

"I'm starting out and don't have enough to meet the fund minimums."

What a drag. If you're just starting out, there's not a lot to allocate. And you've invested all this time learning about funds and asset allocations and selected five funds you want to use. Then you realize that the minimum initial investment for the first fund would force you to deplete all of the money you can invest!

Fear not. You have a couple of easy ways around this problem. First, you can buy the funds one at a time because you plan to save and invest more money, I hope, over the years ahead. I call this little trick *diversifying over time*. One twist on this strategy that will test and perhaps improve your mutual fund investing habits is to start by investing in the type of fund (for example, bond, international stock) that is currently doing the most poorly — that is, you can buy when things are "on sale." Then, the next year, you can add the fund type that is doing the most poorly at *that* time. (Make sure to buy the better funds within the type that is doing poorly!)

Another option is to invest in one of the hybrid funds that invests in all the different types of securities you want. Don't sweat the fact that you can't find one with the exact mix you want. For now, getting close is good enough. (See the "Mobile Mark" example in the "Starting Out" section later in this chapter for more ideas.)

"How do I work out the percentages since funds hold different stuff?"

In the example, our hypothetical 35-year-old investor wants to invest 50 percent of her available investment dollars in U.S. stocks. But you want to buy a hybrid fund and a stock fund. The hybrid fund invests 60 percent in stocks with the balance in bonds, and the stock fund invests about 20 percent overseas. So how the heck do you get 50 percent of your total dollars invested in U.S. stocks?

Divvying up into funds with different investing styles

Suppose that your investment allocation decisions lead you to want to invest 50 percent in U.S. stock funds. Which ones do you choose? As I say in Chapter 8, stock funds differ from one another on a number of levels. You've got your growth-oriented stocks and funds and those that focus on value. Then you've got your basic small-, medium-, and large-company stocks. And *then* there's everyone's favorite fund investing decision — whether to invest in passively managed (index) funds versus actively managed funds that try to beat the market.

Generally, it's a good idea to diversify into different types of funds. You can diversify in one of two ways. Your first option is to purchase many individual funds, each of which focuses on a different style. For example, you can invest in a large-company value stock fund and in a small-company growth fund. I find this approach somewhat tedious. Granted, it does allow a fund manager to specialize and gain greater knowledge about a particular type of stock. But many of the best mutual fund managers invest in more than one narrow range of security — which brings us to your second option.

A second approach is to invest in a handful of funds, each of which covers several bases, and that together cover them all. Remember, the investment delineations are somewhat arbitrary, and most funds do more than just one type of investment. For example, a fund may focus on small-company value stocks but also invest in medium-size company stocks, as well as in some that are more growth oriented.

As for how much you should use index versus actively managed funds, it's really a matter of personal taste. If you're happy as a clam knowing you'll get the market rate of return and knowing that you can't underperform the market, there's no reason you can't index your entire portfolio. On the other hand, if you enjoy the game of trying to pick the better managers and want the potential to earn better than the market level of returns, don't use index funds at all. A happy medium is to do some of both. (You might be interested in knowing that John Bogle, founder of Vanguard and pioneer of index investment funds, has about 40 percent of his money invested in index funds.)

One option is to take Thoreau's advice and simplify your (investing) life: forget about funds that invest in different types of securities. Buy purebreds — a stock fund that has 100 percent (or close to 100 percent) of its stocks in U.S. companies, a bond fund that invests only in bonds, and ditto for an international stock fund.

More difficult for the mathematically challenged is The Other Option — to work it out but keep the number of mixed funds to a minimum. If you don't and you want to invest in four or five mixed funds, trying to end up with the right allocations is a nightmare and requires a Ph.D. in math using simultaneous linear equations with many variables. Yuck!

Getting back to the example of wanting 25 percent in bonds, 50 percent in U.S. stocks, and 25 percent in international stocks, you could allocate your money as follows into these funds:

> 60 % Hybrid fund (60 percent U.S. stocks, 40 percent bonds)
>
> 15 % U.S. Stock fund (100 percent in stocks)
>
> 25 % International Stock fund (100 percent in international stocks)

How did I do this? Well, because the hybrid fund is the only one with bonds, I asked myself what percentage I would need to put into the hybrid fund so that you'd end up with about 25 percent (overall) in bonds. Because 40 percent of the hybrid fund is invested in bonds, the arithmetic looks like this:

> .4 * (Amount to be invested in fund) = .25
>
> Amount to be invested in fund = .25/.4
>
> Amount to be invested in fund = .625 or 62.5 percent

I like nice round numbers so I rounded 62.5 off to 60.

It's easier to work through the numbers with purebred funds, but they seem to fluctuate more because each one is less diversified. But as a portfolio of funds, they fluctuate just the same. Don't worry if you don't come up with the exact percentages.

How many funds and families?

If you're just starting to save and invest money, you very likely don't care how many funds and families are available to you since you don't have enough money to do that many. But if you have a hefty amount to invest already — or hope to have more someday — you should consider how many individual mutual funds to invest in and how many different fund families or companies your funds should come from.

Let's start with the family issue. Given the sheer number and quality of funds that the larger and better fund companies such as Vanguard and Fidelity offer, you could do all of your investing through one family of funds. There's a good argument against doing this, though: even these best firms don't do every type of fund the best. So, by *not* using each family for its particular strength(s), you may be sacrificing a little bit of return.

On the other hand, centralizing your investments in one family saves on administrative hassles by cutting down on the number of applications you need to complete, envelopes to open, statements to file, and so forth. Plus, you're more likely to learn your way around better at a company you spend more of your time interacting with.

Discount brokerage firms offer some of the best of both approaches. You get one-stop shopping and one statement for all of your holdings, but you also have access to funds from many families. On the downside: you pay small transaction fees to purchase many of the better funds through discounters (which I cover in Chapter 4).

There's no one right answer. Choose what works best for your needs. I use a combination of the above approaches by maintaining accounts through some of the giant mutual fund companies, but I also use discount brokers to buy funds from some of the smaller fund families that are more of a hassle to work with. Such a strategy allows me to maximize centralization while minimizing the extra transaction fees I have to pay.

As for the number of individual funds to hold in your portfolio, there are tradeoffs as well. At a minimum, you want to diversify into enough funds so that you can invest in the different types of securities — U.S. and international stocks of different sizes of companies and bonds. If you want, you can achieve fund diversity by investing in just one fund. Although this may seem like a crazy and risky thing to do, it isn't if you use one of the funds of funds described in Chapter 8.

As your savings allow, I generally recommend that you invest at least $3,000 to $5,000 per fund. If you're investing outside a retirement account, most of the better mutual funds will require an investment of this magnitude. Inside a retirement account you may invest far less — typically only $500 per fund — to get going. However, because most retirement accounts annually ding you around $10 per fund as an account maintenance fee, you should aim to invest the higher amounts so that you don't have your small investment devoured by high relative fees. (A $10-per-year fee diminishes a $500 investment by 2 percent per year.) Some fund companies will waive this fee if you keep more than a certain amount — say, $5,000 — in their funds.

It makes sense as you have larger sums to invest to use more funds. Suppose you have $300,000 and want to divide it equally, putting a third each into bonds, U.S. stocks, and an international fund. You could put $100,000 each into three funds: one bond fund, one U.S. stock fund, and one international stock fund.

But I wouldn't do that if I were you — and you shouldn't, either (since you *are* you). With that much money to invest, why not use at least two of each of the different types of funds? That way, if the one international stock fund you've chosen does poorly, all of your money earmarked for overseas investing is not tied up in it. There's no reason that you can't use three different funds within each category. The more money you have, the more sense this strategy makes.

Not everyone agrees with me on this. Recently in a financial publication, an investment advisor who manages client money by allocating it into different mutual funds was quoted as saying, "I'm comfortable putting a multi-million dollar portfolio together with three, four, maybe five funds." His reasoning: ". . . I'm making my job easier."

It is possibly true that more funds mean more paperwork, but if you're setting up three accounts — one each, for example, at Fidelity, Vanguard, and T. Rowe Price — there's no more paperwork to complete in order to invest in several funds at each company. Why not? Because you can exchange and duplicate account registrations via telephone transactions. If you use a discounter, there's no additional paperwork — though you will pay a little more in transaction fees by making more smaller transactions than you'd pay if you invested bigger chunks of money in fewer funds.

Sample Portfolios

Here's where the rubber hits the road. We're going to talk through some real live cases. Of course, the names and details have been changed to protect the innocent! Don't worry that you won't see a situation similar to your own; I've helped people at all different age, income, and asset levels.

My goal in going through these cases is to teach you useful ways to think about investing in funds and to provide specific solutions and ideas. You may feel that you will gain the most benefit from reading those cases that seem closest to your current situation, but I encourage you to read as many as your time allows, perhaps even all of them. Each case raises somewhat different issues, and your life and investing needs will change in the years ahead.

Throughout these cases, I also hope to show you how your investing decisions fit within the context of your overall finances (that's one of the constant themes of this book, you know). The tax impact of your investing decisions is important, and I will emphasize it in all cases. Also, remember the importance of establishing and figuring where you stand with regard to important financial goals you may have, such as retirement planning (the fund-related ins and outs of which are covered in Chapter 5). These examples are arranged somewhat by level of difficulty, from the simpler cases to the more complex.

Starting out

If you're just starting to get your financial goals together, you're hardly alone. If you're still in school or otherwise young and new to the working world, *good for you* to want to get on the right investing road now! Regardless of your age, though, remember that it's never too late. Even a few of my older clients have said that it took them a long time to work up the courage to seek advice. They had delayed, they said, because they were a tad ashamed of their financial affairs and how little they had saved and for waiting so long to plan for retirement.

There's a lesson in that delay if you're just starting out: Don't be ashamed of where you are now. Everyone, including those who have become millionaires and billionaires, had to "start out" sometime.

Ground zero: Zsa-zsa

Zsa-zsa is in her 20s, works as an architect, and loves to watch *Melrose Place* and *Beverly Hills 90210.* She earns decent money, lives in New Jersey, and has no debt and no savings. Financially speaking, she's a blank slate, but because it's January and she made it her New Year's resolution to get her finances in order, she wants to do something.

Her employer offers her health and disability insurance and a profit-sharing retirement plan, which only her firm may contribute to, but to which they've made small contributions in the past. She wants to invest in mutual funds but doesn't want hassle in either paperwork or complications on an ongoing basis. Zsa-zsa is thrifty; she finds saving money easy. She wants to invest for growth. With her money earmarked for long-term future needs such as retirement, she sees no need to invest conservatively (even though she does want some of her investments more conservatively invested). She's in the 28 percent federal tax bracket now, but as her experience in her field increases, she expects to earn more and soon will edge into the 31 percent federal tax bracket.

Recommendations: Zsa-zsa should consider investing $2,000 annually in an IRA. In her case, though, the IRA won't be tax-deductible because her employer offers a retirement plan under which she is considered covered and because she earns more than is allowed ($35,000) to make a tax-deductible contribution to an IRA. The benefit of making this so-called non-deductible IRA contribution is that the earnings on the money compound tax-deferred over time. At her age, she's got several decades at least for the compounding to happen.

On a monthly basis, she figures she can save $600 and could invest it as follows:

✔ **Do the IRA.** It's January, so Zsa-zsa can put $2,000 into an IRA for last tax year as well as another $2,000 for this current tax year. She's willing to be aggressive, so she could split her first two years' IRA contributions between a couple of good funds that invest exclusively in stocks at Fidelity — maybe, for example, Fidelity Disciplined Equity or Stock Selector and Fidelity Low Priced Stock.

Zsa-zsa could establish her IRA account through Fidelity's discount brokerage division, which allows purchasing of Fidelity as well as non-Fidelity funds through one account. Because Fidelity assesses a $12 fee if an IRA fund balance is less than $2,500, sticking with two funds over a few years so as to build each fund's balance above $2,500 would be a wise move. Warburg Pincus International Equity would be a good fund to add.

✔ **Start a monthly investment program.** After funding the IRA, she could divvy up the $600 per month savings into the following funds that are reasonably tax-friendly (which is important because she's investing outside a retirement account and is in a reasonably high tax bracket).

> 50% - 70% in Vanguard Tax Managed Capital Appreciation
> 30% - 50% in Vanguard International Growth

These funds pay very low dividends and, historically, have made modest capital gains distributions. They require a $3,000 minimum initial investment so Zsa-zsa needs to save the minimum before she can invest it. Once the minimum is met and invested in each fund, she can have money sent and deducted electronically from her bank checking account and invested in these mutual funds.

✔ **Start an emergency fund.** Like everyone else, Zsa-zsa should have an emergency source of cash. Although the mutual funds that she's investing in outside her retirement account are liquid and can be sold any day, there's a risk that an unexpected emergency could force her to sell when the markets are hung over.

With family to lean on, she could make do with, say, a cushion equal to three months' living expenses. She could even postpone doing this until after she funds her IRA. (Normally I would recommend doing the emergency fund first but since she has family she could borrow from, I feel it's okay to go for the tax benefits that come long-term with funding the IRA account.) Because she won't keep a large emergency balance, she could keep her emergency fund in her local bank account, especially if it helps to keep her checking account fees down. Otherwise, she could invest in a Vanguard's New Jersey Tax-Free Money Market Fund.

If Zsa-zsa lived in a state for which there's not a good state-specific money market fund available (see Table 6-1 in Chapter 6), she could simply use the Vanguard Municipal Money Market fund which is federally tax-free. If, for example, she lived in Florida, for which USAA offers a Florida money market fund, she'd have to weigh the hassle factor of establishing an account at yet another fund company compared to how much extra yield she'd end up with. Because the USAA fund in Florida has a higher management fee (0.5 percent versus Vanguard's fund at 0.2 percent), it's probably not worth the bother.

Living month to month with debt: Mobile Mark

Mark is a 42-year-old renter who has zero desire to own a home. He doesn't want the feeling of being tied down in case he ever wants to move, something he's done a lot of over the years. Currently he lives in California. Feeling that he's "hit middle age," Mark wants to start socking away money regularly into investments. He has a fairly large folder filled with mutual fund ads and prospectuses but found most of it confusing and intimidating. He has about $5,000 in a bank IRA invested in a certificate of deposit.

Getting started with $100 per month or less to invest

While most mutual funds' minimum initial investment amount of a couple of thousand dollars is quite small compared to private money managers who have six-figure to several-million-dollar entrance requirements, it may still loom large if you're just starting to save and invest. You want to get on with the program, and you don't want to risk spending your savings if it's sitting around in your bank account until you can come up with the cash for high fund minimums.

Here's a way around the problem. Some fund companies allow you to invest in their funds without meeting the minimum initial investment requirements as long as you enroll in their automatic investment program. You can do the trick with these by having a small amount per month deducted from your bank account and sent electronically to the fund company. Neuberger & Berman and T. Rowe Price both waive their initial minimum investment requirements so long as you're investing $50 monthly in a fund through them.

Also remember that fund retirement account minimums are significantly lower — often as low as $500 per month, some even less.

A final strategy is to save for several months until you have enough for some of the funds recommended in Chapters 6 through 8 that have $1,000 minimums. Regardless of which strategy you use to get started, don't compromise your choosing of good funds just because a fund offers low minimums.

Mark feels insecure living month to month and being so dependent on his paycheck. One of the reasons he's feeling some financial pressure is that, in addition to his monthly rent, he has an auto loan payment of about $300 per month and total credit card debt of $6,000. He also doesn't have any family he can depend on for money in an emergency.

Recommendations: Although Mark has the best of intentions, he's a good example of someone who has managed to get his financial priorities *out* of order. Mark's best and most appropriate investment now is to pay off his credit card and auto loan debt and forget about fund investing for a while. At interest rates ranging from 10 to 15 percent, paying off these debts actually is his best investment. Like the millions of others, Mark got into these debts because credit is so easily available and encouraged in our society. Such easy access to borrowing has encouraged Mark to spend more than he's been earning. Thus, one of the first things he should do is to figure just where his money goes in a typical month. By using his credit card statement, checkbook register, and his memory of things he has bought with cash, Mark can determine how much he is spending on food, clothing, transportation, and so on. He needs to make some tough decisions about what expenditures he'll cut so that he can "save" money to use to pay off his debts.

Like Zsa-zsa (you remember her — 20s, architect, sometime TV buff), Mark also should build an emergency reserve. If he ever loses his job, becomes disabled, or whatever, he'd be in real financial trouble. Mark has no family to help him in a financial pinch, and he's close to the limits of debt allowed on his credit cards. Because he often draws his checking account balance down to a few hundred dollars when paying his monthly bills, building up his reserve in his checking account or saving account so as to minimize monthly service charges makes the most sense for him now. Recently, Mark eliminated about $100 per year in service charges by switching to a bank that waives such fees if he direct-deposits his paycheck.

Mainly by going on a financial austerity program — which included sacrifices like dumping his expensive new car and moving so that he can walk or bike to work — within three years, Mark has become debt-free and has accumulated several thousand dollars in his local bank. Now he's ready to invest in mutual funds. Because his employer offers no retirement savings programs, the first investment that Mark should make is to fund a $2,000 individual retirement account (IRA). Mark does not want investments that can get clobbered: he thinks that he has been late to the saving game and doesn't want to add insult to injury by losing his shirt in his first investments. Being a conservative sort, Mark thinks that Vanguard makes sense for him. For his IRA, he can divide his money between a hybrid fund such as Vanguard Wellington (70 percent) and an international stock fund such as Vanguard International Growth (30 percent). In addition to his new $2,000 contribution, Mark also should transfer his bank CD IRA into these funds as well.

Now debt-free, Mark thinks that he can invest about $400 per month in addition to his annual IRA contribution. His income is moderate, so he's in the 28 percent federal tax bracket. He wants diversification but doesn't have a lot of money to start his investing program. He has set up automatic investment plans whereby each month the $400 is invested as follows (note that many of these funds have a minimum initial investment requirement of $1000 and that some of them waive that minimum if you invest via electronic funds transfer):

> 30% in Benham CA Tax-Free Intermediate or Long-Term Bond fund
> 30% in T. Rowe Price Spectrum Growth
> 20% in Neuberger and Berman Focus
> 20% in Warburg Pincus International Equity

Competing goals: Gina and George

George works as a software engineer and his wife Gina works as a paralegal. They live in Virginia, are in their 30s, and have about $20,000 in a savings account, to which they currently add about $1,000 per month. This money is tentatively earmarked for a home purchase that they expect to make in the next three to five years. They figure needing a total of $30,000 for a down payment and expected closing costs; they are in no hurry to buy because they plan to relocate once they have children in order to be closer to family (the allure of free baby-sitting is just too powerful a draw!).

Justifiably, they're pleased with their ability to save money — but they're also disappointed with themselves for leaving so much money earning so little interest in a bank. They figure they need to be serious about investments since they want to retire by age 60, and they recognize that kids will cost money.

George's company, although growing rapidly, does not offer a pension plan. In fact, the only benefits his company does offer are health insurance and a 401(k) plan that George is not contributing to because plan participants cannot borrow against their balances. Gina's employer offers health insurance, $50,000 of life insurance, and disability insurance — but, like George's employer, Gina's does not offer a retirement savings plan.

Recommendations: Deciding between saving for a home or funding a retirement account and immediately reducing one's taxes is often a difficult choice. In George and Gina's case, however, they can and should do some of both. At a minimum, George can save 10 percent of his income in his company's 401(k) plan. Wanting to be somewhat aggressive, George can invest 80 percent in stock funds with the balance in bonds as follows among his 401 (k) plan's mutual fund investment options:

0% in the money market fund option

20% in Vanguard Bond Index Total Bond Market

0% in T. Rowe Price New Income (another bond fund that has much higher management fees than Vanguard's and mediocre investment returns)

15% in Fidelity Magellan (available without its normal sales charge)

15% in Janus

15% in Vanguard Equity Income

35% in Harbor International (an excellent international fund that's still currently closed but available to a 401(k) plan such as this one that has used it in the past)

0% in a so-called guaranteed investment contract (GIC) (which is not a mutual fund but a fixed-return insurance contract) and nothing into the money market account option. See the sidebar on "Investing money in company-sponsored retirement plans" for a discussion of these investment options.

If George contributes the maximum amount through his employer's 401(k) and he and Gina still want to invest more in retirement accounts, they can invest $2,000 each, per year, into a non-deductible IRA.

Gina shouldn't worry that, if she and George should divorce, George would get all of the money in his 401(k) plan. As with non-retirement account assets, these assets can be split between a divorcing husband and wife. A more significant concern would occur if, say, George is an isolated dunce and refuses to talk to Gina about the investment of this money for their retirement and does some not-so-smart things such as frequent jumping from one fund to another. (Try talking about this issue with your spouse. If you don't get anywhere with your spouse, pay a visit to your local marital counselor.)

What about their $20,000 that's sitting in a bank savings account? They should move it, especially because George is a fan of USAA, having benefited from their terrific insurance programs as a member of a military family. Initially, he and Gina can establish a tax-free money market fund such as the USAA Tax-Exempt VA money market fund as an emergency reserve.

Because they don't plan to need the down payment money for the home for another three to five years, they can invest some of their savings — perhaps as much as half — in the USAA Tax-Exempt Intermediate-Term Bond fund. Even though they will pick up a little more yield, they need to know that the bond fund share price declines if interest rates rise (for that weighty subject, see Chapter 7).

Investing money in company-sponsored retirement plans

In some company-sponsored plans, such as 401(k)s, you are limited to the predetermined investment options your employer offers. In most plans, the mutual funds are decent and make you happy that you didn't have to do the legwork to research them. Plans differ in the specific options they offer, but the basic choices are common.

Money market funds offer safety of principal: they don't fluctuate in value. However, there is the risk that your investment will not keep up with or stay ahead of inflation and taxes (which are due upon withdrawal of your money from the retirement account). In most cases, skip this option. One situation in which you might use this option is when you already have a large lump of money accumulated and want a parking place for gradual investment into the riskier investments. For regular contributions coming out of your paycheck, money funds make little sense. If you use the borrowing feature that some retirement plans allow, you may need to keep money in the money market investment option. You also may want to use it if you plan to leave soon and want your money safe and secure while you prepare for your move.

Bond mutual funds pay higher yields than money funds, but they also carry greater risk because their value can fall if interest rates increase. However, bonds tend to be more stable in value than stocks. Aggressive, younger investors should keep a minimum amount of money in these funds, whereas older folks who want to invest more conservatively may want to invest more money this way.

Guaranteed-investment contracts (GICs) are backed by an insurance company and typically quote you an interest rate a little lower than on bond funds. There is, however, no volatility (that you can see). The insurance company however, normally invests your money mostly in bonds and a bit in stocks.

GICs are generally better than keeping your retirement money in a money market or savings account, both of which usually pay a couple of percent less in yield. (See Chapter 7 for more on GICs.)

Balanced mutual funds invest in a mixture primarily of stocks and bonds. This one-stop shopping concept makes investing easier and smoothes out fluctuations in the value of your investments — funds investing exclusively in stocks or bonds make for a rougher ride. These funds are solid options and, in fact, can be used for the majority of your retirement plan contributions.

Stock mutual funds invest in stocks, which usually provide greater long-term growth potential but also wider fluctuations in value from year to year. Some companies offer a number of different stock funds, including those investing overseas. Unless you plan to borrow (if your plan allows) against your funds, for example for a home purchase, you probably should have a healthy helping of stock funds.

Your Employer's Stock. Some companies offer employees the option of investing in the company's stock. Generally I advocate avoiding this option for the simple reason that your future income and other employee benefits are already riding on the success of the company. If the company hits the skids, you may lose your job and your benefits. You certainly don't want the value of your retirement account to depend on the same factors. If you expect your company to conquer the competition, though, investing a portion of your retirement account is fine if you're a risk-seeking sort — but no more than 25 percent. If you can buy the stock at a discount compared to its current market value, so much the better.

George also should get some disability insurance to protect his income (it turns out that his employer offers a cost-effective group coverage plan.) Before Gina becomes pregnant, George and Gina also should purchase some term life insurance.

If George and Gina had little or no money saved and couldn't both save for the home and get the tax benefits of their retirement account contributions, they'd have a tougher choice. They should make their decision based on how important the home purchase is to them. Doing some of both (saving for the home and in the retirement accounts) is good, but the option of not using the retirement account and putting all their savings into the home down payment "account" is fine, too.

We want money, lots and lotsa money: Pat and Chris

Pat and Chris earn good money, are in their 40s, and live in South Dakota. Pat is self-employed and wants to sock away as much as possible in a retirement savings plan. He figures that he can invest at least 10 percent of his income. Chris works for the government, which offers a retirement plan with the following options: a money market fund, a government (big surprise!) bond fund, and a stock fund that invests in larger-company U.S. stocks only.

Pat and Chris want diversification and are willing to invest aggressively. They want convenience and they're willing to pay for it. In addition to Pat's retirement plan, they want and are able to save additional money to invest for other purposes such as Chris's dreams of buying a small business and investing in real estate. They currently own a home that has a mortgage that could easily be supported by one of their incomes. Neither depends on the other's income.

Pat also has an $8,000 IRA account, which is currently divided between the Prudential Growth Opportunity Fund (Class B) and the Prudential GNMA (Class A). Pat has not contributed to the IRA for six years now. He also owns a universal life insurance plan, which he bought from Prudential as well. He bought the life insurance plan five years ago when he no longer could make tax-deductible contributions to his IRA; the life insurance plan is better than an IRA, according to Pat's broker, because he can borrow from it. The broker told Pat last week that his life insurance plan is "paid up" (he need not put any more money into the plan to pay for the $20,000 of life insurance coverage) and has a cash value of $3,300, although he would lose $1,200 if he cashed it in now due to surrender charges.

Recommendations: First, Pat should lose Prudential and his current broker. The broker has sold Pat crummy mutual funds. The Prudential funds have high fees and dismal performance relative to their peers. He could transfer his Prudential fund monies into Vanguard Star or Wellington.

Pat doesn't need life insurance because no one depends on Pat's income. Besides, it's a lousy investment (for the compelling reasons why you're better off not using life insurance for investing, see Chapter 1). Pat should dump the life insurance and either take the proceeds or roll them over into a variable annuity (which I explain later in the chapter).

Pat can establish a Keogh retirement savings plan and stash away up to 20 percent of his net self-employment income per year. A paired plan that offers a high degree of flexibility from year to year in the required contribution is his best bet (paired plans get the marquee in Chapter 5). He could establish his Keogh plan through a discount brokerage account that offers him access to a variety of funds from many firms. He could divide up his Keogh money as follows over the years:

> 15% in PIMCO Total Return
> 15% in Vanguard Bond Index Total Bond Market
> 10% in Mutual Beacon
> 10% in Warburg Pincus Emerging Growth
> 20% in T. Rowe Price Spectrum Growth
> 15% in Vanguard International Growth
> 15% in Warburg Pincus International Equity

Because Chris does not have international stock funds as an investment option, Pat can invest more in these than he normally should if he were investing on his own. In Chris's retirement plan, contributions could be allocated approximately a third into the bond fund, with the balance in the stock fund.

As for accumulating money for Chris to purchase a small business or to invest in real estate, Pat and Chris should establish a tax-free money market fund, such as the Vanguard Municipal Tax-Free Money Market fund, for this purpose. As could George and Gina earlier this chapter, Pat and Chris can invest in a short-to intermediate-term tax-free bond fund if they anticipate not using this money for at least several years and want potential higher returns.

Life changes and starting over

Sometimes you may wish that you were just starting out, but it's never too late to start over. If you have existing investments, they may not make sense for your situation. Perhaps your investment mix is too conservative, too aggressive, too taxing, or not too profitable. Or maybe you've been through a major life change that's causing you to reevaluate or begin to take charge of your investments. Here are some examples sure to stimulate your thinking about an investing makeover.

Education funding: The Waltons

One of the biggest life changes that gets many adults thinking more about investing is the arrival of a child or two. And with all the fear-mongering seen in ads and articles about how you're going to need a gazillion dollars to send your little bundles of joy off to college in 18 years, many a parent goes about investing in the wrong way.

The Waltons — Bill, 36, and Carol, 40, along with their two children, Ted, 1, and Alice, 3 — live in the suburbs of Chicago in a home with a white picket fence and a dog and cat. They own a home with a mortgage of $100,000 outstanding. Their household income is modest because they both teach.

The Waltons have $40,000 in five individual securities in a Shearson brokerage account they inherited two years ago. They also have $20,000 in two Shearson limited partnerships, now worth less than half of what they paid for them five years ago. Bill and Carol prefer safer investments that don't fluctuate violently in value.

They have $25,000 invested in IRAs with American's Washington Mutual Investors fund and $10,000 in a G.T. Global Europe Growth (Class A) mutual fund outside an IRA. Bill has not been pleased with the Europe fund, and Carol is concerned about supporting foreign countries when so many Americans are without jobs. Both like conservative, easy-to-understand investments and hate paperwork. They also have $10,000 apiece in custodial accounts for each of the kids in the Washington Mutual fund, which Bill's dad has contributed for their educational expenses. Bill's dad would like to continue contributing money to the Washington Mutual fund for the kids' college expenses.

Bill just took a new job with a university that offers a 403 (b) retirement savings plan, which he can get with many of the major mutual fund companies. He was not saving through his old employer's 403 (b) plan because, with the kids, they spend all of their incomes. Carol's employer does not have a retirement savings plan.

Recommendations: First, Bill should be taking advantage of his employer's 403 (b) plan. Though he may *think* that he can't afford to, he really can. If need be, he should dump the individual securities and use that money to help meet living expenses while he has money deducted from his paycheck for the tax-deductible 403 (b) account. (Whenever selling securities outside a retirement account, taxes should be an issue. In the Waltons' case, these securities have only been held for a couple of years and were worth about what their tax cost basis was — see Chapter 12).

Fidelity would be a terrific choice for Bill's 403 (b) because he can purchase their solid stock funds without those pesky and costly sales charges he'd get if he were investing in a non-retirement account. He could allocate his money as follows:

25% in Fidelity Puritan
25% in Fidelity Balanced
25% in Fidelity Equity-Income
25% in Fidelity Stock Selector

Bill and Carol could hold onto their Washington Mutual fund investment that they have in their IRAs: This fund has a solid track record and reasonable annual fees of 0.7 percent. Its only drawback is its sales load of 5.75 percent, which is water under the bridge for Bill and Carol because it was deducted when they first bought this fund.

The G.T. Global Europe is not a good fund and has high ongoing management fees of 1.7 percent. They should dump this fund and invest the proceeds in some better and more diversified international stock funds, such as Vanguard International Growth. And regarding Carol's concerns about supporting foreign companies — as a teacher, she should know better! Many companies today have operations worldwide and, besides, money is money. If she's strongly against investing overseas, I suppose that she can choose not to invest her IRA money overseas, but her portfolio likely will be more volatile and less profitable in the long run.

Regarding custodial accounts, Bill and Carol need to remember that their kids will qualify for much less financial aid the more money is saved in their names. Bill's dad should hold onto the money himself or give it to Bill and Carol. (This latter option has the added benefit of increasing Bill's ability to fund his 403(b) account and take advantage of the tax breaks it offers. Bill and Carol (and you as well, if you have children) should read Chapter 18 about ten important things you should know before you invest in funds for college.

The limited partnerships are bad news. They should wait them out until they are liquidated and then transfer the money into some good no-load mutual funds.

Rolling over (but not playing dead): Cathy

It's a surprise to her as much as it is to her friends and family: Cathy has a new job. While she was happily employed for many years with a respected software company, she got smitten with the entrepreneurial bug and signed on with a well-funded start-up software company. Her 401(k) plan investment of about $100,000 is invested in the stock of her previous employer. The company is waiting for Cathy's instructions for what she wants to do with the money. It's been nine months since she got sucked into the vortex of the insane hours of a start-up.

Nearing 40, tired but invigorated from those long days at her new company, Cathy has resolved to make some decisions about where to invest this money. She is comfortable investing the money fairly quickly once she thinks she has a plan. Cathy wants to invest somewhat aggressively; although she enjoys working and working hard, she happily imagines a time when she will not work at all. She likes the idea of diversification, so she thinks she may use a discount brokerage service to invest in a variety of different companies' funds — but she doesn't want the hassle of setting up lots of little IRAs at different fund companies. On the other hand, she doesn't want to pay a bunch of transaction fees, either.

Recommendations: Cathy should sell her stock through her old employer and transfer cash. This will save on brokerage commisions. Having her retirement money in one company's stock like this is risky.

For the best of both worlds, Cathy can have a chunk of money sent to and invested in an IRA at Vanguard, which would give her access to all the valuable Vanguard funds, and another chunk sent to Fidelity's brokerage division, which would give her free access to all the fabulous Fidelity funds, plus access for a small fee to non-Fidelity funds.

At Vanguard she would invest as follows:

15% in Vanguard Bond Index
   Total Bond Market
15% in Vanguard Index 500
10% in Vanguard International
   Growth

At Fidelity she would invest as follows:

10% in Pimco Total Return
10% in Dodge & Cox Stock
10% in Fidelity Disciplined Equity
10% in Fidelity Contrafund
10% in T. Rowe Price International Stock
10% in Warburg Pincus International Equity

Wishing for higher interest rates: Renee the near retiree

Renee is a social worker. Now 59 and single, she wants to plan for a comfortable retirement. In addition to owning her home without a mortgage, she has $150,000 currently invested as follows:

$40,000 in a bank money market account

$75,000 in Treasury bills that will mature this month

$35,000 in an insurance annuity that's invested in a "guaranteed investment contract," yielded 6.75% last year through her employer's non-profit retirement savings 403 (b) plan.

Renee currently earns $30,000 per year and has received pay increases over the years that keep pace with inflation. She has $250 per month deducted from her paycheck for the annuity plan. Her employer allows investments in the retirement plan through almost any insurance company or mutual fund company she chooses. She's also saving about $800 per month into her bank account. She hates to waste money on anything, and she doesn't mind some paperwork.

TIP

Lumping or averaging?

Most of the time, most people invest money as they save it. If you're saving through a company retirement plan, such as a 401(k), this option is ideal: it happens automatically and you're buying at different points in time, so even the world's unluckiest person gets to buy some funds at or near market bottoms.

But what if you have what to you seems like a whole *lot* of money that's lolligagging around in a savings or money market fund awaiting further instructions and direction? Maybe it's just piled up because you're thrifty, or maybe you recently inherited money or received a windfall from work that you've done. You're learning more about how to invest this money but once you decide what types of investments you'd like to purchase, you may be terrified at the thought of actually doing it.

Some people in this situation feel a sense of loss, failure, or even guilt for not making better use of the money than just letting it sit in a savings or money market account. Always remember one important thing: at least you're earning a positive return in the bank or money fund, and it beats the heck out of rushing into an investment you don't understand and in which you may lose 20 percent or more. Of course, there's no reason not to find the best parking spot that you can for your money (see Chapter 6 for recommendations of the best money market funds).

So how do you invest your lump? One approach is to dollar-cost average it into the investments you've chosen. All this means is that you're investing your money in equal chunks on a regular basis, such as once a month. For example, if you have $50,000 to invest, and you want to invest it once a quarter over a year, you would invest $12,500 per quarter until it's all invested. Meanwhile, the money that's awaiting future investment happily continues accumulating interest in a good money market fund.

The attraction of dollar-cost averaging is that it allows you to ease into riskier investments instead of jumping in all at once. The benefit may be that, if the price of the investment drops after some of your initial purchases, you can buy some later at a lower price. If you had dumped all your money at once and then the financial markets get walloped, it's human to think, "Why didn't I wait?"

The flip side of dollar-cost averaging is that if your investments of appreciate in value, you may wish that you had invested your money faster. Another possible drawback is that you may get cold feet continuing to invest money in an investment that's dropping in value. Some who are attracted to dollar-cost averaging are afraid to continue boarding a sinking ship.

Dollar-cost averaging also can cause headaches with your taxes when it's time to sell investments held outside retirement accounts. If you buy an investment at many different times and prices, the accounting is muddied as you sell blocks of the investment. Also, try not to purchase funds, particularly stock funds that have had a good year, late in the year because most of these funds distribute capital gains in December.

Dollar-cost averaging is most valuable when the money you want to invest represents a large portion of your total assets and you can stick to a schedule. It's best to make it automatic so that you're less likely to chicken out.

Most mutual fund companies offer automatic exchange services. Pick a time period that makes sense for you. I like to do dollar-cost averaging once per quarter early in the quarter (the 1st of January, April, July, and October). If you feel comfortable investing and want to get on with the program, "averaging" your money in over a year is fine, but it's riskier. If you've got big bucks to invest and you're cautious, there's no reason you can't average the money over two to five years (you can use some CDs or Treasury bills as holding places in such a case to get a better return than on the money fund).

Renee is concerned about outliving her money; she does not plan to work past age 65. She is terrified of investments that can decrease in value, and she knows a friend who lost thousands of dollars when the stock market crashed in 1987. She says that her CDs and Treasuries were terrific in the early 1980s when she was earning 10% or more on her money. She's concerned now, though: she keeps reading and hearing that many large, reputable companies (such as IBM and Sears) are laying off thousands of workers, yet the stock market seems to be rising to ever-higher levels. She wishes that interest rates would rise again.

Recommendations: First, Renee should stop wishing for higher interest rates. Interest rates are primarily driven by inflation, and high inflation erodes the purchasing power of one's money (see Chapter 7). The problem here is that Renee has all of her money in fixed-income (lending) investments. There's no real potential for growth, no real protection against further increases in the cost of living.

Even though she's planning to retire in six years, she's certainly not going to use or need all of her savings in the first few years of retirement. She won't use some of her money until her 70s and 80s. Thus, she should invest some money in investments that have growth potential. Stock funds are a natural and logical choice.

Renee also could and should invest more through her employer's retirement savings plan because she is saving so much outside that plan and already has a large emergency reserve. In fact she should do the maximum, 20 percent of her salary (see Chapter 5). She also can do better to invest in no-load funds for her 403 (b) plan instead of through an insurance annuity, which carries higher fees. Vanguard and their hybrid funds (which are far less volatile because they invest in many different types of securities) are logical choices for her to use for her 403 (b). I'd recommend the following investment mix for Renee's 403 (b):

> 25% in Vanguard Wellesley Income
> 25% in Vanguard Star
> 25% in Vanguard Wellington
> 25% in Vanguard LifeStrategy Growth

In addition to money that she is newly contributing to her 403 (b) account, Renee also can transfer money from the annuity into these funds. Her insurance annuity account balance statement likely shows that a penalty is assessed for moving the annuity balance (this penalty is not the IRS-imposed tax penalty for withdrawing money — Renee doesn't want or need to do that). The "penalty" results from a commission that was paid to an agent, which means that the commission money is gone. These penalties dissipate over time (because the insurer has use of your money long enough to earn enough to compensate for the agent's commission), and they should not deter one's desire to move money from an insurance annuity. Given Renee's skittishness, leaving that money sit in the GIC is not a bad move. (If you're the more courageous type regarding funds, see Chapter 10 on how to do proper transfers.)

What about the $115,000 in money outside her retirement account? Renee can gradually invest (perhaps once per quarter over two years) a good portion of this money into a mix of funds that, overall, is more conservative than the mix she's using for her 403 (b). She can be more conservative because she likely would tap the non-retirement money first in the future. She should reserve $25,000 in Vanguard's U.S. Treasury money market fund, which pays 1.5 percent more than her bank account; Renee would like to have her emergency reserve in something that's government-backed.

Because she's in a low-to-moderate tax bracket, not far away from retiring, and because it wouldn't be appropriate for her to invest solely in tax-friendly funds (since that would imply that the stock funds need to be growth-oriented — something not appropriate nor likely to be of comfort to Renee), she can use taxable funds for the other $90,000:

15% in Vanguard Bond Index Total Bond Market	15% in Dodge & Cox Balanced
	15% in Lindner Dividend
10% in Benham GNMA	15% in T. Rowe Price Balanced
15% in USAA Mutual Income	15% in Fidelity Balanced

If you're older than Renee, you can use a similar but more conservative mix of funds. For example, if you're in your 70s, for the 403(b), you could substitute the Vanguard Life Strategy Income fund in place of the Life Strategy Growth fund. For the non-retirement money, you could shift the Fidelity Balanced money to the Vanguard Bond Index fund.

More than I dreamed — dealing with a mountain

Sometimes the financial forces are with you and money *pours* your way. Hopefully this will happen for good reasons rather than through something negative. Regardless, a pile of money may overwhelm you. The good news is that a lump sum gives you more financial options. Here's how a couple of people handled it:

I got money, lots and lotsa money: Cash-rich Chuck

Chuck is a successful Pennsylvania entrepreneur in his late 30s. Starting from scratch, he opened a restaurant eight years ago. Today he's reaping the fruits of his labor. After several relocations and remodels, Chuck has built himself quite an operation, with 40 employees on the payroll. It's hard for him to believe, but his restaurant's profit now is running at around $500,000 per year. Not surprisingly, money has been piling up at a fast rate. He now has about $800,000 resting in his business bank checking account paying next to no interest.

He owns a home with a mortgage of about $250,000 but has no money in retirement savings plans. Chuck doesn't want to set up a retirement savings plan at his company because he would have to make contributions for all of his employees in plans such as SEP-IRAs and Keoghs (which I cover in Chapter 5).

The dreaded "d"s: downsizing, divorce, disability and death

Life isn't always what we hope it will be. Sometimes it changes suddenly. You lose your job, your health, or a loved one. Everyone reacts differently to such events. Some maintain a balanced and positive perspective. Other get depressed and lose touch with reality. Some panic and make rash decisions.

If you're making financial decisions you haven't had to make before, you owe it to yourself to be educated about your options and the pros and cons of each.

Be especially careful about hiring financial help because you're in danger of being too dependent and blindly following advice. Take the time to check out the advisor you're considering. And don't go it alone — just make sure to hire competent specialists (attorney, accountant, financial advisor) where appropriate.

The only thing you should rush to do is raise an emergency reserve if you need one. Be careful about selling any investment that you've made a profit on. In one case, a client I had just started working with got laid off. From his perspective, it came out of nowhere; it was a complete shock. He was married and he and his wife were raising their two children. They were heavily in debt, having stretched to buy the most expensive home they could afford and having leased two expensive cars. They had decent savings, but all of it was in the stock market. Luckily for them, this scenario occurred back in 1992 when the market was doing well. This guy's first move was to sell some of their stock to raise cash to tide them over if it took him a while to find a job. This move made sense and was all that he needed to do immediately. The rest of their investments could be left alone.

Chuck has been planning to open another location. He figures that a second location will cost around $400,000, but, as he says, "You just never know with construction work what the total tab may be."

Recommendations: The first thing Chuck should do is get his pile of money out of the bank and into something safer. Bank accounts are federally insured only up to $100,000 — so if his bank fails (and banks have and will continue to fail), he'll have a lot to cry over. Besides, money funds pay much better.

Chuck has several options for investing his excess money. The first is to pay for the cost of a second location; with his savings, he likely can buy a second location with cash. But there are a couple of drawbacks to using too much or all of his cash on a second location. First is the issue of liquidity if he depletes his savings. Second is the issue of diversification. One advantage to not using all of his savings on a second location is that he can invest some of his savings in investments other than his business.

Another option for Chuck is to pay off his mortgage. Yes, he gets a decent tax-deduction (although some of it is lost because of his high income), but because he's got all this extra cash, paying off the mortgage saves interest dollars. That would leave $550,000 in his money fund. If he paid down his mortgage and didn't want to pay all cash for his second restaurant location, he could take out a business loan — but that likely would be at a higher interest rate than the rate he pays on a mortgage for his home because banks consider small business loans riskier. However, because some of the home mortgage interest is not tax-deductible, it's close to a wash in Chuck's case. So he could pay off the mortgage and perhaps use some of his remaining money to pay for part of the second location, and the rest could be financed with a business loan. He should keep a good cushion — say, around $200,000 — for operating purposes for his business.

Some entrepreneurs, including those who have gone on to achieve great success, have violated these principles and more by not only pouring all of their savings into a business but also borrowing heavily. I say: to each his own. There's nothing wrong with going for it if you're willing and able to accept the financial consequences. If you don't have a safety net such as family members who could help with a small short-term loan if things go south and you need some money to live on until you find a way to earn income, be careful.

Because Chuck uses his current bank account for keeping his excess cash as well as for check writing, he could establish a tax-free money market fund in a brokerage account that offers check writing, such as the Fidelity USA account or a SchwabOne account. Beyond the money market fund, Chuck could begin to invest some money ($100,000 to $200,000) in reasonably tax-friendly mutual funds as follows by establishing accounts at Vanguard and Schwab:

> 20% in Vanguard PA Tax-Free Insured Long-Term
> 50% in Vanguard Tax-Managed Capital Appreciation fund
> 10% in Warburg Pincus International Equity
> 10% in Schwab International Equity
> 10% in Vanguard International Growth

Inheritances - Loaded Liz

About a year ago, Liz, who is in her 40s, came into a significant inheritance when her mother passed away. She received about $600,000; $150,000 of this sum was a portfolio of individual large-company, higher-yielding stocks, and the balance came as cash. The stock portfolio is being managed by an advisor out of state who charges 1.5 percent per year as an advisory fee and has trades placed through a brokerage firm. Despite the fact that the portfolio has only about eight stocks in it usually, trade confirmations come in about once per month.

Liz currently is a college professor and makes about $50,000 per year. She has approximately $40,000 invested in the TIAA-CREF retirement plan, with 80 percent in the plan's bond fund and 20 percent in its stock fund. She's saving and investing about $400 per month in the plan because that's what she can afford. Liz also has $110,000 in a bank IRA that will mature soon.

Liz currently owns a home and is happy with it. It has a mortgage of about $90,000 at a fixed rate of 9 percent. She would like to retire early, perhaps before 60, so that she may travel and see the world. She's wary of risk and gets queasy over volatile investments, but she's open to different types of funds. She likes to use many different companies but doesn't want the headache of tons of paperwork. Liz prefers doing business over the phone and through the mail because she's too busy to go to an office.

Recommendations: First, Liz should maximize her retirement contributions even though she thinks that she's saving all that she can afford. She's got all this extra money now that she could draw upon and use to supplement her reduced take-home pay if maximizing her retirement contributions doesn't leave enough to live on.

This extra cash also affords Liz another good move — getting rid of the mortgage. It's costing her 9 percent interest pre-tax (around 6 percent after tax write-offs) and she'd have to take a fair amount of risk with her investments to better this rate of return.

Liz also needs to be more aggressive investing her money, particularly inside her retirement accounts. All of her IRA and 80 percent of her employer's retirement plan money are in fixed-income investments. In the TIAA-CREF plan, she can invest 30 percent in the bond fund, 40 percent in its stock fund, and 30 percent in its global equities fund. With her IRA, she could transfer it to a discount broker and invest it as follows:

> 20% in Vanguard Star
> 20% in Fidelity Balanced
> 20% in SteinRoe Balanced
> 20% in T. Rowe Price Spectrum Growth
> 10% in Neuberger & Berman Guardian
> 10% in Warburg Pincus International Equity

After paying down the mortgage and keeping an emergency reserve of $40,000, as well as another $70,000 for remodeling, Liz would have $250,000 in cash plus the stocks. She should sell the stocks because their dividend income is taxable and she's paying 1.5 percent per year (plus commissions) to have her account managed. The account has underperformed the S&P 500 by an average of 3 percent per year over the past five years. She could transfer these shares to Vanguard's discount brokerage division and then sell them there to save on commissions as well as to have money there to invest in their funds. Then Liz could invest the remaining $400,000 once per quarter over the next three years as follows :

> 20% Vanguard Muni Intermediate-Term Bond fund
> 20% Vanguard Tax-Managed Balanced

Liz could also invest some money in a variable annuity. As explained in Chapter 5, these tax-sheltered investments are beneficial to folks like Liz who have excess money to invest and have many years over which they'd like the money to compound tax-deferred:

>   20% Vanguard Balanced
>   25% Vanguard Equity Index
>   15% Vanguard International Growth

A final word . . .

If you get stumped or perplexed and don't know what to do, always remember one thing: keep it simple.

If you think that your situation differs greatly from those presented here, drop me a letter care of IDG Books with no more than a one-page summary of your circumstances and fund-investing quandaries. If it adds to this chapter, I'll not only write up my advice for you, but I'll also make sure to send you a copy of the next edition of *Mutual Funds For Dummies*! (I cannot personally answer your notes, and if your situation is selected, you may not hear for a number of months.)

Part III
Nuts and Bolts: Indigestion

In this part...

This part covers a lot of things that other mutual fund books assume you know or simply choose to ignore about the nuts and bolts of fund investing. Here you learn how to overcome investor's indigestion (and related gastro-intestinal ailments): how to obtain and accurately complete fund application and transfer forms, how to understand tax forms that your mutual fund companies send you, how to track and manage your funds over the years, and how to fix the rare but downright aggravating technical glitches and problems that pop up in any investing program.

Chapter 10

Application, Transfer, and Some Other Neat Forms

In This Chapter

▶ Explaining application basics

▶ Opening multiple accounts and automatic investing

▶ Applying for checks and debit cards

▶ Understanding retirement account forms

*Y*ou're human — so odds are good that you absolutely, positively *don't* like paperwork. Unfortunately, when you invest money, paperwork is required. But don't despair: I show you how to do the fund application and transfer forms in this chapter.

Although the subject of this chapter may seem dreary, here you learn some extra-nifty things that perhaps you didn't know you could do with fund investing. And, unlike dealing the IRS tax forms year after year, fund paperwork is not that bad once your accounts are opened and up and running. You won't have much (if any) ongoing paperwork to do, except for filing the taxes owed on mutual fund distributions held outside of retirement accounts — but that's the subject of Chapter 12.

The examples I've chosen in this chapter use some of the better firms recommended in this book. Because particular types of applications are so similar from firm to firm, there's no reason you can't, for example, fill out a T. Rowe Price IRA application even if I show you how to complete such an application for Fidelity.

Non-Retirement Accounts

As I discuss in Chapter 4, you can purchase most of the excellent mutual funds I recommend in this book either directly from the mutual fund company that is selling them or through a discount brokerage firm. Though you see many similarities between applications in this section, you also see that brokerage account applications are a different type of animal than mutual fund company applications. Don't worry, though — I show you how to handle both of them.

Application basics

Suppose that you've read the chapters in Part II of this book and you've decided that you want to open a Vanguard Municipal Money Market fund. You call them up on their 800 number (☎800-662-7447) and ask them to "Please send me your account application materials for the Vanguard Municipal Money Market fund."

Several days later, you get a wad of materials in your mailbox; the envelope has enough density and heft to make a great fly swatter! But don't be intimidated. Most of the stuff in the package is marketing propaganda — the fund company wants to convince you to send them gobs of your money. (Some companies actually send some educational stuff.) For example, Vanguard includes a little brochure on the differences among all of their tax-free bond funds. Hunt around until you find the document that says something like "Account Registration Form" or "New Account Application" or "Application."

If you want to invest in several funds within the same fund company, ask when you call if they have a comprehensive or generic account application form that saves you from the drudgery of completing multiple application forms. Alternatively, you can establish a money market fund and then do exchanges by telephone into their other funds. (See Figure 10-1 for a sample form for the Vanguard Municipal Money Market fund.)

1. **Your Account Registration.** Choose in whose name or what organization's name the account is to be registered. Most people choose the first box, which is the option whether you're opening the account for yourself or for yourself and someone else jointly. "Joint tenants with rights of survivorship" is the default classification for jointly registered accounts. A *joint tenancy with rights of survivorship* means the following things:

✔ The person you've jointly registered the account with can do all the things that you can do on the account, such as calling and inquiring about account balances, doing transactions, and writing checks. Neither party needs the other's permission (although it's possible to establish the account so that both signatures are required for check writing).

✔ Each account holder has an equal interest in the account.

✔ If you should die, the entire account balance goes to the other person registered on the account without the hassles and expense of going through probate.

Vanguard
MUNICIPAL BOND FUND

Please do not write in this space. / UEXR 1 2
DLR# Branch

Alpha Code | Soc Code | St Code | Tax Rate | RR | CR | CC

ACCOUNT REGISTRATION FORM

BEFORE YOU COMPLETE THE ACCOUNT REGISTRATION FORM, PLEASE BE SURE TO READ THE INSTRUCTIONS ON THE REVERSE SIDE.

Mail to: The Vanguard Group
Vanguard Financial Center, Valley Forge, PA 19482

For help with this application, or for more
information, call us toll-free: **1-800-662-7447.**

PLEASE PRINT, PREFERABLY WITH BLACK INK.

1 YOUR ACCOUNT REGISTRATION (Check one box)

☐ **Individual or Joint Account**

Owner's Name: First, Initial (if used), Last

Owner's Date of Birth   Owner's Social Security Number

Joint Owner's Name: First, Initial (if used), Last

Joint Owner's Date of Birth   Joint Owner's Social Security Number

Joint accounts will be registered joint tenants with the right of survivorship unless otherwise indicated.

☐ **Gift or Transfer to Minor**

Custodian's Name (One Name Only: First, Initial (if used), Last)

Minor's Name (One Name Only: First, Initial (if used), Last)

under the _____ Uniform Gifts/Transfers to Minors Act
(State of Minor's Residence)

Minor's Social Security Number

☐ **Trust**

Trustee(s)' Name

Name of Trust Agreement

Beneficiary's Name

Taxpayer ID Number   Full Date of Trust Agreement

☐ **Corporation, Partnership, or Other Entity**

Type: ☐ Corp. ☐ Unincorp. Assn. ☐ Partnership ☐ Other

Name of Corp. or Other Entity

Taxpayer ID Number

2 YOUR ADDRESS

Do you have other Vanguard accounts? ☐ Yes ☐ No

Street or P.O. Box Number

City   State   ZIP

Citizenship: ☐ U.S. ☐ Resident ☐ Non-resident _____
              Alien   Alien   Specify Country

(   )
Daytime Phone   Evening Phone

Name of Employer

Occupation

3 YOUR INVESTMENT ($3,000 minimum per Portfolio)

Money Market (45): $ _____   Intermed.-Term (42): $ _____
Short-Term (41): $ _____   Long-Term (43): $ _____
Limited-Term (31): $ _____   Insur. Long-Term (58): $ _____
High Yield (44): $ _____   Total Investment : $ _____

4 YOUR METHOD OF PAYMENT

☐ Check payable to: **The Vanguard Group**-(Portfolio No. _____)
(See Section 3 above for appropriate Portfolio number.)

☐ Exchange $ _____ From _____
                    Name of Vanguard Fund

Account Number

Account Previously Established By:

☐ Phone Exchange ☐ Wire on (Date) _____

Account Number

**5 DIVIDEND AND CAPITAL GAINS
PAYMENT OPTIONS** (Check one box)

Unless a box is checked, all distributions will be reinvested in shares.

☐ Reinvest both income dividends and capital gains in shares.
☐ Pay income dividends in cash and reinvest capital gains in shares.
☐ Pay both income dividends and capital gains in cash.
☐ Send income dividends and capital gains to my bank account
   via Dividend Express.
☐ Send income dividends to my bank account via Dividend Express
   and reinvest capital gains in shares.

**Important: If you select Vanguard Dividend Express, please provide
your bank's telephone number in Section 6 below and attach a voided, preprinted check from your checking account or a preprinted deposit slip from your
checking or savings account. A canceled check or deposit receipt will not be
accepted.**

6 WIRING AND FUND EXPRESS OPTIONS

To arrange for the wire redemption or Fund Express service, please provide your
bank's telephone number below and attach a voided, preprinted check from your
checking account or a preprinted deposit slip from your checking or savings
account. A canceled check or deposit receipt will not be accepted. Passbook
savings accounts are not eligible for Fund Express.

(   )
Bank Telephone Number
Please indicate the type of service you wish to establish:
☐ Wire Redemption
☐ **Automatic Investment Plan (AIP):** On the _____ day each month*,
   transfer $ _____ from my bank account to my Vanguard account.
☐ **Automatic Withdrawal Plan (AWP):** On the _____ day each month*,
   transfer $ _____ from my Vanguard account to my bank account.
   *If you wish to arrange a payment frequency other than monthly (e.g., every other
   month, quarterly, semi-annually, or annually), please circle your choice and
   indicate the month payments are to begin _____.
☐ **Special Purchases and Redemptions (SPR):** To purchase or redeem shares at any
   time, using a bank account to clear the transaction.

7 SIGNATURE (Sign below)

By signing this form, I/we certify that:
■ I/We have full authority and legal capacity to purchase Fund shares.
■ I/We have received a current prospectus of the Fund and agree to be bound
  by its terms.
■ Under penalty of perjury, I/we also certify that —
  a. The number shown on this form is my correct taxpayer ID number.
  b. I am not subject to backup withholding because (i) I have not been notified
     by the Internal Revenue Service that I am subject to backup withholding as
     a result of a failure to report all interest or dividends, or (ii) the IRS has
     notified me that I am no longer subject to backup withholding. (**Cross out
     item "b", if you have been notified by the IRS that you are subject to
     backup withholding because of underreporting interest or dividends on
     your tax return.**)
  c. If I/we have chosen a Fund Express option, I/we authorize Vanguard, upon
     telephonic request, to pay amounts representing redemption(s) made by me/
     us or to secure payment of amounts invested by me/us by initiating credit or
     debit entries to my/our account at the bank named above. I/We authorize
     the bank to accept any such credits or debits to my/our account without
     responsibility for the correctness thereof. I/We further agree Vanguard will
     not be liable for any loss, liability, cost, or expense for acting upon my/our
     telephonic request.

PLEASE SIGN HERE: (If joint account, both owners must sign.)

X
Signature (Owner, Trustee, Etc.)   Date

X
Signature (Joint Owner, Co-trustee)   Date

Welcome to Vanguard!

8 CHECKWRITING OPTION

SUBJECT TO CONDITIONS ON REVERSE SIDE
I/We apply for the privilege of writing checks against this Vanguard Fund account.
I/We guarantee the genuineness of each signature and understand this request is
subject to conditions on reverse side.
ALL REGISTRANTS (MINORS NOT ACCEPTED) MUST SIGN HERE:
(exactly as you will sign checks)

Signature of Owner, Trustee, Etc.   Date

Social Security Number or Employer ID Number

Signature of Joint Owner, Co-trustee, Etc.   Date

Social Security Number or Employer ID Number

Indicate Number of Signatures Required on Checks _____
(Unless a number is indicated, only one signature will be required on checks.)

Figure 10-1:
Vanguard
Municipal
Funds
Account
Registration
Form.

Source: The Vanguard Group

A rarely used option is to register the account as "tenants in common." To have a *tenancy in common*, you can have a legal document drawn up specifying that each tenant owns a certain percentage of the account. Unlike shares of ownership for joint tenants with rights of survivorship, the shares for tenants in common need not be equal. If you die, the account is restricted: your share of the account is distributed to the person whom you chose to receive it, and the surviving account holder is required to set up a new account for his or her share.

If you go to the trouble of setting up the account registration as tenants in common, just scribble in the margin in this section of the form that you want the account set up this way, or attach a short letter that presents the same request. The fund company doesn't want or need to see the legal document. Keep it with your will or other personal financial stuff.

Gift or Transfer to Minor. If you want to open an account in your child's name, check the second box. As the parent, you are the "custodian"; your child is the "minor." Your state's name is asked for because of the two different laws that govern custodial accounts: the Uniform Gift to Minors Act (UGMA) and the Uniform Transfer to Minors Act (UTMA). Each state allows one or the other. The hitch: your child is legally entitled to the money in the account when he or she reaches the so-called age of majority. This is generally age 18 in the states of CA, DC, LA, ME, MI, NV, NY, SC, TN, TX, VT and at an age between 18 and 21 in all other states. Please be sure to read Chapter 18 before you take this plunge.

Trust. Generally, you know if you have a trust because you're either the one who sets it up or you are the recipient of assets that are part of a trust. There are many types of trusts. For example, many folks, by the time they get older, have set up what's known as a living trust that allows their assets to pass directly to heirs without going through probate. If you have a trust agreement, provide the pertinent details at this point in the form.

Corporation, Partnership, or Other Entity. If you want to open a mutual fund account for your corporation, local rotary club, or whatever, this is the registration section you use. You need a taxpayer ID#. If your organization doesn't have one, call the IRS at ☎800-TAX-FORM and request Form SS24.

2. **Your Address.** This part's EZ. You may be wondering why they ask for your phone numbers, your employer, and your occupation. Here's why: The fund company wants your phone numbers so it can call you if needed regarding some issue about your account. The rest of this information is partly required by fund regulators and partly just desired by the fund company itself for what fund companies call "market research"; they want to know what kind of people like to invest in what types of funds. If you wish to remain more private, you can skip this stuff and the fund company will still happily open your account. (The fund company does not share this information with the IRS.)

3. **Your Investment.** Here's where you tell 'em which fund you want. But be careful here. Remember that you are interested in the money market fund, which is the first line in the left column. On the line, simply write the amount you want to deposit.

To ensure that the money was deposited into the correct fund, check the account statement that you receive when you open your account. Although it doesn't happen often, fund companies (and you!) occasionally make mistakes.

4. **Your Method of Payment.** Generally, you're going to send a check to fund your account. Make it payable to the fund (include the fund number if companies number their funds as Vanguard does). Don't worry about someone stealing the check or a mail thief cashing it (remember: you make the check payable to the fund). Alternatively, you could open this account by exchanging money from another account that you have at Vanguard already.

Once you have an account open, you can do exchanges by telephone into other accounts. Exchanges save you the hassle of filling out more application forms every time you open new funds at the same company (although different account types, such as IRAs, do require separate account applications).

Make sure that you have another source of cash during the time it takes for the fund company to open your money fund and for your checks to arrive. Sometimes people send in almost all their money and then, in a few days, realize that they need some of the money and wish they had kept some back.

5. **Dividend and Capital Gains Payment Options.** Most mutual funds make dividend and capital gains payments. If you're not living off this income, it's usually best to reinvest these payments by purchasing more shares in the fund. To do that, just check the first box. This eliminates the hassle of receiving and cashing checks often and then figuring out where to invest the money.

On the other hand, if you're retired, for example, you may want the distributions on your fund sent to you so that you can spend it on whoopee cushions and sports cars. On this form, you can choose to have the money sent to you as a check through the mail. Or, even better, the fund can electronically transfer the money to your bank account. This method gets you the money quicker and means you've got less mail to open and fewer checks to sign and schlep to the bank.

6. **Wiring and Fund Express Options.** This section allows you to establish some other options. *Wire redemption*, if established, allows you to request that money be wired to your bank account. Your mutual fund and your bank may charge for wiring services, though, so don't use wiring as your regular way to move money back and forth to your bank. Save this feature only for when you need money fast that you didn't anticipate needing. (Better to keep enough money in your local bank checking account for needs that arise often.)

If you want to make regular deposits, you can select the *automatic investment plan.* This choice authorizes the fund to instruct your bank to send a fixed amount on a particular day of the month or some other time period. You can do the same in reverse by withdrawing money on a regular schedule, too. The minimum is $50 (that's stated on the other side of this application — it should be stated here to make your life easier). If you want to establish this service for multiple funds, simply attach a letter with your added instructions.

Special purchases and redemptions is an electronic funds transfer — it's like a paperless, electronic check that allows you to move money back and forth between your bank and mutual fund accounts. This process usually takes a full two days to complete because, like a check, the transaction is cleared through the Automated Clearing House (wiring can typically be done same day or next day). The mutual fund and the bank do not charge for this service because it's just like a check — which means that it costs less than wiring.

To establish these additional services, remember to attach a preprinted deposit slip or blank check (write "VOID" in large letters across the front of the check so no one else can use it).

7. **Signature.** Don't forget to sign the form. Not signing delays the opening of your account. (The fund company will mail the application back to you!) Attach your check to the application with a paper clip or staple, and pop everything into the postage-paid envelope that should have come with the application. If you can't find the envelope, the addresses are in the Appendix of this book.

8. **Check writing option.** This is a useful feature to sign up for on a money market fund. Most money funds limit check writing to amounts of $250 or more. I don't recommend establishing check writing for bond funds because it creates tax headaches. Every time you write a check on a bond fund, the transaction must be reported on your annual tax return — yuck! Keep enough cash in your money fund and just write your checks from there.

Opening many fund accounts without getting writer's cramp

As you see in Part II of the book, some of the larger fund companies have a number of good funds, so you may want to invest in multiple funds at one company. Some companies let you invest in multiple funds without having to complete the mountain of paperwork that others make you do.

Vanguard, for example, has a comprehensive "Account Registration Form" that lists almost all of its funds (see Figure 10-2). I say *almost* because Vanguard doesn't update the form every time a new fund comes out — remember that

Vanguard is cheap and hates to waste money. It's possible that one of the funds you want to invest in isn't listed on the form. Don't worry. Just write it in the "Other" section at the bottom of the right column.

B. CHOOSE THE FUND(S) IN WHICH YOU WISH TO INVEST

VANGUARD FUNDS

Please indicate Fund(s) ☒ and fill in the amount of your investment.

NOTE: Windsor Fund is not accepting new accounts.

All Funds and Portfolios require a $3,000 minimum unless otherwise indicated.

*INDICATES FUNDS/ PORTFOLIOS WITH THE CHECKWRITING OPTION AND THE WIRE REDEMPTION OPTION (SEE SECTION C). **WIRE REDEMPTION ONLY.

I/We have read the prospectus for each Fund in which I/we wish to invest and agree to be bound by its terms. I/We wish to open accounts in the following:

MONEY MARKET FUND	INVESTMENT
Vanguard Money Market Reserves*	
☐ Prime Portfolio (30)	$ _____
☐ Federal Portfolio (33)	$ _____
☐ U.S. Treasury Portfolio (50)	$ _____
TAX-FREE INCOME FUNDS	
Vanguard Municipal Bond Fund*	
☐ Money Market Portfolio (45)	$ _____
☐ Short-Term Portfolio (41)	$ _____
☐ Limited-Term Portfolio (31)	$ _____
☐ Intermediate-Term Portfolio (42)	$ _____
☐ Insured Long-Term Portfolio (58)	$ _____
☐ Long-Term Portfolio (43)	$ _____
☐ High-Yield Portfolio (44)	$ _____
Vanguard California Tax-Free Fund*	
☐ Money Market Portfolio (62)	$ _____
☐ Insured Long-Term Portfolio (75)	$ _____
☐ **Vanguard Florida Insured Tax-Free Fund (18)***	$ _____
Vanguard New Jersey Tax-Free Fund*	
☐ Money Market Portfolio (95)	$ _____
☐ Insured Long-Term Portfolio (14)	$ _____
☐ **Vanguard New York Insured Tax-Free Fund (76)***	$ _____
Vanguard Ohio Tax-Free Fund*	
☐ Money Market Portfolio (96)	$ _____
☐ Insured Long-Term Portfolio (97)	$ _____
Vanguard Pennsylvania Tax-Free Fund*	
☐ Money Market Portfolio (63)	$ _____
☐ Insured Long-Term Portfolio (77)	$ _____
TAXABLE INCOME FUNDS	
☐ Vanguard Bond Index Fund (84)*	$ _____
☐ Vanguard/Wellesley Income Fund (27)	$ _____
Vanguard Fixed Income Securities Fund	
☐ Short-Term U.S. Treasury Portfolio (32)*	$ _____
☐ Short-Term Federal Portfolio (49)*	$ _____
☐ Short-Term Corporate Portfolio (39)*	$ _____
☐ Intermediate-Term U.S. Treasury Portfolio (35)*	$ _____
☐ GNMA Portfolio (36)*	$ _____
☐ Long-Term U.S. Treasury Portfolio (83)*	$ _____
☐ Investment Grade Corporate Portfolio (28)*	$ _____
☐ High Yield Corporate Portfolio (29)**	$ _____
ADMIRAL FUNDS*	
☐ Admiral U.S. Treasury Money Market Portfolio (11) ($50,000 min.)	$ _____
☐ Admiral Short-Term U.S. Treasury Portfolio (12) ($50,000 min.)	$ _____
☐ Admiral Intermediate-Term U.S. Treasury Portfolio (19) ($50,000 min.)	$ _____
☐ Admiral Long-Term U.S. Treasury Portfolio (20) ($50,000 min.)	$ _____

BALANCED FUNDS	INVESTMENT
☐ Vanguard Asset Allocation Fund (78)	$ _____
☐ Vanguard Balanced Index Fund (02)	$ _____
☐ Vanguard STAR Fund (56) ($500 min.)	$ _____
☐ Vanguard/Wellington Fund (21)	$ _____
GROWTH AND INCOME FUNDS	
☐ Vanguard Convertible Securities Fund (82)	$ _____
☐ Vanguard Equity Income Fund (65)	$ _____
☐ Vanguard Quantitative Portfolios (93)	$ _____
☐ Vanguard/Windsor II (73)	$ _____
Vanguard/Trustees' Equity Fund	
☐ United States Portfolio (25) ($10,000 min.)	$ _____
Vanguard Index Trust	
☐ 500 Portfolio (40)	$ _____
☐ Total Stock Market Portfolio (85)	$ _____
☐ Value Portfolio (06)	$ _____
Vanguard Specialized Portfolios	
☐ Utilities Income Portfolio (57)	$ _____
GROWTH FUNDS	
☐ Vanguard/Morgan Growth Fund (26)	$ _____
☐ Vanguard/PRIMECAP Fund (59)	$ _____
Vanguard Index Trust	
☐ Extended Market Portfolio (98)	$ _____
☐ Growth Portfolio (09)	$ _____
☐ **Vanguard U.S. Growth Portfolio (23)**	$ _____
AGGRESSIVE GROWTH FUNDS	
☐ Vanguard Explorer Fund (24)	$ _____
☐ Vanguard Small Capitalization Stock Fund (48)	$ _____
Vanguard Specialized Portfolios	
☐ Energy Portfolio (51)	$ _____
☐ Health Care Portfolio (52)	$ _____
☐ Gold & Precious Metals Portfolio (53)	$ _____
INTERNATIONAL FUNDS	
Vanguard/Trustees' Equity Fund	
☐ International Portfolio (46) ($10,000 min.)	$ _____
Vanguard International Equity Index Fund	
☐ European Portfolio (79)	$ _____
☐ Pacific Portfolio (72)	$ _____
☐ **Vanguard International Growth Portfolio (81)**	$ _____
CORPORATE FUNDS	
☐ Vanguard Preferred Stock Fund (38)	$ _____
OTHER	
☐ _____	$ _____
☐ _____	$ _____
☐ _____	$ _____
☐ _____	$ _____
☐ _____	$ _____
☐ _____	$ _____

METHOD OF INVESTMENT

FOR MULTIPLE ACCOUNTS: SEPARATE CHECKS SHOULD BE MADE PAYABLE FOR EACH FUND.

☐ **By Check.** Enclosed: separate check(s) made payable to each Fund for a total investment of $ _____

☐ **By Exchange.** Please exchange $ _____ from _____ _____
Name of Vanguard Fund   _Account No._

into _____   **NOTE:** If registrations are *not* identical, a signature guarantee
Name of Vanguard Fund   will be required to exchange between Fund accounts.

This account previously established by:
☐ Phone exchange ☐ Wire on _____
Date   _Account No. (Previously assigned by Vanguard)_

Figure 10-2: Comprehensive forms list almost every fund you can name at the company.

Source: The Vanguard Group

When you call to order application materials, unless you specifically ask for it, they will not send you this comprehensive or generic account registration form. Don't be shy. Ask!

Not all fund companies offer these comprehensive account application forms. You fill out a separate application for each fund you plan to invest in, but you don't need to. Here are several ways around this paperwork nightmare:

✔ Establish a money market fund first. Then you may do exchanges by phone into any other funds you want. When you call to order the money fund materials, ask for the prospectuses for the other funds that you're interested in. When you do telephone exchanges, fund companies are required by the SEC to ask if you've received the prospectus before they will allow an exchange.

✔ With some fund companies, it's okay for you to attach a separate piece of paper to one application with instructions to the fund company to open "identically registered accounts in the following funds." Next to each fund name, list the amount you want to invest. Don't forget to sign the page and attach your check.

✔ Open a discount brokerage account through a firm such as Charles Schwab, Jack White, or Fidelity that allows telephone exchanges (a subject I cover in the next section).

Discount brokerage accounts

As I discuss in Chapter 4, discount brokerage firms offer you the ability, through a single account, to invest in hundreds of funds from many fund companies. Brokerage firms are different from mutual fund companies. The first difference is that brokerage accounts allow you to hold and trade individual securities, such as stocks and bonds. This feature is handy if you hold individual securities and want them in the same account as your mutual fund.

Another difference is that, in addition to offering mutual funds, brokerage accounts allow you to invest in riskier types of securities and engage in riskier investing strategies. Many brokerage firms, for example, allow investing in options (see Chapter 1), which are volatile, short-term gambling type instruments. Keep your distance.

Most of the sections on a brokerage application are the same as those on a mutual fund application as described in the "Application basics" section earlier in the chapter. Here are the main differences that may give you cause for pause.

Margin what?

Brokers offer (and sometimes encourage) margin trading. Just as you can purchase a home and borrow some money to finance the purchase when you can't afford to pay all cash, you can do the same with your investments. With a home, most banks require that you make a 10 to 20 percent down payment on the purchase price. With a brokerage account, you need to make a 50 percent down payment.

Buying investments on margin, which may only be done for non-retirement accounts, is not something I recommend. First, you pay interest. Although the rate is competitive — nothing approaching the worst credit cards, but it ain't cheap — typically it's a bit less than you would pay on a fixed-rate mortgage on your home.

Also, if your investments fall significantly in value (25 to 30 percent), you get a *margin call*, which means you'll need to add more cash to your account. If you can't or don't, you'll be forced to sell some investments to raise the cash. Of course, if prices increase in value, you'll earn money not only on the "down payment" you invested, but also on the borrowed money invested. (That's called *leverage*.) Margin borrowing can't be done in retirement accounts, which is where you should be doing most of your investing to cut your taxes.

Excessive margin buying and borrowing was one of the reasons that the stock market crashed so precipitously during the Great Depression. Back then, stocks could be purchased with just 10 percent down.

Borrowing on margin can be useful as a short-term source of money. Suppose that you need more short-term cash than you've got in a money fund. What to do? Rather than sell your investments, just borrow against them with a margin loan. This move makes sense especially if you'd have to pay a lot of tax on profits were you to sell appreciated investments.

Getting too personal?

You'll notice in Figure 10-3 in sections 1 and 2 of the brokerage application that several questions ask for what most people consider to be confidential financial information: your driver's license number, your income, your net worth. "Why," you may rightfully ask, "are they being so nosey? Do they really need to know this stuff?"

All brokerage firms ask for this kind of information because of the so-called "Know your customer rule" that the regulators require. Because brokerage accounts allow you to do some risky stuff, regulators believe that the firms should make at least a modest effort to determine whether their clients know enough and have a sufficient financial cushion to invest in riskier stuff.

1. Please complete the following information.

Your Schwab account will allow you to purchase and sell stocks, bonds, mutual funds and other available securities. Please check the box below if you want the margin feature, which allows you to use your securities as collateral to make purchases.

☐ Yes, I want the margin feature. (Please be sure to sign Section 7.)

Please indicate how you wish to title your account: (check only one)

☐ Individual ☐ Joint Tenants with Right of Survivorship
☐ Tenants in Common ☐ Community Property* ☐ Corporate/Sole Proprietor*
☐ Partnership* ☐ Investment Club* ☐ Other*

*Additional documentation required: please contact Schwab.

■ ACCOUNT HOLDER

Account Holder Name (☐Mr. ☐Mrs. ☐Miss ☐Ms. ☐Dr. ☐Other_____)	Social Security/Tax ID number
Your Home Street Address (P.O. Box not sufficient)	Country of Citizenship	Country of Legal Residence	Birth Date
City/State	Zip	Driver's License Number	
Employer Name	Home Phone ( )	Years with Employer	Occupation
Employer Street Address (P.O. Box not sufficient)	Personal Banking Reference (Bank Name and Branch)	Account Number
City/State	Zip	Business Phone ( )	Are You Known By Any Other Name? (state name)

Specify any publicly-traded company of which you are a director, 10% shareholder or policy making officer: Company Name

Specify any security firm with which you are affiliated: Company Name

Check if you are:
☐ Retired RE ☐ Sales/Marketing SM ☐ Skilled/Semi-Skilled SL ☐ Homemaker HW
☐ Self-Employed SE ☐ Professional/Technical PT ☐ Student ST ☐ Unemployed UN
☐ Managerial MA ☐ Clerical CL ☐ Service Worker SW ☐ Attorney AT
                                                        ☐ CPA CP

Where would you like us to send your mail?
☐ Home ☐ Business ☐ P.O. Box (Complete section below)

| P.O. Box Number | City/State | Zip |

■ JOINT ACCOUNT HOLDER

Joint Account Holder Name: (☐Mr. ☐Mrs. ☐Miss ☐Ms. ☐Dr. ☐Other_____)	Social Security/Tax ID number
Employer Name	Country of Citizenship	Country of Legal Residence	Birth Date
Employer Street Address (P.O. Box not sufficient)	Driver's License Number	Are You Known By Any Other Name? (state name)
City/State	Zip	Business Phone ( )	Years with Employer	Occupation

Specify any publicly-traded company of which you are a director, 10% shareholder or policy making officer: Company Name

Specify any security firm with which you are affiliated: Company Name

Check if you are:
☐ Retired RE ☐ Sales/Marketing SM ☐ Skilled/Semi-Skilled SL ☐ Homemaker HW
☐ Self-Employed SE ☐ Professional/Technical PT ☐ Student ST ☐ Unemployed UN
☐ Managerial MA ☐ Clerical CL ☐ Service Worker SW ☐ Attorney AT
                                                        ☐ CPA CP

■ CORPORATION/SOLE PROPRIETOR/PARTNERSHIP/OTHER (SPECIFY)

| Name of Corporation/Sole Proprietor/Partnership/Other | Tax ID Number for Corporation/Sole Proprietor/Partnership/Other |

2. Please provide information about your Financial Profile.

Please furnish the following information to help us identify your investment needs. For joint accounts, please provide household information. (This information will be kept confidential.)

Overall investment objective is:	Federal income tax bracket is:	Investment experience:	Investment knowledge:	Annual income is:	Liquid net worth is:
☐ Capital Preservation	☐ 15%	☐ None	☐ None	☐ Under $15,000	☐ Under $15,000
☐ Income	☐ 28%	☐ Limited	☐ Limited	☐ $15,000 to $24,999	☐ $15,000 to $24,999
☐ Growth	☐ 31%	☐ Good	☐ Good	☐ $25,000 to $49,999	☐ $25,000 to $49,999
☐ Speculation	☐ Other ____	☐ Extensive	☐ Extensive	☐ $50,000 to $99,999	☐ $50,000 to $99,999
				☐ $100,000 or more	☐ $100,000 or more. Please provide approximate figure to the nearest $10,000: $

| Number of Dependents | Birth Dates of Dependents |

Accounts at other Brokerage Firms:

| Brokerage – Firm Name(s) | IRA/Keogh – Firm Name(s) |
| Asset Management Account – Firm Name(s) | |

Figure 10-3:
Brokerage account application — getting to know all about you....

Source: *Charles Schwab & Company, Inc.*

Make your paperwork go faster and your investing less dangerous and skip this stuff! If you're not signing up for the risky account features such as margin and options trading, the brokerage firm does not need to know these things.

Neat brokerage account options — checks and debit cards

Some brokerage accounts offer additional features, such as check writing and a VISA debit card (see Figure 10-4), that allow more convenient ways for you to access the money in your account. The only challenge is that you have to request the application for the special type of brokerage account that offers these features. At Fidelity, for example, their souped-up brokerage account is called a USA account; Schwab's is called a SchwabOne account (see Chapter 6 for more details on these accounts).

Figure 10-4:
Extra services give you more ways to access your money funds.

8 OPTIONAL SERVICES **SAMPLE**
Please complete this section if you would like any of these optional services.

Debit Card. ☐ **Yes, I would like to order a VISA® Gold debit card.** I have indicated the owner(s) to whom a debit card should be issued (names will appear as they are written on this application).

☐ Owner ☐ Joint Owner
Note: Only Individual and Joint registrations are eligible for the debit card feature. Debit cards can not be issued to foreign or P.O. Box addresses. The issuer of this card is Fidelity Trust Company. I authorize Fidelity Trust Company to check my employment and credit history.

Checking. ☐ **Yes, I would like checking privileges.** Name(s) and mailing address as they appear on your account registration will be printed on your checks unless you indicate otherwise below:

☐ Please do not print my address on my checks.

Check here to indicate if more than one signature is required on all checks.

☐ Two signatures are required on all checks. (If no box is checked, only one signature will be required.)
All account holders authorized to write checks must sign the attached signature card.

Bank Wire/EFT. ☐ **Yes, I am interested in transferring money by bank wire and/or EFT** (Electronic Funds Transfer) between my bank and my Fidelity Ultra Service Account. I've attached a voided check to this application and the banking information is referenced in Section 3 of this application. Please note, wire/EFT instructions will be honored provided that at least one common name appears in the bank account and Fidelity USA registrations. Bank must be a member of the Automated Clearing House (ACH).

Additional Services. ☐ **Yes, I would like to take advantage of the extra conveniences** of the Ultra Service Account that enables me to receive imaged copies of my cancelled checks monthly, to code all of my expenses for easier recordkeeping and to have my bills paid directly from this account. Please send me the information on how to take advantage of these features.
Minimum initial investment: $25,000. Monthly service fee: $5. Additional fees are applicable for the bill payment service.

Option Account. ☐ **Yes, I would like to open an option account** and add this feature to my Fidelity Ultra Service Account, please send me an option account application.

Source: Fidelity Investments

Debit cards look just like credit cards and are accepted by stores the same way as credit cards. There's one important difference, however. When you make a purchase with your debit card, the money is generally sucked out of your brokerage account money fund within a day or two. You may also use your VISA debit card to obtain cash from ATMs (which usually costs you a buck or so).

You can use debit cards instead of credit cards. Doing so may simplify your financial life by saving you from writing a check every month to pay your credit card bill. On the other hand, you give up the *"float"* — the free use, until the credit card bill is due, of the money that you owe — because debit cards deduct the money more quickly.

As with a money market mutual fund account, you may obtain checks to write against the money market fund balance in your brokerage account. Don't forget to complete the "signature card" for check writing.

Some brokerage accounts come with even more features that make organizing your finances easier, such as photocopied or imaged copies of checks and a bill payment service. These services cost more money; at Fidelity, for example, you must put more money into your account ($25,000 instead of $10,000) and pay a $5 monthly service fee.

Discount brokerage account transfers

You may have cash, securities, and most mutual funds transferred into a new brokerage account that you establish. All you need is one of their account transfer forms (see Figure 10-5). Using one of these forms saves you the hassle of contacting brokerage firms, banks, and other mutual fund companies that you want to move your money from. Using such a form also saves you the bother and risk of taking possession of these assets yourself.

If you haven't opened an account yet, you also need to complete an account application form. If your account is already open, you don't need to do this. Here's what you need to know to complete a form like the one in Figure 10-5.

A. **Information about your (new) brokerage account.** Fill in your name as you have on your account application or as it's currently listed on your account if it's already opened. If you're sending in your account application with this transfer form, you won't have an account number yet, so just write "NEW" in the space where they ask for your account number.

B. **Information about the account you are transferring.** Write here the name of the brokerage, bank, or fund company that holds the assets you want to transfer; also write in the account number of your account there. *Title of account* simply means how your name appears on the account you are transferring.

Complete one of the following. Complete the relevant section for the brokerage account, mutual fund, or bank account you'll be moving.

C. **Brokerage Account Transfer.** All you have to decide is whether you want to transfer your entire account — which makes your administrative life easier by eliminating an account — or only a part of it. (Another advantage of closing accounts at firms such as Prudential, Merrill Lynch, Dean Witter, Smith Barney Shearson, and Paine Webber is that many of them charge an annual account fee.)

If you're doing a partial transfer, simply list the assets you want to transfer — for example, IBM stock — and list the number of shares, such as 50 or All. With partial transfers that include the transfer of mutual funds, you have to go through the hassle of completing one of these silly forms for each company whose funds you're moving. These funds get listed in the next section, D.

You won't be able to transfer mutual funds into your new brokerage account that are unique (or *proprietary*) to the brokerage firm you're leaving. Funds that cannot be transferred would include funds such as Prudential, Merrill Lynch, Dean Witter, Smith Barney Shearson, Paine Webber, and so on. If there are no adverse tax consequences, you're better off selling them and transferring the cash proceeds. Check out Chapter 11, which walks you through the issues to consider if you're debating whether to hold or sell a fund.

Charles Schwab
Account Transfer Form
(Please use a separate form for each account you transfer.)

(Schwab completes)	❑ Broker change only
❑ Brokerage	❑ ACAT
❑ IRA	❑ Non-ACAT Full
❑ Rollover	❑ Partial
❑ Keogh/Qualified Pension Plan	❑ Mutual Fund

A. Information about your Schwab account.
Schwab Clearing Number: 0164

Name as it appears on your Account

Your Schwab Account Number | Your Social Security or Tax ID

B. Information about the account you are transferring. (Please refer to your statement for the following information.)

Name of Firm | **Broker Clearing #** (Schwab completes)

Your Account Number

Title of Account | ❑ Check here if these assets come from a Qualified Plan

Custodian or trustee of this account (Schwab completes)

Please complete only one of the following: section C, D or E.
(Please use a separate form for each account you transfer.)

Non ACAT transfers only (Schwab completes)
❑ Deliver all securities in kind and uninvested credit balance.
❑ Issue a certificate for all whole shares, liquidate all fractional shares, and discontinue dividend reinvestment.

❑ **C. Brokerage Account Transfer.** (Please check appropriate box.)
  ❑ I wish to transfer my entire account. (Please skip to signature section.)
  ❑ I wish to transfer only the following assets from my account. (Please do not complete the following information if you are transferring your entire account. Section to be used for partial transfers only. Please attach additional forms if necessary.)

Description of Asset (Partial transfers only)	Quantity (Indicate # of shares or "All")	Description of Asset (Partial transfers only)	Quantity (Indicate # of shares or "All")
NOT TO BE USED FOR MUTUAL FUNDS		*NOT TO BE USED FOR MUTUAL FUNDS*	

❑ **D. Mutual Fund Transfer.** Please use one form for each mutual fund you're transferring.

Name of fund | Number of shares or "All"

Transfer (Check One) ❑ In-Kind ❑ Liquidate | Omnibus Account (Schwab completes)

Please indicate how you would like your dividends & capital gains handled (check one): ❑ Reinvested ❑ Credited to your account as cash.

❑ **E. Bank, Savings & Loan, or Credit Union Transfer.**
Check one:

❑ I am only transferring cash. Please transfer:
  ❑ All cash in account
  ❑ Only $_____

❑ I have a CD that I want to transfer. Please:
  ❑ Liquidate it IMMEDIATELY. I am aware of and acknowledge the penalty I will incur from any early withdrawal.
  ❑ Liquidate it AT MATURITY. Maturity Date___/___/___ (Please submit 2-3 weeks before maturity date)

F. Please sign this section.
*If this account is a qualified retirement account, I have amended the applicable plan so that it names Charles Schwab & Co., Inc. as successor custodian.
  Unless otherwise indicated in the instructions above, please transfer all assets in my account to Charles Schwab & Co., Inc. I understand that to the extent any assets in my account are not readily transferrable, with or without penalties, such assets may not be transferred within the timeframes required by NYSE Rule 412 or similar rule of the NASD or other designated examining authority.
  Unless otherwise indicated in the instructions below, I authorize you to liquidate any nontransferrable proprietary money market fund assets that are part of my account and transfer the resulting credit balance to the successor custodian. I authorize you to deduct any outstanding fees due you from the credit balance in my account.*

*If my account does not contain a credit balance, or if the credit balance in the account is insufficient to satisfy any outstanding fees due you, I authorize you to liquidate the assets in my account to the extent necessary to satisfy that obligation. If certificates or other instruments in my account are in your physical possession, I instruct you to transfer them in good deliverable form, including affixing any necessary tax waivers, to enable the successor custodian to transfer them in its name for the purpose of sale, when and as directed by me. I understand that upon receiving a copy of this transfer instruction, you will cancel all open orders for my account on your books.
  I affirm that I have destroyed or returned to you credit/debit cards and/or unused checks issued to me in connection with my securities account."
  Disposition of money market fund assets other than liquidation and transfer: _____*

IMPORTANT: Please be sure to attach a copy of the latest statement of the account you are transferring.

X
Your Signature | Date

X
Joint Account Holder Signature | Date

Delivering Agents: Please refer to the reverse side of this form for delivery instructions.

Letter of Authorization (Schwab completes)
To the prior trustee or custodian: Please be advised that Charles Schwab & Co., Inc. will accept the above captioned account as successor custodian.

Successor Custodian Authorized Signature	Date	Date of Trust

Figure 10-5: Brokerage account transfer form.

Source: Charles Schwab & Company, Inc.

If you were sold some of those awful limited partnerships, check with the discount brokerage to which you're transferring your account to see if they will be able to hold them. Discounters likely will charge you a fee ($25 to $50) to hold LPs, but many of the lousy firms that sold them to you in the first place also charge you just for the privilege of keeping your account open with them. If the costs are about the same, I'd move the LPs to your new account to cut down on account clutter. Another alternative is to speak with the branch manager of the firm that sold them to you and ask that they waive the annual account fee.

D. **Mutual Fund Transfer.** As I explained in the last section, only certain companies' funds may be transferred into a brokerage account. You need to complete one of these forms for each company's funds you're transferring. For each fund you're transferring, list the fund name, your account number, and the amount of shares you want transferred or sold.

If you are transferring the shares "as is" instead of selling them, you need to tell the new firm whether you want the fund's dividends and capital gains distributions reinvested. Unless you need this money to live on, I'd reinvest it.

E. **Bank, Savings & Loan, or Credit Union Transfer.** Use this section on the form to move money from banks and the like. A potential complication occurs when the money is coming from a certificate of deposit. In such a case, you should send in this form several weeks before the CD is set to mature.

If you're like most people and do things at the last minute, you may not think about transferring a CD until the bank notifies you by mail days before it's due to mature. Here's a simple way around your inability to get the transfer paperwork in on time: instruct your bank to place the proceeds from the CD into a money market or savings account when the CD matures. Then you can have the proceeds from the CD transferred whenever you like.

F. **Please sign this section.** Sign it and don't forget to attach a copy of a recent statement of the account you're transferring, as well as your account application if you haven't previously opened an account. At this point . . . you're done! Mail the completed application in the company's postage-paid envelope and the transfer hopefully will go smoothly. If you have problems, see Chapter 13 for solutions.

Retirement Accounts

The applications for retirement accounts pose new challenges. The first part of such applications is just like a non-retirement account application, except that it's easier to fill out. Retirement accounts are only registered in one person's name: you can't have jointly registered mutual fund accounts.

Because mutual fund company retirement account forms are so similar to brokerage account retirement forms, I just use the mutual fund company forms as examples in this section.

Retirement account applications

Individual Retirement Accounts (IRAs) are among the most common accounts you might use at a mutual fund company. Here's what you need to know to complete an IRA application (SEP-IRAs for the self-employed are quite similar). I'll use the Fidelity mutual fund IRA application as an example (see Figure 10-6).

If you plan to transfer money from a retirement account held elsewhere into the one you're opening, you need to be careful of two things before you start: First, make sure that the retirement account type you're opening (such as an IRA or SEP-IRA) matches the type you're transferring. Second, if you want to transfer individual securities from a brokerage account, you need a brokerage account application for whatever type of retirement account you're opening, not a mutual fund account application.

1. **Account Ownership.** An easy section — but make sure, especially if you're going to be transferring IRA money from another firm into your mutual fund IRA, that you list your name exactly as it appears on the account you're transferring. Otherwise, the firm that has your IRA will make the transfer miserable.

2. **Address & Citizenship.** No problems here (are there?).

3. **Type of IRA Investment.** Type? Of course, you want the one that will make you lots of money! You can do several things in this section of the form, from making a contribution to telling them that you're making a transfer or rollover. Here's what each of these little boxes allows:

> ✔ **Regular IRA contribution.** Use this box to indicate that you're making a contribution for the most recent tax year. You have until the time you file your tax return to make a contribution for the previous year.

> ✔ **Direct transfer of an existing IRA.** If you want to move an IRA from another investment firm or bank into your new mutual fund IRA, check this box. You also need to complete an IRA transfer form (which I explain in the next section). This is the best way to move an existing IRA because it presents the least hassle and the fewest possibilities of a tax screw-up.

> ✔ **60-day rollover of an existing IRA.** Withdrawing the money yourself from another IRA and sending it yourself to this new account is not a good way to transfer your IRA. One danger is that if you don't get the funds back into your account within 60 days, you'll owe mega-taxes (current income tax plus penalties).

$LSA

The Fidelity IRA Application

 Fidelity Investments®

P.O. Box 629724
Dallas, TX 75262-9724

Use this application to open a Fidelity IRA invested in Fidelity mutual funds. To transfer your IRA directly to Fidelity from another custodian, you must also complete the enclosed Fidelity IRA Transfer Form. A $10 annual maintenance fee per fund account up to a maximum $60 per individual will be billed separately. Please do not pay the annual maintenance fee before you receive your fee bill, as you may be eligible to have the fee waived. There is also a $10 account liquidation fee. For help with this application, call us at 1-800-544-8888. Mail your completed application in the envelope provided or to Fidelity Investments Southwest Company, P.O. Box 629724, Dallas, TX 75262-9724.

All sections must be completed. Please type or print clearly.

1 Account Ownership

Name (first, middle initial, last):

Social Security Number (used for tax reporting):

Date of Birth (month, day, year):

2 Address & Citizenship

Street Address and Apartment or Box Number:

City:

State: Zip:

Evening Phone:

Daytime Phone:

Citizenship:
☐ U.S. Citizen ☐ Resident Alien
☐ Non-Resident Alien: _____
(Country of Residence)

3 Type of IRA Investment

Select only one category

☐ **Regular IRA contribution. Check tax year** ☐ 1993 ☐ 1994
Check this box if your IRA will be used to make annual contributions up to a maximum of $2,000 per tax year, including sales charges, if applicable.

A separate Spousal IRA can be opened for a spouse earning less than $250. The combined total of the two contributions cannot exceed $2,250, but can be split between the two IRAs, as you wish, as long as no more than $2,000 is contributed to one IRA.

☐ **Direct transfer of an existing IRA**
Check this box if you wish to authorize Fidelity to transfer your existing IRA from another custodian to Fidelity. You must also complete the enclosed IRA Transfer Form. Check type of IRA:
☐ Regular IRA funded with annual contributions
☐ Rollover IRA originally funded with a distribution from an employer-sponsored plan

☐ **60 day rollover of an existing IRA**
Check this box if you are funding this IRA with money you have withdrawn from an IRA at another custodian and are reinvesting at Fidelity. Check type of IRA:
☐ Regular IRA funded with annual contributions
☐ Rollover IRA originally funded with a distribution from an employer-sponsored plan

☐ **Rollover IRA from an employer sponsored plan**
Check this box only if you are funding this IRA with money you accumulated in an employer's retirement plan which is eligible for rollover. Check method of funding:
☐ Enclosed is a check made payable to Fidelity Trust Company.
☐ A check will be sent directly to Fidelity by my employer.

4 Investment Information

The minimum investment is $500 per fund. (Spartan® funds have higher minimums. See each fund's prospectus.) Be sure to read the prospectus(es) for the fund(s) you choose. Please make checks payable to **Fidelity Trust Company.** Write the fund name(s) on the check. If you wish to select more than three funds attach additional instructions indicating the fund name and amount.

1. Fidelity Fund Name:

Investment Amount:
$ ☐,☐☐☐,☐☐☐.☐☐

2. Fidelity Fund Name:

Investment Amount:
$ ☐,☐☐☐,☐☐☐.☐☐

3. Fidelity Fund Name:

Investment Amount:
$ ☐,☐☐☐,☐☐☐.☐☐

3799200

Please continue application on back.

Figure 10-6:
Mutual fund IRA application form.

Source: Fidelity Investments

✔ **Rollover from an employer-sponsored plan.** If you are moving money from an employer plan, you may check this box to establish a rollover IRA. Use the second option here — direct your employer to send a check directly to Fidelity.

Don't have your employer issue you a check (the option the first box gives you) because your employer must withhold 20 percent for taxes. If you want to roll the full amount over — a wise move — you must come up with the missing 20 percent when you deposit the money into your IRA. Otherwise, you owe tax and penalties on it.

Tax advisors usually recommend that money coming from your employer's plan should go into a rollover account. This choice would allow you to someday transfer the money back into another employer's plan. Of course, you can choose investments in your own IRA, so this may sound like a silly reason to use a "Rollover IRA." An advantage to establishing instead a contributory IRA is that you can add to it with future IRA contributions. You also can merge it with other IRA accounts.

4. **Investment Information.** Here's where you get to specify which funds you want your investments placed into. Use this section only for money that you will send in with the application. For money you're transferring, specify (on a form I'll get to in a minute) how you want that money invested.

Bonus question: What's the "$LSA" on top of the application?

Answer: It identifies the branch office (Los Angeles) that this application form came from. The branch office's compensation is partially determined by the assets that they bring into the company. So if you were to mail this form into Fidelity's main office, the branch will receive "credit" for snagging this account.

5. **Beneficiary Designation (see Figure 10-7).** Here's where you get to specify who gets all of this retirement money if you work yourself to an early grave or haven't spent all of it by the time you go. In most cases, people name their spouses, kids, parents, and siblings. You also may list organizations such as charities that you'd like to receive some of your money; it's a good idea to provide their tax identification number and address (just include this information on a separate piece of paper).

If your children are under 18, they don't have access to the money. The money is controlled by a guardian that you identify through your will. If you die without a will, a guardian will be assigned by the courts.

Your *primary beneficiaries* are first in line for the money, but if they've all crossed the finish line by the time that you do, your *contingent beneficiaries* receive the money.

⑤ Beneficiary Designation

Complete this section only if you are opening your first IRA at Fidelity or if you are changing the existing beneficiary designation on your other Fidelity IRAs. If the beneficiary is a trust, please indicate the trust's name and address, the date of the trust, and the trustee's name. If you wish to designate additional beneficiaries, please attach additional instructions providing the necessary beneficiary information.

Your Primary Beneficiaries

I hereby designate the persons named below as primary beneficiaries to receive payment of the value of my IRA account upon my death.

1. Name (first, middle, last):

Share:*   Relationship:

☐☐☐ %

Date of Birth (month, day, year):

☐☐ – ☐☐ – ☐☐

2. Name (first, middle, last):

Share:*   Relationship:

☐☐☐ %

Date of Birth (month, day, year):

☐☐ – ☐☐ – ☐☐

*Shares for each IRA's primary beneficiaries must add up to 100%. Please do not indicate fractional shares (e.g., if you have three beneficiaries, indicate 33%, 33% and 34%).

Your Contingent Beneficiaries

If no primary beneficiary is living at the time of my death, I hereby specify that the balance be distributed to my contingent beneficiaries below.

1. Name (first, middle, last):

Share:**   Relationship:

☐☐☐ %

Date of Birth (month, day, year):

☐☐ – ☐☐ – ☐☐

2. Name (first, middle, last):

Share:**   Relationship:

☐☐☐ %

Date of Birth (month, day, year):

☐☐ – ☐☐ – ☐☐

3. Name (first, middle, last):

Share:**   Relationship:

☐☐☐ %

Date of Birth (month, day, year):

☐☐ – ☐☐ – ☐☐

4. Name (first, middle, last):

Share:**   Relationship:

☐☐☐ %

Date of Birth (month, day, year):

☐☐ – ☐☐ – ☐☐

**Shares for each IRAs contingent beneficiaries must add up to 100%. Please do not indicate fractional shares (e.g., if you have three beneficiaries, indicate 33%, 33% and 34%).

Payment to primary and contingent beneficiaries will be made according to the rules of succession described in the Signature section.

⑥ Employment Information

We are required by the National Association of Securities Dealers (NASD) to ask for this information.

Owner's Occupation, Employer & Employer's Address:

☐ I am affiliated with or work for a member firm of the NASD.

⑦ Signature

Please sign at the end of this section. We must have a signature to open the account.

By signing this application I certify that:

- **I understand that the annual IRA maintenance fee of $10 per fund account up to a maximum $60 per individual will be separately billed or collected by redeeming sufficient shares from each fund account balance. A $10 liquidation fee per fund will be automatically collected from my account(s) when I liquidate it.** Fidelity Investments Southwest Company (FISW) may change the fee schedule from time to time, as provided in the Custodial Agreement. Acceptance will be evidenced by a Letter of Acceptance sent by, or on behalf of Fidelity Trust Company and FISW.

- I understand that if more than one beneficiary is named and no percentages are indicated, payment shall be made in equal shares to my primary beneficiary(ies) who survive me. If a percentage is indicated and a primary beneficiary(ies) does not survive me, the percentage of that beneficiary's designated share shall be divided equally among the surviving primary beneficiary(ies).

- I understand that if I choose not to designate any beneficiary(ies), my beneficiary will be my surviving spouse or, if I do not have a surviving spouse, my estate. I am aware that this form becomes effective when delivered to Fidelity, and will remain in effect until I deliver to Fidelity another form with a later date.

- I understand that the beneficiary information provided herein shall apply to all my Fidelity IRAs for which Fidelity Trust Company (or its affiliate and/or any successor custodian appointed pursuant to the terms of such IRAs) acts as custodian, including regular IRAs, SEP-IRAs, Rollover IRAs, Brokerage IRAs, PAS IRAs and Corporate IRAs, and shall replace all previous designation(s) I have made on any of my Fidelity IRA accounts.

- I hereby adopt the Fidelity IRA, appointing Fidelity Trust Company (FTC) as Custodian, and Fidelity Investments Southwest Company (FISW) or its agent to perform the administrative services. Although FTC is a bank, I recognize that neither Fidelity Distributors nor any mutual fund in which this IRA may be invested is a bank and mutual fund shares are not backed or guaranteed by any bank or insured by the FDIC. **This agreement shall be construed, administered and enforced according to the laws of the Commonwealth of Massachusetts, except as superseded by federal law or statute.**

- I have received and read the Prospectus for the fund(s) in which I am making a contribution, and have read and understand the IRA Custodial Agreement and Disclosure Statement. I hereby certify under penalties of perjury that my Social Security Number (above) is correct and that I am of legal age to enter into this agreement.

- By signing below, I hereby consent to the terms of the Fidelity IRA and to the beneficiary(ies) I have designated in the application.

Your Signature   Date (month, day, year)

SAMPLE

Fidelity Distributors Corporation

IRA-APP-1293R

Figure 10-7:
Fill this out to name your IRA's beneficiary.

Source: Fidelity Investments

6. **Employment information.** You don't have to provide this information if you don't want to.

7. **Signature.** Don't forget to sign and attach any checks.

Stuff to do before transferring retirement accounts

If you have money in a retirement account in a bank, brokerage firm, other mutual fund company, or in a previous employer's retirement plan, you can transfer it to the mutual fund(s) of your choice. Here's a step-by-step list of what you need to do to transfer a retirement account to a mutual fund discount firm. **Note:** If you're doing a rollover from an employer plan, please heed the differences indicated.

1. **Decide where you want to move the account.** Check out Chapter 4 and Part II.

2. **Obtain an account application and asset transfer form.** Call the 800 number of the firm you're transferring the money to and ask for an *account application and asset transfer form* for the type of account you're transferring to — for example, an IRA, SEP-IRA, Keogh, or 403 (b).

You can tell which account type you currently have by looking at a recent account statement; the account type is given near the top of the form or in the section with your name and address. If you can't figure it out on a cryptic statement, call the firm that currently holds the account and ask a representative what type of account you have (just be sure to have your account number handy when you call).

3. **Figure out which securities you'll transfer and which you need to liquidate.** Transferring existing investments in your account to a new investment firm can cause glitches because not everything is transferable. If you're transferring cash (money market assets) or securities that trade on any of the major stock exchanges, transferring isn't a problem.

If you own publicly traded securities, it's often better to transfer them *as is* to your new investment firm, especially if the new firm offers discount brokerage services. (The alternative is to sell them through the firm you're leaving, which may be more expensive.)

Retirement plan applications for the self-employed: SEP-IRAs and Keoghs

If you're self-employed, you should be interested in opening a Simplified Employee Pension Individual Retirement Account (SEP-IRA) or Keogh plan. Why? Because most self-employed people can generally make larger tax-deductible contributions into them than they can into a regular IRA. (You'll find the pros, cons, and contribution limitations of SEP-IRAs and Keoghs covered in Chapter 5.)

SEP-IRA applications are virtually identical to IRA applications, so just follow the instructions for the IRA applications earlier in this chapter (in fact, some firms use the same application form). At those firms that use SEP-IRA applications different from IRA applications, the main difference is that you may see references to "Employer Contribution." You, as the self-employed person, are your employer. If you have employees, they may be eligible for SEP-IRA contributions under your plan (the maximum waiting period is three years of service, where "a year of service" is a year in which an employee earns $400). When employees become eligible for contributions, you set up accounts for them (with their names on them) — they don't establish accounts on their own.

Keogh account applications are more complicated. There's more paperwork to complete,

particularly if you set up the combined profit-sharing and money purchase pension plans that I explain in Chapter 5.

You'll find a few items on a Keogh application that you won't find on an IRA application. First, you'll be asked to supply an *employer tax identification number*. Say what? If your business has obtained a tax identification number from the IRS, plug that in. Otherwise, most small business owners use their Social Security number. You'll also be asked for the name(s) of the *plan administrator*, the person(s) responsible for doing such things as determining which employees are eligible in the plan and making contributions into the accounts. If you're a sole proprietor, you're the administrator. In larger businesses, the administrator is the business owner(s). The Keogh plan documents also ask if your company operates, for tax purposes, on a calendar year (which ends on December 31) or a fiscal year (which has some other end date for the year). Employees are eligible to participate once they have completed two years of service. Different plans define a year of service differently, but most use 500 or 1,000 hours as the threshold.

If you own mutual funds unique to the institution you're leaving, check with your new firm to see if it can accept them. If not, you need to contact the firm that currently holds them to sell them.

4. **(Optional) Let the firm from which you're transferring the money know that you're doing so (you don't need to worry about this step if you're rolling money out of an employer plan).** If the place you're transferring from does not assign a specific person to your account, you definitely should skip this step. If you're moving your investments from a brokerage firm where you've dealt with

a particular broker, though, the decision is more difficult. Most people feel obligated to let their representative know that they are moving their money.

In my experience, calling your representative to tell him the "bad news" is usually a mistake. Brokers or others who have a direct financial stake in your decision to move your money will try to sell you on staying. Some may try to make you feel guilty for leaving, and some may even try to bully you. What to do? I say write a letter if you want to let them know you're moving your account. It may seem the coward's way out, but writing usually makes your departure easier on both sides. With a letter, you can polish what you have to say, but you don't run as much risk of putting the broker on the defensive. Just say that you've chosen to self-direct your investments.

But then again, telling an investment firm that its charges are too high or that it sold you a bunch of lousy investments that it misrepresented to you may help the firm to improve in the future. Don't fret this decision too much. Do what's best for you and what you're comfortable with. Brokers are not your friends. Even though they may know your kids' names, your favorite hobbies, and your birthday, it is a *business* relationship.

Retirement account transfer forms

Transferring retirement accounts isn't too much trouble. In most cases, all you need to do is complete a transfer form. You can use a mutual fund transfer form to move money that's in a bank account, in another mutual fund, or in a brokerage account. You may only use this form to move investment money that you want liquidated and converted to cash prior to transfer.

Figure 10-8 shows the form used for transferring money into a mutual fund IRA. Use one of these forms for each investment company or bank you are transferring IRA money out of. If you're transferring individual securities (for example, stocks or bonds) or want brokerage account features, you'll need a brokerage account transfer form (and brokerage application forms).

1. **Account Ownership.** List your name as it appears on the account you're transferring (look at a recent statement for that account). Write in your Social Security number and the date you entered this here world.

2. **Address.** List the address as it appears on the account you're transferring. Add in your phone numbers in case the mutual fund firm needs to get in touch with you should questions arise.

3. **Type of IRA.** Look at a statement for the account you're transferring and see what type of IRA you have. If you can't figure it out, either call that company and ask them which of the three types you have or just leave it blank, send it in to the mutual fund, and let them figure it out!

The Fidelity Mutual Fund IRA Transfer Form

Fidelity Investments
P.O. Box 660446
Dallas, TX 75266-0446

SAMPLE

Use this form to authorize Fidelity to transfer your IRA directly from another IRA Custodian and invest it in a **Fidelity mutual fund IRA. Please read the instructions on the back of this form before completing the Transfer Form.** Mail your completed form in the enclosed envelope or to Fidelity Retirement Services, P.O. Box 660446, Dallas, TX 75266-0446. If you have any questions, call 1-800-544-4774.

All sections must be completed. Please type or print clearly.

1 Account Ownership

TOA-A

Name (first, middle initial, last):

Social Security Number (used for tax reporting):

Date of Birth (month, day, year):

2 Address

Street Address and Apartment or Box Number:

City:

State: Zip:

Daytime Phone:

Evening Phone:

3 Type of IRA

☐ **Regular IRA** ☐ **Rollover IRA*** ☐ **SEP-IRA**

*Check this box only if you are transferring money originally received as a distribution from an employer-sponsored retirement plan.

4 Where IRA Will Be Invested

A. Please check one of the following:

☐ I am opening a new mutual fund IRA. **Attached is my completed IRA application.**

☐ I already own a Fidelity mutual fund IRA.

B. Please list the name(s) of the Fidelity mutual fund(s) into which the transfer proceeds are to be deposited.

1. Fidelity Fund Name: Percent of Proceeds %

Fund Account Number (if existing):

2. Fidelity Fund Name: Percent of Proceeds %

Fund Account Number (if existing):

If you do not indicate a mutual fund, your transfer proceeds will be invested in Fidelity Cash Reserves, a money market fund.

5 IRA Being Transferred

How your IRA is currently invested:

☐ Mutual Fund Name:

☐ CD/Date of Maturity (month-day-year):
Transfer the proceeds to my Fidelity IRA at maturity unless indicated by checking the box at right for immediate liquidation ☐.
If you liquidate a CD prior to maturity, you may incur a penalty. **Send us this Transfer Form at least three weeks prior to maturity.** If the CD matures in less than three weeks, call 1-800-544-4774 for procedures.

☐ Other/Specify:

Where your IRA is currently located: Please call current custodian for correct address. If this information is not provided, it could significantly delay your transfer.

Name of Transferor Custodian

Name of individual or department responsible for transfers

Address of Transferor Custodian

City

State Zip

Telephone Number of Transferor Custodian

Account Number: **Please attach a copy of your most recent statement.**

6 Authorize Your Other Custodian to Transfer Your IRA

Please transfer all of the IRA account listed in Section 5 **in cash** unless a partial amount is indicated: $

I have received and read the prospectus for the fund(s) in which I am making my investment. If I am over 70½, I attest that none of the amount to be transferred will include the required minimum distribution for the current year pursuant to Section 401(a)(9) of the Internal Revenue Code. If in Section 3 above, I have indicated an IRA which is different than the IRA I currently maintain (e.g., Regular IRA versus Rollover IRA), I hereby establish a new IRA, the terms of which shall be identical to the terms of the agreement for the Fidelity IRA previously established.

Your Signature Date

Signature Guarantee: Please call the custodian or other institution you are transferring from to see if a signature guarantee or other documentation is required.

Name of Bank or Firm Providing Signature Guarantee and Signature of Officer and Title (Be sure to stamp Signature Guarantee)

Fidelity Will Complete This Section. Letter of Acceptance and Instructions for Transfer to a Fidelity Mutual Fund IRA Account

To Transferor Custodian: Fidelity Trust Company (and/or any successor custodian appointed pursuant to the terms of the Fidelity IRA) will accept the transfer described above. Please transfer on a fiduciary-to-fiduciary basis all or part of the designated account as instructed in Section 6, and make check payable to the custodian, Fidelity Trust Company.

Please mail check to Fidelity Retirement Services, P.O. Box 650364, Dallas, TX 75265-0364. **Also include the following information on the check:**

Reference Number FBO Authorized Fidelity Signature Date

2400243

Figure 10-8: Form to transfer your IRA into mutual funds.

Source: Fidelity Investments

4. **Where IRA Will Be Invested.** Here's where you tell the fund company which fund you want the money invested in. If you are opening a new IRA, check the first box. If you already have an IRA at Fidelity, check the second box.

In Part B of the form, list the funds that you want the transferred money invested in and the percentage of the money that is to go into each (the percentages must total 100 percent). If you want to divvy up the money into more than two funds, list the additional funds on a separate piece of paper and attach that to the form.

5. **IRA Being Transferred.** Here, you tell the fund where your IRA is currently held. If it's in another fund, list the name of the fund (if you're transferring more than one fund from the same company, just squeeze those names into the space). If it's money in a CD that you're moving, try to send this form in several weeks before the CD is scheduled to mature. If you're don't get around to doing this until right before your CD matures, buy yourself more time by directing your bank to place the CD proceeds into a money market or savings type account from which you then can do the transfer.

List where the IRA is being held currently. *Custodian* is simply the term for the company holding your IRA — for example, First Low Interest Bank & Trust or Prune Your Assets Brokerage.

You probably won't have a clue as to who or what department handles transfers. If you don't, you can call the company and try to find out. But my advice is, don't bother. Most funds don't burden you with having to find this out — the funds should know from other transfers they've done with that firm. If they don't, let them do the work to find out.

List the mailing address and phone number of the company where your IRA is currently held, and also list your account number there. Attach a copy of the statement for the account you want to move. If you don't know the phone number, don't worry — it ain't critical.

6. **Authorization.** Sign the form. If you only want to transfer some of the cash from the account, fill that amount in the little box. If you want everything to be transferred, leave the box empty.

It's a pain in the posterior, but some firms that you're transferring out of may require that you burn a chunk of your day to go get your signature guaranteed at your local bank (this is not done by a notary). Fortunately, most companies don't require this — but the only way to know for certain is to call and ask.

Stuff this transfer form (along with application form if you're opening a new IRA) in the envelope and send it off.

Automatic Investing Forms

You may have noticed earlier in this chapter that some mutual fund applications have sections that allow you to establish an automatic investment program. Such a program allows the fund to electronically transfer money from your bank account at pre-determined times. If your fund company either doesn't have this option listed on its original application or you didn't fill out that part when you opened the account, or if you're investing through a discount brokerage firm, you need to fill out a separate form to establish this service. Figure 10-9 is an example (see the explanation in "Wiring and Fund Express Options," earlier in this chapter, for how to complete this).

If you have a pile of money sitting in a money market fund and you'd like to ease it into (some call it dollar cost averaging) mutual funds, most fund companies, and discount brokers have services that allow you to do this. They may have separate forms to fill out or, even better, companies such as Fidelity allow you to establish this service by phone once your money fund account is open (see Chapter 9 for a discussion of the pros and cons of dollar cost averaging).

If you're investing outside a retirement account into fund(s) at different points in time, here's a hint: For tax recordkeeping purposes, save your statements that detail all the purchases in your accounts. Most mutual fund companies provide year-end summary statements that show all the transactions you made throughout the year. If you don't save your statements, it won't be the end of the world if you're investing through most of the larger and better fund companies. For purchases made now and in the future, fund companies also should be able to tell you what your average cost per share is when you need to sell your shares.

Other Safety Nets

If you get stuck or just can't deal with filling out forms on your own — not even with the comfort and solace you get from this book — you've got two safety nets:

✔ **Call the fund company's or discount broker's 800 number and ask for help.** (The number usually is listed at the top of the first page of the application.) That's one of the many things those phone representatives are paid to do. If you get someone who's impatient or incompetent, simply call back and you'll get someone else. (If this happens with the companies recommended in this book, please write and let me know!)

Vanguard
FUND EXPRESS

Please print, preferably with black ink.

1. **YOUR NAME AND ADDRESS** *(Please provide the information exactly as listed on your Vanguard Fund account.)*

   Name _____

   Street _____

   City _____ State _____ ZIP _____

   Daytime Telephone Number _____ Evening Telephone Number _____

2. **YOUR BANK INFORMATION** *(Please be sure that your bank is a member of the Automated Clearing House (ACH) network.)*

   Bank or Credit Union _____

   Branch _____ Branch Telephone Number _____

   Please indicate the bank account to be used with your Fund Express transactions:

   Checking account # _____
   OR

   Statement savings account # _____
   OR

   NOW account # _____

   > **IMPORTANT: Please attach a voided preprinted personal check. A cancelled check is not acceptable.**

3. **YOUR FUND EXPRESS SERVICE**

   Vanguard Fund Express may be used for the following:

   - **Automatic Investment Plan (AIP)**—transfers money from your bank account to your Vanguard account on a monthly, bimonthly, quarterly, semi-annual, or annual basis. (Maximum: $100,000; minimum: $50)
   - **Automatic Withdrawal Plan (AWP)**—transfers money from your Vanguard account to your bank account on a monthly, bimonthly, quarterly, semi-annual, or annual basis. (Maximum: $100,000; minimum: $50)
   - **Special Purchases and Redemptions (SPR)**—enables you to transfer money between your Vanguard account and your bank account by toll-free telephone. (Minimum: $100 purchase and $1,000 redemption)

   (over, please)

Please indicate below the Vanguard accounts for which Fund Express is being established, the type of service (AIP, AWP, or SPR), the dollar amount to be transferred (for automatic plans *only*), the transfer schedule (for automatic plans *only*), and the date you wish the transfers to begin (for automatic plans *only*).

Fund Name	Account Number*	Service** (please circle)			Dollar Amount	Transfer Schedule†	Start Date†† (month/day)
_____	_____	AIP	AWP	SPR	$ _____	_____	_____
_____	_____	AIP	AWP	SPR	$ _____	_____	_____
_____	_____	AIP	AWP	SPR	$ _____	_____	_____
_____	_____	AIP	AWP	SPR	$ _____	_____	_____

* If the Vanguard account registrations do not exactly match the bank account registration (including spellings, abbreviations, and initials), all registered shareholders of the Vanguard accounts must have their signatures guaranteed in Section 5 below by an authorized officer of a bank that is a member of the Federal Deposit Insurance Corporation (FDIC), a trust company, or a member of a domestic stock exchange.

** AIP and AWP cannot be established concurrently.

† A monthly, bimonthly (every other month), quarterly, semi-annual, or annual schedule may be selected. If no schedule is indicated, assets will be transferred on a *monthly* basis.

†† The Fund Express service will not begin until *three weeks after* your application has been processed by Vanguard. If the start date you selected falls within this processing period, the transfers will not begin until the next date in your designated schedule.

4. **SHAREHOLDER SIGNATURE(S)** *(Important: All registered shareholders must sign exactly as registered.)*

   I/We authorize Vanguard, upon telephonic request, to pay amounts representing redemption(s) made by me/us or to secure payments of amounts invested by me/us by initiating credit or debit entries to my/our account at the bank I/we have indicated. I/We authorize the bank to accept any such credits or debits to my/our account without responsibility for the correctness thereof. I/We further agree that Vanguard will not be held accountable for any loss, liability, cost, or expense for acting upon my/our telephonic instructions.

   It is understood that this authorization may be terminated by me/us at any time by *written* notification to Vanguard *and* to the bank. The termination request will be effective as soon as Vanguard has had a reasonable amount of time to act upon it.

   _____   _____
   Account Owner's Signature / Date   Joint Owner's Signature / Date

5. **SIGNATURE GUARANTEE** *(If applicable)*

   As stated in Section 3 above, if your bank account registration **does not exactly** match the registration of all of the Vanguard accounts you have listed above, all registered shareholders must have their signatures guaranteed below.

Authorized Officer to place stamp here

   _____
   Authorized Signature of Registered Vanguard Shareholder   Guarantor's Signature

   _____
   Authorized Signature of Registered Vanguard Shareholder   Title

Figure 10-9:
Investing on
auto-pilot.

Source: The Vanguard Group

If you're dealing with a problem that can't be solved in the first phone call and you're working with a representative on it, jot down the person's name and extension number. And don't forget to ask what office location they're in, either; some of the larger fund companies route their 800 calls to many offices, so you never know where your call has ended up unless you ask.

✔ **Visit a branch office.** After all, accessibility is one of the reasons that branch offices are there. Not all companies have them — see Chapter 4 for more details.

Chapter 11

Evaluating Funds:
Sell, Hold, or Buy More?

. . . .

In This Chapter

▶ How to read (and understand) the finer points of fund statements

▶ What figures tell you whether your funds are winning or losing

▶ How to compare the performance of your fund to the real competition

▶ How to decide whether to sell, to hold, or to buy more of a fund

. . . .

*O*nce you've learned about funds, filled out the application forms, and mailed in your money, the hard part is over. Congratulations! You've accomplished what millions of people are still thinking about but haven't gotten off their blessed keisters to do (probably because they haven't read this book yet!).

Now that you've started investing in funds, of course, you want to know how you're doing — specifically, you want to know how much money you're making. It's not that you're greedy; after all, a desire to make money spurred you to invest in funds in the first place. You'd just like some feedback about how your funds are doing. Perhaps you already owned some funds before you and I met. You may be wondering if your prior holdings are greyhounds, basset hounds, or mongrels.

In that case, you've come to the right chapter because in this chapter I explain how to evaluate the performance of your funds and decide what to do with them over time. I also explain why most of the statements you get from funds make your head spin and leave you clueless as to how you're doing. Let's start with the first thing that you receive once you invest money in a fund: an account statement.

Understanding Your Fund Statement

Every mutual fund company has its own unique statement design. But they all report the same types of information, usually in columns. Here's what you find on your statement, along with my short explanations of what it all means (see Figure 11-1).

InvestmentAccountStatement/¹⁹⁹⁴ CALENDAR YEAR					THE**Vanguard**GROUP OF INVESTMENT COMPANIES ®

Figure 11-1: A typical statement.

Source: *The Vanguard Group*

Trade date or date of transaction

This date is the date that the mutual fund company processed your transaction. For example, if you mailed in a check as an initial deposit with your account application, you can see what date they actually received and processed your check. If the fund company receives your deposit by 4:00 P.M. EST, it will purchase shares that same day in the bond and/or stock funds that you intended the check for. Money market funds work a little differently than bond and stock funds. Money market fund deposits don't start earning interest until the day after the company receives your money. Why the wait? Because the fund company must convert your money into federal funds.

Transaction description

In the "transaction description" column, you find a brief blurb about what was actually done or transacted. For example, if you mailed in a deposit, this item may simply say something like *purchase,* or *purchase by check.* If you moved money into a fund from your U.S. Treasury money market fund by phone, this item may say *phone exchange from U.S.T. money fund.*

With retirement accounts, companies use slightly different lingo here. Often, new purchases will be referred to as *contribution* (such as *1995 IRA contribution*).

Also, after you transfer money into your retirement account (as you request to do using a transfer form) from another investment company or bank, this slot typically says something like *asset transfer.* You may also see an entry for annual maintenance fee charge (try paying for these separately so that more of your money continues compounding inside the retirement account).

During the year, you also may see comments such as *dividend reinvestment,* which simply means that the fund paid a dividend that you reinvested by purchasing more shares in your account (see details later in the chapter if you're not sure what a dividend is). Dividends also may be paid out as cash — the company can send a check to you or it can deposit the money into your money market fund. In either case, the transaction description would say something like *income dividend cash.*

Funds pay capital gains, too, so in this column you also see phrases such as *capital gains reinvest.* Capital gains will usually be listed as separate short-term capital gains and long-term capital gains. Only the IRS cares about this (see Chapter 12 for how these are reported differently on your tax return).

On the statement for a money market fund, you may see things such as *check writing redemption* to show the deduction of a check that has cleared your account.

Dollar amount

This simply shows the actual dollar value of the transaction. If you sent in a $5,000 deposit, look to make sure that the correct amount was credited to your account. With dividends and capital gains, fund companies calculate and credit the appropriate amount to your account. There's no way — and really no need — to check such distributions. At any rate, I'm not aware of a fund company making a mistake with these, other than possibly a delay in crediting to shareholder accounts for a few days beyond what was promised.

Share price or price per share

This shows the price per share that the transaction was conducted at. When you're dealing with a no-load (commission-free) fund such as those that I recommend in this book, you get the same price that everyone else who bought or sold shares that day received. Money market funds always maintain a level price of $1 per share.

If you're concerned that a load was charged, check with the company to see what the buy (bid) price and sell (asked) price was that day. If a load was not charged, there should be no difference between these two prices. If a load was charged, the buy price would be higher than the sell price, and the purchase on your statement would be done at the buy price.

Share amount or shares this transaction

This simply shows the number of shares that you purchased or sold with the particular transaction listed. The number of shares is arrived at by default: the fund company takes the dollar amount of the transaction and divides it by the price per share on the date of the transaction. For example, a $5,000 investment in a bond fund at $20 per share would get you 250 shares. You detail-oriented types will be happy to know that fund companies usually go out to three decimal places in figuring shares.

Shares owned or share balance

If money was added to or subtracted from your account, the share balance changes by the amount of shares purchased or redeemed and listed in the prior section, "Share amount or shares this transaction."

There's one unusual instance where the number of shares in your account changes even though no transactions have occurred — when a fund splits. If it splits 2 for 1, for example, you receive two shares for every one that you own. Such a split doesn't increase the worth of what you own; the price per share in a 2-for-1 split is cut by 50 percent. Why do funds do this? It's a gimmick. A company uses it to try to show that the fund has done well. In fact, in such a case a company may want potential buyers to think that the fund has done *so* well that the company has reduced the price; that way, new investors won't think that they're paying a high price. But the high price doesn't matter because fund minimum investment requirements determine whether you can afford to invest in a fund, not the share price. ("Reverse splits" can be done as well to boost the price per share.)

Account value

Typically, on a different part of the account statement separate from the line-by-line listing of your transactions, fund companies show the total *account value* or market value of your fund shares. This value results from multiplying the price per share by the total number of shares that you own.

Four out of five fund investors care about total account value the most (at least according to my scientific surveys of fund investors that I work with!). So you'd think that the fund companies would list out on your statement how this value has changed over time. Well, they don't, and that's one of the reasons why examining your account statement is a lousy way to track your fund's performance over time. Some companies, such as Fidelity, show how your current account value compares to the value when your last statement was issued. This comparison sheds some useful light on your account's performance, but it still doesn't tell you how you've done since you originally invested. See the section later in the chapter for how to determine your funds' performance.

Do fund companies make errors on their statements?

Yes, but not very often. Larger mutual fund companies process billions of transactions a year. Although the transactions are processed with sophisticated computers, human beings are involved, too — and, well, we're not perfect.

If you have several funds at a company, money may get deposited into the wrong fund. With retirement accounts, your contribution might be made for the incorrect tax year. If the error is the fund company's fault, they will happily and quickly fix it once you bring it to their attention (I cover the subject of fixing errors in Chapter 13). You won't know mistakes are made unless you watch your statements.

Fund companies also occasionally make errors reporting share prices and market values. Fidelity, the nation's largest fund company, made numerous errors in 1994. For reporting of fund values held in their brokerage accounts, where they allow holding and trading of funds from other companies, Fidelity made a number of gaffes that I discovered quite by accident.

One case involved Mutual Beacon. Fidelity reflected the reduced share price for this fund at the end of December 1994 because of Mutual Beacon's dividend and capital gains distribu-

tions. Despite doing this, though, Fidelity failed to credit accounts with the additional shares that were distributed on December 29th. Fidelity didn't get the shares credited until the following week, which was too late for the additional shares to be added on the end-of-December statements. So all account holders in Mutual Beacon shares at Fidelity got statements showing a market value of their shares much lower than those values really were. I called Fidelity about this boo-boo. After they looked into it, they said that their dividend department was too busy at year-end to post all distributions and didn't get them all done by the end of December!

Fund companies sometimes make errors reporting share prices and processing distributions on time on the statements they send out. Almost always, though, the fund companies automatically correct such errors on the next statement.

The AcornFund, which is no longer open to new investors, miscalculated its fund's share price for more than two years! When the accounting snafu was caught in 1990, Acorn 'fessed up and had to correct all transactions conducted during those months!

Discount Brokerage Firm Statements

Discount brokerage statements look a bit different than those produced by mutual fund companies. Transactions are listed in a separate section from the summary of the portfolio (see Figure 11-2).

Notice in the *Portfolio Position Detail* section that funds from different companies are listed. As on a mutual fund statement, the *number of shares ("quantity")*, *price per share ("latest price")*, and *market value* of the funds held as of the statement date are listed.

PORTFOLIO POSITION DETAIL

CATEGORY	S T	LONG/ SHORT	QUOTE SYMBOL	QUANTITY	INVESTMENT DESCRIPTION	LATEST PRICE	MARKET VALUE
MUTUAL FUNDS	C C	Long Long	PTTRX SRFBX	1210.897 989.962	PIMCO TOTAL RETURN FUND STEINROE TOTAL RETURN FUND	9.7500 24.5300	$11,806.25 $24,283.77
	C	Long	TBGVX	973.236	TWEEDY BROWNE GLOBAL VAL GLOBAL VALUE FUND	12.0100	$11,688.56
MONEY FUNDS	C C	Long Long	CUIEX	636.451 37.22	WARBURG PINCUS INTL EQTY SCHWAB MONEY MARKET FUND	19.6400 1.0000	$12,499.90 $37.22
Net Portfolio Value					$60,315.70		

ACCOUNT TRANSACTION DETAIL

DATE	TRANSACTION	QUANTITY	DESCRIPTION	PRICE	AMOUNT
*****			Opening Cash Balance		$.00
11/01	Reinvested Shares	5.953	PIMCO TOTAL RETURN FUND	9.8000	($58.34)
11/01	Div For Reinvest		PIMCO TOTAL RETURN FUND		$58.34
11/11	Reinvested Shares	10.569	STEINROE TOTAL RETURN FUND	25.0200	($264.44)
11/11	Div For Reinvest		STEINROE TOTAL RETURN		$264.44
*****			Ending Cash Balance		$.00

Figure 11-2: Discount brokerage account statement.

Source: *Charles Schwab & Co., Inc.*

Long simply means that you bought shares and that you're holding shares you bought. (You may, but I don't recommend that you actually *short* shares held in brokerage accounts. Shorting shares simply means that you sell the shares first, hope they decline in value, and then buy them back). The *C* in this example means that this is a cash holding (as opposed to one purchased with some borrowed money).

What confuses most people about the *Account Transactions Detail* section is that each transaction seems to be repeated. The apparent repetition occurs because of the silly accounting system of debits and credits that brokerage firms use. Note that this account shows that 5.953 shares of PIMCO Total Return were purchased at $9.80 per share for a total purchase of $58.34. Where did this odd amount of money come from for the purchase? The next line tells you — the fund paid a dividend of $58.34. It would be logical and more understandable if these two lines were reversed, wouldn't it? First the money comes in and then it's reinvested into purchasing more shares!

Am I Winning or Losing?

Now that you know how to read your statement, it's time for a more important and interesting issue: how much money you're making. Probably the single most important issue that fund investors care about — how much or little they're making on their investments — is not easy to figure from those blasted statements that fund companies send you. That is, it isn't easy to figure unless you know the tricks of what to look for and what to ignore.

The misleading share price

If you follow the price changes in your fund(s) daily, weekly, monthly, or over whatever period you desire, you won't know how your fund is doing. And you won't know because mutual funds make distributions. When a fund makes a distribution to you, you get more shares of the fund. But distributions create an accounting problem because they reduce the share price of a fund by the exact amount of the distribution. Therefore, over time, following just the share price of your fund doesn't tell you how much money you've made or lost.

The only way to figure out exactly how much you've made or lost on your investment is to compare the *total value* of your holdings in a fund today to the total dollar amount you originally invested. If you've invested chunks of money at various points in time, this exercise becomes much more complicated. (Some of the investment software I recommend in Chapter 15 will help if you want your computer to crunch the numbers. Frankly, though, you have easier, less time-consuming ways to get a sense of how you're doing — and I'll get to those ways soon.)

Total return nuts and bolts

The *total return* of a fund is the percentage change of your investment over a specified period. For example, a fund may tell you that its total return during the year that ended December 31st was 15 percent. Therefore, if you had invested $10,000 in the fund on the last day of December of the prior year, your investment would be worth $11,500 after the year just ended.

The following three components make up the total return on a fund: dividends, capital gains, and share price changes.

How often should I check on my funds?

I recommend that you *don't* track the share prices of your funds on a daily basis. It's time-consuming, nerve-racking, and will make you lose sight of the long term. Worse, you'll be more likely to panic when times get tough.

When you take an airplane trip across the country, do you have to hear from the pilot over the public address system every 60 seconds that weather conditions and other such things are

okay? I didn't think so. If you did, you wouldn't enjoy the flight, and the incessant updates would serve little purpose other than to make you nervous.

A weekly, monthly, or even quarterly check-in is more than frequent enough to follow your funds. I know many successful investors who check on their funds' performance twice or even just once a year.

Dividends

Dividends are income paid by investments. Both bonds and stocks can pay dividends. As I explain in Chapter 7, bond dividends tend to be higher. When a dividend distribution is made, you can receive it as cash (which is good if you need money to live on) or reinvest it into more shares in the fund. In either case, the share price of the fund drops by an amount that exactly offsets the payout. So if you're hoping to strike it rich by buying into a bunch of funds just before their dividends are paid, don't bother.

If you hold your mutual fund outside a retirement account, the dividend distributions are taxable income (unless they come from a tax-free municipal bond fund). If you're ready to buy into a fund outside of a retirement account that pays a decent dividend, you may want to check to see when the fund is next scheduled to pay a dividend. For funds that pay quarterly taxable dividends, you may want to avoid buying in the weeks just prior to such a distribution. (See the Appendix of this book for funds' historic distribution schedules.)

Capital gains

When a stock or bond mutual fund manager sells a security in the fund, any gain realized from that sale (the difference between the sale price and the purchase price) must be distributed, yearly to fund shareholders, as a *capital gain.* Typically, funds make one annual capital gains distribution in December. Some funds make two per year, typically making the other one around mid-year.

As with a dividend distribution, you can receive your capital gains distribution as cash or as more shares in the fund. In either case, the share price of the fund drops by an amount to exactly offset the distribution.

For funds held outside retirement accounts, all capital gains distributions are taxable. As with dividends, capital gains are taxable whether or not you reinvest them in additional shares in the fund.

Sometimes you invest in bond and stock funds outside retirement accounts. When you do, determine when capital gains are distributed if you want to avoid investing in a fund that is about to make a capital gains distribution. (Stock funds that appreciated greatly during the year are most likely to make larger capital gains distributions. Money funds don't ever make such distributions.) Investing in a fund that is soon to make a distribution would increase your current-year tax liability for investments made outside retirement accounts. About a month before the distribution, fund companies should be able to estimate the size of the distribution. (Also, see the Appendix.)

Share price changes

You also make money with a mutual fund when the share price increases. This occurrence is just like investing in a stock or piece of real estate. If your fund is worth more today than when you bought it, you have made a profit (on paper, at least). In order to realize or lock in this profit, you would need to sell your shares in the fund. A fund's share price increases if the securities that the fund has invested in have appreciated in value.

Adding up the total return

Now that you've seen all the different components of total return, you're ready to add them all up. For each of the major types of funds that I discuss in this book, Table 11-1 presents a simple summary of where you can expect most of your returns to come from over the long term. The funds are ordered in the table from those with the lowest expected total returns and share price volatility to those with the highest.

Table 11-1	Components of a Fund's Returns			
	Dividends +	**Capital Gains** +	**Share Price Changes**	**= Total Return**
Money market funds	All returns come from dividends	None	None	Lowest expected return but principal risk is nil
Shorter-term bond funds	Moderate	Low	Low	Expect better than money funds but more volatility
Longer-term bond funds	High	Low to moderate	Low to moderate	Expect better than short-term bonds but with greater volatility
Stock funds	None to moderate depending on stock types	Low to high depending on trading patterns of fund manager	Low to high	Highest expected returns but most volatile

Easiest ways to figure total return

If you've just started investing in funds — or even if you've held funds a long time — you need to realize that what happens to the value of your stock and bond funds in the short term is largely a matter of luck. Don't get depressed if your fund(s) drop from the day you buy them or in the first three or six months. When you invest in bond and stock funds, you should focus on returns produced over longer periods — periods of at least one year, and preferably longer.

As I explained in the section earlier in the chapter about how to read your fund statements, fund companies make it almost impossible for you to determine your total return from the information they provide on their statements. They would make everyone's lives easier if they showed you for each of your funds what your original investment was in the fund. Most fund companies say that their computer systems aren't set up to allow for this — but tell us something we don't already know! In this age of technology, there's no reason why fund companies can't make the appropriate changes to their computer systems. Eventually, you'll probably start to see some companies do what I'm suggesting — even though I don't predict financial market movements, I do predict fund industry practices!

Regardless of the time period over which you're trying to determine your funds' total return, here are the simplest ways to figure total return without getting a headache:

- ✔ **Call the fund company's 800 number.** The telephone representatives can provide you the total return for your funds for many lengths of time (such as for the last three months, the last six months, the last year, the last three years, and so on).

- ✔ **Examine the fund's annual and semi-annual reports.** These provide total return numbers.

- ✔ **Keep a file folder with your investment statements.** That way, you can look up what you originally invested in a fund and compare it to updated market values on new statements you receive. You can make a handwritten table or enter the figures in the software I describe in Chapter 15.

- ✔ **Check fund information services and periodicals.** Fund information services and financial magazines and newspapers carry total return data at particular times during the year. Some, such as the *Wall Street Journal*, carry this information daily.

If you've made numerous purchases in a fund, you may want to know what your effective rate of return is when you also factor in the timing and size of each purchase. The only way to do this is with software. Knowing the rate of return for your overall purchases is not critical for you to successfully evaluate your fund investments. Comparing your funds' performance over various time periods to relevant *performance benchmarks* is sufficient. (Benchmarks? See the next section.)

Which total return figures are best for the long-term?

Over several years, fund companies and others who report on funds typically quote return figures in one of two ways. The better way is the compounded average annual rate of return. For example, over a five-year period, suppose Blue Chip stock fund, which specializes in investing in large-company U.S. stocks, may report that its annualized rate of return is 10 percent per year.

The other way fund returns are reported is by the total return over the entire period in question. For example, over the same five-year period, stock fund XYZ may report that it has returned 98 percent. The total return numbers over the entire period sound much more impressive, don't they? But beware: fund companies like to use these in their marketing materials — for example, by

showing, in a mountain chart, the value today of some amount invested ages ago. Over long periods, though, the stock market typically goes up a lot so most funds can't help but look good over the long haul.

The average annual return numbers are more useful for comparative purposes. For example, if I told you that, over the same five-year period, the index of the large-company stock prices in the U.S. returned 12 percent per year, then you'd know that Blue Chip actually wasn't a stellar fund after all. The absolute total returns over the entire number of years can help you see how much an investment way back when is worth today. Just don't forget that there's inflation over the years, too.

Comparing your funds' performance

Whenever you examine your funds' returns, you should compare those returns to appropriate *benchmark indexes*. Although many investors may have been happy as clams to earn about 10 percent with their stock market investments during the 1980s and early 1990s, they really should not have been because the market averages or benchmark indexes were generating about 15 percent per year.

Each mutual fund should be compared to the benchmark that is most appropriate given the types of securities that a fund invests in; for the bond and stock funds that I recommend in Chapters 7 and 8, I provide descriptions of the types of securities that each fund invests in. Here's a brief rundown of the benchmark indexes you'll find useful. (I've provided benchmarks for the types of funds most people use for longer-term purposes such as retirement account investing.)

Bond benchmarks

A number of bond indexes exist (see Table 11-2) that differ from one another mainly in the maturity of the bonds that they invest in. For example, there are short-term, intermediate-term and long-term indexes.

Table 11-2		Bond Indexes		
Year	Lehman Short-Term Bond Index	Lehman Intermediate-Term Bond Index	Lehman Long-Term Bond Index	Salomon GNMA Index	First Boston High Yield (Junk Bond) Index
1986	11.4%	17.0%	21.4%	13.0%	15.6%
1987	5.1%	0.9%	-0.8%	3.5%	6.5%
1988	6.3%	7.5%	9.7%	8.9%	13.6%
1989	11.7%	14.9%	17.5%	15.6%	0.4%
1990	9.7%	8.2%	6.5%	10.9%	-6.4%
1991	13.2%	17.7%	19.5%	15.9%	43.7%
1992	6.8%	7.9%	8.5%	7.6%	16.7%
1993	7.1%	12.2%	16.2%	6.6%	18.9%
1994	-0.7%	-4.5%	-7.1%	-1.3%	-1.0%
1995	12.9%	21.4%	29.9%	16.9%	17.4%
5-year average	7.8%	10.6%	12.1%	8.9%	18.3%
10-year average	8.3%	10.1%	11.6%	9.6%	11.6%

There are also many more specialized indexes than those listed here. For example, there are indexes for municipal bonds, Treasury bonds, and so on. So if you're looking at these different types of funds, take a look in the fund's annual report to see what index they compare the fund's performance to. Don't assume that they are using the most comparable index.

U.S. stock benchmarks

The major U.S. stock indexes (see Table 11-3) are distinguished by the size of the companies (such as large, small, or all sizes) whose stock they invest in. The Standard & Poor's 500 Index tracks the stock prices of 500 large-company stocks on the U.S. stock exchanges; these 500 stocks account for about 70 percent of the total market value of all stocks traded in the U.S. The Russell 2000 Index tracks 2,000 smaller-company U.S. stocks. All stocks of all sizes on the major U.S. stock exchanges are tracked by the Wilshire 5000 Index. (Trivia fact: There are actually more than 5000 stocks in the Wilshire 5000 Index, which had 5,000 stocks in it when it was created more than 20 years ago — now more than 6,000 stocks are in the index).

Table 11-3	U.S. Stock Indexes		
Year	**Standard & Poor's 500**	**Russell 2000**	**Wilshire 5000**
1986	18.6%	5.7%	16.1%
1987	5.2%	-8.8%	2.3%
1988	16.5%	24.9%	17.9%
1989	31.6%	16.2%	29.2%
1990	-3.1%	-19.5%	-6.2%
1991	30.4%	46.1%	34.2%
1992	7.6%	18.4%	9.0%
1993	10.1%	18.9%	11.3%
1994	1.3%	-1.8%	-0.1%
1995	37.6%	28.4%	36.4%
5-year average	**16.5%**	**20.1%**	**17.3%**
10-year average	**14.9%**	**11.3%**	**14.1%**

If you're evaluating the performance of a fund that invests solely in U.S. stocks, make sure to choose the index that comes closest to representing the types of stocks that a fund invests in. Also, remember to examine a stock fund's international holdings. Suppose, for example, that a particular stock fund typically invests 80 percent in U.S. stocks of all sizes and 20 percent in the larger, established countries overseas. You could create your own benchmark index by multiplying the returns of the Wilshire 5000 index by 80 percent and the Morgan Stanley EAFE international index (discussed in the next section) by 20 percent.

International stock benchmarks

When you invest in funds that invest overseas, you gotta use a comparative index that tracks the performance of international stock markets. The *Morgan Stanley EAFE* (which stands for Europe, Australia, and Far East) index tracks the performance of the more established countries' stock markets. Morgan Stanley also has an index that tracks the performance of the emerging markets in Southeast Asia and Latin America (see Table 11-4).

Even though emerging markets' funds have been quite rewarding in recent years, you also should know that they are volatile and risky. As I discuss in Chapter 8, the diversified international funds that include some investment in emerging markets offer a smoother ride to investors who want some "exposure" (ha! ha!) to emerging markets. More-diversified funds also aren't as constraining on a fund manager who believes, for example, that emerging markets are overpriced.

If you do invest in the more diversified international funds that place some of their assets in emerging markets, as you can see from this table, it's not fair to compare the performance of those funds to the EAFE index. So what do you do to more fairly compare the performance of such a fund? Well, if a fund typically invests about 20 percent in emerging markets, then multiply the EAFE return in the table by 80 percent and add to that 20 percent of the *Emerging Markets* index return. For 1993, for example: 33.0% (*.8) + 74.9% (*.2) = 41.4%. With this computation formula, you can see how any international fund that invested in emerging markets in 1993 couldn't help but look good in comparison to the EAFE index. (These numbers also tell you not to be too impressed with an emerging markets fund that boasts that it returned 70 percent to investors in 1993 — if it did, it was below average!)

The hard part is finding out what percentage a fund typically has invested in emerging markets. Most international funds don't report the total of their investments in emerging markets. For the international funds recommended in Chapter 8, I've given some general idea of what portion they have in emerging markets. Also, you can peek at a fund's recent annual or semi-annual report, in which they detail investments held for each country.

Table 11-4	International Stock Indexes	
Year	*Morgan Stanley EAFE*	*Morgan Stanley Emerging Markets*
1986	69.9%	n/a
1987	24.9%	n/a
1988	28.6%	40.4%
1989	10.8%	65.0%
1990	-23.2%	-10.6%
1991	12.5%	59.9%
1992	-11.8%	11.4%
1993	33.0%	74.9%
1994	8.1%	-7.3%
1995	11.2%	0.2%
5-year average	**9.4%**	**23.6%**
10-year average	**13.6%**	n/a

Don't get too focused on performance comparisons. Indexes don't incur expenses that an actual mutual fund does although, as you hopefully know by now, expenses among funds vary tremendously. Remember all the other criteria such as the fees and expenses and the fund company's and manager's expertise that you should evaluate when you consider a fund's chances for generating healthy returns in the years ahead (see Chapter 3).

Should I Sell, Hold, or Buy More?

I am often asked, "How do I know when I should sell a fund?"

The answer is relatively simple: *Sell only if a fund is no longer meeting the common-sense criteria outlined in Chapter 3 for picking a good fund in the first place.* As long as a fund is

- Generating decent returns relative to appropriate benchmarks and the competition;
- Not raising the fees that it charges and charging more than the best of the competition; and
- Still managed by a competent fund manager,

then stick by its side like a loyal friend!

The only other reason to sell a fund is if your circumstances change. For example, suppose that you're 50 years old and you inherit a big pot of money. You haven't been planning to retire early, but it's amazing what oodles of money can do to your plans — so maybe now you're thinking that early retirement ain't such a bad idea after all. This change in circumstances may cause you to tweak your portfolio so that you have more income-producing investments and fewer growth investments.

Tweaking your portfolio

Over longer periods of time, you may need to occasionally tweak your portfolio to keep your investment mix in line with your desires. Suppose that at the age of 40 you invest about 80 percent of your retirement money in stock funds with the balance in bonds. By the age of 50, you find that the stock funds now comprise an even larger percentage (maybe 85 percent) of your investments because they have appreciated more than the bond funds have. So you do the obvious: you sell some of your stock funds and invest the proceeds in the bond funds. Don't forget to factor the tax consequences into your decisions when contemplating the sale of funds held outside of retirement accounts (see Chapter 12).

Trying to time and trade the markets to buy at lows and sell at highs rarely works in the short-term and never works in the long-term. If you do a decent job *up front* of picking good fund companies and funds to invest in, you should have fewer changes to make in the long haul.

If you've got a good set of funds, keep feeding money into them as your savings allows. But, over time, there's no reason to use just a few funds — broaden the mix as you invest more dollars into funds. Holding a couple or several of each different type of fund makes a lot of sense (I cover that sense of fund diversification in much depth in Chapter 9).

If you own funds currently that you or someone else invested in way back when, use the criteria in Chapter 3 to decide if they are "good" funds or not. Funds that carry high fees, have poor historic performance, and are managed by a parent company not known for investment prowess should be dumped. Just be aware of taxes you may owe selling funds held outside a retirement account (see Chapter 12).

Chapter 12

Understanding Yucky Tax Forms for Mutual Funds

In This Chapter

▶ Form 1099-DIV and distributions from mutual funds

▶ Tax forms and issues to understand when selling funds

▶ Form 1099-R and good stuff to know about retirement fund withdrawals

---

*A*bout the only thing worse than paperwork is paperwork and taxes.

You've got better and more interesting things to do with your time than either paperwork *or* taxes. So do yourself a favor and take advantage of contributing more into tax-sheltered retirement accounts. In addition to saving you on taxes, you'll receive fewer tax documents on the funds that you own and have fewer computations and schedules to complete with your annual tax return. (Although you may have a few more tax hassles in retirement.)

If you invest in mutual funds outside of tax-sheltered retirement accounts or make withdrawals from funds that you hold inside of retirement accounts, you're going to receive tax documents. These forms are sent to you from the mutual fund companies or brokerage firms you're using for fund investing.

In this chapter, I explain how to interpret most of those seemingly Greek-like terms on these terrible-looking documents. Additionally, I discuss issues to consider when selling mutual funds that you hold outside of retirement accounts. I'm also going to highlight how you can use fund tax forms to help you discover whether your mutual fund money is being invested in the most tax-friendly way.

Mutual Fund Distributions: Form 1099-DIV

Mutual funds make distributions. Just as you earn interest on bank accounts, mutual funds (including money market, bond, and stock funds) pay dividends. They also make capital gains distributions when the fund manager sells any of his security holdings at a profit (see Chapter 11). All of these potentially taxable distributions, as well as some other confusing stuff, will be reported to both you and the IRS on Form 1099-DIV (your state tax authorities also get this form). These forms usually arrive in your mailbox in late January and early February.

When it's time to complete your tax return, make sure that you have one of these 1099-DIV forms for each and every nonretirement account that you held money in during the tax year. If you're missing any, get on the horn to the responsible financial institution and request the form(s) you're missing. (And if you're tired of receiving these forms from so many fund companies, take a peak at Chapter 4, where I explain the paperwork-friendly benefits of consolidating your mutual fund holdings into a discount brokerage account.)

Compared to some tax forms, Form 1099-DIV isn't that complicated — but that's compared to the rest of the perplexing tax documents you run into. Here's the Dummies Approved explanation of the boxes you see on your Form 1099-DIVs (see Figure 12-1). Actually, most mutual fund companies display this information in columns, even though a real 1099-DIV has boxes. Once you understand what's in these columns or boxes, if you're unhappy, perk up. I'll tell you some ways to make yourself happier by reducing the taxes and other distributions on your investments!

Box 1a: Gross dividends

This shows you the total of all the taxable distributions (dividends, capital gains, and so on) reported in the boxes that follow on the Form 1099-DIV. A large number here, relative to the amount that you have invested, is not necessarily a good thing. Why? Because you're going to have to pay taxes on this stuff. Stay tuned for whether to be concerned.

If you're starting to invest non-retirement money in mutual funds, you may need to make estimated quarterly tax payments during the year. Contact the IRS (and your state) and request Form 1040-ES. The phone number is ☎ 800-829-1040.

1994 FORM 1099-DIV
Dividends and Distributions

THE**Vanguard**GROUP
OF INVESTMENT COMPANIES®

P.O. BOX 2600 • VALLEY FORGE, PA 19482-2600

PAGE 1 OF 2   1-800-662-2739

JOHN Q SHAREHOLDER
123 MAIN ST
ANYTOWN PA 11111-1111

Recipient's Taxpayer Identification Number
123-12-3123

This is important information and is being furnished to the Internal Revenue Service. If you are required to file a return, a negligence penalty or other sanction may be imposed on you if this income is taxable and the IRS determines that it has not been reported.
DEPARTMENT OF THE TREASURY - INTERNAL REVENUE SERVICE

Fund Name		Fund's Fed. I.D. No.					
Recipient's Account Number	Box 1a: Gross Dividends & Other Distributions on Stock (Total of 1b, 1c, and 1d)	Box 1b: Ordinary Dividends	Box 1c: Capital Gain Distributions	Box 1d: Non-Taxable Distributions	Box 2: Federal Income Tax Withheld	Box 3: Foreign Tax Paid	
VANGUARD BALANCED INDEX		23-2691871					
09892204235	586.60	586.60	0.00	0.00	0.00	0.00	
INDEX-GROWTH PORTFOLIO		23-2695174					
09892204235	136.14	136.14	0.00	0.00	0.00	0.00	
VMMR-PRIME PORTFOLIO		23-6607979					
09892204235	232.88	232.88	0.00	0.00	0.00	0.00	
VFISF-ST US TREASURY		23-2659567					
09892204235	102.49	91.01	11.48	0.00	0.00	0.00	
VFISF-GNMA PORTFOLIO		23-2439154					
09892204235	155.87	98.68	57.19	0.00	0.00	0.00	

Figure 12-1:
Form 1099-DIV reports dividends and capital gains your funds paid.

Source: *The Vanguard Group*

Box 1b: Ordinary dividends

This is where you're actually told the total amount of dividends that your fund(s) paid to you. These dividends are taxed just the same as so-called ordinary income that you earn from work. Money market, bond, and stock funds pay dividends. Dividends generally represent all of the distributions on a money market fund, most of those on a bond fund, and a portion of those on a stock fund.

Short-term capital gains — which represent profits from securities a fund sold within a year of their purchase — are included in this total as well because these also get taxed at ordinary income tax rates.

If you're a higher-income earner, you should avoid investing, outside retirement accounts, in mutual funds that produce taxable dividend income and short-term capital gains since you'll pay a high income tax rate on these distributions. It may be better to seek out investments that do not produce so much taxable distributions.

Even if you're not a high-income earner, you should be concerned if your funds held outside of retirement accounts are producing large capital gains distributions year after year. It's better to hold funds that don't increase your taxes unnecessarily. Funds that produce large capital gains distributions are more typically stock funds (see Chapter 8 for advice on tax-friendly stock funds).

Box 1c: Capital gains distributions

This box or column is used to report long-term capital gains distributions. Your tax rate for receiving these distributions may be different than the rate that you pay on your regular income and short-term capital gains. A fund's long-term capital gain — the profit realized from selling securities that the fund owned more than one year — is taxed on a different tax-rate schedule. However, if your taxable income places you in the federal 28 percent tax bracket (or lower), your capital gains tax rate is identical to your ordinary income tax rate.

If you fall in the 31 percent federal tax bracket (or higher), the good news is that your long-term capital gains tax rate caps at 28 percent. In tax year 1996, the 31 percent tax bracket kicks in above the following income levels for each of these tax filing status categories:

- ✔ Single — $58,150

- ✔ Married filing jointly or qualifying widow(er) — $96,900

- ✔ Married filing separately — $48,450

- ✔ Head of household — $83,050

As I explained in the last section, it's better to invest in mutual funds that tend to minimize capital gains distributions. This is only a concern when investing outside of retirement accounts and mostly with stock funds.

Higher income earners who find themselves in the 31 percent or higher tax bracket (see Chapter 5), need to complete the Schedule D tax worksheet to compute the correct tax owed on their fund's capital gains distributions. Besides the possibility that the IRS wants to make your tax life more difficult , there is some logic behind the capital gains tax limit. Some argue that this limit encourages investment for long-term growth. On the other hand, some complain that it's a tax break for the affluent.

Box 1d: Nontaxable distributions

You rarely see numbers here. (You may think that this is where funds report tax-free dividends, for example, that are paid on municipal bond funds — but they're not reported on Form 1099-DIV because they're not taxable!) This box is where funds report if they made distributions during the year that repaid shareholder's original investments. As with the principal returned to you if a bond or CD you've invested in matures, this chunk of money is not taxable — hence the term here, *nontaxable distributions*.

Why the hubbub over the Fidelity Magellan accounting error?

Late in 1994, Fidelity Investments announced that its Magellan stock fund, the nation's largest mutual fund, would pay its shareholders a capital gains distribution of $4.32 per share in late December. This announcement didn't strike anyone as out of the ordinary because many stock funds make such distributions late in the year.

So why did everybody eventually make such a big deal out of that distribution? Well, it turns out that Fidelity — more specifically, Fidelity's accounting department—made an accounting error. The actual capital gains distribution that should have been reported and that was ultimately paid out at year-end was . . . nothing! The mistake crept into Fidelity's figures through a simple human error. In totaling up the gains and losses on the securities sold during the year, Fidelity's bean-counters overlooked a minus sign in front of a security sold at a loss. So a *losing* transaction appeared as a profit!

The resulting publicity surrounding this snafu was a small nightmare for Fidelity. Some of the reporting was poorly informed — one story, in fact, questioned whether Magellan fund manager Jeff Vinik, who makes investing decisions for the fund and has nothing to do with the accounting, would be held personally responsible for this error!

Ultimately, this fiasco was a nonevent or actually even good news for fund shareholders. When a fund makes a capital gains distribution of, say, $4.32 per year, the price per share of the fund drops by the amount of the distribution. Capital gains distributions paid to shareholders holding this fund outside a tax-sheltered retirement account were spared from paying more taxes! Those holding Magellan inside retirement accounts shouldn't have cared either way.

Unfortunately for Fidelity, this episode wasn't the only accounting glitch they suffered in 1994; I discovered some others myself. See Chapter 11 for more details.

For shares held outside of retirement accounts, these nontaxable distributions factor into your computation of the gain or loss when the shares are sold. Specifically, if and when you sell such shares, you must subtract the money returned to you from what you originally paid for these shares.

Box 2: Federal income tax withheld

It's bad news if there are any amounts here. If there are, it means that you're being subjected to the dreaded *backup withholding*. If you don't report all your mutual fund dividend income (or don't furnish the fund company with your Social Security number), your future mutual fund dividend income is subject to backup withholding of *31 percent!* To add insult to injury, in the not-too-distant future, you will receive a nasty notice from the IRS listing the dividends you didn't report. You end up owing interest and penalties.

Find out right away what's going on here. It's possible that either you or the IRS made a mistake. It's possible that you didn't provide a correct Social Security number or that you have been negligent in reporting to the IRS your previously earned taxable income. Fix this problem as soon as you can. Call the IRS at ☎ (800) 829-1040.

Don't despair about the tax that was withheld by your fund. The withholding wasn't for naught — you receive credit for it when you complete your Form 1040. For tax year 1994, taxpayers subjected to this nastiness reported these withholdings on line 54 ("Federal income tax withheld") on Form 1040.

Box 3: Foreign tax paid

When I first recommended to my parents that they invest in international mutual funds, they actually took my advice — which goes to show you that there really is a first time for everything! Come the following April, dear old Dad turned into a tax-preparing grump. Why? He got a Form 1099-DIV for the international stock fund they invested in and the form had an amount in box 3.

See, if you invest in an international mutual fund, the fund may end up paying foreign taxes on some of its dividends. The foreign taxes paid by the fund are listed here because the IRS allows you two ways to get some of this money back. You can either deduct the foreign tax you paid on Schedule A (line 8, "Other taxes") or claim a credit on Form 1040 (line 43, "Foreign Tax Credit"). The latter move may be more tax-beneficial, but it is also more of a headache because you need to complete yet another IRS Form, Form 1116, which is a bona-fide doozie.

Get out last year's tax return

With all the fuss and muss over mutual fund distributions, you should note how the rest of your non-mutual investments are positioned. Although taxes aren't everything, you may be paying much more than you need to.

Look at your Form 1040 to see how much taxable interest income you had to pay tax on. On Forms 1040 and 1040A, this figure goes on line 8a. If you

filed 1040EZ (don't you just love that name?), the figure goes on line 2.

Now find out what rate of interest you were being paid that generated this interest income. If it came from money in a bank account, odds are quite good that you could be earning more in a money market mutual fund. (See Chapter 6.)

When You Sell Your Mutual Fund Shares

If you sell a mutual fund (or most other investments, for that matter) held outside of a tax-sheltered retirement account, and you sell it for more than you paid for it, you owe capital gains tax on the profit. Conversely, when you sell a fund investment at a loss, it is tax deductible. You should understand the tax consequences of selling your fund shares and factor taxes into your selling decisions.

What's confusing about this talk here of capital gains and losses is that each year your fund(s) may have been paying you capital gains distributions which you then owed tax on. So you may rightfully be thinking, "Hey! I'm being taxed twice!"

It's true you are being taxed twice, but not on just the same profits. You see, the profits the fund distributed, which resulted from the fund manager selling securities in his fund at a profit, are different than those profits that you've realized by selling your shares.

What's your fund's "basis"?

If you sell a fund, in order to compute the taxable capital gain or the deductible capital loss, you have to compute your fund's tax basis. *Basis* is the tax system's way of measuring what you paid for your investment(s) in a mutual fund. I say investments because you may not have made all of your purchases in a fund at once; you may have reinvested your dividends or capital gains or bought shares at different times.

For example, if you purchase 100 shares of the Its Gotta Rise Mutual Fund at $20 per share, your cost basis is considered to be $2,000, or $20 per share. Simple enough. But now suppose that this fund pays a dividend of $1 per share (so that you get $100 in dividends for your 100 shares), and suppose further that you choose to reinvest this dividend into purchasing more shares of the mutual fund. If at the time of the dividend payment is made the $100 dividend purchases four more shares at $25 per share, now you own 104 shares. At $25 per share, your 104 shares are worth $2,600. But what's your basis now? Your basis is your original investment ($2,000) plus subsequent investments ($100) for a total of $2,100. Thus, if you sold all your shares now, you'd have a taxable profit of $500 (current value of $2,600 less the total amount invested or "basis").

For recordkeeping purposes, save your statements detailing all the purchases in your accounts. Most mutual fund companies, for example, provide year-end summary statements that show all transactions throughout the year. For purchases made now and in the future, fund companies also should be able to tell you what your average cost was per share when you need to sell your shares.

Mutual fund accounting 101

So now that you understand concept of *basis* for your fund investments, it's time to put that understanding to work. Now I'm going to walk you through the different ways that the IRS allows you to calculate your basis when you sell your non-retirement account mutual fund investments.

If you sell all your shares of a particular mutual fund that you hold outside a retirement account at once, you can ignore this issue. (After reading through the accounting options that the IRS offers, you have more incentive to sell all your shares in a fund at once!)

Be aware that once you elect one of the following *tax accounting methods* for selling shares in a particular fund, you can't change to another method for the sale of the remaining shares. If you plan to sell only some of your fund shares — and it would be advantageous for you to specify that you're selling the newer shares first — then choose that method. But, regardless of the method you choose, your mutual fund capital gains and capital losses are recorded on Schedule D of IRS Form 1040.

The first fund basis option that the IRS allows you to use when you sell a portion of the shares of a fund is the so-called *specific identification* method. Here's how it works. Suppose that you own 200 shares of Global Interactive Couch Potato fund (you laugh — but there really is a fund with a name similar to this!), and you'd like to sell 100 shares. Suppose further that you bought 100 of these shares ten years ago at $10 per share, and then another 100 shares two years ago for $40 per share. (I'm ignoring or assuming that you didn't make any other purchases from reinvestment of capital gains or dividends — more on this issue later). Today, the fund is worth $50 per share. Being a couch potato has its rewards!

Which 100 shares should you sell? The IRS gives you a choice You can identify the *specific* shares that you sell. With your Global Interactive Couch Potato shares, you may opt to sell the last or most recent 100 shares you bought. Doing so will minimize your tax bill because these shares were purchased at a higher price. If you sell this way, you must identify the specific shares you want the fund company (or broker holding the shares) to sell. Identify the 100 shares to be sold in terms of (1) original date of purchase, (2) cost *when you sell the shares,* or (3) both.

You may wonder how the IRS knows whether you specified which shares before you sold them. Get this: the IRS doesn't know. But if you are audited, the IRS will ask for proof that you identified the shares to be sold before you sold them. It's best to put your sales request to the fund company in writing and keep a copy for your tax files.

Another method of accounting for which shares are sold is the method the IRS forces you to use if you don't specify before the sale which shares are to be sold — the *first-in-first-out* (FIFO) method. FIFO means that the first shares you sell are simply the first shares that you bought. Not surprisingly, because most stock funds appreciate over time, the FIFO method leads to paying more taxes sooner. In the case of the Global Interactive Couch Potato fund, FIFO considers that the 100 shares sold are the 100 that you bought ten years ago at the bargain-basement price of $10 per share.

Although you will save taxes today if you specify selling the shares that you bought last, don't forget (the IRS won't let you) that when you finally sell the other shares, you'll owe taxes on the larger profit. The longer you expect to hold these other shares, the greater the likely value you'll derive from postponing the larger gain and paying more in taxes. Of course, there's always the risk that the IRS will raise tax rates in the future or that your particular tax rate will rise.

Had enough of fund accounting? Well, we're not done yet. The IRS, believe it or not, allows you yet another fund accounting method: the *average cost method.* If you bought shares in chunks over time and/or reinvested the fund distributions (such as from dividends) into more shares of the fund, then tracking and figuring what shares you're selling could be a real headache. So the IRS allows you to take an average cost for all the shares you bought over time.

If you sell all your shares of a fund at once, you'll use the average cost basis method. This method may also be preferred when selling a portion of a fund that you hold. Since many fund companies calculate this number for you, you'll save time and possible fees paid to a tax preparer to crunch the numbers.

Want a real headache? Here you go: The IRS actually gives you a *fourth* method for figuring what shares you are selling — it's called the *average basis, double category method.* This is a twist on the average cost method. With the double category method, you divide your shares of a fund into two pots: a short-term pot, for those shares held a year or less, and a long-term pot for shares held longer than one year. This method may be tax-beneficial if you're in a high tax bracket and do a lot of short-term trading — a financial habit I *don't* recommend. Besides, the accounting you'll need to do to calculate this is tedious and time consuming.

Regardless of which tax cost accounting method you choose for your fund sales, be careful to not overpay your capital gains tax. If you're in the federal 31 percent or higher bracket, remember that the maximum tax rate for long-term capital gains is 28 percent. You need to complete the worksheet in Schedule D of your Form 1040 to ensure that you don't pay more tax than is necessary.

Fund sales reports: Form 1099-B

When you sell shares in a mutual fund, you'll receive Form 1099-B in January of the following year. This is a fairly worthless document because it doesn't calculate the cost basis of the shares that you sold. Its primary value to you is that it nicely summarizes and reminds you of all the transactions that you need to account for on your annual tax return. This form, which is also sent to the IRS, serves to notify the tax authorities of what you sold so that they can check your tax return to see if you report the transaction.

If some of the sales listed on your Form 1099-B are from check-writing redemptions, stop writing checks on those funds! Keep enough stashed in a money market fund and write checks only from that type of account. Money market fund sales are not tax reportable since money funds' share price doesn't change. Thus, fewer tax headaches!

Deciding when to take your tax lumps or deductions

If funds held outside of retirement accounts increase in value, you won't want to sell them because of the tax bite. If on the other hand they decline, you may not know whether to sell them and may not want to dump them and thus lock in your losses. So how do you decide what to do and what role taxes should play in your decisions? As I cover in Chapter 11, several issues can factor into your decision to sell a fund or hold onto it. Taxes are an important consideration. So — what do you need to know about taxes?

First, you do need to realize that taxes are important, but don't let them keep you from doing something you really want to do. Suppose, for example, that you need money to buy a home or take a long postponed vacation — and selling some mutual funds is your only source of money to do this. I say go for it. Even if you have to pay state as well as federal taxes totaling, for example, 35 percent of the profit, you'll have lots left over. Before you sell, however, do some rough figuring to make sure that you'll have enough money to accomplish what you want.

If you hold a number of funds, give preference to selling your largest holdings (that is, those with the largest total market value) with the smallest capital gains. If you have some funds that have profits and some with losses, you can sell some of each in order to offset the profits with the losses. You can use losses to offset gains — as long as both offsetting securities were held for more than one year ("long-term") or both held for less than one year ("short-term"). The IRS makes this delineation because long-term gains and losses are taxed on a different rate schedule than short-term gains and losses (which I discuss earlier in this chapter).

You cannot claim more than $3,000 in short-term or long-term losses in any one year. If you sell funds with losses that total more than $3,000 in a year, you must carry the losses over to future tax years. This situation not only creates more tax paperwork, but it also delays taking the tax deduction. So try not to have *net losses* (losses + gains) that exceed $3,000 in a year.

Selling for tax deductions and the famous *wash sale rule*

Some tax advisors advocate doing *year-end tax-loss selling*. The logic goes something like this: If you hold a mutual fund that has declined in value and you hold that fund outside a retirement account, you should sell it, take the tax write-off, and then buy the fund (or something similar) back.

I don't think this selling just for taking a tax loss is worth the trouble, particularly if you plan on holding the repurchased shares for a long time. Remember that by selling and buying back the shares, you've lowered your basis, which increases the taxable income once you sell the repurchased shares.

If you sell a fund for a tax loss and buy back shares in that same fund within 30 days of the sale, you can't deduct the loss. Why? Because, if you do, you violate the so-called *wash sale rule*. The IRS will not allow deduction of a loss for a fund sale if you buy that same fund back within 30 days. As long as you wait 31 or more days, no problem. If you're selling a mutual fund, you can easily sidestep this rule simply by purchasing a fund similar to the one you're selling.

What to do when you can't find what you paid for a fund

When you sell a mutual fund that you've owned for a long time (or that your parents gave you), you may not have any idea what it originally cost (also known as its *cost basis*).

If you can't find that original statement, start by calling the firm where the investment was bought. Whether it's a mutual fund company or brokerage firm, they should be able to send you copies of old account statements. You may have to pay a small fee for this service. Also, increasing numbers of investment firms (particularly mutual fund companies) automatically calculate and report cost-basis information on investments you sell. Generally, the cost basis they calculate is the average cost for the shares that you purchased.

Fund Retirement Withdrawals and Form 1099-Rs

Someday, hopefully not before you retire, you'll need or want to start enjoying all the money that you will have socked away into great mutual funds inside your tax-sheltered retirement accounts. Here's what you need to know and consider before taking money out of your mutual fund retirement accounts.

Minimizing taxes and avoiding penalties

Although there are many different retirement account types (IRAs, SEP-IRAs, Keoghs, 403 (b)s, and so on), as well as many tax laws governing each, the IRS did one thing to make understanding taxes on withdrawals a little easier. All retirement accounts allow you to begin withdrawing money, without penalty, after age 59^1/$_2$. Why they didn't use a round number like 60 is beyond me.

If you withdraw money from your retirement accounts prior to age 59^1/$_2$, in addition to paying current income tax on the distribution, you also must pay penalties — 10 percent at the federal level and whatever penalties your state charges. (The penalty is computed on Form 5329 — Return for Additional Taxes Attributable to Qualified Retirement Plans). The penalty does not apply to IRA distributions when they're paid because of death or disability, paid over your life expectancy, or rolled over to another IRA.

With early distributions from your employer's retirement plan, the 10 percent penalty does not apply to some additional exceptions, including distributions made

- ✔ After you stopped working (whether by retirement or termination) during or after the calendar year you reach age 55
- ✔ Under a qualified domestic relations court order
- ✔ Because you have deductible medical expenses in excess of 7.5 percent of your adjusted gross income

Of course, you'll pay current income taxes, both federal and state, when you withdraw money that hasn't been previously taxed from retirement accounts. I make this distinction because some of the money invested inside your retirement accounts may have been taxed previously (more on this later).

Issues to consider before making retirement account withdrawals

Generally speaking, most people are better off to postpone drawing on retirement accounts until they need the money. But don't delay if waiting means that you must scrimp and cut corners — especially if you have the money to use and enjoy.

On the other hand, if you have other money you can use, the longer your retirement account money is left alone, the longer it can grow without being taxed. Suppose that you retire at age 60. In addition to money inside your retirement accounts, you have a bunch available outside as well. If you can, you're generally better served living off the money outside of retirement accounts *before* you start to tap the retirement account money.

If you're not wealthy, odds are good that you'll need (and want) to start drawing on your retirement account soon after you retire. By all means, do it. But have you figured out how long your nest egg will last and how much you can afford to withdraw? Most folks haven't. It's worth taking the time to figure how much of your money you can afford to draw on per year, even if you think you have enough. Many good savers have a hard time spending and enjoying their money in retirement. Knowing how much you can safely use may get you to loosen your purse strings.

One danger of leaving your money to compound inside your retirement accounts for a long time —

once you're retired — is that the IRS *requires* you to make withdrawals by April 1st of the year following the year you reach age 70 1/2. If you don't, there's a whopping 50 percent penalty on the amount that you should have taken out but didn't.

It's possible that because of your delay in taking the money out — and the fact that it will have more time to compound and grow — you may need to withdraw a hefty chunk each year. Doing so could push you into higher tax brackets in those years that you are forced to make larger withdrawals.

If you're a high roller, be aware that your delay in withdrawing retirement account money may also cause you to pay an excess distribution penalty of 15 percent tax to the IRS. This penalty is levied *on top of* the regular income tax you owe if you're forced to withdraw more than $150,000 in one year from all your retirement accounts.

If you want to plan how you withdraw money from your retirement accounts in order to meet your needs and minimize your taxes, hire a tax advisor to help. If you have a lot of money in retirement accounts, as well as the luxury of not needing the money until you're well into retirement, tax planning likely will be worth your time and your money.

Individual retirement account (IRA) distributions

By April 1 of the year following the year you turn $70^{1}/_{2}$, you've got to make some important decisions about how your money will come out of your mutual fund

IRA(s). The first choice: whether you receive yearly distributions based on your life expectancy or based on the joint life expectancies of you and your beneficiary. If your aim is to take out as little as possible, you should use a joint life expectancy. That will stretch out the distributions over a longer period.

Next, you've got to decide how you want your life expectancy calculated. With the method known as *term-certain,* you pick the current IRS estimate of your life expectancy, then reduce it by one year every year. So if the IRS figures that as of this year that you'll live another 22.5 years, next year you'd divide the balance of the account by 21.5, and so on. See IRS Publication 590 on how to calculate your life expectancy.

Under the second method, *recalculation*, you go back to the IRS tables and look up your new life expectancy each year. Over time, this method has you taking out a little less money per year than with the term-certain approach. (According to the IRS tables, your life expectancy doesn't decrease by a full year every 12 months.) But there are some serious drawbacks to using this method. For example, if one spouse dies, only the survivor's life expectancy is used. When you both die, the entire balance must be paid out within a year to whoever is next in line for the money. That could mean a big tax bill for whoever is getting the balance of your account (presumably an heir). If you use the term-certain approach, the heir gets to keep taking money out in dribs and drabs, just as you've been doing. Thus, term-certain is preferable for most people.

Making sense of Form 1099-R for IRAs

If you receive a distribution from your mutual fund IRA, the mutual fund company or brokerage firm where you hold your funds will report the distribution on Form 1099-R (see Figure 12-2). These distributions are taxable unless you made nondeductible contributions to the IRA (a situation I'll cover momentarily). Here's a rundown of the important boxes you need to understand on your 1099-R.

Box 1, *Gross distribution,* is the amount of money that you withdrew from your IRA. Make sure that it's correct: check to see if it matches the amount withdrawn from your IRA account statement. This amount is fully taxable if you've never made a nondeductible contribution to an IRA — that's an IRA contribution where you did not take a tax-deduction and therefore filed Form 8606 (Nondeductible IRA Contributions, IRA Basis, and Nontaxable IRA Distributions).

Box 2a, *Taxable amount,* is for the taxable amount of the IRA distribution. However, the payer of an IRA distribution doesn't have enough information to compute whether your entire IRA distribution is completely taxable or not. Therefore, if you simply enter this amount on your tax return as being fully taxable, you overpay on your taxes if you had made nondeductible contributions to your IRA. If you made nondeductible contributions, you compute the nontaxable portion of your distribution on Form 8606, which you need to attach to your annual tax return.

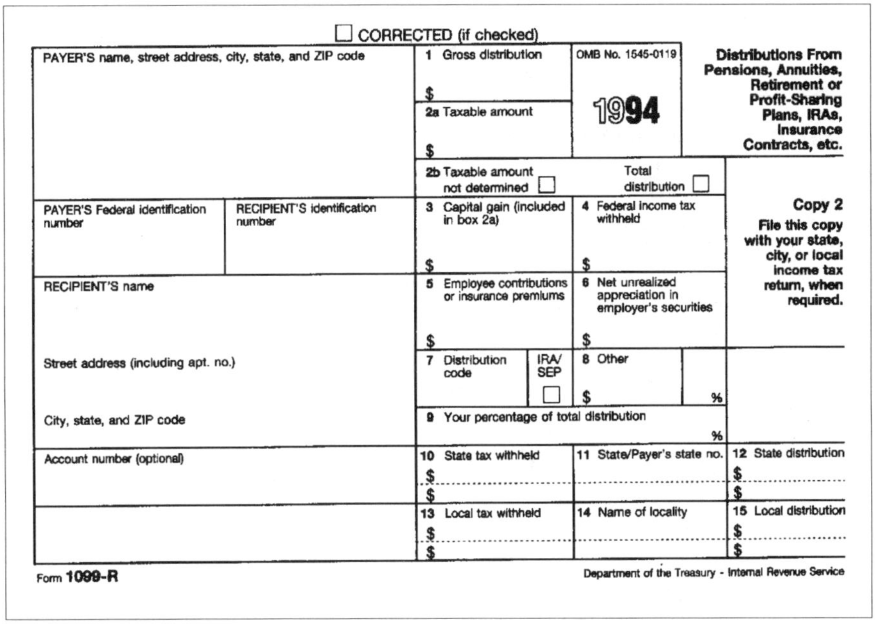

Figure 12-2:
Here's where funds report your retirement plan distributions.

The figure shows IRS Form 1099-R with the following field labels:

CORRECTED (if checked)

PAYER'S name, street address, city, state, and ZIP code

1 Gross distribution $

OMB No. 1545-0119

1994

Distributions From Pensions, Annuities, Retirement or Profit-Sharing Plans, IRAs, Insurance Contracts, etc.

2a Taxable amount $

2b Taxable amount not determined ☐   Total distribution ☐

PAYER'S Federal identification number   RECIPIENT'S identification number

3 Capital gain (included in box 2a) $ 4 Federal income tax withheld $

Copy 2
File this copy with your state, city, or local income tax return, when required.

RECIPIENT'S name

5 Employee contributions or insurance premiums $ 6 Net unrealized appreciation in employer's securities $

Street address (including apt. no.)

7 Distribution code   IRA/ SEP ☐   8 Other $ %

City, state, and ZIP code

9 Your percentage of total distribution   %

Account number (optional)

10 State tax withheld $ $ 11 State/Payer's state no.   12 State distribution $ $

13 Local tax withheld $ $ 14 Name of locality   15 Local distribution $ $

Form **1099-R**   Department of the Treasury - Internal Revenue Service

Non-IRA account withdrawals

Retirement account withdrawals and benefits from non-IRA accounts — such as 401(k), SEP-IRA, or Keogh plans — are taxed depending on whether you receive them in the form of an annuity (paid over your lifetime) or a lump sum. The amount you fill in on your 1040 tax return is reported on a 1099-R that you receive from your employer or another custodian of your plan, which may include an investment company such as a mutual fund company or discount broker.

If you didn't pay or contribute to your employer's retirement plan, or if your employer didn't withhold part of the cost from your pay while you worked, then the amount you receive each year is fully taxable. The amount that you contributed and for which you received a deduction — such as contributions to a 401(k), SEP-IRA, or Keogh — isn't considered part of your cost.

If you made nondeductible contributions to your retirement plan or contributions that were then added to your taxable income on your W-2 — then you are not taxed on the part you contributed. You're not taxed on the portion of such withdrawals because this represents a return of investment dollars that you've already paid tax on. The rest of the amount that you receive is taxable.

As they often do with the rest of our needlessly complicated tax laws, the IRS gives you at least two ways to compute the amount that you owe tax on. These two ways are known as the *General Rule* and the *Simplified General Rule.* The details of these complicated parts of the tax code are beyond the scope of this book — but you can always pick up a copy of *Taxes For Dummies* if you're in this boat.

If you receive a total distribution from a retirement plan, you receive a Form 1099-R. If the distribution qualifies as a lump-sum distribution, Box 3 shows the capital gain amount, and Box 2a minus Box 3 shows the ordinary income amount. Code A is entered in Box 7 if the lump sum qualifies for special averaging. If you do not get a Form 1099-R, or if you have questions about the form, contact your plan administrator.

Understanding form 1099-R for non-IRAs

You report non-IRA retirement account distributions on Form 1099-R, which is the same one used to report IRA distributions. Sometimes people panic when they receive a 1099-R and they intend to rollover their retirement account money into a fund from, say, their employer's retirement plan after they leave their job. Don't worry: as you'll hopefully soon see, you got this form because you did do a legal rollover and therefore won't be subjected to the tax normally levied on distributions.

The following highlights how some of the other boxes on distributions for non-IRA retirement accounts come into play:

- ✔ **Box 3:** If the distribution is a lump-sum and you were a participant in the plan before 1974, this amount qualifies for capital gain treatment.
- ✔ **Box 4:** This indicates Federal Income tax withheld (you get credit for this when you file your tax return).
- ✔ **Box 5:** Your after-tax contribution that you made is entered here.
- ✔ **Box 6:** Securities in your employer's company that you received are listed here. This amount is not taxable until the securities are sold.

✔ **Box 7:** If you are under $59^1/_2$ and your employer knows that you qualify for one of the exceptions to the 10 percent penalty, the employer enters:

Code 2 — separation from service after 55

Code 3 — disability

Code 4 — death

Code A — qualifies for lump-sum treatment

Code G — direct rollover to an IRA

Code H — direct rollover to another retirement plan

✔ **Box 8:** If you have an entry here, seek tax advice.

✔ **Box 9:** This is your share of a distribution if there are several beneficiaries.

Chapter 13

Common Fund Problems and How to Fix 'em

Mutual funds employ people, and people as you well know aren't perfect; some are more competent than others at getting the job done right the first time. Inevitably, just as minor problems crop up with bank accounts, sooner or later, you will have a little snafu that you need to get fixed with your funds.

Established fund companies have hundreds and in some cases thousands of telephone representatives who field phone calls and process stuff you send them in the mail. Most of the bigger and better companies recommended in this book do a good job of training their employees, so you should receive competent assistance. But boobs abound so be prepared.

If you call companies to ask a question or express a concern, sometimes you speak with someone who doesn't know how to fix your problem, who gives you the run-around, or worst — who gives you incorrect information. Here's what you can and should do to ensure getting accurate solutions without investing a lot of your time:

✔ **Know their limitations.** Fund company representatives are there to provide information and assistance. Don't depend on for them for tax advice. (Most of the larger fund companies have retirement account specialists who have more detailed knowledge about tax issues relating to those accounts).

✔ **Talk to someone else.** If you're not getting clear answers or answers that you're satisfied with, don't hesitate to ask for a supervisor. Or you can simply call back on the 800 line and you'll surely get another representative. This is a proven way to get a second opinion to make sure the first person knew what they were talking about.

✔ **Take names and notes for thorny problems.** If you're dealing with a problem that could cost you big bucks if it's not properly solved, make sure to take notes of your conversation, and the name of the person, what office he or she is located in, and their telephone extension. That way, you have some proof of your good efforts to fix things when you need to complain to or are summoned by a higher authority (for example, a supervisor, the IRS, and the like).

While I can't guarantee that this chapter is a page-turner, it can help bail you out and soothe your nerves when you just don't know how to get a problem fixed.

I Can't Figure Out the Loads and Fees

Often when people buy funds, they don't have a clue what it's going to cost them. Sales commissions and ongoing operating fees are sucked out of your money in a way that is transparent to you. So how can you know what a fund is going to cost you to buy and own? Ask the fund company and read the prospectus, which all funds are required by law to send you (see Chapter 3 for how to quickly find this data in this tedious document).

Obtaining a prospectus before you agree to buy is especially critical with funds sold by brokers and brokers who masquerade as "financial planners and consultants." Make sure you know what the fund is costing you as well as the cost of alternative funds.

Do yourself a favor and buy some of the good funds recommended in this book. I recommend no-load funds and always tell you what the fees are.

The Prospectus Isn't Specific about Investments

Most everyone says, "read the prospectus before you invest or send money." You should read some of the early pages in a prospectus — most of the rest is worthless to your needs. But if you do read the prospectus, you may be left with an empty feeling — somewhat like the feeling you have after attending a free seminar hoping to learn about investing when you realize that the instructor's agenda wasn't to teach you how to do things on your own but to sell you the investments.

If you want to know the specific investments that a fund holds, call the fund company's 800 number and ask them to send you their most recent semi-annual or annual report (see Chapter 3 for how to read it). That will list every single investment the fund holds, along with some useful summaries that show what percentage of the fund is invested in different industries (and countries, for international funds). Read the summaries in Chapters 6 through 8 for recommended funds in this book.

I Don't Know Which Fund to Invest In

Fund companies offer a bewildering array of funds. You may be tempted to ask the fund company representatives that you speak with for advice. Most of them won't offer anything terribly specific. The reasons: they don't have the proper training and background to do so, and fund companies don't want the risk and potential legal liability that come from giving advice.

Factoring in your overall financial situation, including your goals and tax bracket, Part II of this book walks you through the logic behind the selection of different types of funds. I also recommend a short list of funds for different needs. Do a little reading and thinking, and you'll soon be able to pick funds that meet your needs.

Establishing Retirement Accounts in a Snap

Okay, so you procrastinate — you're human. Perhaps it's April 14th or 15th and you want to establish an IRA, but you need to do it like now. You don't have time to call an 800 number, wait for days to get applications in the mail, and then wait even more days until the fund company receives your check. All is not lost; here are several proven ways out of your pickle:

✔ **Visit a branch office.** Companies such as Fidelity and Schwab have numerous branch offices. Call them to find the location of the one nearest you. You may also be near other companies' main offices. Check the Appendix of this book for phone numbers and addresses.

Believe it or not, some branch offices are kept open late on tax day. Fidelity, for example, keeps some of its branches open until midnight.

✔ **Use an express mail service.** While not a low-cost option, if you've got a couple of days and a chunk of money at stake, Federal Express or some other overnight express mail service may be worth the cost and save you the time of going to a branch office.

✔ **Go to your local bank.** Establish your retirement account in a savings or money market type account at the bank. Later, when the dust has settled and you have breathing room, call your favorite fund company for its application and transfer forms and move the money.

Bank employees will more than likely try to talk you into a CD or one of the mutual funds that they sell. Skip the CD, since you're looking for a very short-term parking place for your retirement contribution. Bank mutual funds tend to be load (commission-based) funds.

✔ **File a tax extension.** Consider buying yourself more time by filing an extension. While you still must pay any outstanding tax owed by the April 15th deadline, filing an extension through IRS Form 4868 gets you four more months to file your Form 1040 and establish and fund your retirement accounts. Come the middle of August and you're still disorganized or otherwise not ready to get the job done, you can file one last extension (Form 2688) for yet another two months. October 15th is the end.

If you're self-employed, be aware that you need to file the paperwork for a Keogh retirement account by December 31st — there are no extensions (although, as with other retirement accounts, you do have until the time you file your tax forms to fund the Keogh). You can use the strategies discussed above to get the job done by year end. Fidelity even has a fax service, which enables you to put it off until hours before the New Year!

Making Deposits in a Flash

Maybe you have an account open and just need to feed it in a hurry. Most often this happens when you're needing to fund a retirement account, but it may also happen if you've overdrawn your checking account.

If you're dealing with a company that has a branch location near you, simply take a check and deposit it at their office. If the fund company isn't in your neighborhood, don't despair. The next best and fastest way to get money into a fund account you previously established is by wiring it from your bank account. If you have already set up this feature on your fund account, first call your fund company to see what information you need to provide to your bank in order for the wire to be correctly sent. This information usually includes the name of the bank your fund uses for wires, that bank's identification number (the ABA #), the title of the fund company's account at that bank and their account number, your name as it appears on your fund account that the money is to be deposited in, the name of that fund, and your account number. Wiring usually costs money on both ends.

If you don't have the wiring feature established on your account, establishing this feature will take some time because you must request, fill out, and mail a special form to add this whistle to your account.

Another option most fund accounts offer is electronic funds transfer (like a paperless check). You can ask that money be moved this way if you have this option on your account. Electronic funds transfer usually takes a day longer than a wire, but it is free. Simply call your fund company and tell them how much money you want to move. As with wiring, if you don't have this feature, you may establish it by requesting and filling out a form from the fund company.

Messed-Up Deposits and Purchases

With all the sound-alike fund names, you can very well have your money deposited into the wrong fund at some firms. That's why it's a good idea to look at your statement confirming the purchase to verify that the deposit amount and the fund into which the money was deposited are both correct.

If the fund company did make a mistake, they should cheerfully fix the problem (they may need to do a bit of research first). They should credit the correct amount to the fund you requested as of the date the money was originally received.

If the bond or stock fund you intended to buy has declined in value since the deposit should have been made, you get to invest with the benefit of hindsight. Ask that, when the deposit is corrected, it be done as of today. On the other hand, if the fund has appreciated, then you can insist that the original date of purchase be used!

If the screw-up was your fault, sometimes fund companies will cancel out the original trade and give you what you had intended (having lots of money with the company doesn't hurt the chances of this happening). Since companies are leery about people who may take advantage of this to jump out of funds that declined in value, the company will judge whether it appears to be an honest mistake or not.

Specifying Funds to Buy at Discount Brokers

When you invest through most mutual fund companies, their account application and other forms allow you to indicate what fund(s) you wish to make your deposit into. Not so at discount brokerage firms.

If you want to buy funds at the time when the discount broker processes your deposit, write your instructions and send those in with your deposit. For example, if you mail in $2,000 for an IRA deposit to a discount brokerage firm, and you want the money divided between, say, the Neuberger & Berman Guardian fund and the Warburg Pincus International Equity fund, here's how to word the letter:

Dear Sir or Madam:

Enclosed please find a check in the amount of $2,000 that I would like invested in my IRA account as a 1996 contribution (reference your account number or specify if new application is attached) as follows:

> $1,000 into Neuberger & Berman Guardian (NGUAX)
>
> $1,000 into Warburg Pincus International Equity fund (CUIEX)

Please reinvest dividends and capital gains.

Thanks a million,

John Kilcullen
A loyal Dummies book reader

Note the reference about what to do with dividends and capital gains distributions. Try to be as precise as possible with the fund names. The ultimate in precision for a broker is the *trading symbol* that each fund has (trading symbols are listed in the Appendix for funds recommended in this book).

Verifying Receipt of Deposits

When you send money to a fund company, how will you know if the fund company got your money? Unlike with a bank ATM, you won't get a deposit slip with your transaction — at least, not right away. Fund companies will mail you a statement, usually the day after the deposit is received and processed, showing you the transaction. You can keep a log of deposits on paper or with a

Reprinted with permission

If you can't wait for the mail, you can call the fund company's 800 number and verify receipt over the phone. Many of the larger fund companies have automated phone systems that allow you to check on stuff like this quickly, without waiting for a live person.

Getting Money Out in a Hurry

For non-retirement accounts, if you have a money market fund with check writing, writing a check is simple and costs nothing. Another option is to call the fund company and request a *telephone redemption*. The day after the next market close, a check should be cut and mailed to you. If you need the check faster than the mail service can get it to you, you can provide your express mail company (for example, FedEx) account number. Some fund companies also allow you to pick up redemption checks at their headquarters. Call to see if they allow this.

Banks and other recipients of checks from your account may hassle you by placing a hold for an unreasonable number of days on the funds from your checks. For checks that you write yourself, the hold is understandable because the check recipient has no way of knowing if the money will be in the account when the check is ready to clear. But if the check was issued by the fund company from your account, then the money has already been taken from your account, so the check is almost as good as cash to recipients — they just need to wait a couple of days for receipt of the funds.

Banks will normally place up to a five-day hold on out-of-state checks (odds are that your fund company clears checks through an out-of-state bank). If a bank doesn't make the money available to you quickly, ask to speak to the branch manager or some other higher-up. Gently remind them that you can move your bank accounts to a less bureaucratic bank.

What to do about checks lost in the mail

Checks and other stuff do get lost in the mail. If you wrote the check and made it payable to the fund company, there's no big need to stop payment. If you're depositing checks that someone else wrote to you, they may want to stop payment if they are concerned you might cash it.

What's a bigger pain is having to re-do account applications that you may have sent with the check(s). If you do tons of applications and transfer forms, you may want to keep copies.

Registered mail and certified mail don't eliminate the problem of lost mail. They just tell whether or not the mail was received. I wouldn't waste the money or the time needed to go to the post office to do this.

Wiring and electronic funds transfers are other alternatives that you may prefer because you don't need to wait for a paper check to clear. If you just realized you need money to close on a home purchase tomorrow, these are your best bets. See the earlier section on "Making Deposits in a Flash" for how these services work.

For retirement account withdrawals, requests need to be done in writing. Perhaps you need to withdraw money before the end of December due to the IRS mandatory withdrawals following age $70\frac{1}{2}$. The good news here is that you don't need to have received the funds before the end of the year. As long as the distribution is made by the end of December, it doesn't matter to the IRS if the check takes several days to reach you.

Changing Options after You Open Your Account

Perhaps now you wish you had check writing on your money fund. Or you want to establish a regular monthly investment plan so that money is sent electronically from your bank account to some funds. How do you add these features now?

Although you can add some features over the phone, unfortunately most features, particularly those that require your signature — such as check writing — can only be set up through short forms you request by phone. Options previously established, such as reinvestment of dividends, can be changed over the phone.

Changing the registration of your accounts is more of a pain. A letter is generally required, for example, if you marry and change your name or want to add your spouse to the account. A *signature guarantee* may be required — these are provided by banks and brokerage firms. Don't confuse this with getting something notarized, which is different.

Why did my fund plunge?

You don't follow your funds every day, and on the days that you do check the price per share, it typically goes up or down a few cents. One day, usually soon after you talk with a friend and mention how pleased you are with your fund's returns, you receive a rude awakening.

"It dropped $1.21 per share!"

That's what one of my clients said to me after noticing the price of one of her international stock funds in December. Guess what? The fund made a distribution that reduced the price per share but increased the number of shares. So she didn't lose that after all.

If you follow your funds through the daily newspaper and you see such a large price drop, look again to see if any special letters are after the fund's name, such as "x," which indicates that a fund paid its dividend, and "e" for payment of a capital gains distribution.

Making Sense of Your Statements and Profits

Can't understand your fund statement and how much if any money your fund is making for you? Welcome to a large and not very exclusive club. See Chapter 11.

TIP

If you want a tax, financial, or legal advisor or a helpful relative to help you keep an eye on your investments, you can ask that they be listed on your account as an *interested party* to receive duplicate statements. Simply write to the fund company, listing the accounts you'd like the interested party to receive statements for and that person's name and mailing address.

Changing Addresses

Normally fund companies require that you make your change of address in writing, but slowly over time more fund companies are establishing security procedures that allow you to note your change of address by phone. The safeguards include a requirement that you prove that you are you on the phone (give your mother's maiden name and all that); the fund companies also mail confirmations of the changed address to both old and new addresses.

Finding Funds You Forgot to Move with You

Every year, people literally throw away hundreds of millions of dollars in investments, including investments in mutual funds. You may have done this if you've moved around a lot without systematically sending changes of address to fund companies and placing mail-forwarding orders with the post office. After fund companies try for a long time to send mail to your old address, they eventually throw in the towel, and your account becomes dormant. No more statements are sent for a number of years, after which your account is considered abandoned!

By law, the mutual fund company must transfer your abandoned money to the treasurer's office (called *escheatment*, for you Scrabble and Trivial Pursuit buffs) of the state in which the fund company does business or the state in which the last registered address appeared on your account. This may happen from within a few years to more than a decade after the fund company loses contact with you. If you don't claim the property within a certain number of years after that, the state gets to keep it.

If you vaguely recall that you had funds with a particular fund company way back when, call the company. You don't need to remember the specific funds you invested in. Through your name, Social Security number, old mailing addresses, and personal stuff like that, the fund company's computer system can find your accounts and determine whether they were turned over to the state. You can also try contacting the state treasurer's office in the states in which you have lived to see if they have any of your abandoned accounts. If you find your accounts, please write me in care of the publisher and let me know — these things make me feel all warm and fuzzy inside.

Account Transfer Snags

Transferring accounts from one investment firm or bank to another can be a big pain. Even obtaining the correct transfer paperwork and completing it is a challenge. I explain how to do it in Chapter 10.

Problems happen most often with retirement accounts and also with brokerage account transfers. Some firms are reluctant to give up your money and so they drag their feet, doing everything they can to make your life and the lives of employees who transfer accounts at your new investment company a nightmare. The biggest culprits are the supposed "full service" brokerage firms (for instance, Prudential, Smith Barney Shearson, Dean Witter, Merrill Lynch) that employ commission-based brokers. They've lost a lot of money flowing out to no-load and discount brokers' mutual funds, and they do what they can to hang on. The unfortunate reality is that they will cheerfully set up a new account to accept your money on a moment's notice, but they will drag their feet, sometimes for months, when it comes time to relinquish your money.

 Don't be deterred from moving your money into a better investment firm. Remember that the transfer should, under securities industry regulations, be done within 30 days. If it's not, hammer the villains! If the transfer is not completed within a month, get in touch with your new investment firm to determine what the problem is. If your old company is not cooperating, a call to a manager there may help to get the ball rolling. To light a fire under their behinds, tell the manager at the old firm that you're sending letters to the National Association of Securities Dealers (NASD) and the Securities and Exchange Commission (SEC) if they don't complete your transfer within the next week.

In addition to uncooperative brokers, certain assets present problems with transfers. If you purchase any mutual funds at, say, Dean Witter that are Dean Witter house mutual funds, in addition to buying into a relatively crummy family of funds, you also can't transfer their funds as they are. You must first have them liquidated through Dean Witter so that the cash proceeds can be transferred. Most annuities work the same way.

 Transfer individual securities, such as stocks and bonds, to a discount broker. That way, if you later decide to sell them, you save on commission charges. Limited partnerships generally can't be liquidated, and everybody charges decent size fees to hold them — another reason not to buy them in the first place. If you want less account clutter, transfer these to the discount broker you're otherwise going to be using.

Eliminating Fund Marketing Material and Calls

Some mutual fund companies fill your mailbox with tons of marketing materials on all sorts of new funds, old funds, and everything but the kitchen sink.

 If you do business with many companies and their marketing folks are driving you batty, call your fund companies and ask them to code your account on their advanced computer systems so that you won't receive anything other than statements. Fund companies are required under Securities and Exchange Commission regulations to do this. Fund companies are happy to oblige — they don't want irritated customers.

As for all the other junk mail you get thanks to firms that sell mailing lists, fight back, and spare a couple of trees, by sending your request not to receive junk mail to the Direct Marketing Association, Mail Preference Service, 1101 17th St. NW, Suite 900, Washington, D.C. 10036-4704.

Some fund companies and brokers may call you at home soliciting your purchase of investments. They tend to focus on people with large cash balances sitting in their accounts. As Nancy Reagan said to kids about using drugs, "Just say no!" To stop fund sellers from calling you in the future, you've got the Telephone Consumer Act on your side. This act allows you to request the fund company (or anyone else for that matter who solicits you by phone) to cease and desist! The fund company will note on their computers to stop calling you.

Digging Out from Under All Those Statements

If you're being buried in paperwork from statements and transaction confirmations from so many fund companies and can't see the big picture anymore, consider consolidating your fund holdings through a discount broker. There are tradeoffs involved — you'll pay more in fees for the convenience these accounts offer (see Chapter 4).

Getting Account Statements from the Past

Perhaps, for reasons of nostalgia or taxes, you need copies of a statement that's more than a year old. Most companies should have no problem providing it. They may, however, charge you something like $10 per fund per year requested. So be choosy. The main reason you'd think about doing this is for non-retirement accounts in order to identify the cost of some shares bought way back when.

If you're going to sell all the shares that you hold in a fund, check to see if your fund will report the average cost of the shares sold. If their accounting system can do this, you're golden and you don't need to bother with getting the old statements. (See Chapter 12 for more details on tax issues to consider when selling funds.)

Part IV
For the Glutton: More Information and Advice

Reprinted with permission

In this part...

This part covers other stuff you may *want* to know but don't really *need* to know. Perhaps you've received tons of junk (er, I mean, direct) mail from Mr. Fund Knowitall or you've just watched Ms. MarketTiming Guru on television and want to know whether you should follow their prognostications and pearls of wisdom. Or maybe you're one of those impatient types who wants to know now (instead of when your fund company sends you statements) how your funds are doing. This part lets you indulge such gluttonous desires to the hilt. Here you'll master how to evaluate gurus, newsletters, and turn your computer into an investment intelligence agency.

Chapter 14

Fund Ratings, Gurus, and *Still More* Funds? — The Good, the Bad, and the Ugly

. . . .

In This Chapter

▶ Stuff to line your bird cage with

▶ Newsletter Hall of Shame

▶ Use and abuse of fund ratings

▶ The best newsletters and information sources

▶ Closed-end funds

. . . .

*E*ven after an almost-all-you-can-eat meal, some people still aren't satisfied. They want more! Fine, no problem. As the chief chef for this meal, I'm honestly not personally offended.

Consider my father, for example. He loves data and analyzing things. He likes to figure out how things work. I should warn you that when he was still working (he's now retired), he worked as a mechanical engineer (impressively, he worked his entire career in one field). He loves to make charts and graphs. During the months that I wrote this book, he was poring over a veritable truckload of data and information on mutual funds and investing.

So I wrote this chapter for people like my dad. Even if you're not an engineer by training, there may be a bit of a data lover in you. The challenge as you navigate the landscape of mutual fund data, newsletters, references, and gurus is discerning the good from the merely mediocre — as well as from downright useless and dangerous information and advice. Unfortunately, more of the latter are out there waiting to trip you up.

Stuff to Avoid

Why start with the bad stuff? Simple. There's so much of it out there, and odds are good that you may currently be using some of it, or thinking of using it, or it may be pitched to you in the future. Learning the tricks of the trade enables you to better identify the good stuff. But if you're pressed for time and can't bear to see the ugly side of the newsletter business, skip ahead to the good sources that I recommend later in this chapter (software and online services are covered in Chapter 15).

Market timing doesn't work — and neither do crystal balls

Many fund investors believe that they can increase their chances of success if they follow the prognostications of certain gurus. Many gurus say (or imply) that they can tell you when you should be in or out of the markets. Whenever a guru near you treats you to such "wisdom," just repeat after me:

> "No one can predict the future."
>
> "No one can predict the future."
>
> "No one can predict the future."

If you can remember this one simple fact — a fact supported by mountains of evidence and plenty of good old-fashioned common sense — you will dramatically increase your chances for successful investing in funds and decrease the odds of making major mistakes. *And* you'll have a much clearer vision about what resources to use for further reading and research about funds.

If a newsletter writer knows something and you do, too (when you read the newsletter), then it's old news and already reflected in the prices in the securities markets. If newsletter writers did have a knack for unearthing information that no one else typically knew, they wouldn't be wasting their time publishing a newsletter because they could be making millions investing based on their predictions.

Newsletters that purport to time the markets, that tell you the right time to get into and out of certain securities (or the market in general), are doomed to failure in the long run. Over the long term, such a strategy simply will not beat a buy-and-hold approach. In most cases, such timing will lead to inferior returns.

The biggest land mines to avoid in your hunt for good information are the many investment newsletters from self-proclaimed investing gurus eager to make themselves — rather than you — wealthy. Over extended periods of time, very few newsletters beat the market averages. And those that do beat them do so by very tiny amounts — such as a few _tenths_ of one percent per year, after you adjust for the risk that they take. In fact, according to the _Hulbert Financial Digest_ (see next section), only four newsletters over the past decade have kept ahead of the market averages, even by these paltry amounts. The worst have greatly underperformed the market averages and some even would have caused you to lose money during a decade when the financial markets performed very, very well.

But here's the catch: you'd never know about newsletters' dismal performances if all you ever listened to were the claims made by newsletter writers themselves. Most claim that they avoided investing when the stock market crashed in 1987, and they even claim that they told their loyal followers to sell everything just before the bottom fell out. They also usually go on to proclaim that they avoided other major declines and bought at every bottom.

Rated #1 by the Hulbert Financial Digest

Too many mutual fund newsletters claim that they were rated #1 by the _Hulbert Financial Digest_. Mark Hulbert started a very useful business in the 1980s. Almost every investment newsletter was making outrageous claims about how well its previous predictions had done. But how could you, the potential new subscriber, know if a newsletter was telling the truth or blowing smoke? Answer: You couldn't.

Not until Mark Hulbert came along, that is. He tracks how the newsletters' investment picks actually perform. For each newsletter, he creates a portfolio based exactly on the newsletter's recommendations. So, over time, Hulbert knows exactly how the newsletters' picks have done.

Reprinted with permission

But we're also #1 according to . . .

Needing to find others who say that they are *numero uno,* newsletters also cite rankings from other organizations, such as *Timer's Digest.* Again, the same problems that force you to qualify the Hulbert ratings come into play with other newsletter rankings. Given enough time periods and categories of newsletters, many people can claim the coveted #1 spot at some time or another.

Newsletters also refer to awards they've won from the Newsletter Publisher's Association (NPA). My advice: ignore NPA awards. They're meaningless. They have nothing to do with the performance of a newsletter's advice. And because the NPA is an association made up *of the newsletters themselves* (!), they're just giving

themselves a pat on the back! Not a very objective way to dole out awards, eh? (Not being a large association and always doling out awards doesn't hurt newsletter writers' chances of winning, either.)

And, of course, there are the inevitable customer testimonials. Curiously, though, testimonials almost always parrot what's in the promotional material for the newsletter and they never include the person's name. All they provide are the person's initials, such as B.S., and good old B.S.'s home, such as Brooklyn, N.Y. Some of these testimonials are made up — so they really are B.S.!

Has the *Hulbert Financial Digest* stopped the outrageous claims? No, but things seem to be slowly getting better, thanks to Hulbert's influence. The problem still is that people believe the marketing hype of the newsletters and never bother to check with Hulbert's service.

Hulbert's service has created another problem, however. Many newsletters can claim to be #1 by selecting short time periods when they actually were #1. Some falsely lay claim to #1 status by simply comparing their performance to all those that are worse while ignoring the ones that perform better!

Hire us as money managers

Many newsletter writers publish newsletters as a means of drawing people into their money management business. For some, that's the only reason they do the newsletter. So they don't really want to teach you too much about investing — which means that you read articles in their newsletters about how complicated fund investing is and how timing is everything.

Some newsletters that are already short on content plug their money management service *right in the newsletter*. One monthly that sells for more than $100 per year publishes issues that typically are 20 pages long, 16 pages of which are filler; an example of such filler is performance numbers for funds — numbers that you can get for a few bucks a month by picking up one of the many financial magazines that contain such data (or 75 cents for a copy of the *Wall Street Journal*). In the four pages of articles in the typical newsletter, you often confront a plug for the editor's money management business because (according to him) a newsletter's advice can't substitute for the daily oversight of your portfolio.

Please.

Don't believe it. Of course, this isn't what they told you in their marketing materials to get you to subscribe to the newsletter.

Investment Newsletter Hall of Shame

Here are some of the many examples of the really heavy stuff that gets shoveled by some of these folks to sell you on their investment newsletters.

Stephen Leeb's Personal Finance

A veteran newsletter writer, Leeb's newsletter marketing materials issue the following proclamation about Leeb: "A Millionaire Maker Outsmarts the Market. Again." In a glossy, multi-page brochure, Leeb is said to have "the highest I.Q. of them all . . . somewhere between Einstein, Mother Theresa, and an IBM mainframe."

His literature goes on to say, "the reason he can expand your money by 30% to 50% a year is sheer mental horsepower." You're also told that his newsletter is rated #1 by "both of the major rating services."

Leeb's materials assert that he has developed a brilliant and totally awesome proprietary model, which he calls the "Master Key Indicator." His claim is that this model has predicted the last 28 (count 'em, 28) upturns in the market in a row without a single miss. The odds of doing this, according to Leeb, are more than 268 million to 1!

Consider how much money he claims he could have made for you had you invested $10,000 in 1980 according to the prognostications of his Master Key Indicator. His chart shows that, although you would have had to settle for ending up with a measly $176,412 if you had invested in the Fidelity Magellan fund, the best-performing mutual fund over that time period, Leeb's system to beat the system would have allowed you to amass $45,219,074! His marketing materials come complete with charts in case the numbers don't wallop you over your head. Too good to be true? Of course it is! Leeb's figures work out to a 91 percent per year return!

Don't want such high-stakes investing? No problem, says Leeb. Simply "choose your own profit level." Using portfolios of what he calls "stodgy" and "ultra safe" mutual funds, Leeb says that he can make you 32 percent per year and make sure that you never lose more than 1.5 percent in a year.

How good is Leeb at investing? Here's some unadulterated proof. In 1991, Leeb established a mutual fund, Leeb Personal Finance. It's been one of the worst growth stock funds during the almost four years it's been around. His fund has underperformed about 90 percent of its peers and has underperformed the market averages every year of its existence.

Jay Schabacker's Mutual Fund Investing

"America's #1 Mutual Fund Advisor."

I remember Schabacker's name as if it were my own because for a while, it seemed, once a month I would receive a glossy color brochure more than 20 pages long from him in the mail. Like Leeb, Schabacker claims to have been rated #1 by Hulbert. Hulbert says about this, "It is a fabrication. Mutual Fund Investing is not now, nor has it ever been, rated number one by my digest." Hulbert was so incensed by Schabacker's claim that he devoted an entire column, appropriately entitled "Lies and near lies," to setting the record straight in *Forbes* magazine.

Soon after Hulbert's scathing column about Schabacker appeared in *Forbes,* in Schabacker's next mailing he changed his tune a bit. His January 1992 marketing materials displayed a colorful chart showing that his stock and bond fund picks returned 1,517% from 1975 to 1990 — for a nearly 20 percent annualized rate of return, which would have outperformed the famous Fidelity Magellan fund and Peter Lynch. This would imply that his advice had beaten the average stock fund, which returned just 14.7% per year, and the average bond fund, at 9.1% per year, by some distance significantly greater than a country mile.

Like many fund investing newsletter writers, Schabacker also says to avoid index funds — he actually calls them "blind average index" funds because, he says, they are "headed for trouble in the 1990s." Why? Simple: Schabacker reasons that index funds specialize in stocks of large, well-known companies, the very firms that made big bucks in the 1980s from corporate mergers and the like. But as we discussed in Chapter 9 of this book, index funds don't just invest in large-company stocks.

Other investment gurus and the media

I could fill an entire book with all the shameful and deceptive marketing that goes on in the investment newsletter business. Investment gurus come and go. Some of them get their 15 minutes of fame on the basis of one or two successful predictions.

Joe Granville, for example, has long been known for making outrageous and extreme stock market predictions and has been quoted in many financial publications. And his was the #1 newsletter, according to the *Hulbert Financial Digest,* in 1989. That part was true, actually. The only trouble was that, in the decade ending December 31, 1993, one of the best decades ever for the stock market (the Wilshire 5000 index of all U.S. stocks produced a return of 555 percent), followers of Granville's advice *lost* 96 percent!

Then there's Charles Givens, whose books and interviews were chock-full of bad advice in the 1980s. His books advised people to "invest in only one mutual fund at a time" because there can be only one right type depending on the state of the economy. He claimed that if you paid him hundreds of dollars for his audio tapes and financial library, he'd show you how to make more than 20 percent per year in the stock market.

And then there's the former Shearson stock market analyst Elaine Garzarelli, one of the thousands of gurus who supposedly predicted the stock market's crash in the fall of 1987. Garzarelli's fund, Smith Barney Shearson Sector Analysis, was established just before the crash. Supposedly, Garzarelli's indicators warned her to stay out of stocks, which she did, and in so doing saved her fund from the plunge. Shearson quickly motivated its brokers to sell shares in Garzarelli's fund. Thanks to all the free publicity she got from being interviewed just about everywhere, investors soon poured nearly $700 million into this fund.

These investors ended up being sorry. In 1988, Garzarelli's fund was the worst-performing fund among growth stock funds. From 1988 to 1990, Garzarelli's fund underperformed the S&P 500 average by about 43 percent! So even the few investors who were in her fund *before* the crash in 1987 (when Garzarelli's fund outperformed the S&P 500 by about 26 percent) still lost. What she saved her investors by avoiding the crash she lost back (and then some) in the years that followed.

The moral of these stories is simple: Stop guru-watching. And here's an idea for the financial media. Although they have done much good to help educate investors, I challenge them to do their homework before they rush to interview people for predictions. Doing fewer guru pieces would be a step in the right direction as well. Such pieces are detrimental to many investors because they undermine people's confidence in being able to make sense of and succeed in the financial market on their own.

You also should note that this newsletter "all-star team" in 1992 included world income funds in place of U.S. bond funds because, as Schabacker noted, yields were much higher overseas, and such funds were growing fast "for good reason." This call proved to be another bad decision.

Hulbert's tracking of Schabacker's recommendations clearly shows that if a fund investor had followed his advice, the investor would be worse off than he would have been if he had just thrown all of his money in index funds and forgotten about the money. Schabacker's portfolio returns fell well *below* the market averages.

Newsletters cost you time and money — many cost up to several hundred dollars per year. Ignore the predictions and speculations of self-proclaimed gurus (the Jeane Dixons of the investment world). Never use a newsletter for predictive advice. If people were that smart about the future of financial markets, they would be successful money managers making lots more money. The only types of investment newsletters and periodicals that you should consider subscribing to are those that offer research and information rather than predictions. And those publications are what we're going to discuss next.

The Good Stuff

If you want to read more, by all means read more. But read *useful* information. Most of the better financial magazines and newspapers, for example, cost a fraction of what the newsletters do and provide more useful stuff.

Many of the major financial publications — *Barron's*, *Business Week*, *Financial World*, *Forbes*, *Fortune*, *Kiplinger's Personal Finance*, *Money*, *SmartMoney*, the *Wall Street Journal*, and *Worth* — do annual mutual fund roundups. Most newspapers and many large news magazines like *Newsweek*, for example, and television programs such as those on PBS and CNBC provide fund coverage as well.

There are some good newsletters, too. I'll get to those in a moment, but first we must discuss what has become a national obsession: rating mutual funds.

Mutual confusion: misuse of fund ratings

By all means, check out the business and financial magazines, newspapers, and the better newsletters in the rest of this chapter. But, I need to caution you about fund ratings. The most common mistake investors make in using even the better mutual fund publications is focusing too much on the ranking of specific funds. Allow me to illustrate my point with a person who called me not too long ago — a person who made many of the mistakes that can be made when examining fund ratings. Judging from experience, unfortunately, she has lots of company.

In early 1994, I got a call from a woman I'll call Ellen. Ellen asked if she should switch out of her investments in the Vanguard Wellington and Vanguard Star funds and put her money instead into the Fidelity Balanced fund. Fresh from a trip to the local library, she sounded like the financial equivalent of a weatherman spewing forth data on these funds' performance, saying, "Fidelity Balanced returned 19.3% in 1993 and has averaged 14.2% over the past five years, whereas Vanguard's Wellington returned only 13.5% last year and 12.4% over the past five years and Star just 11% last year and 11.7% over the past five years." All of the funds Ellen was reviewing were balanced funds, which hold a diversified mixture of stocks and bonds.

And if the raw performance numbers weren't enough to confirm her sub-par investment selections, Ellen also rattled off the Lipper ratings, which "ranked" the Fidelity Balanced fund as an "A" fund, whereas Vanguard Wellington and Vanguard Star both earned the less-than-stellar grade of "C". Just as in the classroom, "A" is the highest ranking a fund can get (the top 20 percent get it) from the rankings, which are provided by Lipper Analytical Services. Perhaps in order not to insult any fund companies, the bottom 20 percent get an "E" (presumably for making the *E*ffort, instead of a more common "F"). These ratings are largely worthless: there's no accounting for risk, and funds are lumped into broad categories. The performance rankings that wind up in some newspapers can be for periods as short as *one year* (which is the figure that Ellen saw).

Although Ellen said she was calling to get my opinion, she already had out the third and mightiest of nails — the Morningstar ratings — to be hammered into the Vanguard funds' coffin. Fidelity Balanced earned the most coveted five-star rating — the investment equivalent of a Siskel and Ebert movie rating of two thumbs up. "Vanguard Wellington has four stars and Vanguard Star just three," said Ellen with dejection. A true information junkie, Ellen also cited several recent magazine rankings of funds that confirmed her suspicion that something was amiss with her fund investments.

Although I've always enjoyed numbers and statistics, too (it's probably just a genetic condition I got from my dad), I still find it hard to believe how some mutual fund rankings can make such wrong-headed comparisons that lead smart folks like Ellen in the wrong direction. It's completely unfair and invalid to compare the Fidelity Balanced fund with Vanguard's Wellington or Star fund! Fidelity's offering invests a significant portion of its assets overseas, around 50 percent at most times. Vanguard's funds focus on U.S. investments.

A couple of years earlier, Ellen had chosen to invest internationally through separate funds. She held the Vanguard International Growth and Warburg Pincus International Equity funds, which were up 44 percent and 51 percent, respectively, the year before. (These funds weren't on steroids — international funds had a banner 1993.)

So the Fidelity Balanced fund isn't necessarily better just because it has posted higher performance numbers than its balanced peers — remember that we're comparing apples with oranges. To be fair, the Fidelity Balanced fund should be compared with other balanced mutual funds that invest worldwide, not those that invest just in the U.S. Or, as in Ellen's case, it could be compared to creating your own worldwide balanced fund. Ellen's returns, factoring in her separate international fund holdings, actually bested those produced by the Fidelity Balanced fund — she didn't realize this until she did some calculations. When she did, she was happy to keep what she had.

Without going into all the technicalities of how Morningstar calculates its star ratings for funds, I'll just say this: basically, Morningstar looks at what's called *risk-adjusted performance.* Risk is measured by the volatility of a fund's share price over time. Because international securities don't always move in tandem with U.S. securities, a fund's holding of both types generally lessens the volatility of the fund's value. Thus, funds that diversify in this way have an unfair leg up in the Morningstar ratings game.

Morningstar No-Load Funds

Morningstar's mutual fund publication, *No-Load Funds,* is a bit like the cities of Hong Kong and Tokyo. Every square inch of its single-page fund summaries (printed on 8½-by-11-inch pages) is put to use and *packed* with information.

What's most valuable about these one-pagers is that they can save you time. If you want a snapshot summary of lots of data, as well as some thoughtful analysis about a fund you are considering investing in or currently own, Morningstar can't be beat. Most of what's summarized on its pages comes from a fund's prospectus and semi-annual reports. Some of the data that is provided for funds would take you hours to calculate and would require a sophisticated computer software program.

Many public libraries subscribe to Morningstar. A one-year subscription costs $145 per year; a three-month trial subscription costs you $45 (you can take one of these once every two years). Morningstar — as well as discount brokers Charles Schwab and Fidelity — also sells single pages for the funds of your choice. Fidelity and Schwab charge less — typically a few bucks per report if you buy several pages, whereas Morningstar charges $5 each.

Morningstar also produces another publication called *Morningstar Mutual Funds.* This publication covers more funds than *No-Load Funds* does because it includes load funds (funds that carry commissions) as well as no-load funds. As

I explain in Chapter 3, loads are an additional and unnecessary cost to buy funds that are sold through brokers. If you have load funds that you want to evaluate, *Morningstar Mutual Funds* can help (check for it at your local library or get a three-month trial subscription for $55 ☎ 800-876-5005).

Using a Morningstar bond fund page

As I said earlier, Morningstar packs a lot of data on a page, so folks like my father love it (see Figure 14-1). For others, it makes their head spin. The hard part is knowing what to look at and what to make of the information. I'll highlight some of the more useful features to examine for bond funds that you may be considering. I'll jump around their page a bit so that I can work from the bigger picture issues toward more of the details.

Morningstar's pages are hard to read with all of their small print. (Although she and I both have good eyesight, when my wife saw one of their pages she suggested taking it to a copy shop to enlarge it!)

❶ Investment Objectives. From the prospectus, a summary of the general investment objectives and limitations that a fund subjects itself to.

❷ Portfolio Managers. Highlights work and educational background of the fund's managers — good cocktail party chatter! The date the manager(s) started managing the particular fund is noted.

❸ Performance. The first section displays the total amount that investors made or lost (from dividends, capital gains, and share price changes) for each quarter over the past five years. This section can give you a sense of the likely volatility of an investment in the fund (remember, though, that this is history, and the future likely will differ). If you get queasy looking at these numbers, then don't invest.

The "trailing" returns section shows annualized total return information over longer time periods. (Total return numbers do not account for loads, but you're not going to pay any anyway, are you?) The fund's returns are also compared to benchmark indexes, which in some cases aren't so comparable. The Lehman Brothers bond index used here is an intermediate-term maturity index. Such an index isn't valid for comparing all funds, but it isn't bad for this bond fund, which typically invests in intermediate- to longer-term bonds. For some odd reason, Morningstar doesn't compare bond funds to indexes of appropriate maturities — short-, intermediate-, and long-term (see Chapter 11 for more background on benchmarks).

❹ Portfolio Analysis. This data is summarized from a fund's most recent semi-annual report. Note the total number of securities this fund holds (25 bonds) and the listing of the top 25 holdings (which in this case happens to be all of them).

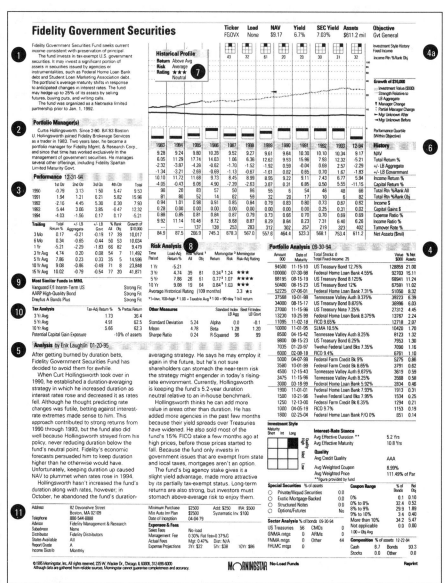

Figure 14-1:
Morningstar
page for a
bond fund.

Source: Morningstar

The *Investment Style Box* shows you what types of bonds the fund mainly holds at the moment (in this case, high-quality, long-term bonds). Interest rate sensitivity measures — average maturity and duration (both of which I explain in Chapter 7) — are provided here, as well as the average credit quality of the fund's bonds. (**4a:** Note the little style boxes for each year so that you can see how the fund's style has varied, if at all, over time.)

The *Special Securities* section highlights the fund's holdings in riskier types of securities, including derivatives (which are discussed in Chapter 1). All things being equal, it's best to see zeros here, but some funds use, for example, options to hedge or reduce the risk of the fund. The empty circle to the left of each risky security name implies that the fund is allowed to hold these types of securities (a dash implies it can't).

Sector analysis quantifies the fund's current holdings of the major types of bonds. See Chapter 7 for definitions. *Composition* details the fund's recent holdings of cash, bonds, and other securities. Composition is worth looking at to determine if a fund really is what it says it is.

5. **Analysis.** Each fund at Morningstar is assigned an analyst. Each analyst then uses available information, as well as interviews with fund company managers (and others) and data on this page, to summarize the fund strategies. This is usually a section well worth reading, especially if you're *not* a numbers kind of person.

6. **History.** Here's a data dump of all sorts of information for the fund over more than the past 11 years. Here you can see how the total return, performance versus benchmarks, dividend (income), capital gains, the fund's annual operating expenses, and trading (turnover) have varied over the years.

7. **Historical Profile.** Without a doubt, the most overused and abused part of the Morningstar page. Funds are given ratings of past performance and volatility from one (worst) to five (best) stars. All things being equal, funds that have produced greater returns with less volatility are given higher ratings. I discussed some problems with fund ratings earlier in this chapter. Another problem with this ranking is this: when a type of fund is out of favor (as international stock funds were from 1990 to 1992, in comparison to U.S. stock funds) they have low star ratings. Funds with track records as short as three years can have the highest rating, even though they may not have endured a down period for the market.

The good folks at Morningstar say that "…funds with 3, 4, and 5 stars often make the most sense for many investors." I think that says it well — you can't really say much more about the star rating system than that. More stars are *not* necessarily better than less and vice versa.

8. Risk Analysis. Here you see more details for the determination of the ranking and how the fund rates over different periods. You also see the fund's average star rating over all the months that it has received a rating. This average rating provides a sense of the consistency of the fund's rating over time.

All sorts of other quantitative measurements of risk are presented here. One of the more useful is *beta,* which helps you to calibrate the volatility of a fund compared to relevant benchmarks. The overall bond market benchmark is assigned a beta of 1.00. Thus, a fund with a beta of 1.2 implies that it is 20 percent more volatile on average (perhaps because it invests in longer-term bonds or lower-credit quality bonds).

9. Most Similar Funds. Names funds that have behaved similarly to this fund. This may help you to identify other comparative funds, but don't assume that these other funds are all that similar — check out the rest of the information on *their* pages.

10. Tax Analysis. This section provides some insightful measures of a fund's tax-efficiency or tax-friendliness. If you're investing in a fund inside a retirement account, ignore this section. If you're not investing inside a retirement account, the tax-adjusted return column shows what your effective return would have been in this fund over various periods if all of the dividend and capital gains distributions that a fund makes are taxed at the highest possible federal tax rate.

Potential Capital Gains Exposure measures how much, if any, unrealized profit exists. The larger the number here, the greater the potential risk of larger distributions in the future, particularly for funds that trade a lot (that is, that have a high turnover), as this one does. Make sure to examine historically how much the fund has distributed (see my discussion of (**6**), *History,* just a few paragraphs ago).

11. Address, telephone, and other such stuff. Here's where you see how to get in touch with the fund, its minimum investment amounts, how often it pays dividends, and so on. Note the last line in the expenses and fees section: *Annual Brokerage Cost.* This cost is the one additional cost of a fund beyond the expense ratio that Morningstar covers in **6**, *History.*

Using a Morningstar stock fund page

Morningstar's stock fund pages carry much of the same types of information that their bond fund pages carry (see Figure 14-2). I won't repeat my explanations of the same sections covered for a bond fund page (to see what I would be repeating if I *did* talk about it here, skip back to the preceding section). Sections 4 and 6 are the only ones with great differences on a stock fund page.

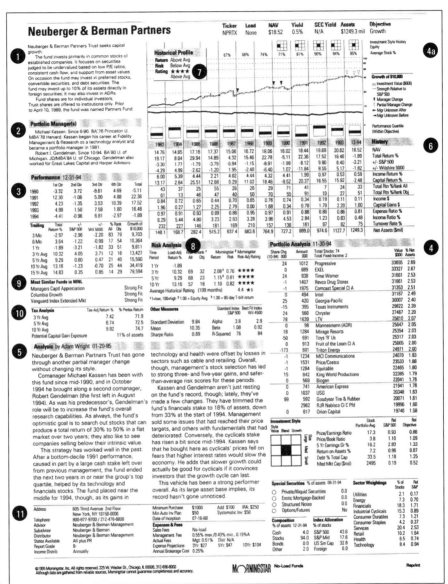

Figure 14-2:
Morningstar page for a stock fund.

Source: Morningstar

4. Portfolio Analysis. The most important area that's different on a Morningstar stock fund page versus one of their bond fund pages is the summary of what's in a fund. That's no surprise, though, because we're talking about funds that invest in quite different securities now: stocks.

As with the bond fund page, the total number of securities held is noted, and a list of the top 25 holdings, along with the number of shares held and how that number has changed recently, also shows up here.

Investment Style here classifies a fund's current stock holdings based on the size of company, as well as on whether those stocks tend to be growth, value, or both (I cover the difference between these types of funds in Chapter 8). A variety of statistical measures are also presented for the stocks that the fund holds. For example, you can see the average rate of growth in the earnings of the companies that this fund invests in and how that rate compares to that of the S&P 500 index.

Composition is also useful for seeing whether a fund is holding major cash positions and whether it invests in securities other than stocks. *Index Allocation* is especially useful for figuring a stock fund's personality even further; it goes into detail about the fund's holdings of different sizes of company stocks and foreign holdings. *Sector Weightings* breaks down a fund's stock holdings by industry and again compares the performances of the fund's holdings to performances of the S&P 500 index. (This particular fund is more heavily invested in financial, service, and retail company stocks.)

6. History. Note the use here of different benchmark indexes suitable for stock funds. The graph also indicates — with small arrow heads — when one of the fund's managers changed.

No-Load Fund Analyst

Those who enjoy doing more reading about funds and the financial markets should consider the *No-Load Fund Analyst* newsletter, which tracks a much smaller universe of the better no-load funds than Morningstar does. This monthly publication carries a lot of commentary and in-depth analysis of trends in the economy, happenings in the fund industry, and fund manager interviews and profiles (see Figure 14-3). In an industry in which many publications claim that they can double your money in a snap if you become a subscriber, the *No-Load Fund Analyst* is a breath of fresh air: it includes no hype or inflated marketing claims.

Personal interviews and the tracking of individual fund managers are unique and valuable aspects of this publication, which is edited by Ken Gregory, Craig Litman, and Mark Headley.

No-Load Fund Analyst

FUND MANAGER UPDATES: JANUS FUND

Janus Fund/Jim Craig: We spoke with Craig on 12/15. Janus Fund's cash position is 41%, up significantly from 13% in July (which was the lowest level in years). Craig reports he sold many large positions after the end of their fiscal year (October). He had intended to use the cash to buy growth stocks (Craig is still optimistic about the resurgence of growth stocks and compressed PEs look attractive), but became extremely pessimistic about the market in the face of an accelerating economy (further fueled by overseas growth), inflation and (in response) continued interest rate hikes. Craig feels he must be patient and avoid "getting killed". He is not sure about the timing, and will not venture to guess about the direction of the markets, but says there must be a real economic slowdown before he feels more comfortable. He is surprised the market has been as strong as it's been. Craig is seeing the threat of inflation at the company level. Price increases may become a serious issue in the early part of 1995. One danger sign: WalMart's average revenue per item is increasing for the first time in years, and the company is not fighting suppliers on price increases. Craig says raw materials prices are way up (the price of an aluminium can is up 30%). He also sees wage inflation as a real problem in a tight labor market except on the coasts. A handful of company executives Craig has met with recently (but the fund does not own) are "panicking" over having to pay higher wages to keep their workers.

The portfolio is very diversified with about 100 stocks. The largest industry concentrations are in health care (12%) and financials (9%). The rest of the fund is an eclectic collection of stocks. Craig has sold economically-sensitive stocks that have had good runs but have peaked, including GM, DuPont and Caterpillar. Freddie Mac, Fannie Mae and Merrill Lynch were sold because of yield curve pressures. He has taken profits in foreign stocks TeleDanmark and Philips Electronics (the fund now has 9% overseas), WalMart (Craig's bet on the success of WalMart's Sams Clubs did not pan out), MCI (suffering from competitive "vengeance" of AT&T) and Gillette (high valuations). He has added to Pfizer, General Re, Lin Broadcasting , Newell and Browning-Ferris. Drug company Astra is a new position, now the second largest holding in the portfolio. Craig still believes in the prospects for Unum (disability insurer) even though the stock has not done well in the wake of the health care debate. The company has bought back 38% of its stock in the last three years. He also remains confident about railroads (3% of the fund), where there is a lot of merger activity. Assets are at $9.4 billion with cash flows mostly flat. Craig says if the market takes off in January, he will sit it out and deploy the cash when he's more comfortable with the inflation/interest rate outlook. Craig has hired two more analysts and reiterated his relief about giving up management duties on small cap Janus Venture ("I should have done it a year earlier").

NLFA Comment: Janus Fund was down 1.1 % for 1994. Jim Craig's move into cash helped the fund avoid serious damage in the tough fourth quarter. Craig frequently retreats to cash when he anticipates market declines. While the fund posted one of the better performances among Mid/Large Cap Growth-at-a-Price funds for the year, Janus trailed a handful of more fully invested (and in some cases, more earnings momentum-oriented) big cap growth funds such as Harbor Capital Appreciation, Yacktman and Vanguard U.S. Growth.

We remain a bit torn about Janus Fund. Its returns have been average since 1991. The gargantuan $9 billion asset base is a negative that is somewhat (but not entirely) mitigated by the Janus organization's research capabilities and Craig's recently renewed focus (he gave up management of the small cap Janus Venture fund late last year). Janus Fund's current defensive stance, while typical for Craig, brings up a lingering issue. It's our (very subjective) opinion that the huge popularity of the Janus Group, and the flagship fund's conservative reputation, has put Craig under considerable pressure to "retain assets" and take fewer risks at the expense of upside performance. We suspect that the bias towards mitigating risk is higher than it was a few years ago.

We believe Janus Fund is still a decent bet to deliver above-average performance within the big cap growth style. However, reaching previous levels of dominance looks less likely. ❖

Figure 14-3: Sample page from No-Load Fund Analyst.

Source: No-Load Fund Analyst

They try to identify talented fund managers at some of the smaller, lesser-known funds. This is, of course, riskier to do. Also, because they recommend funds in numerous fund families, as an investor you must be willing to deal with many fund companies or establish an account at a discount brokerage firm (see Chapter 4).

The editors' primary business has been their investment management business. They manage money for institutions and wealthy individuals in mutual funds — their minimum account size is $2 million. Much to their credit, though, they don't plug their money management business in their newsletter.

The *No-Load Fund Analyst* also follows and discusses closed-end mutual funds, which I cover in the next section. An annual subscription to the *No-Load Fund Analyst* costs $195. For $10, you can obtain a sample issue by calling 800-776-9555.

Closed-End Funds

In Chapter 2, I mention that this book focuses on open-end mutual funds, funds that adjust the number of shares available based on the demand for those shares. Banks operate the same way — a bank doesn't close up shop, unless it fails, just because it happens to have hit, say, $100 million in deposits.

Closed-end funds (which issue a fixed number of shares) are generally inferior to the open-end funds. The better open-end, no-load funds typically offer access to better fund managers, cost less to operate (mainly because of their size), and don't require any commissions to purchase.

Never buy a closed-end fund when it's initially sold or issued. Why not? Because if you do, you'll not only pay a commission of up to 10 percent, but you'll also "lose" money because with most closed-end funds the share price trades at a discount to the fund's net asset value (actual value of the fund's securities).

So why ever buy closed-end funds? Well, some small bargains are occasionally to be had in what's called the secondary market for closed-end funds. Once a closed-end fund starts trading on whatever exchange it trades on, some of the discounts that the funds trade for, relative to the net asset value of its holdings, can be significant — perhaps as much as 15 to 20 percent or more.

Apply the same selection criteria (all of which I outline for you in Chapter 3) that you apply to the open-end funds discussed throughout this book to help you choose prospective closed-end funds, too. The only new criteria for closed-end funds is the fund's *price discount* or *premium* relative to the asset value of its holdings. All things being equal, larger discounts are better. Never pay a premium to buy a closed-end fund. Never buy one without getting at least a 5 percent discount because you will have to pay a broker's commission to buy — and someday to sell — the fund, since these funds trade on a stock exchange. (Use one of the discount brokers I recommend in Chapter 4.)

If you want to learn more about these types of funds, Morningstar has a publication devoted solely to them called *Morningstar Closed-End Funds* ($195 for an annual subscription, $35 for a three-month trial). The *No-Load Fund Analyst* newsletter and some financial magazines and newspapers, mentioned earlier in the chapter, also report on them.

Chapter 15

Computers and Mutual Funds

- -

In This Chapter

▶ Finding your way around mutual funds with software

▶ Tasting fund information online with America Online and CompuServe

▶ Catchin' a wave and surfin' the Internet — mutual funds style

- -

*H*ere's another reason to skip most of the hucksters who pitch investment newsletters: through your personal computer, you can access more and better information at less cost. Along the way, however, you'll find many of the not-so-great newsletters (and others) that I discuss in Chapter 14 hawking their wares.

Of course, if you're not careful, you could end up spending a humongous amount of money on so much computer stuff that you'll suffer from information overload. Always remember that there's a wide variety in the quality of the stuff out there.

Fortunately (for both you and me), this book does not focus on computers. If you're sometimes (or all the time) perplexed by your own bundle of microprocessors, and if you've ever wanted to bludgeon those frequently aggravating boxes that we call computers, then you and I have yet another thing in common. (If you're stumped by computers, you should know, if you don't already, that helping people navigate computers is what the . . . *For Dummies* series started with. So if it weren't for computers, I probably wouldn't be writing this book.)

I've divided this chapter into two parts: (1) *software,* the information contained on the disks you load onto your computer's hard drive or CD-ROM, and (2) *online services,* which access outside data and information via a modem. Some of the stuff I'll discuss does some of both. Those that do are generally placed in the category that they do more of.

Software, Software, Everywhere Software

Most software reviewers can agree that good software must be easy to use. Software that helps you make mutual fund and other investing decisions has the additional need to provide well-founded advice and information. Not all of it does.

Which software is best for you depends on what you're trying to accomplish and on your level of investment expertise. The financial software in the marketplace today can help you with a variety of activities that range from simply tabulating your mutual fund's values and getting current prices to researching investment choices. You can even execute fund trades on your computer.

Investment research software

Investment research software packages usually separate investment beginners (and others who don't want to spend a lot of time managing their money) from those who enjoy wallowing in data and conducting primary research. If you know what funds you want to invest in and just want to get on with investing, you can go straight to the market and invest your money. But even if you don't want to conduct more specific research, some of the packages discussed later in this chapter that offer access to research can help you to conduct transactions online for your investment accounts and track your investment's performance.

A tiny word of caution from one who's been there: there is no lack of information and research available through investment software packages. In fact, you'll probably have the problem of sifting through too much data and differentiating the best from the mediocre and the downright awful. And unless cost is no object, you need to be careful that you don't spend too much of your loot just accessing the information when an online service is offered.

Much of the research investment software available helps people with individual stocks. Before you plunge into the data jungle and try to become the next Peter Lynch or Warren Buffet, be honest about your reasons for wanting to research. Some investors fool themselves into believing that their research will help them beat the markets. As I say many times in this book, though, few of even the so-called "professional" investors ever beat the markets.

The best reason to use research packages is to access quality information in what may or may not be a more cost-effective way than traditional sources of information provide you. Research packages can allow you to peruse more information at lower cost (as long as you don't become an online information junkie) than accessing a paper version of the same.

Some of the other research software on the market is nothing more than printed material that's available on a computer screen. If the raw material is good and the software is thoughtfully laid out, software can allow you to sort and sift through mountains of data. Mutual fund data hounds delight in *Morningstar Mutual Funds OnFloppy* (☎ 800-876-5005), software that provides dozens of statistics on thousands of mutual funds.

If you're a beginner or already suffering from mutual fund information overload, save your software dollars (especially given this package's clunky and non-user friendly DOS interface). If you're the quantitative type who likes to sort and screen megatons of data, this package can save you time and filing space. An add-on to this package, *Portfolio Developer,* allows you to create and track a hypothetical portfolio of funds. I prefer the paper version of Morningstar *No-Load Funds* that I discuss in Chapter 14 because the newsletter contains commentary and more details on a specific fund's investment holdings. The software version (available in DOS format only) costs $95 per year for quarterly updates, $185 for monthly updates, and $45 for a one-time package.

Morningstar Mutual Funds OnDisc is the CD-ROM version of Morningstar's *OnFloppy* product. The main difference is that it comes with more stuff — even more than Morningstar packs onto its paper pages. You can obtain older as well as recent commentaries and historic data also goes back over long time periods — about two decades. This CD-ROM includes the *Portfolio Developer.* The big drawback to *OnDisc* is the cost — $295 for one time, $495 for quarterly updates.

Mutual fund retirement planning software

Some of the best packages to help you develop a long-term strategy for choosing good investments come from the nation's two largest mutual fund providers: Fidelity and Vanguard. Both of their software products are geared to retirement planning (because retirement is the main reason that most people invest for the future).

Fidelity's *Retirement Planning Thinkware* (☎ 800-457-1768) has modules that help you understand the importance of planning and investing for retirement, calculating how much you should be saving and investing annually to reach your goals, developing an investment strategy, and learning about Fidelity's mutual funds.

Both Fidelity's *Retirement Planning Thinkware* and Vanguard's *Retirement Planner* (☎ 800-876-1840) do an excellent job of helping you run different retirement planning scenarios. This feature is critical because you should base the amount of risk you take with your investments as much on your comfort level as on the rate of return you need to earn to reach your goals. For example, these packages show you the impact of earning a couple of percentage points more return per year on your investment balances — thus the software depicts your ability to achieve your retirement goals.

Vanguard's package does a much better job explaining and showing the risks of investing in the stock and bond markets. It allows you to see how portfolios with different mixtures of stocks and bonds performed, all the way back to 1926. Although investment history won't exactly repeat itself, this invaluable feature allows you to go into your investments with realistic expectations so that you won't make the mistake of panicking and selling the first time you weather a drop in stock prices.

Even if you don't invest all (or any) of your money in their funds, the rest of these software packages' retirement planning and investment information and advice is easily worth the $15 purchase price for either package. These packages are available only through the mutual fund companies themselves.

Trading software

The fast-growing investment behemoths Charles Schwab and Fidelity Investments offer software packages that not only provide access to investment research and the ability to track the performance of your accounts; they also offer the ability to trade through your brokerage account at these firms. Like Fidelity's *On-line Xpress,* also known as *FOX, StreetSmart* provides free real-time quotes and up-to-date information on mutual funds and other investments you hold through your brokerage account.

One of the nifty features of these accounts is that you can invest in and track mutual funds from many different fund companies. Fidelity and Schwab reward you if you use your PC (instead of their live personnel) to trade by giving a 10% discount off their regular transaction fee schedule.

With Fidelity's *FOX* package, if you want to access research services such as Dow Jones News/Retrieval and Standard & Poors MarketScope, you need to establish a separate account with each of these companies. The *FOX* package has limited historical mutual fund data (for the most part, it reports returns only for the last five years for Fidelity's mutual funds). With Schwab's *StreetSmart,* you can access and be billed for these information services through your Schwab account or your credit card. Schwab's package doesn't offer any historic mutual fund data.

Both *FOX* and *StreetSmart* charge on a fee-for-service basis every time you access information. Schwab's *StreetSmart* (available in Windows and Macintosh formats) is only available from Schwab (☎ 800-334-4455). Fidelity's *FOX* (DOS only) is available through Fidelity (☎ 800-544-0246) or from Egghead Software stores.

Getting-and-staying-organized software

Quicken, by Intuit, is best known for its checkbook software that helps you to track your spending and pay your bills. Even so, Quicken also allows you to list and track your mutual fund and other investments. In addition to organizing all of your investments into one place, you can track your original purchase price, as well as the current market values and rates of return for your investments.

If you have accounts at numerous investment firms, Quicken (Windows, DOS, Macintosh, and CD-ROM versions) can reduce the clutter and complications involved in tracking your financial empire. In order to calculate your fund returns with the software, you must continually enter your fund's distributions and share price changes. Remember that consolidating your investments at a larger mutual fund company or through discount brokerage account can accomplish the same things for you — without you having to invest hours in learning software and entering data.

Quicken has come out with a so-called Deluxe version of its product recently. I'm not impressed with it. The Deluxe version provides the ability to download, through CompuServe (discussed later in the chapter), mutual fund and other security price quotes. If you don't have or don't want to spend monthly fees for CompuServe, you can dial into a 900 number, which costs $1 per minute. For one important reason, I don't see the benefit of this feature. As I discuss in Chapter 11, tracking the price of a mutual fund is a lousy and inaccurate way to determine your return in a fund. Remember, funds make capital gains and dividend distributions — and you must enter such data *manually* into Quicken to get the correct picture of how you're doing.

The Deluxe CD-ROM version comes with a "Mutual Fund Selector" that in my humble opinion is garbage. My advice: Get the basic Quicken package that costs less. If you want to play around with more mutual fund data and information, use the Morningstar software discussed earlier in the chapter or the better newsletters discussed in Chapter 14.

Online Services and Surfing the Internet

Commercial online services offer anyone with a decent computer and a modem the ability to do some potentially useful things. With these standard gadgets, you can

- ✔ Access tons of articles from major business and financial magazines and newspapers.
- ✔ Search references and other tomes of data.
- ✔ Participate in discussion or "chat" groups.
- ✔ Send e-mail to people around the world!

What you can do through the major online services and the Internet — that Great Information Beyond that you access most easily through the very online services I'll soon discuss — will continue to change rapidly in the years ahead. In a moment, I'll explain what the services are good for with respect to mutual funds. But first a *warning*.

If you're not careful about keeping an eye on the clock, you can spend a small fortune on charges for using the online services. *Time is money when you're on-line.* Most of the services charge a set monthly fee (usually around $10 per month) that covers your first five hours or so; they then charge several bucks per hour for everything over that. Extra charges are levied as well for using particular, so-called *premium*, services such as search and retrieval of magazine articles.

And another thing to be careful of: the company you sometimes keep online. Through online services and the Internet, people and companies often sell stuff you're better off not buying. Online services derive most of their "content" from companies that pay a fee for space on the service.

You also can end up chatting with people who just plain don't know what they're talking about. Remember, there are no entrance exams or license requirements for putting a message into the pile on bulletin boards and chat groups on these services. Therefore, *read with care.*

One final warning: *keep your long-term perspective.* Many of these services offer daily price quotes for your investments — which easily can cause you to lose sight of the bigger picture, especially as it relates to the performance of your mutual funds. Never lose sight of the bigger picture.

America Online

America Online, also known as AOL (available in Windows, DOS, and Macintosh flavors), is the largest online service and provides user-friendly access to the Internet. AOL offers a crisp, clean, user-friendly layout. It has a major personal finance area that started in early 1994.

Morningstar maintains a significant presence on America Online, where you can access performance and other data on thousands of mutual funds. This data is similar to (yet far less substantial than) what is available through the Morningstar single-page summaries that I cover in Chapter 14. Through message boards, you can chat with others about a whole variety of mutual fund topics and even direct questions to the staff at Morningstar.

In 1995, America Online welcomed the Vanguard Group of mutual funds. In what is one of the better company displays I've seen through the online services, *Vanguard Online* offers useful information. Of course, through Vanguard you can obtain recent data and descriptions of Vanguard funds. You also can request — for either mailing or downloading — fund prospectuses, annual reports, and some applications. You even exchange comments, questions, and answers through the message boards.

AOL also carries a fair amount of business news (which is indexed by topic for easy retrieval). You can search current news, for example, for articles on mutual funds. Financial and economic news and financial market highlights are provided as well in case you want to check on recent market happenings.

AOL offers articles from many financial and general interest magazines and newspapers. These include *Consumer Reports, Business Week, Worth, Newsweek,* the *American Association of Individual Investors Journal,* and numerous newspapers. You also can search among past articles on a particular topic.

Most of AOL's other mutual fund services are in a section called Investor's Network, which offers a variety of active investment-related message boards. The message boards on AOL are one of its strengths. Just be careful not to believe all that you read here — anyone can (and usually does) post messages. Be especially wary of brokers and the like who surf around incognito proffering advice — and sometimes try to pick up clients.

Top Advisors Corner contains tips from "top advisors," but these alleged advisors are really just a variety of not-so-hot newsletters (not-so-hot newsletters — as well as a few good newsletters — all get their due in Chapter 14). Also, avoid the *Decision Point Timing and Charts Forum,* which advocates of market timing and technical analysis have been known to frequent.

Mutual fund quotes are available through America Online and you can establish a portfolio (using the ticker symbols located in the Appendix) to track. Values are updated automatically and you can download them into a spreadsheet.

Of the three major online providers, AOL (☎ 800-827-6364) has the most understandable and cost-effective pricing system. It charges just $9.95 a month, which covers your first five hours of usage during the month. Additional hours are $2.95 each. Included in the standard services are E-mail, access to forums, reference tools, newspaper and magazine articles, and all kinds of specialized services. AOL also offers the easiest Internet access of the three biggest online services. (For all the pertinent lowdown on AOL — and a smidgen of impertinent stuff, too — be sure to see the *America Online For Dummies* guide to the service.)

CompuServe

CompuServe (for DOS, Windows, and Macs) offers a service called *FundWatch Online*. FundWatch Online is part of CompuServe's basic package, so you don't pay extra for it — but, given the usefulness of the service, I'd say that you get what you pay for here. It provides much less information on funds than you can obtain through America Online.

Elsewhere, CompuServe forums let you ask fellow investors for information, fund advice, and so on. At the *Investors Forum*, you can browse through all of the recent messages from other members or you can search the messages for information specifically related to mutual funds. Daily mutual fund price quotes, similar to those that are available through AOL, can be retrieved for mutual funds and other securities.

Tickerscreen was an area that caught my eye — I thought it might show an actual stock market ticker tape screen with current prices whizzing by. Wrong! While I perused the "recommended" mutual funds, I couldn't figure out why all the funds being recommended were load funds until I realized that *this was a brokerage firm trying to sell the "recommended" funds!* The lack of disclosure was appalling. (Is the SEC awake, I wonder, to the online world?)

News related to investments can be obtained through *Associated Press Online* (a basic service) or the more expensive *Business News* or *Executive News Service*. These latter two services give you access to thousands of articles and allow you to set up criteria for searching the news databases. The *Magazine Database Plus* can be helpful, but it's relatively expensive to use. You can retrieve the full text of articles from more than 140 magazines, including many financial magazines such as *Kiplinger's* and *Forbes*. Searching for mutual fund articles uncovers hundreds of articles per year. Tons of information are available, but you pay $1.50 for each article, plus the connect time for the search.

The *Business Database Plus* has articles from more than 500 specialized business magazines, trade journals, and newspapers and goes back five years. You find fewer articles here on mutual funds — maybe several dozen or so per year.

CompuServe (☎ 800-848-8990) isn't cheap. It costs $9.95 a month for unlimited connect time on basic services. But most of its better stuff is considered part of "premium services" and are charged at a hefty hourly rate compared to the other online service providers ($4.80 an hour for most modem speeds). Specialized services that involve additional charges include investment quotes, portfolio valuation ($1 each), and executive news service ($15 per hour).

Online runners-up

There are numerous other online services. Many of them aren't all that great, but here's a bit of background on some of the better of the rest.

Prodigy is light on content and heavy on advertising. These two facts are likely related and causal. But it has some useful stuff, too. Financial market news is available on Prodigy through CNBC. An online discount brokerage service (PC Network, division of Donaldson Lufkin & Jenrette) offers the ability to purchase mutual funds. You also can obtain quotes and track your funds over time with Prodigy.

One of Prodigy's services, *Mutual Fund Corner,* contains information on Fidelity (you also find other fund companies presented here that are heavy on advertising and light on good funds and information). Prodigy (☎ 800-776-3449) has pricing identical to AOL — $9.95 per month for first five hours and $2.95 per hour thereafter — but beware: you pay extra for accessing much of their information.

Like Prodigy, GEnie offers many of the specialized services that involve additional charges: Charles Schwab discount brokerage services (which you can access for free using the *StreetSmart* software discussed elsewhere in this chapter), *Dow Jones News/Retrieval,* and a news clipping service. The *Investor's RoundTable* has bulletin boards, real-time conferences, news (*Wall Street Journal* daily highlights, as well as other business and financial highlights). GEnie also has bulletin boards that are subdivided into about two dozen major topics, many covering mutual funds. (As always, beware the plethora of lousy newsletters.)

The news services are extensive — the *Washington Post, Chicago Tribune,* and numerous other papers are on GEnie. There's even an electronic newsstand that gives access to the full text of articles from more than 900 magazines. GEnie's (☎ 800-638-9636) charges are comparable to Prodigy's.

For the real data and information hounds

If you've got lots of money to invest or you just love to wallow in data, there's still more! Be careful, though. Some of this stuff can become addictive and gobble up lots of your time — and money.

Reuters Money Network

Reuters Money Network, available in Windows, DOS, and Macintosh formats and distributed by Reality Technologies (☎ 800-346-2024), is a software package that also offers online access to financial information and news. In addition to mutual fund data from Morningstar (which is updated monthly) and research reports on stocks and bonds from Standard & Poor's, users also can access financial information and news from Dow Jones, Reuters itself, and many other sources for a fixed monthly fee ranging from $9.95 to $19.95. For an additional $6.95 per month, you can partake of Reuters' "Personalized News Clipping Service," which culls articles from a number of publications on your specific mutual fund(s) of interest, as well as on other investments in your portfolio. Thus, this software may save you the time and work of reviewing so many publications to track news items on your investments.

Telescan

If you want to access mutual fund pricing data that goes back 20 years, *The Telescan System* can produce graphically pleasing charts that give you just such data. Through this package, you also can access other mutual fund data from Morningstar that's similar to the information on Morningstar's *Mutual Funds OnFloppy* software. This package is more expensive than most and is best suited for those who want to do more comprehensive screening of individual stocks. Telescan also offers news through Reuters.

Ignore this package's touting of "industry renowned newsletters" — almost all of them have mediocre to dismal long-term track records. The best newsletters — the few that there are — seem to have opted not sell their wares on-line (yet). Also, skip Telescan's "technical analysis" data. Technical analysis is a branch of investment analysis that resembles using a Ouija board to predict your future. Also bypass the program's information on investing in stock options, which are sure loser gambles on the short-term direction of a stock's price.

The cost of Telescan (☎ 800-324-4692) depends on how you use it and what billing method you select. If you use it periodically, their Per Minute Plan is your best bet. It charges you $0.42 to $0.94 per minute (the higher cost gets you during prime time, which runs from 7:00 A.M. to 6:00 P.M. local time) plus $0.10 per graph and $2.00 per search. Investment junkies can buy unlimited access with Telescan's Flat Rate Plans, which range from $45 per month for unlimited non-prime-time usage to $500 per month for unlimited access at any time.

There's no charge for the software, but there is a $13 fee for shipping and handling and a $50 annual fee for using the software — in addition to the basic usage charges.

Dow Jones News Retrieval

Dow Jones News Retrieval is the ultimate for news and information junkies. It provides access to

- ✔ Dow Jones Newswire and various international newswires, plus a wire service reporting on business-related government activity

- ✔ Tons of newspapers (38 of the top 50 U.S. papers plus 120 international papers); in many cases, article files go back more than five years and hundreds of magazines are available online

- ✔ A clipping service that can collect articles as they are written for particular topics of your choosing

The Mutual Funds Performance Report, which covers 1,500 mutual funds, gives you information on historical performance, assets, and basic background. Not a lot of meat here.

Everything you do through Dow Jones News Retrieval costs money. Most text retrieval services cost $1.50 per 1,000 characters retrieved. Every letter, space, and so forth, constitutes a character, so the bill can run up in a hurry. They offer a service called *Dow Jones Market Monitor* which provides you with eight hours of usage per month for $29.95. This flat-rate service has two major catches, however. The first is that you can't use it weekdays between 6 A.M. and 7 P.M. Also, you don't have access to nearly as many publications. ☎ 1-609-520-4000.

The Internet

For mutual funds and investing, there's not really any need to use the Internet, what with the abundance of software and online services and "old-fashioned" paper resources that can keep you busy around the clock. Software and online services also have the virtue of being easier to access.

There are a few Internet newsgroups that provide access to a larger (and probably more diverse) resource for sharing information. All told, the effort for you to figure out the system would not be worth the benefits just for mutual funds or personal investing.

But you never listened to your parents, so why should you listen to me?! There are some other things on the Internet, and, besides, you may already have a ramp onto the Information Superhighway. You can access the Internet in different ways. Using one of the online services described in the previous section is the easiest. You can also access the Internet through any one of a number of Internet access providers. Charges and services vary.

My advice on accessing the Internet: take a class or workshop and read a basic book (such as *The Internet For Dummies,* which you'd better believe is on my desk). Once you get on, you can join one of the thousands of UseNet Newsgroups, add your name to a mailing list, download free software, or search one of the countless databases around the world. The possibilities are endless. But you could easily forget about the rest of your life!

UseNet Newsgroups are bigger versions of the forums (a.k.a. *message boards* or *chat groups*) that are found in the online services. Anyone can participate in the Internet groups, and these groups tend to maintain much commotion — some of which may be interesting to you. Essentially, they're groups of E-mail messages pertaining to a single theme, though their interrelatedness may not always be obvious! Some groups have moderators who screen messages, but most are verbal free-for-alls.

You can find an interesting newsgroup through trial and error, but there's also an organizational method to the Cybermadness; the method is based on a few broad categories. Business and consumer groups are in *misc.* You might try *misc.invest.funds,* which gets a lot of traffic and includes tips on mutual funds and investment strategies. A recent check there revealed that *misc.invest.funds* contained almost 10,000 posted messages!

You'll also find various *ClariNet News Services*, which you can get directly from ClariNet or through some commercial Internet access providers. ClariNet enables you to create your own electronic newspaper. The "newsgroups" contain copyrighted news articles, complete with meaningful headlines and other journalistic goodies. The articles come from Associated Press, Reuters, and other major news services. You can screen newsgroups for articles about a specific topic by using a screen or filter called *NewsClip.*

One of the neatest features is *clari.news.top,* which covers the top U.S. news stories with continuous updates. Specifically, try *clari.biz.economy* which covers economic news and indicators, and *clari.biz.finance.personal* and *clari.biz.invest,* which cover personal investing and finance, respectively. Some groups cover the various stock markets as well as late-breaking business news in general.

Overall, you probably should look at newsgroups more as recreation than research — a little like a cocktail party with your business colleagues. You may hear some new ideas or sharpen an idea of your own, but you're probably not going to solve all your investment problems while you're there.

Part V

The Part of Tens: Desserts, for the Mind

Reprinted with permission

In this part...

Why lists of ten-somethings? Why not? Life is all about priorities, and more than ten of anything is too many to remember and follow. Fewer than ten leaves you with that empty feeling you have after eating a hearty plate of bean sprouts for lunch. So — ten it is. Like Goldilocks, here you get just the right amount of information about some other important fund concepts and concerns.

Chapter 16

Ten Negative Fund-Investing Thoughts to Overcome

⋯⋯⋯⋯⋯⋯⋯⋯⋯⋯⋯⋯⋯⋯⋯⋯⋯⋯⋯⋯⋯⋯⋯⋯⋯⋯

*T*hinking too much and acting in what seem common-sense ways are your own worst enemies when investing in mutual funds. If you've thought the thoughts enumerated in this chapter (or think them in future), it's a sign that you're a normal person. Overcome these ten detrimental ways of thinking and tendencies and you're well on your way to avoiding common painful and costly fund investing mistakes.

"Why should I bother with so little to invest"

You gotta start somewhere. You actually benefit more from mutual funds the less you have to invest than do those investors with heftier balances (although they benefit a lot as well). With several hundred or a few thousand dollars to invest, you can't diversify well or avoid big commissions when you buy individual securities. With mutual funds you can. And you pay no more than those with big bucks to invest.

When investing money for the longer term, especially inside of retirement accounts, start with hybrid or all-in-one funds such as Vanguard's Star or LifeStrategy funds (see Chapter 8). These have low minimum initial investment requirements of just $500 and subsequent investment amounts of just $100 per deposit ($50 if you're signed up for automatic investment such as electronic withdrawal from a bank account).

Consider this. Invest just $500 today in good mutual funds and add just $50 per month. In 20 years, with funds that average a 10 percent per year return, you'll have about $41,000! Do it over 40 years, and you'll have about $314,000. If you can manage $100 per month, you'll have about $79,000 in 20 years, $606,000 in 40 years!

"My funds went down so I must have made a bad decision"

Don't be so hard on yourself. If you invested in the funds recommended in this book and used good selection criteria in picking funds on your own, then 99 times out of 100, a fund that goes down does so because the types of securities it focuses on (for example, bonds, U.S. stocks, international stocks) are down.

If, for example, your fund is down about 5 percent over the past year, find out how similar funds have done over the same time period. If the average comparable fund is down more than 5 percent, you have cause to be happy; if it's up 20 percent, you've got reason to worry. See Chapter 11 for some ground rules for deciding whether to dump or hold your laggard fund.

"I don't want the risk of being in investments that aren't insured"

Lack of insurance, such as that from the FDIC on bank accounts, is not what makes funds risky. Mutual fund risks are driven by the price changes of the securities, such as bonds and stocks, that they invest in. Unlike banks and insurance companies, mutual fund companies can't go bankrupt (see Chapter 2).

Mutual funds that invest in municipal bonds may have insurance against the default of the bonds. Otherwise, insurance isn't necessary or available for funds.

Don't overlook other, not so obvious, types of risk. Bank accounts don't carry the price, risk, or volatility that bond and stock mutual funds do. However, bank accounts are exposed to the risk that the value of your money may not grow fast enough to keep ahead of inflation and taxes.

If you don't like the volatility that comes from stock and bond funds, even with money you have earmarked for longer-term purposes, invest more of your money in balanced or hybrid funds. These tend to mask the volatility of their individual stock and bond components because they're all mixed together (see Chapter 8).

"I'll buy the funds doing best now"

Most people want to jump on board the winning bandwagon. But the best performers all too often turn into tomorrow's losers and mediocre funds (see Chapter 3).

The types of securities that do best inevitably change. You may actually increase your chances of fund-investing success by minimizing exposure to recent hot performers and investing more into fund types that are currently depressed.

"I can do better investing in individual securities"

Perhaps you've read about how investment legends like Peter Lynch and Warren Buffet make wise investments, so you figure that if you do what they do, so can you. (After all, many of these books say and imply that you can.)

Nothing personal, but it ain't going to happen. You're likely at best a part-time amateur. If you enjoy playing pick-up basketball games, it would be fun, if somewhat humbling, to play against the great Michael Jordan. But I'd assume that you'd play Jordan for the fun of it rather than an expectation or vain hope of beating him. Buying individual stocks is the same — don't do it thinking you'll beat the better mutual fund managers.

And don't fool yourself into thinking you're an expert just because you know more than most people about a particular industry or company. Many others have this knowledge, and if you have truly inside information that a company is about to be acquired, for example, and invest your money based on this, you'll end up with a large fine or jail sentence or both.

"I shouldn't invest without knowing what's happening with the economy, trade agreements, tax and budget reform..."

While I don't advocate sticking your head in the sand, all these big-picture issues are well beyond your (or, really, anyone else's) ability to accurately forecast. Besides, investors' expectations are already reflected in the prices of securities in the financial markets.

By all means, read, listen, and absorb what's going on in the world around you. But don't use this information in an attempt to time the markets.

"I'm going to sell because interest rates are rising and the economy is tanking"

The financial markets tend to lead these sorts of economic changes. The stock market, for example, often peaks six months to a year before the economy does. Conversely, stock prices usually head back up in advance and in anticipation of an actual economic recovery. Interest rates and bond prices typically have the same kind of interaction. By the time everyone's talking about rising interest rates, the bond market has usually hit bottom.

For example, in late 1994, after interest rates had already substantially increased, depressing bond prices, bond fund investors dumped a lot of their holdings. While I'm not foolish enough to think that I can predict which way interest rates are heading, I do know that selling when the bond market is "having a sale" is the opposite of a wise investment strategy (see Chapter 7 to learn about bonds).

"I'm going to wait for a correction for a buying opportunity"

Some stock market investors like to wait for a big drop before they start investing. This seems logical, especially coming on the heels of years of advancing prices. It also fits the philosophy of buying when prices are discounted.

Problem is, how do you know when the decline has run its course? A 10 percent drop? 20, 30, 40 percent? If you're waiting for a 20 percent drop and the market only drops 15 percent before it then rises 100 percent over the coming years, you'll miss out.

Especially if you're just starting to save and invest money, forget about trying to wait and buy at lower prices. Invest regularly so that, if prices drop, you'll buy some at lower prices. That way, if prices don't decline, you won't miss out on the advance. If you have a large amount of money awaiting investment, average the money monthly or quarterly over a year or two into different types of funds (see Chapter 9).

"I need to stay on top of my funds to make sure nothing bad happens"

There's a big difference between monitoring and obsessing. There's no need to follow the daily price changes of your mutual funds. Following daily prices of mutual funds is a lousy way to discern what the return of your fund is.

Tracking and hovering over your funds increase your chances of panicking and making emotionally based decisions. The investors I know who bail out when prices are down almost always are those who follow things too closely. Keep in sight the big picture: why you bought the fund in the first place and what financial goal you are trying to fulfill.

Funds make dividend and capital gains distributions that reduce the price per share of a fund. These distributions either get reinvested into more shares in the fund or come to you in cash and must be factored as well into determining your fund's performance.

"My fund isn't in the Top Ten for its category so it's not the best"

Stop looking at the Top Ten lists. Most such lists completely ignore risk. Many of these lists rank funds based on short time periods. The funds on top are constantly changing.

If a fund is taking so much risk that it's in the Top Ten, that also means that it's risky enough to end up in the Bottom Ten some day (see the many examples in Chapter 3).

The categories that are used in these types of lists are also flawed, since many of the funds aren't really comparable. Ignore the Top Ten performance lists. Read Chapter 11 to learn appropriate ways to evaluate and track the performance of your funds.

Chapter 17

Ten Questions More Fund Investors Should Ask

● ●

*I*nvestors and market followers ask a lot of questions. Asking questions is a good thing, since the answers, if provided by knowledgeable people, will help you to learn. As I noted in the last chapter, questions based on fear are particularly important to clear up. Otherwise, you could make a bad move.

While plenty of questions are asked, however, not enough of the right kind of questions are asked. So, here are some queries and issues to ponder that can not only make you a better investor but can also help make the fund industry and even our government better oriented to serving your needs.

Why so many funds?

So many funds exist because so many companies and people want a slice of the very profitable mutual fund pie. Investors certainly don't need this many funds and, thus far, these extra funds and companies selling them haven't led to as much price competition that benefits investors as you see in other industries with as many players. The reason: it's hard for the uninformed to comparison shop.

Over time, you are likely to see more competition, particularly on the fees that funds charge. This competition will inevitably lead to the merging of smaller companies into larger ones to help contain costs. In the meantime, take the proliferation of funds as a sign that it pays to shop around because some companies are charging much more than others for the same types of funds and performance.

What is this fund going to cost me?

You don't buy groceries, dinner out, or tickets to a play or baseball game without knowing the cost. Why should mutual funds be any different?

Since funds charge you every year you're in them (and load funds hit you with sales commissions up-front or at other times as well), check out what a fund is going to cost you over, say, ten years of ownership. This information is now required in a fund's prospectus. On a $5,000 investment, you may see a range from about $10 to $1,500!

Why is Fidelity's Magellan fund (and other large stock mutual funds) still charging an annual fee of about one percent per year?

Under the management of Peter Lynch, now almost a household name, the Fidelity Magellan fund amassed the best ten-year track records among stock funds. *After* that happened (and after Lynch left), money poured into Magellan as Fidelity advertised the heck out its performance.

Today, Magellan has approximately $55 billion under management. Yet it still charges an annual operating fee of around one percent. While this isn't an unreasonable fee for a stock fund to be charging, it is for a large fund. Consider that Fidelity is raking in $550 million in fees from this fund. Compare this to 1984, when Magellan had about $2 billion dollars in assets, was charging one percent annually, and was collecting about $20 million as a yearly fee.

Does it cost Fidelity 27 times as much to manage this fund as it did ten years ago? Of course not. This extra money is going into the pockets of the owners of Fidelity. If Fidelity were sharing the economies of scale that come with managing this amount of money in Magellan, the annual expense fees on this fund should be much less — perhaps anywhere from 70 to 90 percent less than current levels. As the mutual fund industry continues to grow, there are increasing numbers of companies and funds that do not share the economies that come from running larger funds.

Magellan's not a bad fund (although its performance in recent years has been mediocre), but its fees are much higher than necessary. Fidelity also charges a sales commission to purchase this fund even though no broker is involved. This fee also falls into Fidelity's coffers, a fact that I ignored in the above analysis. Funds comparable to Magellan are available at lower cost (see Chapter 8), including from Fidelity.

Why doesn't the Social Security system allow taxpayers to invest their money into mutual funds?

The tiny country of Chile, for example, allows taxpayers to invest their money in mutual funds. This not only ensures segregation of taxpayers' funds for their retirement years, it also ensures good growth and returns on their investments.

The Social Security trust fund is somewhat bogus in that the assets are part of the overall federal pool of money. The government claims that the Social Security money is invested in Treasuries. The money is not really invested there because the federal government issues Treasuries; therefore, the money flowing in from Social Security simply reduces the amount of Treasury bonds the government needs to issue to finance the national debt.

As more people like me direct the investment of their own retirement funds, instead of having a company pension fund manager do the job, isn't there a danger we'll screw it up?

Yes, individuals who direct their own retirement investments can make major mistakes. The average person has but a fraction of the training and experience with investing money that a company pension fund manager has. So people are more likely to not save enough, to underinvest in growth-oriented investments such as stocks, and to try to time the financial markets. These are among the downsides of self-directed retirement plans such as 401(k) plans.

Of course, not all pension managers do superb jobs; but as a group, they've done well. Companies like to do away with traditional pension plans because many employees don't seem to value them as they should and because the plans are expensive to maintain. With 401(k)-type plans, the responsibility and most of the "cost" of saving gets dumped onto the employee's shoulders.

You must educate yourself and learn how to properly and intelligently invest your money!

Why doesn't our company retirement savings plan allow investing through the best mutual funds?

Sometimes, the well-intentioned people at a company who establish a retirement savings plan, such as a 401(k) or 403(b) plan (see Chapter 5), may not know any more than you do about investments. They may even know less or have gotten bad advice when the plan was established.

One of the ways that company retirement plan investment options get improved is because of suggestions from employees like you! So, speak up with constructive suggestions and ideas.

Why isn't there more money invested in index funds?

Index funds which track the performance of the markets still account for a minuscule percent of the $3 trillion now invested in funds. The main reason there's so little investors' money in index funds is because of all the ratings and rankings of funds. So much attention is paid to which funds are at the head of the pack today that most people lose sight of the fact that over longer time periods, index funds beat the vast majority of their actively managed peers.

Index funds also seem sort of boring and ego-deflating because you're admitting you can't beat the market and you're resigning yourself to the market rate of return. Swallow your ego and learn the benefits of using these funds (see Chapter 8).

Did this mutual fund or advisor invest in securities comparable to the index they are comparing themselves to?

If a fund or advisor's fund recommendations looks like it's beaten the pants off a comparative index, odds are they are using an unfair index for comparison. A fair comparative benchmark is one that invests in the same types of securities as the fund or advisor.

Examine and ask what portion of the money invested typically was invested in the major types of securities — such as large-, medium- and small-company U.S. stocks, foreign stocks, etc. Suppose, for example, that a fund or an advisor who invests in funds says that they generated annual returns averaging 15 percent over the past five years and compares their performance to the Standard & Poor's Index of 500 large-company U.S. stocks. If the fund or advisor invested in international stocks or smaller company stocks or bonds or all of the above, then the S&P 500 isn't a fair yardstick (see Chapter 11).

Can you show me independent, audited proof that your privately managed fund or newsletter recommendations produced the returns that you're claiming they did?

Most of the time they can't prove their claims. And if they can, they'll choose shorter time periods and ones in which they look the best.

Privately managed funds can produce such proof only through an accountant's audit. Newsletters are tracked by the *Hulbert Financial Digest*. Over long time periods, the "best" newsletters" just barely keep up with the market rates of return that you can obtain with near 100 percent certainty with index funds (see Chapter 14).

Why don't more fund companies adopt Vanguard's operating structure?

Most businesses and business founders want to reap the full financial rewards if their business succeeds. That's what capitalism is all about. Fewer are as concerned about the impact that their business structure has on the customer's best interests (witness tobacco manufacturers). John Bogle, founder of Vanguard, was far more concerned about his customer's needs than maximizing profits.

What's most appealing about Vanguard's structure is that their funds have an incentive to control costs, since their funds are solely owned by its shareholders and don't kick profits back to the management company. Vanguard's incentive system has also managed to reward fund managers for producing good performance.

At other mutual fund companies, the supposedly independent boards of directors should be asking tougher questions, such as why management fees aren't being reduced as some funds mushroom in size. The problem is that most directors are afraid if they raise these issues they'll be shown the door from these cushy jobs that often pay tens of thousands of dollars per year for very little work.

Chapter 18

Ten Things You Should Know and Do *Before* You Invest in Mutual Funds to Pay for College Expenses

● ●

*F*ew subject areas have more misinformation and bad advice than what is dished out on paying for your children's college expenses. Some mutual fund companies, including a few of the better ones discussed in this book, publish free guides that are rife with poor advice and some scare tactics.

Their basic premise is that, by the time your tikes reach age 18 or so, it's going to cost more money than you can possibly imagine to pay for college. Thus, you had better start saving a lot of money as soon as possible. Otherwise, you'll have to look your 18-year-old in the eyes some day and say something like, "Sorry, we can't afford to send you to the college you have your heart set on."

Investing in mutual funds to help pay for college costs may be a wise move, but if you're like most parents, you're bound to make some easily avoidable and costly mistakes. Here are ten important things you should know and consider doing before setting out to amass a fortune to meet the bills for your children's tuition, room, board, textbooks, trips home, and late night pizza runs.

Fund your retirement accounts first

Self-centered as it may seem, you're really doing yourself and your kids a tremendous financial favor if you fully fund your retirement accounts. First, you save yourself a boatload in taxes. As discussed in Chapter 5, 401(k), 403(b), SEP-IRAs, and Keogh plans give you an immediate tax deduction at the federal and state level. And once the money is inside these retirement accounts, it compounds without taxation over the years.

You should also know that the more money you save and invest outside of retirement accounts, the less financial aid (loans and grants) you'll qualify for. Strange as it may seem, the financial aid system ignores 100 percent of the money you have *inside* retirement accounts, but it counts all of it *outside*.

The financial aid system penalizes investing in your child's name

The financial aid system even more heavily penalizes money held in your child's name by assuming that about 35 percent of the money in your child's name (for example, in custodial accounts) will be used toward college costs. By contrast, only 6 percent of the non-retirement money held in your name is assumed to be used to pay for college costs.

You should also know that when you place money in your child's name, your child has the legal right to that money in most states at age 18 or 21.

College costs rise faster than general inflation

Every year, one of the many things that the federal government spends our tax dollars on is calculating how the cost of living is changing. In recent years, the cost of living has been growing around 3 to 4 percent per year. While this is a modest rate of inflation, the average increase in the cost of a college education has been growing at about double the rate: 7 percent annually.

College costs tend to rise more rapidly because teaching, in its present form, is labor intensive. College price increases are not likely to continue outstripping overall price increases, however. As many companies have learned to do, increasing numbers of colleges are getting leaner. Technology-based and other labor-saving teaching methods, once implemented, should make education even more efficient and cost-effective.

To keep up with and ahead of college price increases, you must invest for growth, at least somewhat. The younger your child is, the more years you have before you need to tap the money and, therefore, the greater the risk you can take. A simple rule of thumb: add 30 (to invest more aggressively) to 50 (to invest more conservatively) to your child's age. Got that number? Now make that a percentage and invest that amount into bonds with the remainder in stocks, preferably using mutual funds.

Reduce the risk in the mix as your kids get older

Although you want to have a healthy percentage of their college money in stock funds, the closer your children get to going to college, the more conservative you should be with their money. (The rule of thumb will accomplish that.)

Balanced or hybrid mutual funds are an ideal choice for college investing (see Chapter 8). If you put together your own portfolio of stock and bond funds, as your children get within a few years of going to college, consider selling the "star" funds and dump the money into a short-term bond fund.

Children under 14 have a distinct tax system

Parents used to have an incentive to transfer money into their children's names in order to reduce their own income taxes. The "Kiddie Tax" system changed all that and led to today's somewhat complicated system for children under the age of 14.

The first $1,300 of what's known as unearned income (which includes distributions from mutual fund and other investments) is taxed at a favorable rate that is likely to be less than the parents' rate. The first $650 is not taxed, and the next $650 is taxed at 15 percent at the federal level. Earnings above $1,300 are taxed at the parents' rate.

Before you rush to transfer money into your child's name in order to take advantage of the likely lower tax rate on their first $1,300 of unearned income, consider the financial aid implications discussed earlier in the chapter. Unless you're sufficiently wealthy that you're going to pay all your child's college costs without any financial assistance (including loans), think at least twice before putting money in your child's name. Doing so reduces your financial aid eligibility.

All income earned at age 14 and over is taxed at kid's rate

Once your children turn 14 years of age, they pay taxes at whatever rate their income leads to. So if you don't expect to apply for any financial aid, you can place as much in their names as you like in anticipation of college expenses and save yourself on taxes. Be aware that in most states, children have legal access to the money at age 18 (see Chapter 10).

You can choose mutual fund investments for your children before your kids turn 14 so that the income produced from these investments approximately equals up to but no more than $1,300 per year. Most growth-oriented investments can be used to defer gains until the year when sold (see Chapter 8). Just wait until the child reaches 14 before you consider selling.

Don't assume that junior can't afford expensive colleges

The financial aid system examines your income, assets and liabilities, number of children in college, and stuff like that. Based on an analysis, the financial aid process may determine that you can afford to spend, for example, $8,000 per year on college for your child. That doesn't mean that your child can only consider schools that cost up to that amount. In fact, if your son or daughter desires to go to a $25,000 per year private school, loans and grants may be able to plug the gap between what you can afford and what it costs.

Apply for aid. Otherwise, you may never know what you and your child are missing out on.

Make sure the rest of your financial house is in order

Investing for college costs is important, but other financial issues should take priority. We already talked about the importance of funding retirement accounts in order to get the tax breaks.

You should also review your insurance coverage (life and disability) to make sure your family is financially prepared if you become unable to earn an income. Before you start investing in funds, also get rid of high-interest credit card and auto debts. The odds are against your earning a higher rate of return on your mutual funds than you're paying on these types of loans.

Don't try to pay for college costs all by yourself

College is expensive and, unless you're affluent, you and your child will need to borrow some money. Consider these educational loans investments in your family. There is financial aid that's available regardless of need, including grants and loans. Don't make the mistake of not applying.

In addition to financial aid, you may be able to use other sources to help pay college expenses. If you're a homeowner, for example, you may be able to tap home equity. The kids' grandparents also may be financially able to help out (it's better for them to hold the money themselves until it's needed).

Teach your children the value of working, saving, and investing

If you're one of the fortunate few who can pay for the full cost of college yourself, more power to you. But even if you can, you may not be doing as well by your children as you may like to believe.

When children set goals and learn to work, save, and make wise investments, these values pay dividends for a lifetime. So does your spending time with your children rather than working so hard to try and save enough to pay for college. Besides, lazy, dependent children may never leave home!

If you want to learn more about getting your finances in order and planning for college costs, read *Personal Finance For Dummies.*

Chapter 19

Ten Things to Consider or Ask Before Hiring a Financial Advisor

• •

*T*his chapter is this far back in the book for a reason. Millions of investors have successfully invested in mutual funds on their own. The vast majority of these folks were like you. Maybe they had an idea about what a mutual fund was, but they weren't sure or were uncomfortable about how to go about investing in funds. Some people didn't even know what a mutual fund was — perhaps you didn't when you started reading this book. But investing in mutual funds is not difficult; common sense and a modicum of financial sense is all you need.

There's no compelling reason that you cannot or should not invest in mutual funds without hiring someone like me or another financial advisor. So, if you jumped to this chapter first, STOP right there! While you can read this chapter before you've read the rest, I recommend that you march back to Chapter 1 and start learning more about funds and investing. You'll be better able to understand this chapter once you've read those that come before it, not to mention the fact that you'll be improving your ability to save yourself possibly thousands of dollars in financial advisory fees.

But if you've arrived here because you just don't want to deal with handling fund investing or financial planning decisions on your own, keep on keepin' on.

Financial planner or money manager?

As you search the landscape for help, you will confront a variety of different advisors eager to assist you with investing your money. As we discussed in Chapter 5, those who claim to be advisors but who derive commissions from the products that they sell are salespeople and not advisors.

If you want objective help, those who are true financial planners generally help with a variety of issues such as retirement planning, decisions relating to the use and payoff of debt, investing, insurance, and perhaps even real estate. The charge for these services should be a fee based on the time that's involved. I'll talk about fees later in the chapter.

Money managers or financial advisors who perform *money management* will invest your money and charge you a fee — usually expressed as a percentage of assets under management. Some advisors only do money management, but increasing numbers of financial planners offer money management services as well.

The benefit of a good planner is that he or she should help restructure your financial situation before your money gets invested in mutual funds. If a planner provides specific mutual fund recommendations, you can implement them on your own and save yourself a bundle in ongoing advisory fees.

Using advisors who only perform money management can make sense for people who have finished their planning and need someone to help manage their money. Money managers will argue that, because they devote full-time to investing, they are more adept at it.

But here's an increasingly common problem that has been surprisingly little discussed — when financial planners add the second hat of money manager, a number of conflicts of interest can arise with the planning services that they offer. First, planner/money managers may be reluctant to recommend, and in fact have an incentive to ignore, planning strategies that deplete the money you have to invest. Why? Because the more you have to invest, the greater the total money management fees they earn.

All of the following planning moves result in less money that you can invest with the planner/money managers, so they may not recommend these:

- ✔ Maximizing saving through your employer's retirement saving plan(s)
- ✔ Spending more on real estate — either through purchasing a larger primary home or investing in rental property
- ✔ Buying and investing in your own business or someone else's privately held business
- ✔ Paying down debt of all types, such as credit cards, auto loans, mortgages, business loans, and the like.

Another problem with planners who also manage money is that they may be short on specific advice in the planning process. Sadly, I've seen more than a few cases where people have paid planners upwards of several thousand dollars for a largely boilerplate computer-generated financial plan and have received little if any specific financial planning and investment advice. If you want to invest in no-load funds, the planner should willingly and happily provide specific fund recommendations and help you build a portfolio for the fee that you pay him.

Active versus passive management

The vast majority of the value that comes from making investing decisions is deciding on the overall allocations and selection of funds that meet your needs. If your needs and situation are relatively stable and you do your homework right the first time, you shouldn't need to be bouncing from fund to fund.

Much of what you're paying a planner for is the time spent reviewing your financial situation and matching your needs and goals to a suitable portfolio of funds. If you hire a money manager on an ongoing basis to manage your investment portfolio, you must fundamentally believe that the changes that will be made over time will enhance your portfolio's returns sufficiently to more than cover the cost of the money manager's services. This belief may not be well-founded. Remember, you can touch base from time to time with an advisor who charges a fee for their time.

Another risk of constantly tinkering with your mutual fund portfolio is that it can lead to being in the wrong place at the wrong time. This is the same issue I cover in Chapter 14 on the perils of blindly following some newsletters' and gurus' timing advice to switch into this fund and out of that one. Trading in non-retirement accounts also increases your tax burden.

Who's in control?

If you hire a money manager, another issue you should consider and be aware of is that they will require that you turn control of the account over to them. Specifically, you will sign or initial a form granting the advisor authority to execute trades in your account — otherwise known as granting them a *limited power of attorney* (that's what the first line in Figure 19-1, a section of a discount brokerage application, is authorizing).

Figure 19-1:
When you initial this section, you give your financial advisor control over investing your funds.

7. Please **INITIAL** any of the following statements which apply to your Financial Advisor ("FA").

Please Note: If more than one person is listed on the account, **EACH** account-holder must initial the information below.

Account Holder	Joint Account Holder	
Initial	Initial	I authorize FA to execute trades in my account.
Initial	Initial	I grant FA authority to authorize disbursal of funds by check, wire transfer, withdrawal, and other forms of disbursement, 1) to other financial institutions, for my benefit, or 2) to me at my address of record. (NOTE: This option is only effective if FA is authorized to execute trades and is not permitted for Custodial accounts.)
Initial	Initial	I authorize Schwab to deduct FA's fees and expenses from my account as directed by FA.
Initial	Initial	I authorize Schwab to send duplicate copies of my trade confirmations and account statements to FA.

Source: Charles Schwab & Company, Inc.

The second line on this sample form gives your advisor power to move money out of your account. I generally recommend against giving your advisor this power unless you need to withdraw money from your account frequently and find that it's more convenient to have your advisor do it for you.

The third line allows your advisor to have their ongoing fees deducted from the account. I would definitely not allow this for retirement accounts because it diminishes the amount of money that you have compounding tax deferred. For non-retirement accounts, it's up to you, although many advisors insist on this feature since it makes it easier for them to collect their fees.

The fourth line requests the brokerage firm to send duplicate copies of your account statements and trade confirmations to your advisor. That's acceptable and to be expected.

Almost all money managers manage money on what's called a discretionary basis — they make decisions to buy this fund and sell that fund without your prior approval. In other words, you're turning control over to them. You find out about transactions being performed in your investment account(s) when you receive the trade confirmations in the mail and through your monthly or quarterly statement.

At a minimum, before you turn control over to the money manager, make sure you discuss your investment objectives with them. These overall goals should drive how the manager manages your money.

If you don't like the idea of turning control over to someone else, remember that you can hire a financial advisor who will provide specific advice that you can implement. This will likely not only be more cost effective but will also keep you in the driver's seat.

Fees — What's it going to cost?

If you hire a planner on an hourly basis, expect to pay anywhere from $50 or so all the way up to several hundred dollars per hour. Expect to pay at least $100 per hour — you can easily pay more; those planners with the $300 per hour billing rates tend to work exclusively with the well-heeled who can afford the freight.

Here's an example of a fee schedule for a money management firm that manages money by investing in a variety of mutual funds. This firm charges a percentage of assets under management:

Amount You Invest	Fee Percentage	Fee in Dollars
$ 100,000	1.00%	$ 1,000
$ 250,000	1.00%	$ 2,500
$ 500,000	0.95%	$ 4,750
$1,000,000	0.85%	$ 8,500
$2,000,000	0.70%	$14,000
$5,000,000	0.50%	$25,000

What's amazing about this type of fee schedule is that, while the percentage charge declines slightly as the amount you invest increases, look at how the total charges increase. This firm sends the same quarterly reports out to the client with $1,000,000 invested, who pays $8,500 per year, as it does to the client with $100,000 invested, who pays $1,000 per year for the same service.

This advisory firm, in fact, claims, "every client regardless of whether they have $100,000 invested or $1,000,000, receives the same personal attention." If that's true, then their fee schedule shouldn't look like it does! Either this firm ain't making any money on their small accounts or (more likely) they're making a truck load on the larger ones. Keep this in mind since advisors' fees are negotiable.

Also, ask what sort of transaction and other fees you can expect to pay in addition to the advisory fee paid to the money manager. Most money managers will ask that you establish an account at one of the discount brokerage firms, such as Schwab or Jack White, or with a mutual fund company such as Vanguard. Ask who they use and why.

If you're going to consider hiring a mutual fund money manager, take the time to add up all of the costs. Here's a quick and dirty table (see Table 19-1) to help you to do the job:

Table 19-1	Adding Up All the Costs
Cost	**Annual Percentage of Your Assets**
Money manager's fee	for example, 1.0 % _____
Operating fees on mutual funds invested in (don't let the advisor say they can't figure this because the funds they use vary over time — they can base it on their current portfolio or what they used over the past year)	for example, 1.0 % _____
Transaction and other fees	for example, 0.2 % _____
Total	for example, 2.2 % _____

Remember that, over the long haul, a diversified portfolio primarily invested in stocks has returned around 10 percent. If you're paying a total of 2.5 percent to have your money managed, you're giving away 25 percent of your expected return. And don't forget, because the IRS sure won't, that you'll owe taxes on your non-retirement account profits so you're giving away an even greater percentage of your after-tax returns.

How do you make investing decisions?

Throughout this book, I've discussed the good and bad ways people can and have invested in mutual funds over the years. Chapter 3 in particular walks you through the methodology and logic behind selection of funds. It isn't rocket science — it can be as simple as picking any other product or service. You want value — where can you invest in funds that meet your needs managed by a fund company and fund managers that have good track records and that charge competitive fees?

Most advisors try to factor their economic expectations and prognostications into their investment strategies. But this is much easier said than done. In their marketing materials and more so in their marketing conversations with you, advisors will sell you on their past shrewd moves. No doubt some advisors can honestly claim they've avoided being involved in certain investment disasters or been in on the ground floor of some winners.

The fundamental problem with some money managers is that they would have made better snake oil salesmen. They will try and convince you that they have a crystal ball. Specifically, some will claim that they can time the markets; they say they'll get you out of the market before it falls and put your money back in time to catch the next rise. Sounds good in theory, and you figure that those advisors must be able to do this since they use big financial words and wear nice suits.

You saw for yourself the record of the supposed gurus in Chapter 14 — over long time periods, it is virtually impossible for even the acknowledged experts to beat the markets. Great investors such as Warren Buffet and Peter Lynch say that you can't time the markets. Believe 'em!

What's your track record?

In the world of mutual funds, fund companies must have their performance records audited and reviewed by the Securities and Exchange Commission. Most also provide an independent auditors report. Private money managers face no such requirement. A few — very few — provide independent audits.

Of course, what you really want to know are the performance facts about the money manager you are considering for ongoing management of your funds — what rate of return have they earned year by year? How have they done in up and down markets? How much risk have they taken, and how have their funds performed versus comparable benchmarks (see Chapter 11)? These are important questions. But it is difficult, if not impossible, to get objective and meaningful answers from the majority of investment advisors who manage money on an ongoing basis.

Money managers will play a number of marketing games to pump themselves up. If all the money managers out there are telling the truth, then 99 percent are beating the market averages, avoided being invested in the stock market in a big way when the 1987 crash hit, and just happened to be in the best-performing funds last year. Here are the major marketing ploys too many money managers use to pump up their supposed past performance, and to seduce you into turning your money over to them:

✔ **Select accounts.** If you can get the money manager to give you performance numbers and charts, all too often there will be a little asterisk that refers you to some microscopic footnote somewhere near the bottom of the page. If you have your magnifying glass handy, you will see that the asterisk says something like "select" or "sample accounts." What this means, and what they should have said instead is: "We picked the accounts where we did best, used the performance numbers from those, and ignored the rest." (Interestingly, using smaller type in this way is a violation of SEC regulations.)

Advisory firms also may select the performance time periods where they look best. Many of the track records being touted in sales brochures don't cover periods when the stock market took a major hit, such as Black Monday in October, 1987. Finally, and most flagrantly, some firms simply make up the numbers.

✔ **Free services.** Many money managers will produce performance numbers that presume they're giving their services away for nothing. Remember, money managers charge a fee (percentage of assets) for their services — these fees (according to SEC regulations) should be deducted from the returns that were earned to clearly show what you as an investor using their services would have made. Since most money managers place their mutual fund trades through discount brokers who charge transaction fees, these fees should be deducted from returns as well.

✔ **Bogus benchmarks.** It's not bad enough that some money managers make their performance numbers higher than they really are. They also try to make themselves look good in relation to the overall market by comparing their performance numbers to inappropriate benchmarks. A common problem in recent years has been money managers who invest worldwide (including international stocks) yet compare their investment performance to U.S.-based indexes.

Any worthy money manager who invests in mutual funds diversifies and invests money overseas. In 1993, for example, the average international stock fund rocketed up more than 38 percent, whereas the average U.S. stock fund returned less than 13 percent. So money managers who invested around the globe and then compared their performance in 1993 to U.S. indexes can't help but look good.

✔ **Switching into (yesterday's) stars.** Money managers don't want to send out performance updates that show they're sitting on yesterday's losers and missed out on yesterday's winners. So guess what? They sell the losers and buy into some of yesterday's winners, thus creating the illusion that they're more on top of things than they really are (some mutual fund newsletters do this as well). This strategy, also known as "window dressing," is also potentially dangerous because they may be making a bad situation worse by selling funds that have already declined and buying into others after they've soared.

What are your qualifications and training?

The answers you receive to the question of qualifications and training will vary all over the map. An advisor should have experience in the investing or financial services field — generally, the more the better. But also look for someone with intelligence and ethics who can converse with you in plain English.

In terms of credentials, check 'em out but don't be overly impressed by some, such as the CFP (Certified Financial Planning) degree. Most planners with this "credential," which can be earned by taking a self-study course at home, sell products. Other common credentials that advisors may have include the following

✔ CFA (Chartered Financial Analyst). This is a plus since it means that the advisor should know how to analyze securities and investments and the fundamentals of portfolio management.

✔ MBA (Master's in Business Administration). This is a plus since it hopefully means the advisor has had coursework dealing with investments and finance. Check out where the MBA was earned.

✔ PFS (Personal Financial Specialist) is a credential conferred on accountants who pass an exam similar to the CFP. As noted later in this chapter, those with the PFS are less likely to work on commission the way many CFPs do.

✔ CLU (Chartered Life Underwriter) & ChFC (Chartered Financial Consultant) are insurance credentials and carry little if any value in advising on mutual fund investing. It may be a red flag that you're dealing with a salesperson rather than a real advisor.

The term "Registered Investment Advisor" denotes that the advisor is registered with the U.S. Securities and Exchange Commission as an investment advisor. The SEC does not require a test; however, it does require that the advisor file *Form ADV,* also known as the Uniform Application for Investment Advisor Registration. This lengthy document asks for very specific information from investment advisors, such as a breakdown of where their income comes from, relationships and affiliations with other companies, each advisor's educational and employment history, the types of securities the firm recommends, and the firm's fee schedule. (Many states require passing a securities exam, such as a Series 2, 63, or 65.)

Credentials are a little bit like mutual fund ratings — they don't always mean what you'd expect. Good advisors do tons of reading and will tell you that reading 20 good investment books taught them as much or more than any degree program they took.

In a pitch over the phone or in marketing materials sent by mail, an advisor is much more likely to gloss over or avoid certain issues. Although it's possible for an advisor to lie to the SEC on Form ADV (it has happened on numerous occasions), it's likely that an advisor will be more truthful on this form than in her own marketing to you. You can ask the advisor to send you a copy of her Form ADV, or call the SEC for a copy at ☎202-272-7450.

Check references

Take the time to ask other people how the advisor benefitted them. This is a terrific way to verify the rates of return the advisor may claim (although you're smart enough to recognize that the advisor will refer you to the clients who have done the best with him). Also inquire about the advisor's strengths and weaknesses.

Virtually all money managers offer a "free" introductory consultation if you meet their minimum investment requirements. Some financial planners who work an hourly basis will not offer a free consultation. Most planners who offer free sessions work on commission, or they will try to sell you a money management service. So the "free" consultation ends up being a sales pitch to convince you to buy certain products or services through them.

Advisors willing to work with you by the hour and who are busy can't afford to burn an hour of their time for an in-person "free" session. Such advisors should be willing to spend some time on the phone answering background questions, however. They should also be able to send background materials by mail and provide references if you ask.

Do you carry liability insurance?

Financial planners and money managers should carry liability (sometimes it's called errors and omission) insurance. This provides you (and the advisor) with protection in case a major mistake is made for which the advisor is liable. Make sure he carries enough coverage given what he'll be helping you with.

Some advisors may be surprised by this question or may think you're a problem customer looking for a lawsuit. On the other hand, if your advisor gets you into some disasters, you'll be glad for the insurance.

Part VI
Appendix: Other Useful Stuff about the Best Mutual Funds

Reprinted with permission

In this part...

To round it off — how about performance numbers and other good stuff about the best mutual funds? It's all here to help get you started. Here are my favorites.

Appendix

How to Find Fund Companies and Discount Brokers

Benham Funds
1665 Charleston Road
Mountain View, CA 94043
☎ (800) 472-3389

Brandywine Fund
3908 Kennett Pike
P.O. Box 4166
Greenville, DE 19807
☎ (800) 656-3017

Cohen & Steers Realty Shares, Inc.
757 Third Avenue
New York, NY 10017
☎ (800) 437-9912

Columbia Funds
1301 SW 5th Avenue
P.O. Box 1350
Portland, OR 97207
☎ (800) 547-1707

Dodge & Cox Funds
One Sansome St., 35th Floor
San Francisco, CA 94104
☎ (800) 338-1579

Domini Social Equity Fund
6 St. James Avenue, 9th Floor
Boston, MA 02116
☎ (800) 762-6814

Fidelity Funds
82 Devonshire Street
Boston, MA 02109
☎ (800) 544-8888
Fidelity Discount Brokerage
☎ (800) 544-8666

Lindner Funds
7711 Carodelet, Suite 700
P.O. Box 11208
St. Louis, MO 63105
☎ (314) 727-5305

Mutual Series Funds
51 John F. Kennedy Parkway
Short Hills, NJ 07078
☎ (800) 448-3863

Neuberger & Berman Funds
605 Third Avenue
New York, NY 10158
☎ (800) 877-9700

PIMCO Funds
840 Newport Center Drive Suite 360
Newport Beach, CA 92660
☎ (800) 927-4648

Schwab Funds
101 Montgomery Street
San Francisco, CA 94104
☎ (800) 526-8600

SteinRoe Funds
300 W. Adams St.
Chicago, IL 60606
☎ (800) 338-2550

T. Rowe Price Funds
100 E. Pratt Street
Baltimore, MD 21202
☎ (800) 638-5660

Tweedy Browne Funds
52 Vanderbilt Avenue
New York, NY 10017
☎ (800) 432-4789

USAA Funds
USAA Building
9800 Fredericksburg Rd.
San Antonio, TX 78288
☎ (800) 531-8100

The Vanguard Group
P.O. Box 2600
Valley Forge, PA 19482
☎ (800) 662-7447

Warburg Pincus Funds
466 Lexington Avenue
New York, NY 10017
☎ (800) 888-6878

Jack White & Company
9191 Town Center, 2nd Floor
San Diego, CA 92122
☎ (800) 323-3263

Table A-1 — Bond Funds

Fund Name	Trading Symbol	(Total Return — Percent)										Capital Gains*	Dividends*
		1986	1987	1988	1989	1990	1991	1992	1993	1994	1995		
Taxable													
Vanguard Short-Term Corporate	VFSTX	11.4	4.4	7.0	11.5	9.2	13.1	7.2	7.1	-0.1	12.7	D	Monthly
PIMCO Low Duration	PTLDX	-	-	8.2	11.5	9.1	13.5	7.7	7.8	0.6	11.8	D	Monthly
Vanguard IndexTotal Bond Market	VBMFX	-	1.5	7.3	13.6	8.6	15.2	7.1	9.7	-2.7	18.1	D	Monthly
PIMCO Total Return	PTTRX	-	-	9.5	14.2	8.1	19.5	9.7	12.5	-3.6	19.8	D	Monthly
Vanguard GNMA	VFIIX	11.7	2.2	8.8	14.8	10.3	16.8	6.8	5.9	-1.0	17.0	D	Monthly
Benham GNMA	BGNMX	11.3	2.7	8.5	13.9	10.2	15.6	7.7	6.6	-1.7	15.7	D	Monthly
USAA Federal Securities GNMA	USGNX	-	-	-	-	-	-	6.1	7.1	0.0	16.7	D	Monthly
Vanguard Long-Term Corporate	VWESX	14.3	0.2	9.7	15.2	6.2	20.9	9.8	14.6	-5.3	26.3	D	Monthly
Vanguard High Yield Corporate	VWEHX	16.9	2.6	13.6	1.9	-6.0	29.2	14.2	18.2	-1.7	19.1	D	Monthly
U.S. Treasury													
Vanguard Short-Term Treasury	VFISX	-	-	-	-	-	-	6.7	6.3	-0.6	12.1	D	Monthly
Vanguard Admiral Short-Term Treasury	VASTX	-	-	-	-	-	-	-	6.5	-0.3	12.2	D	Monthly
Vanguard Intermediate-Term Treasury	VFITX	-	-	-	-	-	-	7.8	11.4	-4.3	20.4	D	Monthly
Vanguard Admiral Intermediate-Term Treasury	VAITX	-	-	-	-	-	-	-	11.3	-4.2	20.5	D	Monthly
Vanguard Long-Term Treasury	VUSTX	-	-2.9	9.2	17.9	5.8	17.4	7.4	16.8	-7.0	30.0	D	Monthly
Vanguard Admiral Long-Term Treasury	VALGX	-	-	-	-	-	-	-	16.7	-6.9	30.0	D	Monthly

* Capital gains and dividend schedules may change over time, but these are the typical months that the fund has, in the past, declared such distributions payable to shareholders of the fund.

(continued)

Table A-1 *(continued)*

Fund Name	Trading Symbol	(Total Return — Percent)										Capital Gains*	Dividends*
		1986	1987	1988	1989	1990	1991	1992	1993	1994	1995		
Federally Tax-Free													
Vanguard Municipal Short-Term	VWSTX	7.4	4.1	5.6	7.0	6.6	7.2	4.7	3.8	1.6	6.0	D	Monthly
Vanguard Municipal Inter.-Term	VWITX	16.2	1.6	10.0	10.0	7.2	12.2	8.9	11.6	-2.1	13.6	N	Monthly
Vanguard Municipal Long-Term	VWLTX	19.4	-1.1	12.2	11.5	6.8	13.5	9.3	13.5	-5.8	18.7	N	Monthly
Vanguard Municipal Insured Long-Term	VILPX	18.6	0.1	12.8	10.6	7.0	12.5	9.2	13.1	-5.6	18.5	N	Monthly
State and Federally Tax-Free													
Benham CA Tax-Free Intermediate	BCITX	12.6	0.8	5.9	7.9	7.0	10.4	7.1	10.7	-3.7	13.5	D	Monthly
Fidelity Spartan CA Inter. Muni	FSCMX	-	-	-	-	-	-	-	-	-4.7	15.1	Ap,D	Monthly
Schwab CA Intermediate	SWCSX	-	-	-	-	-	-	-	-	-2.1	10.4	D	Monthly
Vanguard CA Tax-Free Insured Intermediate	VCAIX	-	-	-	-	-	-	-	-	-	13.1	D	Monthly
Fidelity Spartan NY Intermed. Muni	FSNMX	-	-	-	-	-	-	-	-	-4.3	14.4	D	Monthly
Benham CA Tax-Free Long-Term	BCLTX	19.2	-4.6	10.4	9.8	6.6	11.8	8.1	13.7	-6.5	19.8	D	Monthly
Fidelity Spartan CA Muni Income	FSCAX	-	-	-	-	8.2	11.5	8.8	14.0	-9.0	19.0	Ap,D	Monthly
Vanguard CA Tax-Free Insured Long-Term	VCITX	-	-3.9	12.1	10.5	7.0	11.0	9.3	12.8	-5.7	18.5	D	Monthly
Fidelity Spartan CT Muni Income	FICNX	-	-	10.1	10.4	6.6	10.6	8.2	12.9	-7.0	17.1	Jn,D	Monthly
Fidelity MA Muni Income	FDMMX	16.9	-1.3	10.7	9.3	7.4	11.3	9.3	12.9	-6.1	18.1	S,D	Monthly
Fidelity MI Muni Income	FMHTX	18.9	-2.8	13.0	10.2	5.1	12.0	9.5	13.8	-7.5	15.4	F,D	Monthly
Fidelity MN Muni Income	FIMIX	17.0	-3.8	12.6	9.2	7.2	8.5	7.6	12.4	-6.0	16.0	F,D	Monthly
Vanguard NJ Tax-Free Insured Long-Term	VNJTX	-	-	-	10.4	7.7	11.2	9.4	13.4	-5.2	17.3	D	Monthly
Vanguard NY Insured Tax-Free	VNYTX	-	-3.5	12.0	10.3	6.3	12.8	9.7	13.1	-5.7	17.7	D	Monthly

* Capital gains and dividend schedules may change over time, but these are the typical months that the fund has, in the past, declared such distributions payable to shareholders of the fund.

(continued)

Table A-1 (continued)

Fund Name	Trading Symbol	(Total Return — Percent)										Capital Gains*	Dividends*
		1986	1987	1988	1989	1990	1991	1992	1993	1994	1995		
USAA NY Bond	USNYX	-	-	-	-	-	13.8	9.0	13.5	-9.1	18.1	My,N	Monthly
Vanguard OH Tax-Free Insured Long-Term	VOHIX	-	-	-	-	-	12.0	9.5	12.8	-5.2	16.8	D	Monthly
Vanguard PA Tax-Free Insured Long-Term	VPAIX	-	-1.3	12.3	10.6	6.9	12.2	10.2	12.7	-4.6	16.4	D	Monthly
USAA VA Bond	USVAX	-	-	-	-	-	11.7	8.5	12.6	-6.3	17.1	My,N	Monthly

Table A-2

Stock Funds

Fund Name	Trading Symbol	(Total Return — Percent)										Capital Gains*	Dividends*
		1986	1987	1988	1989	1990	1991	1992	1993	1994	1995		
Hybrid													
Vanguard Tax-Managed Balanced	VBINX	-	-	-	-	-	-	-	-	-	28.6	D	Jn,D
Vanguard Wellesley Income	VWINX	18.2	-1.9	13.5	20.8	3.8	21.4	8.6	14.6	-4.4	28.9	D	Mr,Jn,S,D
Vanguard Star	VGSTX	13.8	1.6	19.0	18.6	-3.6	24.1	10.5	10.9	-0.3	28.2	D	Ja,Jl
Dodge & Cox Balanced	DODBX	18.8	7.2	11.6	23.0	0.9	20.6	10.6	15.9	2	28.0	D	Mr,Jn,S,D
Vanguard Wellington	VWELX	18.3	2.3	16.1	21.5	-2.8	23.5	7.9	13.5	-0.5	32.9	D	Mr,Jn,S,D
Fidelity Balanced	FBALX	-	1.9	16.0	19.7	-0.4	26.7	7.9	19.3	-5.3	14.9	S,D	Mr,Jn,S,D
Fidelity Asset Manager	FASMX	-	-	-	15.3	5.3	23.5	12.7	23.2	-6.6	18.1	D	Mr,Jn,S,D
Fidelity Puritan	FPURX	20.7	-1.7	18.8	19.6	-6.2	24.4	15.4	21.4	1.8	21.4	S,D	Mr,Jn,S,D
Lindner Dividend	LDDVX	20.7	-4.1	24.1	11.8	-6.5	27.3	21.1	14.9	-3.3	21.5	Mr,D	Mr,Jn,S,D
T. Rowe Price Balanced	RPBAX	23.1	-3.4	9.0	20.7	7.1	22.0	7.3	13.3	-2.1	24.9	D	Mr,Jn,S,D
SteinRoe Balanced	SRFBX	17.1	0.6	7.9	20.2	-1.7	29.4	7.9	12.3	-4.1	22.6	D	F,My,Ag,N

* Capital gains and dividend schedules may change over time, but these are the typical months that the fund has, in the past, declared such distributions payable to shareholders of the fund.

(continued)

Table A-2 (continued)

Fund Name	Trading Symbol	1986	1987	1988	1989	1990	1991	1992	1993	1994	1995	Capital Gains*	Dividends*
		(Total Return — Percent)											
U.S. Stock													
Vanguard Index 500	VFINX	18.0	4.7	16.2	31.4	-3.3	30.1	7.5	9.8	1.2	37.4	D	Mr,Jn,S,D
Schwab 1000	SNXFX	-	-	-	-	-	-	8.5	9.6	-0.1	36.6	D	Ju,D
Vanguard Index Total Market	VTSMX	-	-	-	-	-	-	-	10.6	-0.2	35.8	D	Mr,Jn,S,D
Dodge & Cox Stock	DODGX	18.3	11.9	13.8	26.9	-5.0	21.4	10.8	18.3	5.2	33.4	D	Mr,Jn,S,D
Mutual Qualified	MQIFX	16.9	7.6	30.3	14.4	-10.1	21.0	22.7	22.7	5.7	26.6	Jn,D	Jn,D
Mutual Shares	MUTHX	16.9	6.3	30.6	14.8	-9.8	20.9	21.3	20.9	4.5	29.1	Jn,D	Jn,D
Mutual Beacon	BEGRX	15.4	12.7	28.9	17.4	-8.1	17.5	22.9	22.9	5.6	25.9	Jn,D	Jn,D
T. Rowe Price Spectrum Growth	PRSGX	-	-	-	-	-	29.8	7.2	21.0	1.4	29.9	D	D
Fidelity Equity Income	FEQIX	16.9	-1.6	22.5	18.7	-14.0	29.3	14.6	21.2	0.2	31.8	Mr,D	Mr,Jn,S,D
Fidelity Equity Income II	FEQTX	-	-	-	-	-	46.5	19.0	18.9	3.2	26.4	J,D	Mr,Jn,S,D
Fidelity Fund	FFIDX	15.6	3.3	17.9	28.7	-5.0	24.1	8.4	18.3	2.6	32.8	Fe,Ag,D	Mr,Jn,S,D
Vanguard Tax-Managed Capital Apprec.	VMCAX	-	-	-	-	-	-	-	-	-	34.4	D	Jn,D
Fidelity Disciplined Equity	FDEQX	-	-	-	36.3	-0.6	35.9	13.2	13.9	3.0	29.0	D	D
Fidelity Contrafund	FCNTX	13.1	-2.0	21.0	43.3	3.9	54.9	15.9	21.4	-1.1	36.2	D	D
Fidelity Low Priced Stock	FLPSX	-	-	-	-	-0.1	46.2	28.9	20.2	4.8	24.9	S,D	S,D
Fidelity Stock Selector	FDSSX	-	-	-	-	-	46.0	15.4	14.0	0.8	36.5	D	D
Warburg Pincus Growth & Income	RBEGX	-	-	-	21.1	4.0	13.1	9.1	37.0	7.6	20.4	D	Mr,Jn,S,D
Warburg Pincus Emerging Growth	CUEGX	-	-	-	21.8	-9.9	56.1	12.1	18.0	-1.4	46.3	D	Jn,D
Neuberger & Berman Guardian	NGUAX	11.9	-1.0	28.0	21.5	-4.7	34.3	19.0	14.4	1.4	32.1	D	Mr,Jn,S,D
Neuberger & Berman Partners	NPRTX	17.3	4.3	15.4	22.7	-5.1	22.4	17.5	16.5	-1.9	35.2	D	D
Neuberger & Berman Focus	NBSSX	10.1	0.6	16.5	29.8	-5.9	24.7	21.1	16.3	0.9	36.2	D	D

* Capital gains and dividend schedules may change over time, but these are the typical months that the fund has, in the past, declared such distributions payable to shareholders of the fund.

(continued)

Table A-2 (continued)

Fund Name	Trading Symbol	1986	1987	1988	1989	1990	1991	1992	1993	1994	1995	Capital Gains*	Dividends*
Vanguard Primecap	VPMCX	23.5	-2.3	14.7	21.6	-2.8	33.0	9.0	18.0	11.4	35.5	D	D
Columbia Growth	CLMBX	6.9	14.7	10.8	28.9	-3.3	34.2	11.8	13.0	-0.6	32.9	D	D
Columbia Special	CLSPX	15.6	3.0	42.5	31.8	-12.4	50.3	13.7	21.7	2.3	29.3	D	D
Brandywine	BRWIX	16.3	2.6	17.7	32.8	0.6	49.2	15.7	22.6	0	35.7	O,D	O,D
International Stock													
Schwab International Index	SWINX	-	-	-	-	-	-	-	-	3.8	14.2	D	D
T. Rowe Price International Stock	PRITX	61.2	7.9	17.9	23.7	-8.9	15.8	-3.5	40.1	-0.8	11.4	D	D
Vanguard International Growth	VWIGX	56.7	12.4	11.6	24.8	-12.0	4.7	-5.8	44.7	0.8	14.9	D	D
Warburg Pincus International Equity	CUIEX	-	-	-	-	-4.6	20.6	-4.3	51.3	0.1	10.3	D	Jn,D
USAA Investment International	USIFX	-	-	-	-17.4	-9.3	13.4	-0.1	40.0	2.7	8.3	N	N
Tweedy Browne Global Value	TBGVX	-	-	-	-	-	-	-	-	4.4	10.7	D	D
Specialty													
Fidelity Real Estate	FRESX	-	7.7	10.3	13.8	-8.6	39.1	19.4	12.5	2.0	10.9	Mr,D	Mr,Jn,S,D
Cohen & Steers Realty Shares	CSRSX	-	-	-	-	-	-	20.1	18.7	8.3	11.1	D	Mr,Jn,S,D
Vanguard Gold	VGPMX	49.8	38.7	-14.2	30.3	-19.9	4.3	-19.4	93.3	-5.4	-4.5	D	D
Benham Global Gold Fund	BGEIX	-	-	-	29.9	-19.5	-11.2	-8.7	81.2	-16.7	9.2	D	Jn,D
Fidelity Utilities	FIUIX	-	-	14.8	25.8	1.8	21.1	10.9	15.5	-5.3	30.6	Mr,D	Mr,Jn,S,D

* Capital gains and dividend schedules may change over time, but these are the typical months that the fund has, in the past, declared such distributions payable to shareholders of the fund.

Index

• **E** •

• **F** •

• G •

• H •

• *N* •

• *O* •

• W •

• •

• Z •

Notes

Notes

7/29/96

The Internet For Macs® For Dummies® 2nd Edition	by Charles Seiter	ISBN: 1-56884-371-2	$19.99 USA/$26.99 Canada
The Internet For Macs® For Dummies® Starter Kit	by Charles Seiter	ISBN: 1-56884-244-9	$29.99 USA/$39.99 Canada
The Internet For Macs® For Dummies® Starter Kit Bestseller Edition	by Charles Seiter	ISBN: 1-56884-245-7	$39.99 USA/$54.99 Canada
The Internet For Windows® For Dummies® Starter Kit	by John R. Levine & Margaret Levine Young	ISBN: 1-56884-237-6	$34.99 USA/$44.99 Canada
The Internet For Windows® For Dummies® Starter Kit, Bestseller Edition	by John R. Levine & Margaret Levine Young	ISBN: 1-56884-246-5	$39.99 USA/$54.99 Canada

MACINTOSH

Mac® Programming For Dummies®	by Dan Parks Sydow	ISBN: 1-56884-173-6	$19.95 USA/$26.95 Canada
Macintosh® System 7.5 For Dummies®	by Bob LeVitus	ISBN: 1-56884-197-3	$19.95 USA/$26.95 Canada
MORE Macs® For Dummies®	by David Pogue	ISBN: 1-56884-087-X	$19.95 USA/$26.95 Canada
PageMaker 5 For Macs® For Dummies®	by Galen Gruman & Deke McClelland	ISBN: 1-56884-178-7	$19.95 USA/$26.95 Canada
QuarkXPress 3.3 For Dummies®	by Galen Gruman & Barbara Assadi	ISBN: 1-56884-217-1	$19.95 USA/$26.99 Canada
Upgrading and Fixing Macs® For Dummies®	by Kearney Rietmann & Frank Higgins	ISBN: 1-56884-189-2	$19.95 USA/$26.95 Canada

MULTIMEDIA

Multimedia & CD-ROMs For Dummies® 2nd Edition	by Andy Rathbone	ISBN: 1-56884-907-9	$19.99 USA/$26.99 Canada
Multimedia & CD-ROMs For Dummies®, Interactive Multimedia Value Pack, 2nd Edition	by Andy Rathbone	ISBN: 1-56884-909-5	$29.99 USA/$39.99 Canada

OPERATING SYSTEMS:

DOS

MORE DOS For Dummies®	by Dan Gookin	ISBN: 1-56884-046-2	$19.95 USA/$26.95 Canada
OS/2® Warp For Dummies® 2nd Edition	by Andy Rathbone	ISBN: 1-56884-205-8	$19.99 USA/$26.99 Canada

UNIX

MORE UNIX® For Dummies®	by John R. Levine & Margaret Levine Young	ISBN: 1-56884-361-5	$19.99 USA/$26.99 Canada
UNIX® For Dummies®	by John R. Levine & Margaret Levine Young	ISBN: 1-878058-58-4	$19.95 USA/$26.95 Canada

WINDOWS

MORE Windows® For Dummies® 2nd Edition	by Andy Rathbone	ISBN: 1-56884-048-9	$19.95 USA/$26.95 Canada
Windows® 95 For Dummies®	by Andy Rathbone	ISBN: 1-56884-240-6	$19.99 USA/$26.99 Canada

PCS/HARDWARE

Illustrated Computer Dictionary For Dummies® 2nd Edition	by Dan Gookin & Wallace Wang	ISBN: 1-56884-218-X	$12.95 USA/$16.95 Canada
Upgrading and Fixing PCs For Dummies® 2nd Edition	by Andy Rathbone	ISBN: 1-56884-903-6	$19.99 USA/$26.99 Canada

PRESENTATION/AUTOCAD

AutoCAD For Dummies®	by Bud Smith	ISBN: 1-56884-191-4	$19.95 USA/$26.95 Canada
PowerPoint 4 For Windows® For Dummies®	by Doug Lowe	ISBN: 1-56884-161-2	$16.99 USA/$22.99 Canada

PROGRAMMING

Borland C++ For Dummies®	by Michael Hyman	ISBN: 1-56884-162-0	$19.95 USA/$26.95 Canada
C For Dummies® Volume 1	by Dan Gookin	ISBN: 1-878058-78-9	$19.95 USA/$26.95 Canada
C++ For Dummies®	by Stephen R. Davis	ISBN: 1-56884-163-9	$19.95 USA/$26.95 Canada
Delphi Programming For Dummies®	by Neil Rubenking	ISBN: 1-56884-200-7	$19.99 USA/$26.99 Canada
Mac® Programming For Dummies®	by Dan Parks Sydow	ISBN: 1-56884-173-6	$19.95 USA/$26.95 Canada
PowerBuilder 4 Programming For Dummies®	by Ted Coombs & Jason Coombs	ISBN: 1-56884-325-9	$19.99 USA/$26.99 Canada
QBasic Programming For Dummies®	by Douglas Hergert	ISBN: 1-56884-093-4	$19.95 USA/$26.95 Canada
Visual Basic 3 For Dummies®	by Wallace Wang	ISBN: 1-56884-076-4	$19.95 USA/$26.95 Canada
Visual Basic "X" For Dummies®	by Wallace Wang	ISBN: 1-56884-230-9	$19.99 USA/$26.99 Canada
Visual C++ 2 For Dummies®	by Michael Hyman & Bob Arnson	ISBN: 1-56884-328-3	$19.99 USA/$26.99 Canada
Windows® 95 Programming For Dummies®	by S. Randy Davis	ISBN: 1-56884-327-5	$19.99 USA/$26.99 Canada

SPREADSHEET

1-2-3 For Dummies®	by Greg Harvey	ISBN: 1-878058-60-6	$16.95 USA/$22.95 Canada
1-2-3 For Windows® 5 For Dummies® 2nd Edition	by John Walkenbach	ISBN: 1-56884-216-3	$16.95 USA/$22.95 Canada
Excel 5 For Macs® For Dummies®	by Greg Harvey	ISBN: 1-56884-186-8	$19.95 USA/$26.95 Canada
Excel For Dummies® 2nd Edition	by Greg Harvey	ISBN: 1-56884-050-0	$16.95 USA/$22.95 Canada
MORE 1-2-3 For DOS For Dummies®	by John Weingarten	ISBN: 1-56884-224-4	$19.99 USA/$26.99 Canada
MORE Excel 5 For Windows® For Dummies®	by Greg Harvey	ISBN: 1-56884-207-4	$19.95 USA/$26.95 Canada
Quattro Pro 6 For Windows® For Dummies®	by John Walkenbach	ISBN: 1-56884-174-4	$19.95 USA/$26.95 Canada
Quattro Pro For DOS For Dummies®	by John Walkenbach	ISBN: 1-56884-023-3	$16.95 USA/$22.95 Canada

UTILITIES

Norton Utilities 8 For Dummies®	by Beth Slick	ISBN: 1-56884-166-3	$19.95 USA/$26.95 Canada

VCRS/CAMCORDERS

VCRs & Camcorders For Dummies™	by Gordon McComb & Andy Rathbone	ISBN: 1-56884-229-5	$14.99 USA/$20.99 Canada

WORD PROCESSING

Ami Pro For Dummies®	by Jim Meade	ISBN: 1-56884-049-7	$19.95 USA/$26.95 Canada
MORE Word For Windows® 6 For Dummies®	by Doug Lowe	ISBN: 1-56884-165-5	$19.95 USA/$26.95 Canada
MORE WordPerfect® 6 For Windows® For Dummies®	by Margaret Levine Young & David C. Kay	ISBN: 1-56884-206-6	$19.95 USA/$26.95 Canada
MORE WordPerfect® 6 For DOS For Dummies®	by Wallace Wang, edited by Dan Gookin	ISBN: 1-56884-047-0	$19.95 USA/$26.95 Canada
Word 6 For Macs® For Dummies®	by Dan Gookin	ISBN: 1-56884-190-6	$19.95 USA/$26.95 Canada
Word For Windows® 6 For Dummies®	by Dan Gookin	ISBN: 1-56884-075-6	$16.95 USA/$22.95 Canada
Word For Windows® For Dummies®	by Dan Gookin & Ray Werner	ISBN: 1-878058-86-X	$16.95 USA/$22.95 Canada
WordPerfect® 6 For DOS For Dummies®	by Dan Gookin	ISBN: 1-878058-77-0	$16.95 USA/$22.95 Canada
WordPerfect® 6.1 For Windows® For Dummies® 2nd Edition	by Margaret Levine Young & David Kay	ISBN: 1-56884-243-0	$16.95 USA/$22.95 Canada
WordPerfect® For Dummies®	by Dan Gookin	ISBN: 1-878058-52-5	$16.95 USA/$22.95 Canada

Fun, Fast, & Cheap!™

NEW!

The Internet For Macs® For Dummies® Quick Reference
by Charles Seiter

ISBN:1-56884-967-2
$9.99 USA/$12.99 Canada

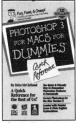

NEW!

Windows® 95 For Dummies® Quick Reference
by Greg Harvey

ISBN: 1-56884-964-8
$9.99 USA/$12.99 Canada

SUPER STAR

Photoshop 3 For Macs® For Dummies® Quick Reference
by Deke McClelland

ISBN: 1-56884-968-0
$9.99 USA/$12.99 Canada

SUPER STAR

WordPerfect® For DOS For Dummies® Quick Reference
by Greg Harvey

ISBN: 1-56884-009-8
$8.95 USA/$12.95 Canada

Title	Author	ISBN	Price
DATABASE			
Access 2 For Dummies® Quick Reference	by Stuart J. Stuple	ISBN: 1-56884-167-1	$8.95 USA/$11.95 Canada
dBASE 5 For DOS For Dummies® Quick Reference	by Barrie Sosinsky	ISBN: 1-56884-954-0	$9.99 USA/$12.99 Canada
dBASE 5 For Windows® For Dummies® Quick Reference	by Stuart J. Stuple	ISBN: 1-56884-953-2	$9.99 USA/$12.99 Canada
Paradox 5 For Windows® For Dummies® Quick Reference	by Scott Palmer	ISBN: 1-56884-960-5	$9.99 USA/$12.99 Canada
DESKTOP PUBLISHING/ILLUSTRATION/GRAPHICS			
CorelDRAW! 5 For Dummies® Quick Reference	by Raymond E. Werner	ISBN: 1-56884-952-4	$9.99 USA/$12.99 Canada
Harvard Graphics For Windows® For Dummies® Quick Reference	by Raymond E. Werner	ISBN: 1-56884-962-1	$9.99 USA/$12.99 Canada
Photoshop 3 For Macs® For Dummies® Quick Reference	by Deke McClelland	ISBN: 1-56884-968-0	$9.99 USA/$12.99 Canada
FINANCE/PERSONAL FINANCE			
Quicken 4 For Windows® For Dummies® Quick Reference	by Stephen L. Nelson	ISBN: 1-56884-950-8	$9.95 USA/$12.95 Canada
GROUPWARE/INTEGRATED			
Microsoft® Office 4 For Windows® For Dummies® Quick Reference	by Doug Lowe	ISBN: 1-56884-958-3	$9.99 USA/$12.99 Canada
Microsoft® Works 3 For Windows® For Dummies® Quick Reference	by Michael Partington	ISBN: 1-56884-959-1	$9.99 USA/$12.99 Canada
INTERNET/COMMUNICATIONS/NETWORKING			
The Internet For Dummies® Quick Reference	by John R. Levine & Margaret Levine Young	ISBN: 1-56884-168-X	$8.95 USA/$11.95 Canada
MACINTOSH			
Macintosh® System 7.5 For Dummies® Quick Reference	by Stuart J. Stuple	ISBN: 1-56884-956-7	$9.99 USA/$12.99 Canada
OPERATING SYSTEMS:			
DOS			
DOS For Dummies® Quick Reference	by Greg Harvey	ISBN: 1-56884-007-1	$8.95 USA/$11.95 Canada
UNIX			
UNIX® For Dummies® Quick Reference	by John R. Levine & Margaret Levine Young	ISBN: 1-56884-094-2	$8.95 USA/$11.95 Canada
WINDOWS			
Windows® 3.1 For Dummies® Quick Reference, 2nd Edition	by Greg Harvey	ISBN: 1-56884-951-6	$8.95 USA/$11.95 Canada
PCs/HARDWARE			
Memory Management For Dummies® Quick Reference	by Doug Lowe	ISBN: 1-56884-362-3	$9.99 USA/$12.99 Canada
PRESENTATION/AUTOCAD			
AutoCAD For Dummies® Quick Reference	by Ellen Finkelstein	ISBN: 1-56884-198-1	$9.95 USA/$12.95 Canada
SPREADSHEET			
1-2-3 For Dummies® Quick Reference	by John Walkenbach	ISBN: 1-56884-027-6	$8.95 USA/$11.95 Canada
1-2-3 For Windows® 5 For Dummies® Quick Reference	by John Walkenbach	ISBN: 1-56884-957-5	$9.95 USA/$12.95 Canada
Excel For Windows® For Dummies® Quick Reference, 2nd Edition	by John Walkenbach	ISBN: 1-56884-096-9	$8.95 USA/$11.95 Canada
Quattro Pro 6 For Windows® For Dummies® Quick Reference	by Stuart J. Stuple	ISBN: 1-56884-172-8	$9.95 USA/$12.95 Canada
WORD PROCESSING			
Word For Windows® 6 For Dummies® Quick Reference	by George Lynch	ISBN: 1-56884-095-0	$8.95 USA/$11.95 Canada
Word For Windows® For Dummies® Quick Reference	by George Lynch	ISBN: 1-56884-029-2	$8.95 USA/$11.95 Canada
WordPerfect® 6.1 For Windows® For Dummies® Quick Reference, 2nd Edition	by Greg Harvey	ISBN: 1-56884-966-4	$9.99 USA/$12.99/Canada

IDG BOOKS WORLDWIDE™

Order Center: **(800) 762-2974** *(8 a.m.–6 p.m., EST, weekdays)*

Quantity	ISBN	Title	Price	Total

Shipping & Handling Charges

	Description	First book	Each additional book	Total
Domestic	Normal	$4.50	$1.50	$
	Two Day Air	$8.50	$2.50	$
	Overnight	$18.00	$3.00	$
International	Surface	$8.00	$8.00	$
	Airmail	$16.00	$16.00	$
	DHL Air	$17.00	$17.00	$

*For large quantities call for shipping & handling charges.
**Prices are subject to change without notice.

Ship to:

Name _____

Company _____

Address _____

City/State/Zip _____

Daytime Phone _____

Payment: ☐ Check to IDG Books Worldwide (US Funds Only)

☐ VISA   ☐ MasterCard   ☐ American Express

Card # _____ Expires _____

Signature _____

Subtotal _____

CA residents add
applicable sales tax _____

IN, MA, and MD
residents add
5% sales tax _____

IL residents add
6.25% sales tax _____

RI residents add
7% sales tax _____

TX residents add
8.25% sales tax _____

Shipping _____

Total _____

Please send this order form to:

**IDG Books Worldwide, Inc.
Attn: Order Entry Dept.
7260 Shadeland Station, Suite 100
Indianapolis, IN 46256**

*Allow up to 3 weeks for delivery.
Thank you!*

IDG BOOKS WORLDWIDE REGISTRATION CARD

Title of this book: Mutual Fund$ For Dummie$

My overall rating of this book: ❑ Very good [1]   ❑ Good [2]   ❑ Satisfactory [3]   ❑ Fair [4]   ❑ Poor [5]

How I first heard about this book:

❑ Found in bookstore; name: [6]

❑ Advertisement: [8]

❑ Word of mouth; heard about book from friend, co-worker, etc.: [10]

❑ Book review: [7]

❑ Catalog: [9]

❑ Other: [11]

What I liked most about this book:

What I would change, add, delete, etc., in future editions of this book:

Other comments:

Number of computer books I purchase in a year: ❑ 1 [12]   ❑ 2-5 [13]   ❑ 6-10 [14]   ❑ More than 10 [15]

I would characterize my computer skills as: ❑ Beginner [16]   ❑ Intermediate [17]   ❑ Advanced [18]   ❑ Professional [19]

I use ❑ DOS [20]   ❑ Windows [21]   ❑ OS/2 [22]   ❑ Unix [23]   ❑ Macintosh [24]   ❑ Other: [25]_____
(please specify)

I would be interested in new books on the following subjects:
(please check all that apply, and use the spaces provided to identify specific software)

❑ Word processing: [26]

❑ Data bases: [28]

❑ File Utilities: [30]

❑ Networking: [32]

❑ Other: [34]

❑ Spreadsheets: [27]

❑ Desktop publishing: [29]

❑ Money management: [31]

❑ Programming languages: [33]

I use a PC at (please check all that apply): ❑ home [35]   ❑ work [36]   ❑ school [37]   ❑ other: [38] _____

The disks I prefer to use are ❑ 5.25 [39]   ❑ 3.5 [40]   ❑ other: [41]_____

I have a CD ROM: ❑ yes [42]   ❑ no [43]

I plan to buy or upgrade computer hardware this year: ❑ yes [44]   ❑ no [45]

I plan to buy or upgrade computer software this year: ❑ yes [46]   ❑ no [47]

Name: _____   Business title: [48] _____   Type of Business: [49] _____

Address (❑ home [50] ❑ work [51]/Company name: _____)

Street/Suite# _____

City [52]/State [53]/Zipcode [54]: _____   Country [55] _____

❑ **I liked this book!** You may quote me by name in future
IDG Books Worldwide promotional materials.

My daytime phone number is _____

IDG BOOKS

THE WORLD OF
COMPUTER
KNOWLEDGE

 # YES!

Please keep me informed about IDG's World of Computer Knowledge.
Send me the latest IDG Books catalog.

COMPUTER
BOOK SERIES
FROM IDG